BARRON'S

CHSPE

8TH EDITION

Sharon Weiner Green, M.A.
Former Instructor in English
Merritt College, Oakland, California

Michael Siemon, M.A.
Former Instructor
Malay College, Kuala Kangsar, Malaysia

Lexy Green, B.A.
The College Preparatory School
Oakland, California

BARRON'S

All inquiries should be addressed to:
Barron's Educational Series, Inc.
250 Wireless Boulevard
Hauppauge, New York 11788
www.barronseduc.com

ISBN: 978-1-4380-0123-4

ISSN: 1095-0176

PRINTED IN THE UNITED STATES OF AMERICA

9 8 7 6 5 4 3 2 1

10%
POST-CONSUMER
WASTE
Paper contains a minimum
of 10% post-consumer
waste (PCW). Paper used
in this book was derived
from certified, sustainable
forestlands.

Contents

Preface

We have prepared this book to help those students who wish to take advantage of California's special opportunity—the California High School Proficiency Examination (CHSPE). In addition to providing three chapters reviewing essential basic skills, we have included three practice tests in this book. However, tests change and from time to time the testing authorities will include new types of questions to see how well they work as indicators of student ability. We hope that students who use our book to prepare for this exam will let us know how closely our model tests reflect today's CHSPE. Anyone interested in reaching us should email us at sharongreen@post.harvard.edu.

We have had a lot of help in putting together this book, and we would like to thank the people who assisted and/or put up with us. In particular, we thank our fellow Barron's authors who allowed us to use review materials from their books *Barron's How to Prepare for the Test of Standard Written English* and *Barron's How to Prepare for the New High School Equivalency Examination (GED)*. In addition, we thank Deborah Abramovitz, Nathan Oliver, Rachel Phillips, and Chris Waters, who all passed the test; our painstaking editor, Jennifer Giammusso; and David Green and the two John Seals, our constant supports.

Introduction

WHAT THE TEST IS LIKE AND HOW TO STUDY FOR IT

Who May Take the Test?

If you are 16 or older, you may take the California High School Proficiency Examination. There is no upper age limit: the test is open to older nongraduates as well as to currently enrolled high school students.

If you are younger than 16, you may also take the test if, on the date the test is given, you have already finished a full year of tenth grade or are enrolled in your second semester of tenth grade.

You do not need your parents' permission to take the test. If you are under 18, you need to have a school official sign your registration form to verify that you are eligible to take the test.

What Happens Once You Pass the Test?

Once you pass the test, you will receive a Certificate of Proficiency from the State Board of Education. The Certificate of Proficiency is legally equivalent to a high school diploma, but it is not a diploma. Even if you have received your Certificate of Proficiency, you may still have to continue to attend high school: California state law provides that students younger than 18 who do not have a regular high school diploma may not leave high school until they

1. have turned 16 years of age, *and*
2. have received their Certificate of Proficiency, *and*
3. have presented their school with signed parental permission forms allowing them to leave school.

What Happens Once You Leave High School?

Once you leave high school with a Certificate of Proficiency, you have many options. Your Certificate of Proficiency will qualify you for admission to a California community college. The equivalent of the high school diploma, it is accepted by community colleges throughout the state. Outside California, community colleges differ from state to state in accepting the Certificate of Proficiency for admission; however, more and more states are developing proficiency examinations of their own, and the proficiency certificates are becoming more widely accepted each year. In addition, some four-year colleges, such as Bard College at Simon's Rock, admit students without high school diplomas.

You may also find your Certificate of Proficiency helpful if you want to enlist in the armed services; some branches of the service treat it as fully equal to a high school diploma (other branches may treat it the way they treat passing the GED and give it limited credit). You will definitely find it useful if you intend to apply for a federal civil service job: the U.S. Civil Service Commission has directed that the Certificate of Proficiency is acceptable in applications for civil service positions. Your options are those of a regular high school graduate: college, work, travel, military service. You also have one additional option: if you leave high school with a Certificate of Proficiency, at any time before you turn 18 years of age you may re-enter high school and resume your course work there.

How Do You Sign Up for the CHSPE?

First, you must fill out a registration form. You can download one from the CHSPE website: www.chspe.net. If you lack Internet access, you should be able to get a copy of the CHSPE *Information Bulletin* from your high school counselor or at your local public library. If you have trouble finding a copy, call the CHSPE office at (866) 342-4773.

Send the completed registration form and a cashier's check or money order (made out to California Department of Education) to CHSPE Office, Sacramento County Office of Education, P.O. Box 269003, Sacramento, CA 95826-9003. The Department of Education will not accept personal checks, cash, or credit card payments.

When Is the Test Given?

The CHSPE is generally given three times each year, in March, June, and October. Dates for the test and the deadlines for registration are posted on the website and printed in the information bulletin. Your registration must be received at least four weeks prior to the date of the test in order for the CHSPE Office to send you an admission ticket for the test. Get your registration in sooner if that's at all possible. That way you'll have a better chance of being assigned to the testing center of your choice.

If you miss the regular registration deadline, you may still be able to register for the test. There is a late registration deadline about two and a half weeks before the test, and an emergency registration deadline four days before the test. However, you are really better off if you manage to get your paperwork in before the regular registration deadline. The late registration and emergency registration fees are much higher than the regular registration fee, and if you register late, there's a strong chance you won't be able to get into the testing center of your choice.

If you need to make special testing arrangements because of physical access needs or religious observance, you must contact the CHSPE Office at least four weeks before the test date. You must provide evidence of your need, such as a letter from an appropriate authority verifying your physical status or your religious conviction.

There are special rules for cell phones. Although official policy discourages their use, the test makers are realistic enough to recognize that many students will need to have their cell phones in order to communicate with their rides. Therefore, cell phones are allowed in the test center. However, they must be turned off while the test is being administered.

Where Is the Test Given?

There are now 70 test centers in high schools and colleges throughout California. The locations are posted on the website, and you should select the one that is most convenient for you.

What Should You Bring to the Test?

You must bring the admission ticket and a photo ID. Acceptable identification includes a school ID card with your photograph, a permanent driver's license or a DMV ID. The *Information Bulletin* lists a few more possibilities, and you can call the testing service if you have questions about your ID. This is important. If you don't have acceptable ID, you will not be permitted to take the test. The admission ticket is also important. If you don't receive this by the Tuesday eight days after the registration deadline, you must call the testing service to confirm whether you are registered for the test.

You should also bring several No. 2 pencils with erasers. Do not bring anything like paper, rulers, books, or other aids. These are forbidden, and if you use them, you can be kicked out of the test. The list of what not to bring is enormous. Do not bring iPods, iPads, PDAs, pagers, cameras, spell checkers, dictionaries, laptops, notebooks, backpacks, briefcases, markers, or pens. The list goes on and on. You may bring a cell phone, but it must be turned off and not make any noises during the test. You may bring a simple numerical calculator: one that has the basic arithmetic functions ($+ - \times \div$). It may have percent (%), square root ($\sqrt{\ }$), sign-change ($+/-$), and memory keys (M+, M−, MC, MR) as well. Snacks and beverages are forbidden, although you may bring in a bottle of water without a label.

How Do You Find Out the Test Results?

About a month after the test date, unofficial results of the CHSPE will be posted on the Internet. If you want to be able to get access to your unofficial results online, be sure to give your e-mail address and provide a password when you register to take the test.

A few days after the unofficial test results are posted, you should receive your score report in the mail. In addition, if you have passed both the language arts and mathematics sections of the test, you will receive your Certificate of Proficiency in the mail. If you are enrolled in a public high school and pass the test, your name and the names of other students who pass the test will be reported to your school.

How Is the Test Organized?

The 3½-hour High School Proficiency Examination is divided into two parts, an English language arts section and a mathematics section. The English language arts section is made up of two subtests. One subtest covers reading comprehension and vocabulary; the other subtest deals with essay writing and grammar skills. These two subtests are organized as follows:

Reading Subtest	54 reading comprehension questions
	30 vocabulary questions
Language Subtest	48 multiple-choice questions
	one persuasive essay

The mathematics section is simply made up of 50 multiple-choice questions.

You need to pass both English subtests *and* the mathematics section to earn your Certificate of Proficiency. However, you do not have to pass all these sections of the test on the same day. Once you have passed a particular section or subtest, you have passed it; you do not have to retake it. If necessary, you can earn your Certificate of Proficiency one section at a time.

One useful thing to remember about the CHSPE is that it is not timed. You have a total of 3½ hours for the test. You can spend all that time on the mathematics section if you like, or you can devote the entire 3½ hours to taking the reading subtest. If you think you need extra time in order to do well on a section, you can take that extra time. However, no matter how many or how few test sections you take on the day of the test, your test fee will be the same. You have to decide how much you can handle on the day of the test, and whether you can afford to take the test more than once.

If you intend to take the entire CHSPE on one day, you will need to organize your time. Here's a possible plan for you to follow.

8:30 A.M.	Write your essay
9 A.M.	Take the language subtest
10 A.M.	Take the reading subtest
11 A.M.	Take the mathematics section

Obviously, you can follow a different order when you take the test; this is just one possibility. However, if you allow half an hour for the essay and an hour for each of the multiple-choice sections, you should be able to finish the entire test in the allotted time.

How Is the Test Scored?

Most of the questions on the CHSPE are multiple-choice questions. Your raw score will be based on the number of questions that you answer correctly. The mathematics section, for example, consists of 50 multiple-choice questions. If you answer 30 questions correctly, you will have a math raw score of 30. However, the number you see on your score report will not be 30. It will be what the test makers call a scale score and will generally range from 250 to 450.

Some tests are harder than others. The student who earns a math raw score of 25 in March, for example, may earn a 32 raw score on the October test. By converting raw scores to scale scores, the test makers hope to make up for any differences in difficulty among the tests.

What is a passing score? On the mathematics section and on the reading subtest, a passing score is a scale score of at least 350. On the language subtest, a passing score will be based on a combination of your raw score on the multiple-choice questions and your performance writing the essay. Don't worry too much about raw scores and scale scores; you'll do just fine on the test if you answer 65 to 70% of the questions correctly.

What the Test Is Like

Here's what you will face on the three parts of the test.

THE READING SUBTEST

The reading subtest consists of 54 reading comprehension questions and 30 vocabulary questions. The reading comprehension questions test your ability to read a variety of material, from newspaper articles to poetry. Some reading passages may be practical: you may have to master instructions for doing a particular task, for example. Others will be simply informative or entertaining. The vocabulary questions test your ability to work with words. Some questions will test your knowledge of synonyms; others will test your understanding of words with multiple meanings; still others will test your ability to grasp the meaning of words from their contexts.

THE LANGUAGE SUBTEST

The language subtest requires you to write a short (one or two page) persuasive essay. Topics vary, but they generally deal with questions that concern students in your age group. Your task will be to take a stand on an issue and to argue your point, convincing your reader.

Here is a typical persuasive essay topic:

> Some believe that people under the age of 18 should not be allowed to drive. Do you agree or disagree? Write a letter to the editor of your local newspaper to convince the public to agree with your position.

In addition to the essay task, the language subtest includes 48 multiple-choice questions. These test your mastery of basic English grammar. Some questions will ask you to identify and repair errors in grammar, punctuation, and sentence structure. Others will ask you to select the wording that makes the strongest sentence—the clearest, the smoothest, the most concise. Still others will have you polish a passage by combining sentences or manipulating sentence parts. You may need to rearrange sentences to improve the passage's logical organization or to cut sentences that do not belong in the passage.

THE MATHEMATICS SECTION

The mathematics section of the test consists of 50 multiple-choice questions. These range from simple computation to basic algebra and geometry problems. A few questions may involve statistics and probability.

Some require you to read graphs or tables. Others require you to calculate the area or volume of a given shape. You will be asked to determine averages and calculate percentages.

Many of the questions on the CHSPE test practical skills or knowledge. As a citizen you need to be able to interpret the ballot and voting materials you receive in the mail. You need to be able to read the newspaper in order to assess the performance of the public officials you elect. You need to be able to fill out common legal forms, such as requests for absentee ballots, and to interpret legal ordinances and rules. You need to be able to read the graphs and charts published by government agencies. As an employee or job seeker, you need to be able to read help wanted advertisements and fill out job applications. You may be required to prepare a resume and write cover letters to potential employers. You need to be able to compare pay scales and to figure out your take-home pay. As a consumer, you need to be able to calculate which product is your best buy. You need to be able to interpret advertisements, product labels, and instructions. You also need to be able to read warranty information and credit contracts. These are your basic skills, skills covered in the multiple-choice sections of the test.

Hints on Studying for the Test

You may not realize it, but you are already actively studying for the High School Proficiency Examination. Every time you go to the supermarket and compare the prices of the items on sale, you are practicing for the test. Every time you fill out a form or follow a written direction, you are practicing for the test. As you go through the model tests in this book, pay attention to the sorts of questions you come across. Then, when you come across a similar question in your daily life, think about it the way you would think about a question on the test. Read the label on the package and ask yourself questions about what it says. Compare costs of similar items at a store to figure out the best buys. Read the help wanted advertisements in the newspaper and figure out which job is best for you. Use odd moments: while you wait for your bus, read the bus schedule; while you stand in line at the post office, read the official notices. Above all else, *read*. The more you read, the better you will be able to understand what you read. Nothing improves reading comprehension as much as practice. Read anything you like, but READ.

Similarly, the more you write, the better able you will be to express your ideas in writing. As you go through the model tests, pay attention to the sorts of essay questions you come across. Then try to think up essay questions of your own. Here are some sample essay questions:

PERSUASIVE ESSAY QUESTIONS

1. Should school athletics receive financial support?
2. Should high school students be allowed to elect their own courses?
3. Should children be allowed to choose their own religion?
4. Should cities have a curfew for teenagers?
5. Should the drinking age be lowered in California?
6. Should high schools be coeducational?

Don't try to cram for the test. The only thing a study session lasting several hours will do for you is tire you out. If, in the course of taking the model tests, you find out you have trouble reading and interpreting graphs, spend a half hour or hour each day studying graphs. Don't try to do everything all at once. Set up a study schedule, one you can keep, and follow it. Regular practice handling particular problem areas will pay off.

In the review sections that follow the self-assessment test, you will find all the practice materials you need to review the basic skills covered on the test. Even if you feel you have done well on the self-assessment test, go over the review sections as well. Concentrate on the sorts of problems that slowed you down on the self-assessment test. If you know you have difficulty dealing with certain questions—word problems, fractions, graphs—concentrate on these problems as well. Again, don't cram, but pace yourself and allow yourself sufficient time for review.

Hints on Handling Essay Questions

The essay questions on the test call for straightforward persuasive writing: you are asked to convince somebody of something. Where do you begin? Obviously, begin with the question. Consider once more the following sample essay question:

> Some believe that people under the age of 18 should not be allowed to drive. Do you agree or disagree? Write a letter to the editor of your local newspaper to convince the public to agree with your position.

You probably already have an opinion on this question. Your job is to come up with evidence to support your opinion, evidence that would persuade your readers to agree with you. This type of essay should be relatively simple for you to write. First, there is no right or wrong answer. You are free to take either side. Second, you will have a writer's checklist supplied to you by the CHSPE test makers. Here are some of the points it tells you to observe:

- Keep on topic. Don't digress.
- Write in complete sentences.
- Provide enough details to back up your ideas.
- Arrange your thoughts in a logical order. Make it easy for the reader to follow your reasoning.
- Provide a topic sentence for each paragraph.

- Capitalize the beginning of each sentence.
- Print or write neatly and clearly.
- Check your spelling and punctuation.

If you carefully observe these points, you should do just fine.

Here are some additional writing hints for you:

1. Never use a long word where a short one will do.
2. Keep your sentences short.
3. If you can cut out a word, do so.
4. Use the active voice, not the passive. (Write "Younger teenage drivers have more accidents than older teenagers do," not "More accidents are had by younger teenage drivers than are had by older teenagers.")
5. Be sure to cover each of the required elements in your essay, and do not forget to include the title (if one is requested).

Again, if you feel underprepared in writing skills, be sure to work your way through Chapter 1. Its sections on grammar, punctuation, and usage are sure to be helpful to you.

Hints on Handling Reading Comprehension Questions

As you go through the passages on our model tests, try asking yourself the following questions:

1. What is the *main idea* of the passage?
2. What *key phrases and ideas* are there in the passage?
3. Are there any words or phrases in a question that change or qualify its meaning? Watch out for the following words: *no, some, many, all; sometimes, never, always; not at all, partly, completely,* etc.

Some of the passages will be several paragraphs long. Don't expect to find all the answers to all the questions in the first paragraph you read. Read *all* the paragraphs belonging to the passage. When hunting for the answer to a particular question, hunt through the entire passage. Don't expect the questions to follow the order in which the material in the passage is organized: your first question may ask you for information found in the passage's fourth paragraph, whereas your second question may ask you for information found in the first paragraph.

Remember that the sort of reading involved in many of the comprehension passages is practical reading, reading to locate specific factual information. You will find additional practice in both practical and general reading in Chapter 2.

Hints on Handling Mathematics Questions

There are special skills needed for the different kinds of math problems. You will find a basic math review in Chapter 3, covering these skills. Whenever you do a calculation, or read an answer from a graph, or solve a word problem, think about the question *before* you start to do calculations. Many times, you can find an easy way if you look for it; we will point out some ways in the answers to the model test questions. When you are done with your work, *always* ask yourself "Does the answer make sense?" If the answer doesn't seem reasonable, you have probably made a mistake.

Even though different types of questions require different techniques, you can follow some general rules:

1. Check your work. Everyone makes errors in arithmetic, but you can catch yours if you try. If you arrived at the answer by subtracting, add the answer and the number you subtracted to check it out. If you divided to get the answer, check it by multiplying.

2. When a problem involves fractions or other complicated numbers, it helps to get an approximate answer by simplifying the numbers. For example, $\frac{9}{16} \times 30$ has to be a bit more than half ($\frac{8}{16}$) of 30, that is, it has to be more than 15. By finding an approximate answer, you can be confident that the more difficult calculation is correct.

3. For word problems, you have to translate sentences into numbers and equations. Read *all* the sentences of the question; then go back and write down any numbers or relationships mentioned in the question. Stop and think about the question. Many times you are expected to fill in some more information from your own experience, maybe a formula like "distance = rate $\times$ time." The arithmetic will usually be straightforward once you know *what number* the question is asking for.

4. For questions using graphs, you are expected either to interpret the patterns on the graph or to estimate values at significant points on the graph. Typically, there will not be a grid of horizontal and vertical lines such as you see on graph paper, but there will be scales or numbers along the axes of the graph. You should practice using a piece of paper like a ruler, moving it parallel to the vertical or horizontal axes of the graph to get an estimate of the y (vertical) or x (horizontal) value at points on the graph. During the test, you can use your answer sheet this way. When doing this, you will not need to be terribly precise; just get an estimate that is good enough to allow you to choose among the answers listed for each question.

5. Some questions test general mathematical reasoning—you are expected to know what it is reasonable to think, given a description of some circumstances or a graph of some data. If you have enough time, it is worthwhile to "explore" the situation, thinking about what you see, or to think while you are reading the question what you *might* be able to figure out from the data or picture you are given. Don't spend much time doing this. When you get a look at the answer choices for each question, see if any of them stand out as very unusual or unlikely—that may give you a clue about what the test question, in the other answers, does consider it possible to decide. Then, look at each answer and see if there is some wording in the question statement, or some detail of the graph, that makes it easy to see the suggested answer is wrong. Turn that around in

your mind, to see if saying what is correct matches one of the other answers. If you do not see the right answer immediately, look at each answer in turn and decide if it makes sense or not, from what the question gives you as the starting point.

Remember that many of the questions on the test deal with everyday situations and the sort of mathematics you can use and practice anywhere—at the store, reading the newspaper, balancing your checkbook, or any time you encounter numbers. Some require you to apply what you learned in your basic algebra and geometry classes in high school. You can find additional study materials in Chapter 3.

General Test-Taking Tips

1. **Answer every question.** There is no penalty for guessing on the High School Proficiency Exam. You get one point for each correct answer in the multiple-choice section. No points will be subtracted for incorrect answers. Therefore, it will help you to guess whenever you do not know the answer to a question. Blind guessing should give you correct answers and earn you points roughly 25 percent of the time.

2. **Make educated guesses.** You can improve the odds of getting the right answer when you guess by crossing out answers you know are incorrect. If you do not know the correct answer, but you can rule out two of the possibilities, your guesses should be correct approximately 50 percent of the time.

3. **Skip difficult problems and return to them later.** If you find that you have trouble answering all of the questions on the test in the allotted time, you should skip the difficult test questions and return to them later. Mark the skipped questions in your test booklet (not on the answer form) so that you will see them easily. Move on to the questions that you can answer with ease. When you have completed all of the easy questions, return to the more difficult ones. Each question is worth just one point, whether it is easy or difficult. You do not want to miss an easy point at the end of the test because you got bogged down on a tough one early on. Remember to go ahead and guess on any answers that remain blank in the last few minutes of the test.

4. **Take care of yourself.** Be sure to get enough sleep the night before the test. This is far more valuable than any last minute review that you can do. Wake up early enough to eat breakfast before the test. Studies show that people perform better on tests when they have had something to eat recently. Bring a snack to eat during the break. Your body will require fuel if your brain is to keep working effectively.

YOUR STUDY PROGRAM

There are many ways to use this book in studying for the CHSPE. People have different styles and study habits that work for them; you may need to modify our suggestions below so that they fit your own patterns. We suggest a study program that involves 30 sessions of about one hour each. You could complete this program in six weeks of five sessions each, or five weeks of six sessions; you could even stretch it over two months with a session every other day.

The study program follows an underlying plan, which you can adapt to create your own, customized program instead. Here's how it works:

- Take the self-assessment test, and review the answers to locate your weak spots.
- Use about half of your planned time to study the review material in this book, concentrating on any weak spots identified by the self-assessment test.
- Take Model Test A. Again, check for areas that still need improvement.
- Go through the review material covering these areas; ask a friend or a teacher for advice if you are having difficulties working through the review material.
- At least one week before the test, take Model Test B under "test conditions." (Spend the full 3½ hours on the test to get a feel for what taking the actual test is like.)
- Carefully review the answer explanations for questions you missed on this test.

If you follow the 30-hour program, mark your calendar so that you schedule yourself to finish your study program about a week before you are due to take the test; this will give you some additional time to review anything you still feel uncertain about, or just to relax and take a breather before the test.

The 30-Hour Study Program

Each session here should take about one hour to complete; you can do more than one session a day if you like, or spend longer than an hour on a session, but be sure to take a break if you wind up working for more than an hour. The 30-hour study program does not include the time you will spend taking the tests in this book, so plan the additional time you need for this as well.

- Take the language arts subtest of the self-assessment test. This subtest includes the essay and the 48 multiple-choice questions on language skills. If you prefer, you may just write the essay now, and postpone the multiple-choice portion until after Study Session 2.

Study Session 1. Read Chapter 1, The Basics of Writing, up to the section *Developing Your Essay Writing Skills*. Choose one of the practice essay topics in that section, and take 30 minutes to write an essay.

Study Session 2. Read the Chapter 1 section *Advanced Outlining* and practice by writing another essay from the list of topics in *Developing Your Essay Writing Skills.*

Study Session 3. Check your self-assessment test answer sheet against the answer key in Chapter 1. Read the answer explanations there, paying special attention to any questions you missed. For the questions you got right, just scan the explanations to see how they confirm or clarify your choice. Read the Chapter 1 section *Punctuation for Sentence Sense.*

Study Session 4. Start reading *Common Problems in Grammar and Usage* in Chapter 1. Do at least one practice exercise in each part of this section, focusing on areas that you missed on the self-assessment test. Aim to reach the exercises on "Problems Involving Verbs" in this session. Look for review material in the *General Grammar Review* section that cover areas you need to study.

Study Session 5. Continue reading *Common Problems in Grammar and Usage*, doing at least one practice exercise in each part. Do about half of the exercises in any area you had problems with on the self-assessment test (save the rest for the next round of study).

• Take the reading subtest of the self-assessment test.

Study Session 6. Check your answer sheet for the reading subtest against the answer key. Read the answer explanations, again paying special attention to questions you missed. Read the opening section, *General Reading*, from Chapter 2 up to the illustration on page 161. Answer the three questions on that passage, and read the answer analysis there. Continue reading, and answer the questions on the first practice passage. Check the answers at the end of the section, and write your own answer analysis for these answers.

Study Session 7. Complete the *General Reading* practices. Write answer analyses for any questions you missed (ask a friend or a teacher for help if you aren't sure).

Study Session 8. Read the *Practical Reading* section of Chapter 2, up to the illustrations. Work through these, and study the answer explanations given for them.

Study Session 9. Work through the practice exercises in *Practical Reading*; write your own answer explanations for any questions you missed.

Study Session 10. Write two more essays from the list of topics in *Developing Your Essay Writing Skills* in Chapter 1.

• Take the Math section of the self-assessment test.

Study Session 11. Check your answer sheet for the mathematics section against the answer key. Read the answer explanations, concentrating on questions you missed. Read the opening section, *Interpreting Math Problems*, from Chapter 3. Skim through the *Arithmetic* section up through I. E-10 (that is, as far as multiplying, dividing, adding, and subtracting fractions). If you are weak on fraction arithmetic, do a couple of the practice exercises in each group.

Study Session 12. Continue through the *Arithmetic* section of Chapter 3. Do about five or ten of the practice exercises in Section I. E-11 (Problems Involving Fractions), and also five or ten of the practice exercises in Section I. G-2 (Problems on Percents). Skim through the remaining parts of this section looking for any questions similar to ones that gave you trouble on the self-assessment test. Read the relevant examples and answer several practice questions that follow.

Study Session 13. Skim the *Algebra* section of Chapter 3. Do one or two practice exercises for each section, except for Sections II. E (Solving Word Problems) and II G (Ratio and Proportion), which deserve special attention. Do half of the practice exercises for these two sections.

Study Session 14. Read the *Basic Graphs* and *Measures* sections (III and IV) of Chapter 3. Do approximately half of the practice exercises given for these two sections.

Study Session 15. Read the *Geometry* section (V) of Chapter 3. Do all of the practice exercises for this section.

Study Session 16. Read the *Data, Graphs, and Statistics* section (VI) of Chapter 3. Do all of the practice exercises for this section.

Study Session 17/18. Review your answer sheet for the math section of the self-assessment test to locate any weak areas that are not covered by the "Basics of Mathematics" material in Chapter 3. You may have more advanced math books or be able to borrow some from a friend or a library to help you study these areas.

Note: if you feel you should spend more time than 3 hours practicing the material in the *Arithmetic* and *Algebra* sections, you may use sessions 17 and 18 for that as well as for other supplementary studying.

- Take Model Test A. You may take the entire test on one day if you wish, but if so please take breaks between the parts. Do not, at this stage, try to complete the test in $3\frac{1}{2}$ hours. Do make notes of how long it takes you to do each section.

Study Session 19. Review the Chapter 2 sections *How to Write an Essay in 30 Minutes* and *Advanced Outlining*. Evaluate yourself on how well you followed the guidelines in these sections, and compare your essay for Model Test A with your essay for the self-assessment test. Ask a friend who writes well, or a teacher, to give you feedback on the Model Test A essay.

Study Session 20. Check your answer sheet for the language subtest against the answer key in Chapter 4. Read the answer explanations there. If any grammar questions caused you problems, read the relevant parts of the *General Grammar Review* in Chapter 1.

Study Session 21. Review any parts of the *Common Problems in Grammar and Usage* section that apply to the areas you noted in session 20, and do any exercises in theses areas that you did not do earlier (in sessions 4 and 5).

Study Session 22. Mark your answer sheet for the reading subtest, read the answer explanations, and review any parts of the *General Reading* or *Practical Reading* sections of Chapter 2 covering areas that troubled you in Model Test A.

Study Session 23. Go back to the self-assessment test, and redo the reading subtest questions you missed the first time as exercises. Write another essay.

Study Session 24. Check your answer sheet for the math section of Model Test A, and read the answer explanations for the questions you missed. If any of these involved arithmetic (fractions, decimals, or percentages), do more exercises in these areas from Section I of Chapter 3. Look for "word problems" in the later parts of Section I that are similar to those that bothered you on the test.

Study Session 25. Do more exercises from Sections II (*Algebra*), III (*Basic Graphs*), and IV (*Measures*), emphasizing areas that bothered you on the test.

Study Session 26. Do the other half of the exercises in (*Geometry*), Section V. Go back to the self-assessment test and redo the math questions you missed the first time.

- Set aside a full $3\frac{1}{2}$ hours in which you won't be interrupted to take Model Test B. Try to get through the full test. If you don't finish in the allotted time, take a break and come back to finish the rest later. Remember, you don't have to answer every question to do well on the test.

Study Session 27. Check your answer sheet for Model Test B against the answer key in Chapter 5. Read the answer explanations, and list the areas you did well on (congratulate yourself!), and the areas you did not do as well as you hoped but think you can improve with just a little more work.

Study Session 28. Review any language arts (writing or reading) areas you want to improve. Redo some exercises in these areas (or do any you may have skipped before).

Study Session 29. Review any math areas you want to improve. Redo exercises from this book, or find other exercises (from other math books if you have them) to practice in these areas.

Study Session 30. Go back to Model Test A and redo any questions you missed when you took it before. Do the same for Model Test B. Write one more essay. Relax!

Answer Sheet

SELF-ASSESSMENT TEST

ENGLISH LANGUAGE ARTS SECTION

Language Subtest

1 Ⓐ Ⓑ Ⓒ Ⓓ	13 Ⓐ Ⓑ Ⓒ Ⓓ	25 Ⓐ Ⓑ Ⓒ Ⓓ	37 Ⓐ Ⓑ Ⓒ Ⓓ
2 Ⓐ Ⓑ Ⓒ Ⓓ	14 Ⓐ Ⓑ Ⓒ Ⓓ	26 Ⓐ Ⓑ Ⓒ Ⓓ	38 Ⓐ Ⓑ Ⓒ Ⓓ
3 Ⓐ Ⓑ Ⓒ Ⓓ	15 Ⓐ Ⓑ Ⓒ Ⓓ	27 Ⓐ Ⓑ Ⓒ Ⓓ	39 Ⓐ Ⓑ Ⓒ Ⓓ
4 Ⓐ Ⓑ Ⓒ Ⓓ	16 Ⓐ Ⓑ Ⓒ Ⓓ	28 Ⓐ Ⓑ Ⓒ Ⓓ	40 Ⓐ Ⓑ Ⓒ Ⓓ
5 Ⓐ Ⓑ Ⓒ Ⓓ	17 Ⓐ Ⓑ Ⓒ Ⓓ	29 Ⓐ Ⓑ Ⓒ Ⓓ	41 Ⓐ Ⓑ Ⓒ Ⓓ
6 Ⓐ Ⓑ Ⓒ Ⓓ	18 Ⓐ Ⓑ Ⓒ Ⓓ	30 Ⓐ Ⓑ Ⓒ Ⓓ	42 Ⓐ Ⓑ Ⓒ Ⓓ
7 Ⓐ Ⓑ Ⓒ Ⓓ	19 Ⓐ Ⓑ Ⓒ Ⓓ	31 Ⓐ Ⓑ Ⓒ Ⓓ	43 Ⓐ Ⓑ Ⓒ Ⓓ
8 Ⓐ Ⓑ Ⓒ Ⓓ	20 Ⓐ Ⓑ Ⓒ Ⓓ	32 Ⓐ Ⓑ Ⓒ Ⓓ	44 Ⓐ Ⓑ Ⓒ Ⓓ
9 Ⓐ Ⓑ Ⓒ Ⓓ	21 Ⓐ Ⓑ Ⓒ Ⓓ	33 Ⓐ Ⓑ Ⓒ Ⓓ	45 Ⓐ Ⓑ Ⓒ Ⓓ
10 Ⓐ Ⓑ Ⓒ Ⓓ	22 Ⓐ Ⓑ Ⓒ Ⓓ	34 Ⓐ Ⓑ Ⓒ Ⓓ	46 Ⓐ Ⓑ Ⓒ Ⓓ
11 Ⓐ Ⓑ Ⓒ Ⓓ	23 Ⓐ Ⓑ Ⓒ Ⓓ	35 Ⓐ Ⓑ Ⓒ Ⓓ	47 Ⓐ Ⓑ Ⓒ Ⓓ
12 Ⓐ Ⓑ Ⓒ Ⓓ	24 Ⓐ Ⓑ Ⓒ Ⓓ	36 Ⓐ Ⓑ Ⓒ Ⓓ	48 Ⓐ Ⓑ Ⓒ Ⓓ

Reading Subtest

1 Ⓐ Ⓑ Ⓒ Ⓓ	22 Ⓐ Ⓑ Ⓒ Ⓓ	43 Ⓐ Ⓑ Ⓒ Ⓓ	64 Ⓐ Ⓑ Ⓒ Ⓓ
2 Ⓐ Ⓑ Ⓒ Ⓓ	23 Ⓐ Ⓑ Ⓒ Ⓓ	44 Ⓐ Ⓑ Ⓒ Ⓓ	65 Ⓐ Ⓑ Ⓒ Ⓓ
3 Ⓐ Ⓑ Ⓒ Ⓓ	24 Ⓐ Ⓑ Ⓒ Ⓓ	45 Ⓐ Ⓑ Ⓒ Ⓓ	66 Ⓐ Ⓑ Ⓒ Ⓓ
4 Ⓐ Ⓑ Ⓒ Ⓓ	25 Ⓐ Ⓑ Ⓒ Ⓓ	46 Ⓐ Ⓑ Ⓒ Ⓓ	67 Ⓐ Ⓑ Ⓒ Ⓓ
5 Ⓐ Ⓑ Ⓒ Ⓓ	26 Ⓐ Ⓑ Ⓒ Ⓓ	47 Ⓐ Ⓑ Ⓒ Ⓓ	68 Ⓐ Ⓑ Ⓒ Ⓓ
6 Ⓐ Ⓑ Ⓒ Ⓓ	27 Ⓐ Ⓑ Ⓒ Ⓓ	48 Ⓐ Ⓑ Ⓒ Ⓓ	69 Ⓐ Ⓑ Ⓒ Ⓓ
7 Ⓐ Ⓑ Ⓒ Ⓓ	28 Ⓐ Ⓑ Ⓒ Ⓓ	49 Ⓐ Ⓑ Ⓒ Ⓓ	70 Ⓐ Ⓑ Ⓒ Ⓓ
8 Ⓐ Ⓑ Ⓒ Ⓓ	29 Ⓐ Ⓑ Ⓒ Ⓓ	50 Ⓐ Ⓑ Ⓒ Ⓓ	71 Ⓐ Ⓑ Ⓒ Ⓓ
9 Ⓐ Ⓑ Ⓒ Ⓓ	30 Ⓐ Ⓑ Ⓒ Ⓓ	51 Ⓐ Ⓑ Ⓒ Ⓓ	72 Ⓐ Ⓑ Ⓒ Ⓓ
10 Ⓐ Ⓑ Ⓒ Ⓓ	31 Ⓐ Ⓑ Ⓒ Ⓓ	52 Ⓐ Ⓑ Ⓒ Ⓓ	73 Ⓐ Ⓑ Ⓒ Ⓓ
11 Ⓐ Ⓑ Ⓒ Ⓓ	32 Ⓐ Ⓑ Ⓒ Ⓓ	53 Ⓐ Ⓑ Ⓒ Ⓓ	74 Ⓐ Ⓑ Ⓒ Ⓓ
12 Ⓐ Ⓑ Ⓒ Ⓓ	33 Ⓐ Ⓑ Ⓒ Ⓓ	54 Ⓐ Ⓑ Ⓒ Ⓓ	75 Ⓐ Ⓑ Ⓒ Ⓓ
13 Ⓐ Ⓑ Ⓒ Ⓓ	34 Ⓐ Ⓑ Ⓒ Ⓓ	55 Ⓐ Ⓑ Ⓒ Ⓓ	76 Ⓐ Ⓑ Ⓒ Ⓓ
14 Ⓐ Ⓑ Ⓒ Ⓓ	35 Ⓐ Ⓑ Ⓒ Ⓓ	56 Ⓐ Ⓑ Ⓒ Ⓓ	77 Ⓐ Ⓑ Ⓒ Ⓓ
15 Ⓐ Ⓑ Ⓒ Ⓓ	36 Ⓐ Ⓑ Ⓒ Ⓓ	57 Ⓐ Ⓑ Ⓒ Ⓓ	78 Ⓐ Ⓑ Ⓒ Ⓓ
16 Ⓐ Ⓑ Ⓒ Ⓓ	37 Ⓐ Ⓑ Ⓒ Ⓓ	58 Ⓐ Ⓑ Ⓒ Ⓓ	79 Ⓐ Ⓑ Ⓒ Ⓓ
17 Ⓐ Ⓑ Ⓒ Ⓓ	38 Ⓐ Ⓑ Ⓒ Ⓓ	59 Ⓐ Ⓑ Ⓒ Ⓓ	80 Ⓐ Ⓑ Ⓒ Ⓓ
18 Ⓐ Ⓑ Ⓒ Ⓓ	39 Ⓐ Ⓑ Ⓒ Ⓓ	60 Ⓐ Ⓑ Ⓒ Ⓓ	81 Ⓐ Ⓑ Ⓒ Ⓓ
19 Ⓐ Ⓑ Ⓒ Ⓓ	40 Ⓐ Ⓑ Ⓒ Ⓓ	61 Ⓐ Ⓑ Ⓒ Ⓓ	82 Ⓐ Ⓑ Ⓒ Ⓓ
20 Ⓐ Ⓑ Ⓒ Ⓓ	41 Ⓐ Ⓑ Ⓒ Ⓓ	62 Ⓐ Ⓑ Ⓒ Ⓓ	83 Ⓐ Ⓑ Ⓒ Ⓓ
21 Ⓐ Ⓑ Ⓒ Ⓓ	42 Ⓐ Ⓑ Ⓒ Ⓓ	63 Ⓐ Ⓑ Ⓒ Ⓓ	84 Ⓐ Ⓑ Ⓒ Ⓓ

Answer Sheet

SELF-ASSESSMENT TEST

MATHEMATICS SECTION

1 (A) (B) (C) (D)   14 (A) (B) (C) (D)   27 (A) (B) (C) (D)   40 (A) (B) (C) (D)
2 (A) (B) (C) (D)   15 (A) (B) (C) (D)   28 (A) (B) (C) (D)   41 (A) (B) (C) (D)
3 (A) (B) (C) (D)   16 (A) (B) (C) (D)   29 (A) (B) (C) (D)   42 (A) (B) (C) (D)
4 (A) (B) (C) (D)   17 (A) (B) (C) (D)   30 (A) (B) (C) (D)   43 (A) (B) (C) (D)
5 (A) (B) (C) (D)   18 (A) (B) (C) (D)   31 (A) (B) (C) (D)   44 (A) (B) (C) (D)
6 (A) (B) (C) (D)   19 (A) (B) (C) (D)   32 (A) (B) (C) (D)   45 (A) (B) (C) (D)
7 (A) (B) (C) (D)   20 (A) (B) (C) (D)   33 (A) (B) (C) (D)   46 (A) (B) (C) (D)
8 (A) (B) (C) (D)   21 (A) (B) (C) (D)   34 (A) (B) (C) (D)   47 (A) (B) (C) (D)
9 (A) (B) (C) (D)   22 (A) (B) (C) (D)   35 (A) (B) (C) (D)   48 (A) (B) (C) (D)
10 (A) (B) (C) (D)   23 (A) (B) (C) (D)   36 (A) (B) (C) (D)   49 (A) (B) (C) (D)
11 (A) (B) (C) (D)   24 (A) (B) (C) (D)   37 (A) (B) (C) (D)   50 (A) (B) (C) (D)
12 (A) (B) (C) (D)   25 (A) (B) (C) (D)   38 (A) (B) (C) (D)
13 (A) (B) (C) (D)   26 (A) (B) (C) (D)   39 (A) (B) (C) (D)

Self-Assessment Test

ENGLISH LANGUAGE ARTS SECTION

Writing Task

Some people believe that high school students should be required to do volunteer work in order to graduate. Do you agree or disagree? Write a letter to the editor of your local newspaper to convince its subscribers to agree with your position on this issue. Be specific about your reasons for taking this position.

LANGUAGE SUBTEST

> **Directions:** Look at the underlined words in each sentence. You may see a mistake in punctuation, capitalization, or word usage. If you spot a mistake in the underlined section of a sentence, select the answer choice that corrects the mistake. If you find no mistake, choose Choice D, *Correct as is*.

1. Every one of the girls in the contest is trying to do <u>their</u> best.

    (A) there
    (B) her
    (C) they're
    (D) *Correct as is*

2. Our first impression of a person <u>can affect</u> us for years to come.

    (A) may effect
    (B) can effect
    (C) affect
    (D) *Correct as is*

3. <u>Theirs</u> no business like show business.

    (A) Theres
    (B) Their's
    (C) There's
    (D) *Correct as is*

4. By next January, Jerry Brown <u>will be</u> governor of California for three years.

    (A) had been
    (B) will have been
    (C) have been
    (D) *Correct as is*

5. "Give me liberty or give me <u>death!" exclaimed Patrick Henry.</u>

    (A) death"! exclaimed Patrick Henry.
    (B) death!" exclaimed Patrick Henry!
    (C) death," exclaimed Patrick Henry!
    (D) *Correct as is*

6. I do not know where <u>Merritt College is?</u>

    (A) is Merritt College?
    (B) is Merritt college.
    (C) Merritt College is.
    (D) *Correct as is*

7. I <u>can't hardly</u> hear what the professor is saying.

   (A) cannot hardly
   (B) couldn't hardly
   (C) can hardly
   (D) *Correct as is*

8. She told her secret to Marjorie <u>as well as myself</u>.

   (A) as well as I
   (B) as well as me
   (C) as good as myself
   (D) *Correct as is*

9. <u>Let's go</u> to the movies.

   (A) Lets go
   (B) Lets' go
   (C) Let's us go
   (D) *Correct as is*

10. I <u>had ought to like</u> coffee, but I don't.

    (A) ought to like
    (B) should of liked
    (C) had ought like
    (D) *Correct as is*

11. If you work <u>less</u> hours, you will receive less pay.

    (A) fewer
    (B) lesser
    (C) least
    (D) *Correct as is*

12. <u>When I went to the hospital I</u> got to ride in an ambulance.

    (A) When I have gone to the hospital; I
    (B) When I went to the hospital, I
    (C) I went to the hospital, I
    (D) *Correct as is*

13. My grandmother often <u>said: "Haste makes waste"</u>.

    (A) said, "Haste makes waste."
    (B) said "Haste makes waste."
    (C) said, "Haste makes waste".
    (D) *Correct as is*

14. We're waiting to see which college <u>excepts</u> Alisa first.

    (A) excepted
    (B) accepting
    (C) accepts
    (D) *Correct as is*

15. She <u>did not keep no</u> receipts.

    (A) does not keep no
    (B) did not keep any
    (C) did not keep none
    (D) *Correct as is*

16. After her walk, she <u>lay</u> down for a short nap.

    (A) lied
    (B) laid
    (C) laying
    (D) *Correct as is*

17. <u>Me and Johnny</u> had pizza for dinner.

    (A) Johnny and myself
    (B) Johnny and me
    (C) Johnny and I
    (D) *Correct as is*

18. Many special occasions in life <u>requires</u> formal clothing.

    (A) require
    (B) are required
    (C) does require
    (D) *Correct as is*

Directions: Look at each sentence. You may see a mistake in sentence structure. If you spot a mistake in the sentence's structure, select the answer choice that rewrites the sentence so that it is clear, concise, and correct. If you find no mistake, choose Choice D, *Correct as is*.

19. These were issues which were, in the main, having to do with finances.

    (A) These issues, which, in the main, they had to do with finances.
    (B) Mainly, these were issues that were having to do with finances.
    (C) These were mainly financial issues.
    (D) *Correct as is*

20. At art school Angelina is studying painting, sculpting, and how to make collages.

    (A) At art school Angelina is studying painting, sculpting, and collage-making.
    (B) At art school Angelina is studying to paint, to sculpt, and how to make collages.
    (C) Angelina is studying painting, sculpting, and to make collages at art school.
    (D) *Correct as is*

21. Ben ran down the stairs, charged through the front door, and, without a pause, jumped on his bike.

    (A) Ben ran down the stairs and he charged through the front door and he jumped on his bike without a pause.
    (B) Running down the stairs, charging through the front door, Ben jumping on his bike without a pause.
    (C) Ben ran down the stairs charged through the front door and jumped on his bike without a pause.
    (D) *Correct as is*

22. The reason why she stayed home from the dance was because she had a cold.

    (A) The reason why she had stayed home from the dance was because she was having a cold.
    (B) She stayed home from the dance because she had a cold.
    (C) Why she stayed home from the dance, it was because she had a cold.
    (D) *Correct as is*

23. Blue whales weighing over 120 tons are among the world's largest sea mammals.

    (A) Blue whales, among the world's largest sea mammals, are weighing over 120 tons.
    (B) Weighing over 120 tons, blue whales are among the world's largest sea mammals.
    (C) The world's largest sea mammals, weighing over 120 tons are blue whales.
    (D) *Correct as is*

24. If our football team wins the state championship later this season, they won for four straight years.

    (A) If our football team wins the state championship later this season, they will have won for four straight years.
    (B) If our football team wins the state championship later this season, they would have won for four straight years.
    (C) If our football team wins the state championship later this season, they had won for four straight years.
    (D) *Correct as is*

25. Maggie wrote an article about the problem with mice in the cafeteria in the school newspaper.

    (A) Maggie wrote an article about the problem with mice in the school newspaper in the cafeteria.
    (B) In an article in the school newspaper, Maggie wrote about the problem with mice in the cafeteria.
    (C) In the school newspaper, Maggie wrote about the problem with mice in the cafeteria in an article.
    (D) *Correct as is*

26. A scholar is a person who is studious, intelligent, and has a good education.

    (A) A scholar is a person who is studious, has intelligence, and a good education.
    (B) A scholar is a person who is studying, intelligent, and has a good education.
    (C) A scholar is a person who is studious, intelligent, and well-educated.
    (D) *Correct as is*

27. Because the test was difficult, I did just fine.

    (A) Even though the test was difficult, I did just fine.
    (B) Being that the test was difficult, I did just fine.
    (C) Since the test was difficult, I did just fine.
    (D) *Correct as is*

28. I was hindered by the thick underbrush and the branches hanging from the trees running through the woods.

    (A) Running through the woods, I was hindered by the thick underbrush and the branches hanging from the trees.
    (B) Running through the woods, the thick underbrush and the branches hanging from the trees hindered me.
    (C) I was hindered through the woods running by the thick underbrush and the branches hanging from the trees.
    (D) *Correct as is*

29. The proposed cuts in the welfare program are going to hurt the poor, who will have no place to go for relief.

    (A) The proposed cuts in the welfare program are going to hurt the poor, they shall have no place to go for relief.
    (B) The proposed cuts in the welfare program are going to hurt the poor, which will have no place to go for relief.
    (C) The proposed cuts in the welfare program are going to hurt the poor, they will have no place to go for relief.
    (D) *Correct as is*

30. I have enjoyed the films of Christopher Guest not only for their plots but also because they are witty.

    (A) I have enjoyed the films of Christopher Guest not only for their plots but because they are also witty.
    (B) I have enjoyed the films of Christopher Guest not only for their plots but also for their wit.
    (C) I have enjoyed the films of Christopher Guest not only for their plots but for their wit also.
    (D) *Correct as is*

31. After the visitor signed the historic guest book, which held the signatures of the great and near-great who had visited the estate during the past fifty years.

    (A) After the visitor had signed the historic guest book, which held the signatures of the great and near-great who had visited the estate during the past fifty years.
    (B) Afterwards the visitor signed the historic guest book it held the signatures of the great and near-great who had visited the estate during the past fifty years.
    (C) The visitor signed the historic guest book, which held the signatures of the great and near-great who had visited the estate during the past fifty years.
    (D) *Correct as is*

32. When Anita Yu comes back from her sales trips, she usually submitted her expense account to the chief bookkeeper.

    (A) When Anita Yu comes back from her sales trips, usually she had submitted her expense account to the chief bookkeeper.
    (B) When Anita Yu comes back from her sales trips, she usually submits her expense account to the chief bookkeeper.
    (C) Anita Yu comes back from her sales trips, and she usually submitted her expense account to the chief bookkeeper.
    (D) *Correct as is*

33. By the time we arrive in Italy, we have traveled through four countries.

    (A) By the time we arrive in Italy, we had traveled through four countries.
    (B) By the time we arrive in Italy, we will have traveled through four countries.
    (C) By the time we arrive in Italy, four countries have been traveled through.
    (D) *Correct as is*

34. J.K. Rowling, a British novelist, whose fame in the field of fantasy may come to equal that of J.R.R. Tolkien.

    (A) A British novelist, J.K. Rowling, whose fame in the field of fantasy may come to equal that of J.R.R. Tolkien.
    (B) J.K. Rowling, who is a British novelist, and whose fame in the field of fantasy may come to equal that of J.R.R. Tolkien.
    (C) J.K. Rowling is a British novelist whose fame in the field of fantasy may come to equal that of J.R.R. Tolkien.
    (D) *Correct as is*

35. The rock star always had enthusiastic fans and they loved him.

    (A) The rock star always had enthusiastic fans which loved him.
    (B) The rock star always had enthusiastic fans who loved him.
    (C) The rock star always had enthusiastic fans, and they loved him.
    (D) *Correct as is*

36. Familiar with the route from her driving lessons, the student driver's road test was easy for her to pass.

    (A) Familiar with the route from her driving lessons, the student driver's road test was easily passed by her.
    (B) Being that she was familiar with the route from her driving lessons, the student driver's road test was easy for her to pass.
    (C) Because she was familiar with the route from her driving lessons, the student driver found the road test easy to pass.
    (D) *Correct as is*

Directions: Read the passage. Then read the questions that come after the passage. Choose the correct answer based on what you know about writing good essays.

The Try-Out

Danny was in first grade the first time he tried out for a basketball team. This was Little League basketball, and every first grader who tried out was assigned to a team. It didn't matter if someone who tried out did things wrong. Nobody was left out. Danny loved playing basketball and wanted to play it forever. Each year the try-outs got harder and harder. Now he was in seventh grade, and today's try-out would decide whether he would earn a spot on the seventh-grade travel team, the Middletown Vikings. Danny's father Richie had been on the travel team when he was a boy. When he was on the team, he had even led the Vikings to the finals of the Little League Basketball World Series that year. More than anything else in the world, Danny wanted to follow in his father's footsteps. He had studied the game until he knew more about basketball than anyone else in the school. Given that, Danny was afraid he wouldn't make the cut for the travel team. To his dismay, he had stopped growing back in fifth grade. As he looked at himself in the mirror, he knew in his heart that he was just too short to be a Viking.

It didn't matter if someone who tried out <u>did things wrong</u>.

37. Consider the underlined words in the sentence above. Good writing uses concrete examples. Choose the answer that replaces the underlined words with a concrete example.

    (A) was lacking in ability
    (B) performed inadequately
    (C) was a weak player
    (D) missed every free throw

38. Which sentence would NOT belong in this paragraph?

    (A) Danny thought his father was the best basketball player he had ever seen.
    (B) Little League basketball tryouts are very different from Little League baseball tryouts.
    (C) Danny was only fifty-five inches tall.
    (D) He had spent hour after hour practicing his jump shots and building up his speed.

Danny's father Richie had been on the travel team when he was a boy. When he was on the team, he had even led the Vikings to the finals of the Little League Basketball World Series that year.

39. Consider the two sentences above. What is the BEST way to combine these sentences?

    (A) Danny's father Richie having been on the travel team when he was a boy, when he was on the team, he had even led the Vikings to the finals of the Little League Basketball World Series that year.
    (B) Danny's father Richie had been on the travel team when he was a boy; he had even led the Vikings to the finals of the Little League Basketball World Series that year.
    (C) When he was a boy, Danny's father Richie had been on the travel team; and, when he was on the team, he had even led the Vikings to the finals of the Little League Basketball World Series that year.
    (D) When Danny's father Richie was on the travel team, he was a boy, and he had even led the Vikings to the finals of the Little League Basketball World Series that year.

Given that, Danny was afraid he wouldn't make the cut for the travel team.

40. Which word or phrase would BEST replace the underlined phrase in the sentence above?

    (A) Even so,
    (B) Therefore,
    (D) Consequently,
    (D) Being that

41. Which of these would be the best topic sentence for this paragraph?

    (A) The Middletown Vikings travel team went to the finals of the Little League Basketball World Series.
    (B) Danny's father had bought him new sneakers for the try-out.
    (C) For almost as long as he could remember, Danny had wanted to play on the Vikings travel team.
    (D) All seventh-graders are eligible to try out for the Middletown Vikings basketball travel team.

42. Which of the following ideas is supported by details or evidence in the passage?
    (A) Danny is wholly convinced that he will make the travel team.
    (B) All seventh-graders are required to try out for the basketball team.
    (C) Danny is highly motivated to become a skilled basketball player.
    (D) Everyone who tries out for the seventh-grade travel team is automatically accepted.

Archbishop Desmond Tutu

When he was a child in South Africa, Desmond Tutu wanted to be a doctor. Because his family did not have enough money to pay for medical training for him, he had to give up this dream. He became a school teacher instead. For four years he was happy working as a
(5) *teacher, but then the South African government enacted a new law. It was called the Bantu Education Act. The provisions of the act appalled Tutu. Discriminating against South Africa's black and Asian students, it set up a deliberately inferior system of education for them. Tutu could not cooperate with this law. He resigned from his*
(10) *teaching job and began to study to be an Anglican priest.*

As a priest, Tutu fought for equal rights for all South Africans. He preached and did things to call the world's attention to the evils of apartheid *(the South African system of racial segregation that barred blacks from white areas and deported them to bleak homelands). He*
(15) *became famous throughout the world for his nonviolent resistance to apartheid, and for his support for oppressed people everywhere.*

Even though he is famous, Archbishop Tutu has always made time for people. On the day in 1984 that he was named winner of the Nobel Peace Prize, reporters and photographers converged on the
(20) *seminary where he was staying. The school administration quickly set up a press conference in a central courtyard. That way Archbishop Tutu could speak to all the reporters at once. Just as the press conference was going to begin, the archbishop's student assistant came through the courtyard. She was returning from a family funeral.*
(25) *Right away the archbishop left the microphones and cameras, and he went to comfort her. The world press could wait; her grief could not.*

43. Which of these would be the best topic sentence for the opening paragraph?

    (A) Desmond Tutu taught at the Johannesburg Bantu High School for four years.
    (B) Even if you don't always get what you want in life, that can be a good thing.
    (C) One of the world's most famous crusaders for social justice and peace is South Africa's Archbishop Desmond Tutu.
    (D) Desmond Tutu is the name of a very famous clergyman who is known all around the world for his fight for social justice.

44. As used in line 6, the word "provisions" most nearly means

    (A) requirements
    (B) supplies
    (C) predictions
    (D) food

He preached and <u>did things</u> to call the world's attention to the evils of apartheid.

45. Consider the underlined words in sentence above. Good writing uses concrete examples. Choose the answer that replaces the underlined words with a concrete example.

   (A) was willing
   (B) gave lectures
   (C) he managed
   (D) took actions

He preached and did things to call the world's attention to the evils of apartheid (the South African system of racial segregation that barred blacks from white areas and deported them to bleak homelands).

46. What is the purpose of the words in parentheses in the sentence above?

   (A) to argue a point
   (B) to define a term
   (C) to ask a question
   (D) to make a suggestion

The school administration quickly set up a press conference in a central courtyard. That way Archbishop Tutu could speak to all the reporters at once.

47. What is the BEST way to combine the two sentences shown above?

   (A) The school administration quickly set up a press conference in a central courtyard, that was where Archbishop Tutu could speak to all the reporters at once.
   (B) Quickly the school administration set up a press conference in a central courtyard, the reason was because Archbishop Tutu could speak to all the reporters at once.
   (C) When the school administration quickly set up a press conference in a central courtyard, because that way Archbishop Tutu could speak to all the reporters at once.
   (D) The school administration quickly set up a press conference in a central courtyard so that Archbishop Tutu could speak to all the reporters at once.

48. Which sentence would NOT belong in the final paragraph?

   (A) Desmond Tutu has visited many countries in his crusade for social justice.
   (B) The young woman looked tired and drawn.
   (C) The quiet seminary grounds were transformed into a mob scene.
   (D) Individuals matter deeply to him.

READING SUBTEST

Directions: Read the passage. Then read each question about the passage. Make up your mind which is the best answer to the question. Then mark the answer you have chosen on your answer sheet.

THE ASS AND THE LOAD OF SALT
A Fable from Greece

A merchant was driving his donkey homeward from the seashore with a heavy load of salt. They came to a river crossed by a shallow ford. They had crossed this river many times before without accident, but this time the donkey slipped and fell when halfway over. When the merchant at last got the donkey to his feet, much of the salt had melted away. Delighted to find how much lighter his burden had become, the donkey finished the journey very cheerfully. The merchant, however, was much less pleased.

The next day the merchant led his donkey back to the seashore for another load of salt. On the way home the donkey, remembering what had happened at the ford, purposely let himself fall into the water, and again got rid of most of his heavy load.

The merchant was furious. He immediately turned around and drove the donkey back to the seashore, where he loaded him with two great baskets filled with sponges. At the ford the donkey again purposely stumbled and fell into the water; but this time, when the donkey had scrambled to his feet, his load was not lighter, and it was a very unhappy donkey that dragged himself homeward under a load ten times heavier than before.

1. What did the merchant plan to do with the salt?

   (A) Feed it to the donkey.
   (B) Dissolve it in liquid.
   (C) Carry it to the seashore.
   (D) Sell it to customers.

2. What made the donkey's load grow lighter the first time he fell in the river?

   (A) One of the baskets fell into the water.
   (B) The merchant lightened the donkey's load.
   (C) The salt dissolved in the water.
   (D) The load was able to float.

3. After falling in the river the first time, the donkey was cheerful because

   (A) he enjoyed getting wet
   (B) his load was easier to carry
   (C) his master was angry
   (D) he knew the journey was almost over

4. The merchant was much less pleased because

   (A) his donkey had been injured
   (B) he still had a long distance to travel
   (C) the donkey had refused to get back on its feet
   (D) he had less salt to sell

5. The second time the donkey fell in the river, he did so

   (A) clumsily
   (B) heavily
   (C) intentionally
   (D) absentmindedly

6. People like the merchant in this story can be described as

   (A) shrewd
   (B) wicked
   (C) greedy
   (D) honest

7. This story was probably told in order to

   (A) share a true experience
   (B) help the reader train animals
   (C) help the reader sell merchandise
   (D) teach a lesson

SYSTEMS OF BREEDING

In planning a breeding program for rabbits, you first need to understand the concept of the gene pool. Any breed or other foundation stock selected for breeding constitutes a pool or group of many, perhaps thousands, of hereditary units, commonly referred to as genes. Genes are specifically located in the chromosomes, very small threadlike bodies found in every cell of the body. In a rabbit there are 22 pairs, and their segregation (one member of each pair going to each egg or sperm) in the production of eggs or sperm, plus the ultimate union of egg and sperm at mating and conception, provides the mechanism for transmission of hereditary characteristics from one generation to the next. It also provides the mechanism that in nature ensures sufficient variability for adaptation of the species to minor changes in the environment and for its perpetuation.

The gene pool of the rabbit has been modified in many ways by domestication and by selection to establish the different breeds. This pool, in the rabbits at hand, is the breeder's capital stock, and intelligent breeding depends on knowing as much as possible about the pool. How well does it perpetuate itself? How much variation does it transmit that is either good, bad, or indifferent, particularly with respect to reproductive capacity? How much of it is immediately apparent to the breeder, and how much can become apparent only after long breeding experience? In spite of all that humans know about genetics and reproduction, nature is still the most successful breeder. If this were not so, we would not have the infinite number and variety of species that exist in the world, many of which are known to have existed for many, many centuries. But even nature slips. Species have been lost as a result of circumstances with which they were unable to cope; malformed offspring occur sometimes in the wild. Nature's success is essentially due to the size of the gene pools of each species, plus the ruthless elimination of the unfit as they appear. These combine to ensure a high proportion of successful individuals, including some individuals adaptable to any ordinary change that may occur in the environment in which they live. The ability to adapt to differing environments is the feature that helps promote survival and is the mechanism by which species have evolved.

8. This article is probably addressed to

 (A) professional geneticists
 (B) commercial rabbit raisers
 (C) successful individuals
 (D) environmental specialists

9. What are chromosomes?

 (A) genes
 (B) species
 (C) breeds of rabbits
 (D) parts of cells

10. Which of the following statements are TRUE?

 I. Breeders need genetic information to plan breeding programs intelligently.
 II. The gene pool consists of 22 chromosome pairs.
 III. Successful species survive by adapting to their environment.

 (A) Statements I and II only
 (B) Statements I and III only
 (C) Statements II and III only
 (D) all of the statements

Self-Assessment Test

11. What does the phrase "even nature slips" most nearly mean?

    (A) It is natural to let things slide.
    (B) Nature is steadily successful.
    (C) Nature moves smoothly but gradually.
    (D) Even nature makes mistakes.

CHILDREN OF THE HARVEST
An Autobiographical Essay by Lois Phillips Hudson

When school was out, I hurried to find my sister and get out of the schoolyard before seeing anybody in my class. But Barbara and her friends had beaten us to the playground entrance and they seemed to be waiting for us. Barbara said, "So now you're in the A class." She sounded impressed.

"What's the A class?" I asked.

Everybody made superior yet faintly envious giggling sounds. "Well, why did you think the teacher moved you to the front of the room, dopey? Didn't you know you were in the C class before, way in the back of the room?"

Of course I hadn't known. The Wenatchee fifth grade was bigger than my whole school had been in North Dakota, and the idea of subdivisions within a grade had never occurred to me. The subdividing for the first marking period had been done before I came to the school, and I had never, in the six weeks I'd been there, talked to anyone long enough to find out about the A, B, and C classes.

I still could not understand why that had made such a difference to Barbara and her friends. I didn't yet know that it was disgraceful and dirty to be a transient laborer and ridiculous to be from North Dakota. I thought living in a tent was more fun than living in a house. I didn't know that we were gypsies, really (how that thought would have thrilled me then!), and that we were regarded with the suspicion felt by those who plant toward those who do not plant. It didn't occur to me that we were all looked upon as one more of the untrustworthy natural phenomena, drifting here and there like mists or winds, that farmers of certain crops are resentfully forced to rely on. I didn't know that I was the only child who had camped on the Baumanns' land ever to get out of the C class. I did not know that school administrators and civic leaders held conferences to talk about the problem of transient laborers.

I only knew that for two happy days I walked to school with Barbara and her friends, played hopscotch and jump rope with them at recess, and was even invited into the house for some ginger ale— an exotic drink I had never tasted before.

12. The person telling this story is

    (A) an understanding teacher remembering a favorite pupil
    (B) a mature adult recalling an episode from her youth
    (C) an envious student upset with a schoolmate
    (D) a concerned parent worried about her child

13. Barbara is impressed because

    (A) the narrator and her sister live in a tent
    (B) only the best students are assigned to the A class
    (C) she thinks highly of the teacher
    (D) she knows how much the narrator wanted to be in the A class

14. The narrator had most probably been placed in the C class because

    (A) she was a poor reader
    (B) she had come from a small school
    (C) all migrant children were assigned to the C class
    (D) the A and B classes were both filled to capacity

15. The people in the community distrusted the transient laborers because the laborers were

    (A) drifters with no ties to the community
    (B) unwilling to help with the planting
    (C) people with little or no education
    (D) afraid of strangers

16. After the narrator was moved to the A class, how did Barbara and Barbara's group of friends view her?

    (A) They disliked her as a competitor.
    (B) They accepted her as a playmate.
    (C) They felt superior to her as a student.
    (D) They admired her for being a gypsy.

17. People like the natives of Wenatchee in this story can be described as

    (A) dishonest
    (B) shrewd
    (C) generous
    (D) intolerant

18. To the narrator, ginger ale was an exotic drink because

    (A) it came from a foreign country
    (B) it was associated with gypsies
    (C) she had not encountered it before
    (D) Barbara had refused to give her any

ARMY RESERVE BENEFITS: MONEY FOR THE FUTURE

Maybe you're young and don't want to think about it now. Maybe you're not so young and are thinking about it. The "it" refers to life after service—your retirement and survivor benefits. Let's take a look at them.

Retirement pay

As a reservist attending regular monthly drills and two weeks of annual training, you are building up points towards retirement pay, pay that you are entitled to when you reach the age of 60 after 20 years of qualifying service. Retirement pay is something to think about, especially when it's tacked on to income from Social Security and a civilian or civil service pension.

Retirement benefits

When you start drawing your retirement pay from the Reserve, the benefits don't stop there. In fact, some of them just begin or are an extension of those which you received prior to retirement. For example:

Medical Care. *When you start receiving retirement pay, you and your legal dependents become eligible for medical care at a military medical facility. In some cases, medical care is authorized at a civilian hospital, for which the Army pays a major part of the cost.*

Dental Care. *Providing facilities are available, you can receive unlimited dental care. There are restrictions on the amount of care extended to dependents.*

PX and Commissary Shopping Privileges. *You and your spouse can make as many trips to these stores as you like, any time you like.*

Travel. *There may be other kinds of trips in store for you as well. One of the retirement benefits you and your dependents can enjoy is the chance to travel on military aircraft (space-available basis) anywhere in the world. When the cost of transportation can take a large chunk out of a vacation fund, this benefit can make the difference between going 50 miles or 5000 miles from home.*

There's More. *There are other benefits, too, that you receive as a Reserve retiree drawing retirement pay. Some are limited, but well worth exploring. These include legal assistance, veterinary aid, and use of recreation and other facilities (such as tennis courts and craft shops) on military posts. In addition, many military installations maintain recreation areas on lakes, by seashores, or in the mountains that are also available to retirees.*

19. This article was probably taken from

   (A) a congressional report on military spending
   (B) an Army Reserve combat training manual
   (C) an Army Reserve recruiting pamphlet
   (D) a civil service pension guide

20. Which of the following statements are FALSE?

    I. A retired Reservist's husband or wife may shop at the commissary.

    II. Army Reserve retirees are always able to get on military flights.

    III. The Army pays only for medical treatments performed at military hospitals.

    (A) Statements I and II only

    (B) Statements I and III only

    (C) Statements II and III only

    (D) all of the statements

21. Which of the following is NOT a retirement benefit provided by the Reserve for its retirees?

    (A) care for sick pets

    (B) access to athletic facilities

    (C) help with legal difficulties

    (D) unlimited dental care for dependents

22. Which of the following statements is TRUE?

    (A) The Reserve always provides dental treatment for retirees.

    (B) The PX is a store used by both active and retired military personnel.

    (C) You begin receiving your retirement pay 20 years after you reach the age of 60.

    (D) Retirees are entitled to use only on-post military recreation facilities.

In the following selection from the novel A Tale of Two Cities, *Charles Dickens describes the journey of a coach carrying mail and passengers to the seaport town of Dover.*

THE DOVER ROAD
From a Novel by Charles Dickens

It was the Dover road that lay, on a Friday night, late in November, before the first of the persons with whom this history has business. The Dover road lay, as to him, beyond the Dover mail, as it lumbered up Shooter's Hill. We walked uphill in the mire by the side of the mail, as the rest of the passengers did; not because they had the least relish for walking exercise, under the circumstances, but because the hill, and the harness, and the mud, and the mail, were all so heavy, that the horses had three times already come to a stop, besides once drawing the coach across the road, with the mutinous intent of taking it back to Blackheath.

With drooping heads and tremulous tails, the horses mashed their way through thick mud, floundering and stumbling between whiles as if they were falling to pieces at the larger joints. As often as the driver rested them and brought them to a stand, with a wary "Wo-ho!

So-ho then!" the near leader violently shook his head and everything upon it — like an unusually emphatic horse, denying that the coach could be got up the hill. Whenever the leader made this rattle, the passenger started, as a nervous passenger might, and was disturbed in mind.

23. The passengers are walking up the hill because

    (A) they need fresh air and exercise
    (B) they are afraid of the horses
    (C) there is no room for them in the coach
    (D) the coach cannot carry them uphill

24. In the first paragraph, the word "lumbered" most nearly means

    (A) was made of wood
    (B) moved heavily
    (C) cut down timber
    (D) became useless

25. The passengers are not enjoying their walk because

    (A) the road is muddy and hard to climb
    (B) they want to return to Blackheath
    (C) they had paid to go to Dover
    (D) they prefer other forms of exercise

26. In the second paragraph, the phrase "brought them to a stand" means

    (A) led them to a booth
    (B) made them get back on their feet after a fall
    (C) caused them to come to a halt
    (D) fetched them to the station

27. In the passage, the horse do all of the following EXCEPT

    (A) drag the coach
    (B) stagger and lurch
    (C) stop in their tracks
    (D) attempt to gallop

28. The near leader (second paragraph) is

    (A) the driver
    (B) one of the horses
    (C) one of the passengers
    (D) the narrator

29. The passenger starts because

    (A) the sudden noise frightens him
    (B) it is time to begin his journey
    (C) the driver has shaken his whip
    (D) they cannot reach the top of the hill

FUEL RESOURCES

California's mineral fuel resources are primarily oil and gas. The few bituminous and subbituminous coal seams in the state have not been mined for many years. Output from the one remaining lignite mine near Ione, in Amador County, is now processed not as fuel, but for its content of montan wax, used as an additive in making shoe polish and rubber products. Peat from four counties is used only for soil conditioning or other agricultural purposes.

Despite its huge output, California's liquid fuels industry cannot meet the demands of the consumers within the state. Crude petroleum and gasoline and other refinery products must be imported each year in constantly increasing quantities by ocean tankers and pipeline. Natural gas is imported by pipeline from as far away as Canada. This demand stems from a combination of ever-rising population, lack of solid fuels, and the requirements of more than 10 million motor vehicles registered in the state.

Production of crude petroleum reached its peak in 1953 and began to decline the following year. It has recently averaged about 300 million barrels annually. Increasing emphasis on secondary recovery methods and federal oil and gas leasing on the ocean bottom miles seaward from older tidelands drilling are slowing the decline, but have not fully compensated for the reduced output from older oilfields. More than a quarter of the crude oil being processed by California's two-score refineries now is obtained outside the state. Most of the in-state production is in the five adjoining counties of Los Angeles, Kern, Ventura, Orange, and Santa Barbara, although Fresno and Monterey counties to the north also report significant quantities.

California has begun exploring its offshore resources of oil and gas hidden in the submerged lands of the Outer Continental Shelf. Oil and gas reserves beneath the ocean's depths may open a promising source of fuel for California and the nation. With advanced technology, drilling for possible reserves in depths encountered outside the three-mile limit off the California coast has become practical.

30. Which of the following is one of California's chief natural fuel resources?

    (A) coal
    (B) lignite
    (C) oil
    (D) peat

31. Lignite's high content of montan wax is used

    (A) in making shoe polish
    (B) in processing oil and gas
    (C) for fuel
    (D) for soil conditioning

32. The rising demand for liquid fuels within California has been caused by all the following EXCEPT the
    (A) increasing air pollution
    (B) increasing number of motor vehicles
    (C) increasing population
    (D) lack of solid fuels

33. California's liquid fuels industry hopes to find new sources of liquid fuel by

    (A) coal mining
    (B) offshore drilling
    (C) refining montan wax
    (D) tidelands drilling

34. Which of the following statements about California's liquid fuels industry is TRUE?

    (A) It is less important than California's solid fuel industry.
    (B) It is increasingly capable of meeting the demands of California's consumers without relying on imports.
    (C) It is increasingly involved in the processing of lignite.
    (D) It is increasingly involved in exploring offshore resources of oil and gas.

A NARROW FELLOW IN THE GRASS
A Poem by Emily Dickinson

A narrow fellow in the grass
Occasionally rides;
You may have met him. Did you not,
His notice sudden is.

(5)   *The grass divides as with a comb,*
A spotted shaft is seen,
And then it closes at your feet
And opens further on.

He likes a boggy acre,
(10)   *A floor too cool for corn,*
Yet when a boy and barefoot,
I more than once at noon

Have passed, I thought, a whip-lash
Unbraiding in the sun,
(15)   *When, stooping to secure it,*
It wrinkled, and was gone.

Several of nature's people
I know, and they know me;
I feel for them a transport
(20)   *Of cordiality;*

But never met this fellow,
Attended or alone,
Without a tighter breathing
And zero at the bone.

Emily Dickinson (1830–1886)

35. The "narrow fellow" of the title is most likely a

   (A) barefoot boy
   (B) blade of grass
   (C) rider with a whip
   (D) spotted snake

36. In line 7, "it" most likely refers to the

   (A) comb
   (B) grass
   (C) shaft
   (D) narrow fellow

37. Who is the speaker of this poem?

    (A) a young boy
    (B) an expert naturalist
    (C) an adult male
    (D) a woman who loves nature

38. What is the speaker's attitude toward the "narrow fellow" of the title?

    (A) grudging respect
    (B) marked fear
    (C) breathless wonder
    (D) cordial goodwill

POLAR BEARS

*Exquisitely adapted for life in one of earth's harshest environ-
ments, polar bears can survive for twenty years or more on the Arctic
Circle's glacial ice. At home in a waste where temperatures reach
minus 50 degrees Fahrenheit, these largest members of the bear fam-
(5) ily are a striking example of natural selection at work. Because
nature has provided them with two layers of fur covering an underlying coating of blubber, polar bears are well adapted to resist heat
loss. Their broad, snowshoe-like paws and sharp, curved claws
enable them to traverse the ice with ease. They even possess the
(10) capacity to scent prey from a distance of 20 miles.*

39. How does the author feel about the polar bear's adaptation to its environment?

    (A) ambivalent
    (B) admiring
    (C) disapproving
    (D) indifferent

40. Polar bears' bodies are well adapted to

    (A) conserving heat
    (B) surviving despite little water
    (C) escaping from their prey
    (D) wearing snowshoes

41. In line 10, "capacity" most nearly means

    (A) ability
    (B) quantity
    (C) spaciousness
    (D) intelligence

In the following selection from the novel Martin Eden, *Jack London describes his hero's first visit to an unfamiliar residence.*

AN AWKWARD VISIT
A Selection from *Martin Eden* by Jack London

The one who opened the door with a latch-key went in, followed by a young fellow* who awkwardly removed his cap. He wore rough clothes that smacked of the sea, and he was manifestly out of place in the spacious hall in which he found himself. He did not know what to do with his cap, and was stuffing it into his coat pocket when the other took it from him. The act was done quietly and naturally, and the awkward young fellow appreciated it. "He understands," was his thought. "He'll see me through all right."

He walked at the other's heels with a swing to his shoulders, and his legs spread unwittingly, as if the level floors were tilting up and sinking down to the heave and lunge of the sea. The wide rooms seemed too narrow for his rolling gait, and to himself he was in terror lest his broad shoulders should collide with the doorways or sweep the bric-a-brac from the low mantel. He recoiled from side to side between the various objects and multiplied the hazards that in reality lodged only in his mind. Between a grand piano and a centre-table piled high with books was space for a half a dozen to walk abreast, yet he essayed it with trepidation. His heavy arms hung loosely at his sides. He did not know what to do with those arms and hands, and when, to his excited vision, one arm seemed liable to brush against the books on the table, he lurched away like a frightened horse, barely missing the piano stool. He watched the easy walk of the other in front of him, and for the first time realized that his walk was different from that of other men. He experienced a momentary pang of shame that he should walk so uncouthly. The sweat burst through the skin of his forehead in tiny beads, and he paused and mopped his bronzed face with his handkerchief.

"Hold on, Arthur, my boy," he said, attempting to mask his anxiety with a flippant remark. "This is too much all at once for yours truly. Give me a chance to get my nerve. You know I didn't want to come, an' I guess your fam'ly ain't hankerin' to see me neither."

"That's all right," was the reassuring answer. "You mustn't be frightened at us. We're just homely people—Hello, there's a letter for me."

*The young fellow is Martin Eden.

42. This selection is best described as

    (A) biography
    (B) fiction
    (C) essay
    (D) screenplay

43. The person who opens the door is a

    (A) burglar
    (B) young boy
    (C) sailor
    (D) family member

44. Which of the following BEST describes the relationship between Arthur and Martin?

    (A) Arthur is Martin's brother.
    (B) Arthur and Martin are members of the same sailing crew.
    (C) Arthur and Martin are old friends.
    (D) Arthur and Martin are acquaintances from different backgrounds.

45. How does Martin feel about his visit?

    (A) He feels eager to embark on a new adventure.
    (B) He feels proud to be in such a beautiful home.
    (C) He feels uncertain of his welcome.
    (D) He feels distrustful of Arthur's motives.

46. To Martin, the room seems filled with

    (A) treasures
    (B) obstacles
    (C) arms and hands
    (D) family

47. In the fourth paragraph, the word "homely" most nearly means

    (A) unattractive
    (B) uncultured
    (C) ordinary
    (D) stay-at-home

A DEFENSE AGAINST SMALLPOX

Few people today know about the efforts of an 18th-century English noblewoman to fight smallpox, then an often fatal disease. Lady Mary Wortley Montagu (1689–1762) was a gifted English writer. As a young woman, she ran away from home to marry Edward Wortley Montagu. Early in the marriage, Lady Montagu came down with a severe case of smallpox that badly scarred her face. However, she did not hide from society, but played an active role at court.

Two years later Lady Montagu once again defied convention by traveling to Turkey with her husband and three-year-old son. In Constantinople she learned of the Eastern custom of giving people a mild case of the pox to prevent them from coming down with the deadly form of the disease. (Nowadays people call this technique inoculation.) Lady Montagu described the practice in letters to her friends back home. "There is a set of old women who make it their business to perform the operation," she wrote. Instead of treating the operation as a risky medical procedure, the Turks looked on it almost as a diversion. Whenever a family decided it was time for their young people to be inoculated, they would invite friends and relatives for a long visit—a sort of house party. Then an old woman with a large needle would come by. She would treat a dozen or more patients, cutting open veins and injecting tiny amounts of pus taken from someone with a mild case of the disease. After about a week the patients would become feverish and show signs of the pox, but in another ten days they would be good as new.

Lady Montagu thought it was her patriotic duty to bring this method of fighting smallpox to the attention of people in England. She believed the operation to be completely safe. Every year thousands of Turks were inoculated, and there was no record that anyone inoculated had died of the pox. In Constantinople, she had her young son inoculated, and, after the Montagus returned from Turkey, their three-month-old daughter Mary became the first person in England to be inoculated.

Despite opposition from religious and medical groups, thanks to Lady Montagu's efforts inoculation caught on. It was the chief defense against death by smallpox for the next 80 years until the discovery of vaccination by Jenner.

48. Lady Mary Wortley Montagu is an example of

    (A) a scientist who studied epidemics
    (B) a mother who was troubled by foreign medical practices
    (C) a traveler who brought back word of a new way to fight disease
    (D) a writer who did not understand English medical traditions

49. As used in the second paragraph, "convention" most nearly means

    (A) a house party
    (B) a gathering of delegates
    (C) the medical profession
    (D) accepted behavior

50. People like Lady Montagu can best be described as

    (A) proud
    (B) cheerful
    (C) daring
    (D) gentle

51. Why did Lady Montagu assume that it was safe to have her young son inoculated against smallpox?

    (A) She had survived smallpox as a young woman.
    (B) She knew that no one had died from the procedure.
    (C) She believed that boys were stronger than girls.
    (D) She thought that children did not generally catch smallpox.

52. Lady Montagu tried to fight smallpox in England because

    (A) her son had become very ill
    (B) she was no longer welcome in Constantinople
    (C) she hoped to make a profit by doing so
    (D) she wanted to help her fellow countrymen

53. This passage was probably written in order to

    (A) help the reader fight smallpox
    (B) introduce a historical figure
    (C) encourage the reader to travel
    (D) prove the Turks were wrong

54. What tone does the author maintain in this passage?

    (A) straightforward
    (B) disapproving
    (C) ironic
    (D) hopeful

Directions: Select the word or group of words that has the same, or nearly the same meaning as the word that is in **boldface.**

55. **Gratify** most nearly means

   (A) make unnaturally sensitive
   (B) make welcome
   (C) please
   (D) lure

56. **Preliminary** most nearly means

   (A) extravagant
   (B) detailed
   (C) inexpensive
   (D) preparatory

57. **Specimen** most nearly means

   (A) tube
   (B) sample
   (C) injection
   (D) group

58. **Cite** most nearly means

   (A) build upon
   (B) denounce
   (C) refer to
   (D) disregard

59. **Disdain** most nearly means

   (A) resemble
   (B) scorn
   (C) perceive
   (D) defy

60. **Prosper** most nearly means

   (A) thrive
   (B) please
   (C) deceive
   (D) struggle

61. **Affirm** most nearly means

    (A) take for granted
    (B) assert
    (C) repent
    (D) see clearly

62. **Notify** most nearly means
    (A) inform
    (B) remind
    (C) discourage
    (D) withhold

63. **Disclose** most nearly means
    (A) hold back
    (B) disguise
    (C) reveal
    (D) avoid

64. **Summit** most nearly means
    (A) base
    (B) total
    (C) bulk
    (D) top

Directions: Read the sentence below, paying special attention to the word in **boldface.** Then look at the sentences below it. Select the answer choice in which the **boldfaced** word is used in the same way that it is in the original sentence.

*My grandfather served with **distinction** in the armed forces during the Korean War.*

65. In which sentence does the word "distinction" mean the same thing that it does in the sentence above?
    (A) Do you know the distinction between right and wrong?
    (B) Death plays no favorites; it comes to all without distinction.
    (C) Charles Shaw wine, known popularly as Two-buck Chuck, has the distinction of being the cheapest wine you can buy.
    (D) William's parents are proud their son graduated from college with distinction.

*No matter how much they differ in looks and in cost, the elegant mansion of the millionaire and the **rude** dwelling of the frontiersman are both houses.*

66. In which sentence does the word "rude" mean the same thing that it does in the sentence above?

    (A) After the recent storm, we saw that the rude bridge across the creek was in need of repairs.
    (B) I was awakened from a sound sleep by the rude cries of the crows.
    (C) The contractor gave us a rude first estimate of the cost of remodeling the house.
    (D) Mother complained to the store manager that the clerk had been rude to her.

*Sharon tried to **model** herself on her grandmother, the kindest person she knew.*

67. In which sentence does the word "model" mean the same thing that it does in the sentence above?

    (A) Ben decided to model his teaching style on his favorite professor's manner.
    (B) Even though my car is a 1996 model, it still runs extremely well.
    (C) Elegant and slender, Kate was born to be a fashion model.
    (D) Before the sculptor set to work on casting the bronze statue, he first constructed a clay model.

*With no job and no high school diploma, Tom found his prospects for the future were **bleak**.*

68. In which sentence does the word "bleak" mean the same thing that it does in the sentence above?

    (A) A bleak wind from the north whipped across the prairie.
    (B) Above the tree line, the hillside is bleak and bare, with no shelter to protect a hiker from the elements.
    (C) The bleak, a small freshwater fish related to the carp, is pale silver in color.
    (D) It was a bleak holiday season for us this year, for Grandfather was in the hospital again.

*You may pet the kitten if you **stroke** her gently; otherwise she will scratch.*

69. In which sentence does the word "stroke" mean the same thing that it does in the sentence above?

(A) Cinderella's carriage turned back into a pumpkin at the stroke of midnight.
(B) My boss believes that every weird idea he has is a stroke of genius.
(C) As he sat in his easy chair, Grandfather thoughtfully would stroke his long white beard.
(D) A stroke of lightning hit the old church tower.

*Instead of having to pay a fine for reckless driving, Tim was sentenced to pick up **litter** along the highway.*

70. In which sentence does the word "litter" mean the same thing that it does in the sentence above?

(A) Our cat gave birth to her first litter in my bedroom closet.
(B) The princess traveled to the palace in a curtained litter carried by six slaves.
(C) We were appalled by the amount of litter in the streets after the parade.
(D) The soldiers put together a makeshift litter for their wounded comrade.

*According to the terms of my **contract** with the publisher, I have to revise this text every two years.*

71. In which sentence does the word "contract" mean the same thing that it does in the sentence above?

(A) When you shine a light in a patient's eyes, the pupils of the eyes quickly contract.
(B) If you don't want to contract the flu this winter, ask your doctor for a flu shot early in the fall.
(C) Contract bridge is a card game for four players.
(D) The quarterback signed a multimillion-dollar contract with the Oakland Raiders.

*Julia's air of **reserve** sometimes caused strangers to think she was unfriendly; actually, she was merely shy.*

72. In which sentence does the word "reserve" mean the same thing that it does in the sentence above?

    (A) Sue wished she could break through John's formal reserve to let him know how much she cared.
    (B) I want to reserve a midsize car for next weekend.
    (C) In case of emergency, keep a reserve of food and medical supplies handy.
    (D) Wendy spent a summer working at a fire lookout tower in a forest reserve.

*Afraid of being swept overboard, the boy held **fast** to the rope.*

73. In which sentence does the word "fast" mean the same thing that it does in the sentence above?

    (A) Did you know that Muslims fast during the month of Ramadan?
    (B) His boot was stuck fast in the mud.
    (C) I can always depend on Ramon; he is a fast friend.
    (D) If you start out at too fast a pace, you may exhaust yourself before the race is over.

*The President and his wife enjoyed their vacation at the family **compound** near Kennebunkport.*

74. In which sentence does the word "compound" mean the same thing that it does in the sentence above?

    (A) Soap is a compound substance composed of fat, ashes, and lye.
    (B) Set off by barriers and protected by security guards, the compound was a safe place for the movie star and her children.
    (C) The recent rainstorm will only compound the problems of the people still cleaning up after the flood.
    (D) It is the job of the pharmaceutical company's research division to compound drugs to create new medicines.

> **Directions:** In each of the sentences below, the word in **boldface** may be unfamiliar to you. Use the other words in the sentence to help you decide what the word in **boldface** means.

*In their single-minded drive to discover ways to **prolong** human life, doctors do not always consider that longer lives are not always happier ones.*

75. As used in the sentence above, "prolong" most nearly means

   (A) ease
   (B) lengthen
   (C) diagnose
   (D) dissect

*Because it is strong, adhesive, and invaluable as a nest-building material, many species of birds **incorporate** silk into their nests.*

76. As used in the sentence above, "incorporate" most nearly means

   (A) smuggle
   (B) dissolve
   (C) crumble
   (D) include

*The Cabinet member's resignation was not totally **unanticipated**: rumors of his departure from office had been making the rounds in Washington for a week.*

77. As used in the sentence above, "unanticipated" most nearly means

   (A) successful
   (B) unexpected
   (C) welcome
   (D) uneventful

*The wagon train leaders chose to change their route when they realized that the heavy rains had made crossing the river too **impracticable** a task.*

78. As used in the sentence above, "impracticable" most nearly means

   (A) practical
   (B) watery
   (C) roundabout
   (D) impossible

*Because fruit juice fills babies' small stomachs and ruins their appetite for foods that contain the nourishment they need, consuming large quantities of juice can actually be **detrimental** to babies less than 24 months old.*

79. As used in the sentence above, "detrimental" most nearly means

   (A) harmful
   (B) supplemental
   (C) squeamish
   (D) profitable

*One by one, the mayor **estranged** all of her supporters until, at the end, only a few of her closest allies really wanted her to stay in office.*

80. As used in the sentence above, "estranged" most nearly means
   (A) regretted
   (B) alienated
   (C) advocated
   (D) rewarded

*Though Phil had expected to be overawed when he met Joe Montana, he found that the world-famous quarterback was friendly and not at all **intimidating**.*

81. As used in the sentence above, "intimidating" most nearly means

   (A) approachable
   (B) frightening
   (C) welcoming
   (D) remarkable

*Although the realtor had said that the apartment was in **pristine** condition, when we inspected it, we were surprised to discover that it was shabby and run-down.*

82. As used in the sentence above, "pristine" most nearly means

   (A) vacant
   (B) average
   (C) dreadful
   (D) perfect

*The Widow Douglas and her sister Miss Watson had very different ideas about how to bring up Huck Finn. While Miss Watson did nothing but scold the boy, Widow Douglas was more understanding and often **condoned** Huck's minor offenses.*

83. As used in the sentence above, "condoned" most nearly means

(A) punished
(B) pardoned
(C) exaggerated
(D) rebuked

*Despite her father's **admonition** that a woman's place was in the home and an unfriendly reception from her professors and fellow students, Marion Cleeves went on to become the first woman to receive a doctorate in anatomy from the University of California at Berkeley.*

84. As used in the sentence above, "admonition" most nearly means

(A) warning
(B) surprise
(C) encouragement
(D) refusal

MATHEMATICS SECTION

Directions: Each of the following statements, questions, or problems is followed by four suggested answers or completions. Choose the *one* that best completes each of the statements or answers the question. Mark the oval on the answer sheet whose letter corresponds to the answer you have selected.

1. What is the value of the expression $\dfrac{3 \times 2^2 - 3^2}{(3 \times 2)^2 - 2^4}$ written as a decimal?

   (A) 0.10
   (B) 0.15
   (C) 0.20
   (D) 0.30

2. Monica wants to buy a game console as a present. She looks up prices for the model she wants on an Internet price comparison website, and finds a list of sellers, with the following prices:

merchant 1	$149.99
merchant 2	$157.89
merchant 3	$149.99
merchant 4	$169.99
merchant 5	$149.98
merchant 6	$179.51
merchant 7	$149.95
merchant 8	$148.95

   What is the median price for the game console in this listing?

   (A) $148.95
   (B) $149.98
   (C) $149.99
   (D) $150.00

3. For the table of prices in the previous question, which of the following is true?

   (A) The median price is the same as the mode.
   (B) The median price is the same as the mean.
   (C) The median price is greater than the mode.
   (D) The median price is greater than the mean.

4. The average distance from the Earth to the Sun is about 150 million kilometers. Since 1 mile is approximately 1.6 km (kilometer), which value below is the best estimate of this distance in miles, to one significant digit?

    (A) 1.0×10^8 miles
    (B) 9.0×10^7 miles
    (C) 9.0×10^6 miles
    (D) 1.0×10^6 miles

5. If Morgan tosses a fair coin four times, what is the probability that he will get exactly two heads and two tails?

    (A) 1/4
    (B) 3/8
    (C) 1/2
    (D) 5/8

6. Pyramid Records is selling CDs at $1 off its usual price of $8.35 per disk. What is the percentage reduction, to the nearest whole percent, on these disks?

    (A) 10%
    (B) 12%
    (C) 15%
    (D) 20%

Refer to the graph below to answer the next three questions.

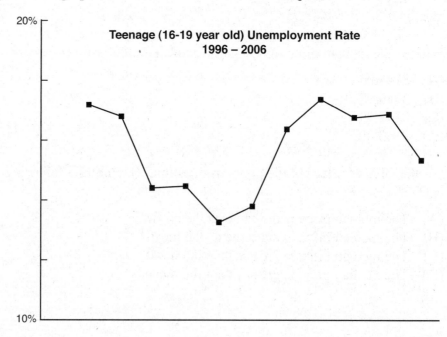

7. In which year on this graph was the unemployment rate for 16- to 19-year olds the highest?

   (A) 1996
   (B) 2000
   (C) 2003
   (D) 2006

8. Which year showed the greatest increase in teenage unemployment over the previous year?

   (A) 1999
   (B) 2000
   (C) 2001
   (D) 2002

9. Approximately how great was the average (mean) difference in the unemployment rate per year from the lowest year to the highest in this time period?

   (A) 0.75%
   (B) 1%
   (C) 1.3%
   (D) 25%

10. According to the 2010 U. S. Census, the population of the United States in that year was 308,745,538. Which of the following represents this number in scientific notation correct to three significant digits?

    (A) 308×10^6
    (B) 3.08×10^8
    (C) 3.09×10^8
    (D) 3.09×10^7

11. A family is planning a trip of 550 miles. Their car gets an average of 22 miles to the gallon. They expect to pay an average price of $2.40 for each gallon of gas they purchase. How much do they expect to spend on gas for the trip?

    (A) $55
    (B) $60
    (C) $75
    (D) $77

12. A woman is three times as old as her daughter and four times as old as her son. If the daughter is 12 years old, how old is the son?

    (A) 8
    (B) 9
    (C) 10
    (D) 36

13. The Wallaces have a circular pond in their backyard that is 20 feet across and has a depth of 2 feet. About how many cubic feet of water does it hold?

   (A) 315
   (B) 525
   (C) 630
   (D) 2,500

14. What is the next number in the sequence 7, 10, 14, 19, 25?

   (A) 29
   (B) 31
   (C) 32
   (D) 36

15. A man travels from Kingston to Yorkville, a distance of 40 miles. For the first 30 miles he travels on the freeway, averaging a speed of 60 miles per hour. The last 10 miles he averages a speed of 30 miles per hour. How many minutes does it take him to travel from Kingston to Yorkville?

   (A) 30 minutes
   (B) 40 minutes
   (C) 45 minutes
   (D) 50 minutes

16. On his tenth birthday a boy stands 4 feet, 8 inches tall. On his twelfth birthday he stands 5 feet, 4 inches tall. What was his average growth per year in that period?

   (A) 2 inches
   (B) 3 inches
   (C) 4 inches
   (D) 5 inches

Refer to the graph below for the next question.

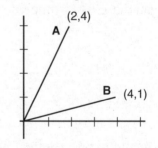

17. What is the ratio of the slope of line *A* to line *B*?

   (A) 1 : 1
   (B) 2 : 1
   (C) 4 : 1
   (D) 8 : 1

18. A right-angled triangle has two of its sides 2 inches long; which of the answers below is closest to the length of the other side?

    (A) 2 inches
    (B) 3 inches
    (C) 4 inches
    (D) 5 inches

19. Craig Leonard went with eight friends to Chang's Chinese Kitchen for lunch. All the others ordered the lunch special, but Craig had a dish (from the dinner menu) that cost $2 more than the others' lunches. If the bill came to $38.45, how much did Craig owe?

    (A) $3.80
    (B) $4.05
    (C) $6.05
    (D) $6.45

20. Calculate the value of $C(10,3) = \dfrac{10!}{3!7!}$

    (A) 720
    (B) 240
    (C) 120
    (D) 90

Refer to the table below to answer the next two questions.

1 gallon	4 quarts
1 gallon	3.785 liters
1 quart	2 pints
1 pint	2 cups
1 pint	16 ounces

21. A woman buys a half-gallon of milk. During the day, she drinks two 8-ounce glasses from the full container, and uses one cup of milk in cooking. How much milk does she have left in the container?

    (A) 20 ounces
    (B) 28 ounces
    (C) 40 ounces
    (D) 108 ounces

22. Approximately how many ounces are there in a liter?

    (A) 17 ounces
    (B) 34 ounces
    (C) 45 ounces
    (D) 64 ounces

23. A woman pays $396 a year for medical insurance. At the end of three years she is hospitalized briefly. The insurance company reimburses her for her hospital expenses, minus a deductible amount of $300. If the hospital bill was $2,278.60, how much money has she saved by carrying medical insurance?

    (A) $396.00
    (B) $790.60
    (C) $800.00
    (D) $1,090.60

Refer to the chart below to answer the next three questions.

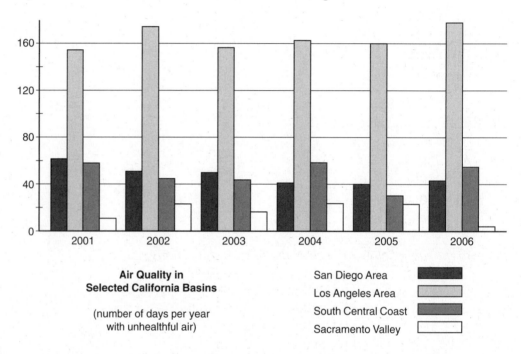

**Air Quality in
Selected California Basins**

(number of days per year
with unhealthful air)

San Diego Area
Los Angeles Area
South Central Coast
Sacramento Valley

24. About what fraction of the year does Los Angeles have unhealthful air quality?

    (A) $\frac{1}{4}$

    (B) $\frac{1}{3}$

    (B) $\frac{1}{2}$

    (D) $\frac{1}{10}$

25. Which of the areas shown in this chart has had the fewest unhealthful days between 2001 and 2005?

    (A) San Diego
    (B) Los Angeles
    (C) South Central Coast
    (D) Sacramento Valley

26. A circle has one square circumscribed around it and another one inscribed in it. What is the ratio of the area of the circumscribed square to that of the inscribed one?

    (A) $\sqrt{2}:1$
    (B) $2:1$
    (C) $3:1$
    (D) $4:1$

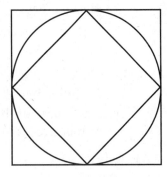

27. Nancy is purchasing ice cream for a party, having collected $5 apiece from the six people who signed up to contribute to the ice cream fund. If the actual cost for the ice cream was $25, how much change does she owe each of the six contributors?

    (A) $0.57
    (B) $0.83
    (C) $0.87
    (D) $0.89

28. Raymond needs boards of $1\frac{3}{8}$ feet, $2\frac{3}{8}$ feet, and $5\frac{1}{2}$ feet to complete a carpentry project. What is the total length of the boards he needs?

    (A) $8\frac{3}{8}$ feet

    (B) $9\frac{1}{4}$ feet

    (C) $9\frac{3}{8}$ feet

    (D) $9\frac{1}{2}$ feet

Refer to the following table to answer the next two questions.

BUDGET AND EXPENSE RECORD								
	January		February		March		April	
Item	Budget	Actual Expense	Budget	Actual Expense	Budget	Actual Expense	Budget	Actual Expense
Rent	$125	$124.53	$125	$126.25	$125	$123.75	$125	$121.16
Food	$65	$62.48	$65	$64.18	$65	$60.43	$65	$62.35
Clothes	$20	$12.62	$20	$9.93	$20	$18.68	$50	$36.22
Phone	$5	$3.45	$5	$5.86	$5	$3.45	$5	$4.20

29. Martha Acton keeps a record of her monthly budget and expenses. The rent on her studio apartment varies from month to month, depending on how great her share of the utility bill is. In what month did the amount she paid in rent exceed the amount she had budgeted for rent?

    (A) February
    (B) March
    (C) April
    (D) None of the above

30. What were Martha's total actual expenses in April?

    (A) $215.00
    (B) $221.83
    (C) $223.93
    (D) $245.00

Refer to the following graph to answer the next three questions.

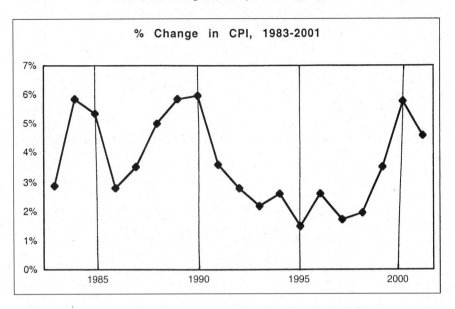

Inflation, San Diego Metropolitan Area

31. Which year saw the smallest change in CPI in San Diego?

    (A) 1986
    (B) 1994
    (C) 1995
    (D) 1997

32. Which pattern best describes the trends shown by this graph?

    (A) Increase, decrease, increase
    (B) Decrease, increase, level off
    (C) Level, decrease, increase
    (D) Irregular variation between 1% and 6%

33. How much greater was the inflation rate at its highest than at its lowest point in the time period from 1983 to 2001?

    (A) 4 times
    (B) 6 times
    (C) 3 times
    (D) 2 times

34. Kathy can wash a car in 15 minutes, and her friends Emily and Nancy can each wash a car in 20 minutes. If the girls work for three hours washing cars at a Student Council sponsored fund-raiser, what is the greatest number of cars they can wash during that time?

    (A) 27
    (B) 30
    (C) 32
    (D) 36

35. What is the equation of the slanted line shown in the following graph?

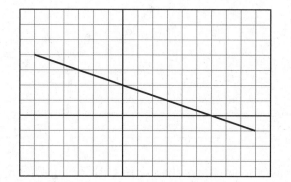

    (A) $y = 2 - x/3$
    (B) $y = x/3 + 2$
    (C) $y = x/2 + 3$
    (D) $y = 3 - x/2$

36. A woman bought a sedan for $16,700. In the first year she owned it, it depreciated 50% in value, and in the second year it depreciated an additional 20% of its original value. What was the car worth at the end of the second year?

    (A) $3,340
    (B) $5,010
    (C) $8,350
    (D) $10,690

37. A box office cashier sells 528 theater tickets in six hours. What is his hourly average of theater tickets sold?

    (A) 83
    (B) 87
    (C) 88
    (D) 93

38. Examine the following arrangement of numbers:

$$
\begin{array}{c}
1 \\
1\ 2\ 1 \\
1\ 3\ 3\ 1 \\
1\ 4\ 6\ 4\ 1 \\
1\ 5\ 10\ ?
\end{array}
$$

What number should appear next (at the question mark)?

(A) 5
(B) 10
(C) 15
(D) 20

39. A woman is buying a house. The price of the house is $96,000. She makes a down payment of $17,500, and finances the rest by a loan. If she takes a home loan at an interest rate of 12% per year, what will the amount of interest be for the first year?

(A) $942
(B) $1,750
(C) $9,420
(D) $11,520

40. In the triangle shown below, with two of the angles given in degrees, which of the following pieces of information cannot be determined from the given data?

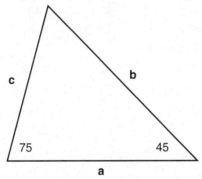

(A) The length of the longest side of the triangle
(B) The size of the largest angle of the triangle
(C) Which angle of the triangle is the largest
(D) Which side of the triangle is the largest

41. A man knows he will have to pay $900 in property taxes on November 15. He decides to set aside $150 on the first of each month and save that money so that he can pay his taxes on November 15. On what date should he start saving if he is to follow his plan, skipping no month's deposit?

(A) June 1
(B) July 1
(C) August 1
(D) November 15

42. A man has a choice of buying a digital watch for $31.95 in cash or of paying $15 down and three monthly payments of $7.95 each. How much will he save if he pays cash?

(A) $6.90
(B) $7.40
(C) $7.80
(D) $7.90

43. LuckSafe Market makes a profit of 1.5% on all its sales. One week it sold $17,980 worth of merchandise. How much was its profit that week?

(A) $268.60
(B) $269.70
(C) $2,696.00
(D) $2,698.00

44. A handyman has to cut a board one yard long into three unequal pieces. If the second piece he cuts is to be 1 inch longer than the first piece cut, and if the third piece is to be 1 inch longer than the second piece, how long should the first piece be?

(A) 11 inches
(B) 12 inches
(C) 13 inches
(D) 14 inches

45. Six times as many boys as girls are enrolled in Court Hall Military Academy. The total enrollment of the military academy is 196. How many girls are enrolled?

(A) 26
(B) 28
(C) 44
(D) 168

Refer to the following table to answer the next three questions.

MEDICAL INSURANCE PROGRAM QUARTERLY RATES

Member's Age on Premium Due Date	Member Only	Member & Spouse or Member & Children	Member, Spouse, & Children
Less than 35	$43.86	$89.58	$128.08
35–39	$62.96	$128.72	$161.90
40–49	$68.48	$136.92	$175.44
50–59	$87.66	$175.34	$211.02
60–64	$112.88	$219.66	$252.40

Select the quarterly premium according to your current age. Include a check for that amount with your enrollment form. You will be billed thereafter for each quarterly premium, as it becomes due, at the rate appropriate to your age at that time.

46. A 58-year-old unmarried man enrolls in the Medical Insurance Program. What quarterly premium is he most likely to be paying?

(A) $68.48
(B) $87.66
(C) $112.88
(D) $175.34

47. A 43-year-old man and his 28-year-old wife are both eligible to enroll in the Medical Insurance Program. They wish to pay the least expensive quarterly premium they can. What quarterly premium are they most likely to pay?

(A) $43.86
(B) $68.48
(C) $89.58
(D) $136.92

48. By how much will their quarterly premium increase when the wife turns 35?

(A) $36.94
(B) $39.12
(C) $39.14
(D) $62.96

49. A woman earns $21.60 an hour for a 30-hour work week. For any extra hours she works, she receives 60% of her regular hourly pay. If she works 33 hours one week and 35 hours the next, how much will she be paid for the two-week pay period?

(A) $699.84
(B) $1,296.00
(C) $1,399.68
(D) $1,468.80

50. In the National League baseball standings, which of the following teams has a winning percentage of 45%?

(A) Los Angeles, Won 15, Lost 7
(B) San Diego, Won 11, Lost 11
(C) Houston, Won 10, Lost 12
(D) Atlanta, Won 5, Lost 17

ANSWER KEY

English Language Arts Section

LANGUAGE SUBTEST

[There is no correct answer for the Writing Task.]

1. B	9. D	17. C	25. B	33. B	41. C
2. D	10. A	18. A	26. C	34. C	42. C
3. C	11. A	19. C	27. A	35. B	43. C
4. B	12. B	20. A	28. A	36. C	44. A
5. D	13. A	21. D	29. D	37. D	45. B
6. C	14. C	22. B	30. B	38. B	46. B
7. C	15. B	23. B	31. C	39. B	47. D
8. B	16. D	24. A	32. B	40. A	48. A

READING SUBTEST

1. D	10. B	19. C	28. B	37. C	46. B
2. C	11. D	20. C	29. A	38. B	47. C
3. B	12. B	21. D	30. C	39. B	48. C
4. D	13. B	22. B	31. A	40. A	49. D
5. C	14. C	23. D	32. A	41. A	50. C
6. A	15. A	24. B	33. B	42. B	51. B
7. D	16. B	25. A	34. D	43. D	52. D
8. B	17. D	26. C	35. D	44. D	53. B
9. D	18. C	27. D	36. B	45. C	54. A

55. C	60. A	65. D	70. C	75. B	80. B
56. D	61. B	66. A	71. D	76. D	81. B
57. B	62. A	67. A	72. A	77. B	82. D
58. C	63. C	68. D	73. B	78. D	83. B
59. B	64. D	69. C	74. B	79. A	84. A

Mathematics Section

1. B	11. B	21. C	31. C	41. A
2. C	12. B	22. B	32. D	42. A
3. A	13. C	23. B	33. A	43. B
4. B	14. C	24. C	34. B	44. A
5. B	15. D	25. D	35. A	45. B
6. B	16. C	26. B	36. B	46. B
7. C	17. D	27. B	37. C	47. C
8. D	18. B	28. B	38. B	48. C
9. C	19. C	29. A	39. C	49. C
10. C	20. C	30. C	40. A	50. C

ANSWER EXPLANATIONS

English Language Arts Section

LANGUAGE SUBTEST

1. **(B)** her
   Error in pronoun agreement. The subject of the sentence, *one*, is singular; a pronoun referring to a singular subject should be singular as well.
   Note: Many grammarians now accept *their* in sentences like this one. However, the test-makers still consider the use of *their* in this context an error. Don't argue with the test-makers. Just follow the rule, and you'll be marked right.

2. **(D)** Correct as is.
   To affect something is to influence or have an effect on it. It is spelled correctly in the sentence.
   Although Choice C spells *affect* correctly, it introduces a new error. The subject of the sentence, *impression*, is singular; for Choice C to be correct, the verb would have to be singular as well.

3. **(C)** There's
   Don't confuse *There's* (short for *There is*) with *Theirs* (something belonging to them). *There's no business like show business* is correct.

4. **(B)** will have been
   Error in sequence of tenses. The future perfect tense (*will have been*) is used to indicate a time that comes after the present moment and before a time in the future.

5. **(D)** Correct as is.
   When an exclamation point applies only to the statement you are quoting, you should place it in between the quotation marks.

6. **(C)** Merritt College is.
   Error in punctuation. Use a period to mark the end of an indirect question. (*Where is Harry Potter?* is a direct question. To make it an indirect question, you invert the word order and substitute a period for the question mark: *I wonder where Harry Potter is.*)

7. **(C)** can hardly
   Double negative. *Hardly* and *scarcely* are words that have negative force. If you use them with an unnecessary negative (for example, *not*, *nothing*, or *without*), most grammarians consider the result nonstandard. Eliminate the unnecessary negative.

8. **(B)** as well as me
   Incorrect pronoun form. Grammarians do not accept *myself* as a replacement for the subjective pronoun *I* or the objective pronoun *me*. In this sentence, the pronoun is the object of the preposition *to*. Therefore, the correct answer is Choice B, *as well as me.*

9. **(D)** Correct as is
   Here, *Let's* is used correctly as a contraction or shortened form of *Let us.*

10. **(A)** ought to like
    Error in usage. *Had ought* is nonstandard for *ought*. You ought to eliminate nonstandard expressions from your prose.

11. **(A)** fewer
    Error in usage. In formal writing, *fewer* refers to things you can count (how many), while *less* refers to amount or extent (how much). For working *fewer hours,* you receive *less pay.*

12. **(B)** When I went to the hospital, I
    Error in punctuation. Use a comma after an introductory adverb clause.

13. **(A)** said, "Haste makes waste."
    Error in punctuation. Choice A correctly places the period within the quotation marks.

14. **(C)** accepts
    Error in usage. Do not confuse *to except* (exclude or make an exception of) with *to accept* (admit formally, as to a college).

15. **(B)** did not keep any
    Double negative. Both *not* and *no* are words that have negative force. If you use them together in a *not...no* construction, most grammarians consider the result nonstandard. Eliminate the unnecessary negative.

16. **(D)** Correct as is
    Lay here is correctly used as the past tense of the verb *to lie.*

17. **(C)** Johnny and I
The pronoun here is part of the subject of the sentence and should be in the subjective case. The correct answer is *Johnny and I.*

18. **(A)** require
Subject-verb agreement. The subject of the sentence, *occasions,* is plural; the verb should be plural as well.

19. **(C)** These were mainly financial issues.
Wordiness. Choice C restructures the original sentence to cut out its wordiness without changing its fundamental meaning.

20. **(A)** At art school Angelina is studying painting, sculpting, and collage-making.
Lack of parallelism. *Painting* and *sculpting* are gerunds, verb forms that end in *–ing* and function like nouns. *Painting* and *sculpting* are the first two items in a series of three items; all three items in the series should be gerunds as well.

21. **(D)** Correct as is
The sentence is correctly punctuated and has no grammatical errors.

22. **(B)** She stayed home from the dance because she had a cold.
Wordiness. The expression *the reason . . . was because* is both informal and redundant (unnecessarily wordy). You can correct the sentence either by replacing *because* with *that* (*the reason . . . was that*) or by rephrasing the sentence. Choice B rephrases the sentence, cutting out the wordiness.

23. **(B)** Weighing over 120 tons, blue whales are among the world's largest sea mammals.
Misplaced modifier. By recasting the sentence in this way, you make it clear that your subject is the blue whale family as a whole and not simply a random assortment of whales who happen to weigh over 120 tons.

24. **(A)** If our football team wins the state championship later this season, they will have won for four straight years.
Error in sequence of tenses. The future perfect tense (*will have been*) is used to indicate a time that comes after the present moment and before a time in the future.

25. **(B)** In an article in the school newspaper, Maggie wrote about the problem with mice in the cafeteria.
Misplaced modifier. By recasting the sentence in this way, you make it clear both that the mice are in the cafeteria and that the cafeteria is not in the newspaper.

26. **(C)** A scholar is a person who is studious, intelligent, and well-educated.
Lack of parallelism. *Studious* and *intelligent* are both adjectives, words that modify nouns. *Studious* and *intelligent* are the first two items in a series of three items; all three items in the series should be adjectives.

27. **(A)** Even though the test was difficult, I did just fine.
Incorrect conjunction. The author is setting up a contrast between what was expected ("It was a tough test, Mom, so I didn't do too well.") and what actually happened ("It was a tough test, Mom, but I got an A!"). The conjunction *Even though* signals this contrast.

28. **(A)** Running through the woods, I was hindered by the thick underbrush and the branches hanging from the trees.
Misplaced modifier. Ask yourself just who was running through the woods. The trees? No way! To correct a dangling participle, you must move the participial phrase ("running through the woods") so that it is near "I," the word it modifies.

29. **(D)** Correct as is
Choices A and C incorrectly link two independent clauses with a comma (the dreaded comma splice); Choice B incorrectly replaces *who* with *which*: the poor, after all, are people, and should be referred to as *who*, not *which*. The original sentence is correct.

30. **(B)** I have enjoyed the films of Christopher Guest not only for their plots but also for their wit.
Lack of parallelism. Correlatives (connective words that come in pairs, such as "either . . . or," "both . . . and," and "not only . . . but also") usually connect parallel structures. In Choice B, the correlatives

"not only…but also" correctly connect two nouns, *plots* and *wit*.

31. **(C)** The visitor signed the historic guest book, which held the signatures of the great and near-great who had visited the estate during the past fifty years.
Sentence fragment. The original sentence has no main clause. Instead, it links two dependent clauses (one that begins with the subordinating conjunction *After*, and one that begins with the relative pronoun *which*) with a comma. Choice C corrects the fragment by cutting out the subordinating conjunction *After*. This simple correction eliminates the fragment. The sentence now has a main clause: *The visitor signed the historic guest book.*

32. **(B)** When Anita Yu comes back from her sales trips, she usually submits her expense account to the chief bookkeeper.
Error in sequence of tenses. Note the word *usually*. Choice B correctly uses the present tense to indicate a habitual or customary action.

33. **(B)** By the time we arrive in Italy, we will have traveled through four countries.
Error in sequence of tenses. The future perfect tense (*will have been*) is used to indicate a time that comes after the present moment and before a time in the future.

34. **(C)** J.K. Rowling is a British novelist whose fame in the field of fantasy may come to equal that of J.R.R. Tolkien.
Sentence fragment. The original sentence has a subject but no verb. The addition of the linking verb *is* corrects the sentence fragment.

35. **(B)** The rock star always had enthusiastic fans who loved him.
Why is Choice B the best answer? Choice B takes two simple independent clauses and, by turning one of them into a subordinate clause, creates a slightly more complex (and less babyish sounding) sentence.

36. **(C)** Because she was familiar with the route from her driving lessons, the student driver found the road test easy to pass.

Dangling modifier. Who was familiar with the route? The road test certainly wasn't familiar with it! Fortunately, the student driver was familiar with the route, and so she found the test easy to pass.

37. **(D)** missed every free throw
The phrase "did things wrong" is vague. Missing free throws, however, is a concrete example of a problem a novice basketball player might have.

38. **(B)** Little League basketball tryouts are very different from Little League baseball tryouts.
The subject of the passage is a young boy's try-out for a Little League *basketball* team. Nothing in the passage discusses Little League baseball.

39. **(B)** Danny's father Richie had been on the travel team when he was a boy; he had even led the Vikings to the finals of the Little League Basketball World Series that year.
The clause "When he was on the team" is redundant: if Richie had not been on the Vikings, he couldn't have led the team to the World Series finals.

40. **(A)** Even so,
Look at the sentence in the passage that immediately precedes the sentence you are analyzing. It praises Danny for his knowledge of basketball. You would expect the next sentence also to be positive. However, it is not. "Danny was afraid he wouldn't make the cut." You need a transitional phrase between these two sentences that signals a change in direction. The transitional phrase *Even so* (nevertheless, in spite of that) serves this function. Choice A is correct.

41. **(C)** For almost as long as he could remember, Danny had wanted to play on the Vikings travel team.
The entire paragraph deals with Danny's reasons for wanting to make the team and with his fear that he will fail to reach his goal.

42. **(C)** Danny is highly motivated to become a skilled basketball player.

Several sentences in the paragraph provide evidence in support of the statement that Danny is highly motivated to become a skilled basketball player. Consider these two in particular: "More than anything else in the world, Danny wanted to follow in his father's footsteps. He had studied the game until he knew more about basketball than anyone else in the school."

Use the process of elimination to confirm your answer choice. Is Danny wholly convinced that he will make the travel team? No. He is convinced he *won't* make the team: "As he looked at himself in the mirror, he knew in his heart that he was just too short to be a Viking." You can eliminate Choice A. Are all seventh-graders required to try out for the basketball team? No. Nothing in the paragraph suggests that. You can eliminate Choice B. Is everyone who tries out for the seventh-grade travel team automatically accepted? No. Only first-graders who try out for the first-grade team are automatically accepted. By seventh grade, would-be players have to earn their spots. You can eliminate Choice D. Only Choice C is left. It is the correct answer.

43. **(C)** One of the world's most famous crusaders for social justice and peace is South Africa's Archbishop Desmond Tutu.
Generally found at the beginning of a paragraph, a topic sentence expresses the paragraph's main or essential idea. It should be neither too broad in focus nor too narrow and should be grammatically and clearly expressed.
Use the process of elimination to answer this question. Choice A is too narrow in focus to be a good topic sentence for an essay about Archbishop Tutu; it serves only to provide a detail about Tutu's teaching career. You can eliminate Choice A. Choice B is too broad and vague to be a good topic sentence for an essay about Archbishop Tutu; it fails to mention him at all. You can eliminate Choice B. Although Choice D does manage to focus on Archbishop Tutu, the sentence is wordy and awkward. You

can eliminate Choice D. Only Choice C is left. Not only is it clear and to the point, it also focuses on Archbishop Tutu. It is the correct answer.

44. **(A)** requirements
The provisions of a law are its stipulations or *requirements*.

45. **(B)** gave lectures
The only answer choice that provides a concrete example of an action taken by Archbishop Tutu in his fight against apartheid is Choice B: he *gave lectures*, speaking out against the evils of the system and calling the world's attention to them.

46. **(B)** to define a term
The words in the parentheses serve to define *apartheid*, the foreign word in italics.

47. **(D)** The school administration quickly set up a press conference in a central courtyard so that Archbishop Tutu could speak to all the reporters at once.
Choice D correctly uses the conjunction *so that* to introduce a clause that gives the reason for or purpose of an action.
You can use the process of elimination to answer this question. Choice A incorrectly links the two sentences with only a comma, creating a comma splice. Cross out Choice A. Choice B both repeats the comma splice error and introduces the redundant construction, *the reason was because.* Cross out Choice B. Choice C incorrectly uses two subordinating conjunctions, *When* and *because*; the sentence thus has no main clause. Cross out Choice C. Only Choice D is left. It is the correct answer.

48. **(A)** Desmond Tutu has visited many countries in his crusade for social justice.
The final paragraph describes an incident that illustrates Archbishop Tutu's compassion. A sentence focusing on the Archbishop's travels has no place in this context.

READING SUBTEST

1. **(D)** Sell it to customers.
By definition, a merchant is someone who sells articles of trade for profit. In this case,

the merchant has traveled to the seashore to fetch back home a load of salt that he intends to sell.

2. **(C)** The salt dissolved in the water.
Here's what happened. The containers holding the salt were not watertight. When the river water came in contact with the salt, the water dissolved the salt. The salty water that resulted flowed back into the river. Very little, if any, salt was left in the containers. Thus, the donkey's load was lighter.

3. **(B)** his load was easier to carry
Clearly, a lighter load would be easier to carry, and having a lighter load to carry would cheer up a poor beast of burden.

4. **(D)** he had less salt to sell.
To the donkey, the load of salt means work; he is pleased to have less of it to carry. To the merchant, the load of salt means profit; he is displeased to have less of it to sell.

5. **(C)** intentionally
The donkey "purposely let himself fall into the water." In other words, he did so on purpose or *intentionally.*

6. **(A)** shrewd
Shrewd means clever. The clever merchant knew the donkey would try his trick again and figured out a way to outsmart the tricky beast. Consider what the merchant did. He went back to the seashore and loaded the donkey with two baskets of sponges. What happened when the river water came into contact with the sponges? Did it dissolve them? No. Instead, the sponges soaked up the river water, becoming heavier with every drop of water they absorbed. The donkey's load became heavier, not lighter, and the shrewd merchant taught his donkey not to try that particular trick any more.

7. **(D)** teach a lesson
This story is a fable. Like most fables, it has a moral or lesson to teach. The lesson this fable teaches is that "the same actions will not suit all circumstances." In other words, what worked once will not necessarily work the next time you try it.

8. **(B)** commercial rabbit raisers
The title of this passage tells you that its subject is systems of breeding, in this instance, systems of breeding or raising rabbits. While the opening paragraph *does* refer to genetic concepts, it does so only to emphasize the usefulness of these ideas to breeders. The passage is a summary of information a breeder or commercial rabbit raiser needs, not a summary of information a professional geneticist would need.

9. **(D)** parts of cells
The opening paragraph describes chromosomes as "very small threadlike bodies found in every cell of the body." They are therefore parts of cells. (Note that the definition of this technical term immediately follows the first use of the term, set off from the term itself by a comma. This technique, known as apposition, is very common in texts, so that if you come across an unfamiliar technical term in a passage, you should take a close look at the words immediately following the new term to see if they define it.) You can also come up with the answer by ruling out the other answer choices. Chromosomes are not genes; they are locations for genes. Therefore, Choice A is incorrect. Chromosomes are not species (classes of animals); therefore, Choice B is incorrect. Chromosomes are certainly not types of rabbits; therefore, Choice C is incorrect. The correct answer must be Choice D.

10. **(B)** statements I and III only
Once again, apply the process of elimination to answer this question. The opening sentence states that "in planning a breeding program for rabbits, you first need to understand the concept of the *gene pool.*" In other words, breeders need genetic information to plan their breeding programs. Therefore, statement I is correct. You can cross out Choice C. The paragraph goes on to describe the gene pool as a "group of many, perhaps thousands, of hereditary units, commonly referred to as genes." Although there are 22 chromosome pairs in

each rabbit, the gene pool itself consists of all the genes of all the rabbits who make up the breed. Therefore, statement II is false. You can cross out both Choices A and D. The correct answer must be Choice B. To check your reasoning, examine statement III. The passage's concluding sentence states that the ability to adapt "makes for survival and is the mechanism by which species have evolved." Statement III is indeed true, and the correct answer is, as you suspected, Choice B.

11. **(D)** Even nature makes mistakes.
Look at the sentence immediately following "But even nature slips." What does it discuss? Lost species, species that failed to survive because they could not cope with a change in circumstances. Malformed offspring, infant creatures that fail to survive because they are born with serious flaws. These are examples of nature's failures as a breeder: although nature is still the most successful breeder, even nature cannot claim complete success, for "even nature makes mistakes."

12. **(B)** a mature adult recalling an episode from her youth
Consider the next-to-last paragraph. In this paragraph, the writer lists the many things she did not yet know. Clearly she is looking back on her childhood, recalling a special event.

13. **(B)** only the best students are assigned to the A class
The writer, who had been assigned to the C class, has been moved to the A class, and Barbara and her friends are both envious and impressed. They are envious and impressed because the class subdivisions are based on academic standing, and only the best students are assigned to the A class.

14. **(C)** all migrant children were assigned to the C class
In the next-to-last paragraph, the narrator states that she "was the only child who had camped on the Baumann's land ever to get out of the C class." This suggests that all the migrant children, the children camping

on the Baumann's land, were automatically placed in the lowest subdivision.

15. **(A)** drifters with no ties to the community
The members of the community looked on the migrant workers "as one more of the untrustworthy natural phenomena, drifting here and there like mists or winds, that farmers of certain crops are resentfully forced to rely on." Thus, the local farmers distrusted the migrant workers because they considered them to be drifters.

16. **(B)** They accepted her as a playmate.
For two days, the narrator walked to school with Barbara and her friends and played games with them. Clearly they accepted her as a playmate.

17. **(D)** intolerant
The natives of Wenatchee look on the migrant workers as dirty and disgraceful. They stereotype them as gypsies, and consider them a community problem. Their attitude toward the migrant workers reveals the Wenatchee natives' underlying bias and intolerance.

18. **(C)** she had not encountered it before
To most Americans, ginger ale is an everyday, ordinary drink. To the narrator, however, it was exotic, a foreign beverage, something she had never tasted.

19. **(C)** an Army Reserve recruiting pamphlet
The passage discusses the pay and benefits to which a retired member of the Reserve is entitled. It talks about them in personal terms: they are *your* retirement and survivor benefits, good things that you can get if you serve in the Reserve for 20 years. Such a list showing the advantages of joining the service belongs most naturally in a Reserve recruiting pamphlet aimed at persuading potential reservists to enlist. The correct answer is Choice C. Though Choice D may appeal to you, it is incorrect—a civil service pension guide provides information about civilian administrative pensions, not military ones.

20. **(C)** statements II and III only
Use the process of elimination to answer this question. Under the heading "PX and

Commissary Shopping Privileges," the passage states that spouses (wives or husbands) may shop at these stores. Therefore statement I is true. You can rule out Choices A, B, and D. Both statements II and III are false. Under the heading "Travel," the passage states retirees may ride aircraft on a space-available basis. That means that, if a particular military flight were fully booked, the retiree would not be able to get on it. Similarly, under "Medical Care," the passage specifically states that medical treatments at civilian hospitals may sometimes be paid for by the Army.

21. **(D)** unlimited dental care for dependents
Use the process of elimination to answer this question. The final paragraph lists veterinary aid as a benefit for retirees. Therefore, the Reserve does provide care for sick pets belonging to retirees. You can cross out Choice A. The paragraph also states retirees may use such on-post facilities as golf courses and tennis courts. Therefore, the Reserve does provide access to athletic facilities for its retirees. You can cross out Choice B. The paragraph also mentions legal assistance as a retirement benefit. You can cross out Choice C. Only Choice D is left. It is the correct answer. While the Reserve provides unlimited dental care for its retirees, it does not provide unlimited care for their dependents: "There are restrictions on the amount of care" that dependents receive.

22. **(B)** The PX is a store used by both active and retired military personnel.
Again, use the process of elimination to reach the right answer. Note the phrase that begins the paragraph on dental care. "Providing facilities are available," the Reserve offers dental treatment for retirees. If no facilities are available, the Reserve cannot offer dental care. Therefore, it is false to claim that the Reserve *always* provides dental treatment for retirees. Choice A is incorrect. The second paragraph states that you are entitled to retirement pay "when you reach the age of 60 after 20

years of qualifying service." If you have served for 20 years, you will begin receiving your retirement pay when you turn 60. It is false that you would have to wait until you were 80 (20 years *after* you reach 60). Choice C is incorrect. According to the last paragraph, retirees can use military-maintained recreation areas "on lakes, by seashores, or in the mountains." Thus, they are entitled to use both off-post and on-post military recreation facilities, not just on-post ones. Choice D is incorrect. Only Choice B is left. It is true that both active and retired military personnel may shop at the PX. The correct answer is B.

23. **(D)** the coach cannot carry them uphill
The passengers are walking uphill through the mud, not because they enjoy exercising in mud, but because the horses are having a hard time hauling the mail coach up the muddy hill. In fact, the horses have been having such a hard time that they've had to stop three times already.

24. **(B)** moved heavily
To lumber is to move clumsily or heavily, especially when weighed down by a great weight.

25. **(A)** the road is muddy and hard to climb
The muddiness and steepness of the road, which make it hard to climb, are the circumstances that prevent the passengers from relishing or enjoying their walk.

26. **(C)** caused them to come to a halt
The driver rests the horses by bringing them to a stand. That is, he stops them, causing them to come to a halt.

27. **(D)** attempt to gallop
The poor, tired horses never *attempt to gallop*.
Use the process of elimination to answer this question. Do the horses drag the coach? Yes, they draw it across the road, as if trying to turn around and return to Blackheath. You can eliminate Choice A. Do the horses stagger and lurch? Yes, they are described as floundering and stumbling. You can eliminate Choice B. Do the horses stop in their tracks? Yes, they do so at least three times.

You can eliminate Choice C. Only Choice D is left. It is the correct answer.

28. **(B)** one of the horses
The near leader shakes his head "and everything upon it." The horse is shaking his harness, causing it to jangle, making a rattling sound.

29. **(A)** the sudden noise frightens him
To start is to give a sudden involuntary jump or twitch from shock or alarm. The rattle alarms the passenger, frightening him and causing him to jump.

30. **(C)** oil
The question asks whether coal, lignite, oil, or peat is one of California's chief mineral fuel resources; this is answered by the first sentence of the passage: "California's mineral fuel resources are primarily oil and gas." All the other resources mentioned are secondary. Gas is not one of the answers given. Oil, however, is Choice C; it is the correct answer.

31. **(A)** in making shoe polish
First, scan the passage for the key words "lignite" and "montan wax." "Lignite" occurs only in paragraph 1, in a sentence discussing "the one remaining lignite mine" in the state. The last part of the sentence states that lignite is "now processed . . . for its high content of montan wax, used as an additive in making *shoe polish* and rubber products." Montan wax serves as an ingredient in shoe polish; the correct answer is Choice A.

32. **(A)** increasing air pollution
To answer this question, you must eliminate all those answer choices that do increase the demand for liquid fuels in California. You'll find the "rising demand for liquid fuels" discussed in paragraph 2. The last sentence of this paragraph gives the causes for the rising demand: "This demand stems from a combination of ever-rising population, lack of solid fuels, and the requirements of more than 10 million motor vehicles registered in the state." *Increasing population* creates a rising demand for liquid fuels; therefore, you can eliminate Choice C. *Lack of solid*

fuels creates a rising demand for liquid ones; therefore, you can eliminate Choice D. With the increase in population you find a corresponding increase in the number of motor vehicles in the state, and, with the increase in the number of motor vehicles, you find a corresponding increase in the demand for liquid fuel. Therefore, you can eliminate Choice B. Only Choice A is left. *Increasing air pollution* is a *result* of increased fuel consumption, not a *cause* of increased demand for fuel. The correct answer is Choice A.

33. **(B)** offshore drilling
The final paragraph discusses California's offshore resources of oil and gas. Because California's liquid fuel industry cannot meet the state's rising demand for fuel, it "has begun exploring" these resources, hoping to find new fuel sources "hidden in the submerged lands of the Outer Continental Shelf." The offshore oil and gas reserves "may open a promising source of fuel." The correct answer is clearly Choice B.
You can use the process of elimination to answer this question. Coal and montan wax are solid fuels, not liquid fuels; therefore, you can eliminate Choices A and C. While tidelands drilling is a source of liquid fuel, it is an old source, one declining in production. Thus, the tidelands are not a place where industry could hope to find new sources of liquid fuel; you can eliminate Choice D. Only Choice B is left; it is the correct answer.

34. **(D)** it is increasingly involved in exploring offshore resources of oil and gas
Once again, use the process of elimination to answer this question. Compare each of the answer choices with what the passage states or implies, and cross out the ones that seem false or unsupported by the passage.
A. The liquid fuel industry is less important than the solid fuel industry in California. False. Paragraph 1 states that the chief mineral fuel resources in California are oil and gas, the liquid fuels. It also states there are only a few coal mines in the state, and no

other solid fuel resources (since lignite and peat are not used as fuels). Paragraph 2 also mentions the lack of solid fuels. Everything in the passage indicates that California's liquid fuel industry is much more important than its solid fuel industry.

B. California's liquid fuel industry is increasingly capable of meeting the demands of California's consumers without relying on imports. False. Paragraph 2 says "Crude petroleum and gasoline...must be imported each year in constantly increasing quantities."

C. California's liquid fuel industry is increasingly involved in the processing of lignite. False. Lignite is not used as a fuel in California; therefore, the liquid fuel industry can hardly be increasingly involved in processing it.

D. California's liquid fuel industry is increasingly involved in exploring offshore resources of oil and gas. True. The last paragraph explains that "with advanced technology, drilling for possible reserves in depths encountered outside the three-mile limit . . . has become practical."

35. **(D)** spotted snake
Many clues in the poem lead you to this correct answer. The movement in the grass (think of the archetypal "snake in the grass"), the physical images (the spotted shaft, the supposed "whiplash" that wriggles off when the speaker tries to pick it up), the identification of the narrow fellow as one of "nature's people"—all of these point to the narrow fellow's being a spotted snake.

36. **(B)** grass
This question is tricky. You really need to know that the "spotted shaft" is the snake's body glimpsed through the grass and not a hole in the ground (like a mine shaft) that miraculously closes and then opens in a different place. What Dickinson is describing here is the snake's movement through the grass, which first parts or separates ("divides as with a comb") to let him through and then closes behind him once he has moved on.

37. **(C)** An adult male
In the third and fourth verses, the speaker refers to incidents in his youth, when he was "a boy and barefoot." This suggests that he is now no longer a boy but *an adult male*. Despite his acquaintanceship with nature's people, however, there is no evidence that he is an expert naturalist.

38. **(B)** marked fear
What causes the speaker's "tighter breathing" and his sense of being chilled to the core? His intense, *marked fear* of the snake. The correct answer is Choice B. Choice D is incorrect: though the speaker feels cordial goodwill toward other living creatures, he fears snakes.

39. **(B)** admiring
The author describes the polar bear as "exquisitely adapted" to its bleak environment and calls it "a striking example of natural selection at work." His view of the polar bear clearly is an *admiring* one.

40. **(A)** conserving heat
The author states that polar bears are "well adapted to resist heat loss." Instead of losing heat easily, as less well-padded animals do, polar bears keep warm because their bodies are adapted to *conserving heat*.

41. **(A)** ability
The capacity in question is the bear's remarkable *ability* to smell its prey from a phenomenal distance away.

42. **(B)** fiction
Fiction is defined as literature that is the work of the imagination and is not necessarily based on fact. Novels by definition are fiction; thus, the novel *Martin Eden* is fiction. Choice B is correct.
Choice D is incorrect. Although the selection contains some dialogue, a screenplay would have far more dialogue in proportion to description and narration.

43. **(D)** family member
What do we know about the person who opens the door? We know he opens it with a key. He has a key to the house; he belongs there. In fact he is a member of the family.

44. **(D)** Arthur and Martin are acquaintances from different backgrounds.
The entire selection establishes how very different Arthur and Martin are. Martin is rough, awkward, bronzed from being out in the sun. Arthur is easy, assured, at home in his middle-class surroundings. The two young men clearly are *acquaintances from different backgrounds*.

45. **(C)** He feels uncertain of his welcome.
Martin clearly states, "I didn't want to come, an' I guess your fam'ly ain't hankerin' to see me neither." He is all too aware of how out of place he is, and plainly *feels uncertain of his welcome*.

46. **(B)** obstacles
Paragraph 2 describes the various objects in the room that Martin feels he will bump into, knock over, or otherwise damage. Books, tables, bric-a-brac, piano stools—all these are *obstacles* in his way.

47. **(C)** ordinary
In trying to reassure Martin that he needn't be frightened, Arthur describes his family as "just homely people." He does not mean that they are bad looking people. Instead, he means that they are normal, everyday, ordinary folks—people with whom Martin could feel at home.

48. **(C)** a traveler who brought back word of a new way to fight disease
Use the process of elimination to answer this question. Was Lady Mary Wortley Montagu a scientist who studied epidemics? No, she was a writer, not a scientist. You can eliminate Choice A. Was Lady Mary Wortley Montagu a mother who was troubled by foreign medical practices? No, she was a mother who was impressed by foreign medical practices. You can eliminate Choice B. Was Lady Mary Wortley Montagu a writer who did not understand English medical traditions? Nothing in the passage suggests that Lady Montagu failed to understand English medical traditions. You can eliminate Choice D. Only Choice C is left. It is the correct answer.

49. **(D)** accepted behavior
Lady Montagu was a nonconformist. Instead of marrying the man her parents wanted her to marry, she eloped. Instead of staying safely at home in England, she traveled to Turkey with her husband the ambassador. In doing so, she defied convention, rejecting what was regarded as *accepted behavior* for young women at that time.

50. **(C)** daring
Lady Montagu undertook dangerous voyages and exposed her family to unfamiliar medical practices. A risk taker, she was *daring*.

51. **(B)** She knew that no one had died from the procedure.
The next-to-last paragraph states that "Every year thousands of Turks were inoculated, and there was no record that anyone inoculated had died of the pox." Thus, Lady Montagu believed the operation was completely safe because *she knew that no one had died* from it.

52. **(D)** she wanted to help her fellow countrymen
The next-to-last paragraph opens with the statement that Lady Montagu thought it was her patriotic duty to bring this method of fighting smallpox to the attention of people in England. She was a patriotic Englishwoman *who wanted to help her fellow countrymen*.

53. **(B)** introduce a historical figure
Lady Mary Wortley Montagu was a real woman who lived in the 18th century. This passage serves to introduce us to the achievements of Lady Montagu, *a historical figure*.

54. **(A)** Straightforward
The passage presents a factual account of Lady Mary Wortley Montagu's fight against smallpox. Its tone is straightforward and direct.

55. **(C)** pleases
To gratify is to please or satisfy. Think of being "gratified by making straight A's."

56. **(D)** preparatory
Preliminary means preparatory or introductory. Think of "a preliminary survey."

57. **(B)** samples

A specimen is a sample or part of some-thing, especially one collected to be ana-lyzed. Think of "a blood specimen."

58. **(C)** refer to

To cite is to mention or refer to something or someone. Think of "citing an example."

59. **(B)** scorn

To disdain means to scorn or feel contempt. Think of someone "disdaining stupid fools."

60. **(A)** thrive

To prosper is to thrive or do well. Think of someone's "business prospering."

61. **(B)** assert

To affirm is to assert or state firmly. Think of "affirming one's innocence."

62. **(A)** informed

To notify is to inform or tell. Think of "notifying the police" about an accident.

63. **(C)** reveal

To disclose is to reveal or make known. Think of "disclosing a secret."

64. **(D)** top

The summit is the top or highest point of something. Think of "the summit of Mount Everest."

65. **(D)** William's parents are proud their son graduated from college with distinction.

Distinction as used in both sentences means honor or recognition of achievement: to graduate with distinction and to serve with distinction both are achievements. It is a noun.

66. **(A)** After the recent storm, we saw that the rude bridge across the creek was in need of repairs.

Rude as used in both sentences means crudely or roughly built: the rude dwelling and the rude bridge both are crudely built. It is an adjective.

67. **(A)** Ben decided to model his teaching style on his favorite professor's manner.

As used in both sentences, to model is to make someone or something conform to a chosen standard. It is a verb.

68. **(D)** It was a bleak holiday season for us this year, for Grandfather was in the hospi-tal again. As used in both sentences, bleak means gloomy and depressing, without hope. It is an adjective.

69. **(C)** As he sat in his easy chair, Grandfather thoughtfully would stroke his long white beard.

As used in both sentences, to stroke is to rub lightly with one's hand, as in a caress. It is a verb.

70. **(C)** We were appalled by the amount of lit-ter in the streets after the parade.

As used in both sentences, litter is trash or rubbish. It is a noun.

71. **(D)** The quarterback signed a multimillion-dollar contract with the Oakland Raiders.

As used in both sentences, a contract is a formal binding agreement. It is a noun.

72. **(A)** Sue wished she could break through John's formal reserve to let him know how much she cared.

As used in both sentences, reserve means formality or coolness of manner. It is a noun.

73. **(B)** His boot was stuck fast in the mud.

As used in both sentences, fast means firmly or tightly. It is an adverb.

74. **(B)** Set off by barriers and protected by security guards, the compound was a safe place for the movie star and her children.

As used in both sentences, a compound is a cluster of residences, a group of houses generally belonging to a family. It is a noun.

75. **(B)** lengthen

To prolong something is to make it longer or lengthen it. Think of "prolonging a visit."

76. **(D)** include

To incorporate silk into a nest is to mix it in or include it, adding it to the whole. Think of "incorporating revisions into a text."

77. **(B)** unexpected

Unanticipated means unexpected or unfore-seen. Think of "unanticipated delays."

78. **(D)** impossible

Impracticable means impossible or inca-pable of being put into practice. Think of "impracticable plans."

79. **(A)** harmful

Detrimental means harmful or damaging. Think of something "detrimental to the environment."

80. **(B)** alienated

To estrange is to alienate or make unfriendly. Think of "friends becoming estranged."

81. **(B)** frightening

Intimidating means frightening or making fearful. Think of "an intimidating bully."

82. **(D)** perfect

Pristine means immaculately clean or perfect. Think of "a pristine white handkerchief."

83. **(B)** pardoned

To condone is to pardon or overlook. Think of being "unwilling to condone cheating."

84. **(A)** warning

An admonition is a word of caution or warning. This is our admonition to you: if you want to succeed, read!

Mathematics Section

1. **(B)** 0.15

Simplify the expression as a fraction before dealing with converting it to a decimal value.

Numerator: $3 \times 2^2 - 3^2 = 3 \times 2 \times 2 - 3 \times 3 = 12 - 9 = 3$

Denominator: $(3 \times 2)^2 - 2^4 = (3 \times 2) \times (3 \times 2) - 2 \times 2 \times 2 \times 2 = 6 \times 6 - 16 = 36 - 16 = 20$

The fractional value is $\dfrac{3}{20}$. You can convert this to a decimal by making the denominator 100 (multiply numerator and denominator by 5):

$$\frac{3}{20} \times \frac{5}{5} = \frac{15}{100} = 0.15$$

Alternatively, notice that 3/20 is half as much as 3/10 (which is 0.3), so that its decimal value must be $0.30 \div 2 = 0.15$.

2. **(C)** $149.99

To find the median price, it helps to re-list the prices in order from lowest to highest (or the other way), or to mark them on the test booklet. You don't have to make a complete list—as soon as you get to the fifth one in order, you have enough information to find the median price. Here, the lowest price is that for merchant 8 ($148.95), next is merchant 7 ($149.95), then merchant 5 ($149.98), and then two at $149.99. With an even number of prices, the median would "split the difference" between the fourth and fifth prices if they were different, but in this case they are the same, so the median price is the price of these two central values in the list. (There are three prices in the list higher than $149.99 and three prices lower than that.)

3. **(A)** The median price is the same as the mode.

The mode is the most common value in a table or list of data. In the price listing above, only $149.99 appears more than once, so it is the mode. It is also the median (read the answer explanation for Question 2 if you need a refresher on finding the median). If you are sure of your ground, you don't need to look at the other answers once you have decided that A is a true statement. However, it may be worthwhile to look at the others to check yourself. C and A are mutually exclusive—since the median and the mode are the same in this example, C cannot be true. B and D involve the mean as well as the median, so you should give some thought to what the mean would be—you don't need to calculate it by adding up all eight prices and dividing by 8! The lowest five prices are all very close—$148.95 to $149.99, but the top three are substantially higher, about $158, $170, and $180. These three together add roughly $10, $20 and $30 excess above the low end. That's almost $60 extra, which when you divide by 8 to get the average will push the average $7–$8 higher than if the top three were in the same range as the bottom five prices. The mean (the arithmetic average formed by adding all the values and dividing by how many of them there are) will be at least $7 higher than the low value at about $149. Since the median is about $1 more than that low value, the mean must be significantly higher than the median; both Choices B and D must be false.

4. **(B)** 9.0×10^7 miles
To convert 150 million km to miles, you would divide that by 1.6:

$$150,000,000 \text{ km} \times \frac{1 \text{ miles}}{1.6 \text{ km}}$$

Without actually doing the division, you should see that the result would be somewhat less than 100,000,000, which is 1.0×10^8. Therefore, you can eliminate Choices C and D (9 million miles and 1 million miles, respectively). All you need to do is choose whether Choice A or B is the better estimate. To do that, you can perform the long division

$$1.6\overline{)1500\ldots} \quad \overset{93\ldots}{}$$

far enough to see that it rounds down to 90 rather than up to 100. Or, you can select Choice B by noticing that 100 million (Choice A) $\times$ 1.6 = 160 million, but 90 million (Choice B) $\times$ 1.6 = 144 million, and that is closer to 150 million than the other answer. Choice B is the best estimate of the four given.

5. **(B)** $\dfrac{3}{8}$

The probability of exactly two heads (and therefore, two tails) is the number of ways Morgan can get two heads in four tosses, divided by the total number of possible results. Since there are two equally likely possibilities with each toss (H or T), there are $2 \times 2 \times 2 \times 2 = 16$ possibilities for the four tosses all together. You could try writing out all the outcomes, but it is easy to overlook some cases, so it is better to compute the total this way. There are two ways to get the number of outcomes with two heads—either list them directly, or figure out how many outcomes do *not* have exactly two heads.

(i) Make a systematic listing:

first toss
is heads: H H T T   H T H T   H T T H
first toss
is tails: T T H H   T H T H   T H H T

(*Put the second H in each possible position, treat the second T the same way.*)
There are six outcomes with 2H and 2T, so

$$\frac{6}{16} = \frac{3}{8} \text{ is the probability.}$$

(ii) Count the outcomes that don't have exactly 2H and 2T. That may sound harder than listing the desired outcomes directly, but you may actually find it easier. In any case, this is a good check on whether you really did get the full list if you tried to do that:

0 heads: T T T T
1 head: H T T T   T H T T   T T H T   T T T H
1 tail: H H H T   H H T H   H T H H   T H H H
                                    (*3 heads*)

0 tails: H H H H

This gives a total of 10 outcomes, so the 2H and 2T outcomes are $16 - 10 = 6$ of them.

6. **(B)** 12%
The percentage reduction is $100 \times$ amount off $\div$ original price. In this case, you need to find $100 \times 1 \div 8.35$ to the nearest whole percent. Anything between 11.5% and 12.4% rounds off to 12%.

$$8.35\overline{)100.00} \rightarrow$$

$$\begin{array}{r} 11.9\ldots \\ 835\overline{)10000.0} \\ \underline{835} \\ 1650 \\ \underline{835} \\ 815\,0 \\ 751\,5 \end{array}$$

7. **(C)** 2003
The left-most data point on the graph is from 1996, the right-most point from 2006; therefore, each point marks one year in the period. You can label these points, or just mark off the ones in the listed answers.

1996 is almost the highest point, but if you carefully line up your answer sheet parallel to the horizontal axis, you'll see that at the level of the 1996 data, the paper cuts through the graph at one place. Counting the data points to that one shows it is the value for 2003. (You can also rule out 2000, which clearly has the lowest unemployment value, and 2006, which is near the middle of the graph.)

8. **(D)** 2002

In 1999, the unemployment rate increased slightly over that for 1998, and in 2000 the rate dropped (to the lowest value in this period). You should be able to see that the change from 2000 to 2001 is less than from 2001 to 2002; the line is visibly less step, and shorter than the line from 2001 to 2002.

9. **(C)** 1.3%

The lowest year, 2000, had an unemployment rate about 13% (roughly half way between the tick marks for 12% and 14%; again, use your answer sheet as a ruler to see where the data point is on the vertical scale). Three years later, 2003 had unemployment of about 17% or a bit higher. That is about 4% in 3 years, which is closer to 1.3% per year than to any of the other answers.

10. **(C)** 3.09×10^8

The Census count of 308,745,538 people rounds up to 309 million. Since a million (1,000,000) is the same as 10^6, consequently the population to three significant digits could be expressed as 309×10^6. However, scientific notation conventionally uses a single digit to the left of a decimal point, with the remaining two significant digits following that. Each leftward shift of the decimal point adds one to the exponent of 10, so $309 \times 10^6 = 30.9 \times 10^7 = 3.09 \times 10^8$.

11. **(B)** $60

Calculate the number of gallons the family will need to complete the 550-mile trip and then multiply the number of gallons by the price ($2.40) they expect to pay per gallon. To find the number of gallons they will

need, divide the length of the trip (550 miles) by the average mileage (22 miles per gallon) of their car:

$$\begin{array}{r} 25 \\ 22\overline{)550} \\ 44 \\ \hline 110 \\ 110 \\ \end{array}$$ gallons; multiplying by $2.40 per gallon:

$$\begin{array}{r} \$2.40 \\ \times\, 25 \\ \hline 12.00 \\ 48.0 \\ \hline \$60.00 \end{array}$$

12. **(B)** 9

The woman is three times as old as her daughter, and her daughter is 12 years old. Therefore we can figure out that the woman is $3 \times 12 = 36$ years old. The woman is four times as old as her son, and we are asked to find how old the son is. We can figure this out by an equation or by simply rephrasing the question until we see how to answer it.

By equation: "The woman is four times as old as her son" becomes (woman's age) $= 4 \times$ (son's age) or $36 = 4 \times s$. To find s (the son's age) divide both sides of the equation by 4:

$$\frac{36}{4} = \frac{4 \times s}{4}$$
$$\frac{36}{4} = 9$$

By words: "The woman is four times as old as her son" means the same as "the son is $\frac{1}{4}$ as old as the woman," and (since we know she is 36) we can figure out $\frac{1}{4}$ of $36 = 36 \div 4 = 9$.

13. **(C)** 630

The pond is a cylinder, with a radius of 10 feet (20 feet across gives the diameter). The volume of a cylinder is $\pi r^2 h = \pi \times 10^2 \times 2 = 200 \times \pi \approx 200 \times 3.14\ldots = 628$. You don't actually need to remember the formula for the volume of a cylinder if you know the general rule that the volume of a solid that has the same cross section at every height is the height times the area of the surface, in this case the area of the 20-foot diameter circle.

14. **(C)** 32

Find the change from each number to the next in the sequence (subtract each one from the following one).

$10 - 7 = 3$
$14 - 10 = 4$
$19 - 14 = 5$
$25 - 19 = 6$

At each step, the difference increases by 1; therefore the next number is $25 + 7 = 32$.

15. **(D)** 50 minutes

The man traveled 30 miles at 60 miles per hour and the last 10 miles of his trip were at 30 miles per hour. To find how long the trip lasted, you need to calculate how much time each part of the trip took. The first part is easiest; if he was traveling at 60 miles per hour, he covered 30 miles (half of 60 miles) in half an hour—that is, the first part took 30 minutes. The second part is a bit harder to figure, but the same idea works; think of it as a proportion or fraction problem: The man traveled 10 miles at 30 miles per hour, so in one hour he would have traveled 30 miles. He actually traveled only $\frac{1}{3}$ of this distance (10 miles = $\frac{1}{3}$ of 30 miles), so he must have taken $\frac{1}{3}$ of an hour to go that far. $\frac{1}{3}$ of 60 minutes = 20 minutes and adding this to the first part of the trip gives 30 minutes + 20 minutes for the total time in minutes for the man to travel from Kingston to Yorkville.

16. **(C)** 4 inches

The boy's average growth rate for the two years (10th birthday to 12th birthday) is the total number of inches he grew divided by 2. Convert the heights to inches to make this easier:

at age 10 he was 4 feet 8 inches tall =
$4 \times 12 + 8 = 48 + 8 = 56$ inches

at age 12 he was 5 feet 4 inches tall =
$5 \times 12 + 4 = 60 + 4 = 64$ inches
The difference ($64 - 56 = 8$ inches) is the total growth; the average is $8 \div 2 = 4$ inches.

17. **(D)** 8 : 1

You need to find the slope of both lines to determine their ratio. Remember that the slope of a line is the "rise" divided by the "run"—that is, change in y over change in x. The slope of line A is 2, since it goes through the point (2,4) and the origin; that is a rise of 4 units divided by a run of 2 units. For line B, the rise is 1 over a run of 4, so the slope is 1/4. Therefore, the slope of A has the ratio of 2 : 1/4 to the slope of B. Reduce this to unit terms by multiplying both sides of the ratio by 4, and you get slope (A): slope (B) = $4 \times (2 : 1/4) = 8 : 1$, which is Choice D

18. **(B)** 3 inches

Try to eliminate the answers that do not work. If the other side is 2 inches, then all three sides are equal, and the triangle would be equilateral, with all angles 60°, not a right triangle. If the other side is 4 inches, then the 2-inch sides couldn't meet except by collapsing onto the 4-inch side, so that there is no triangle. A 5-inch side is even worse! The only good choice is B, 3 inches. You can also calculate the side by recognizing that it must be the diagonal of a square:

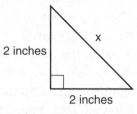

The side opposite the right angle has to be larger than the others (since the right angle is the largest angle). Now you can either use the Pythagorean formula, so that $x^2 = 2^2 + 2^2 = 8$; or remember that the diagonal of a square is $\sqrt{2}$ times the side, so that $x = 2\sqrt{2} = 2 \times 1.41 \ldots = 2.82$.

You don't need to be exact about the value of $\sqrt{2}$ or actually calculate the square root of 8 to see that 3 is closer to it than any of the other choices.

19. **(C)** $6.05

This question is a natural candidate for algebra, since the amount Craig and his friends paid for lunch is "unknown." Let x stand for the cost of the luncheon special, which Craig's eight friends had; then the cost of Craig's dish was $x + 2$ and the total cost has the equation:

$$8x + (x + 2) = 38.45$$
$$9x + 2 = 38.45$$
$$9x = 38.45 - 2 = 36.45$$

Therefore, $x = \$36.45/9 = \$4.05$, and Craig owed $x + 2 = \$6.05$.

20. **(C)** 120

The factorial notation $n!$ means multiplying the integer n by each smaller positive integer, so $10! = 10 \times 9 \times 8 \times 7 \times 6 \times \ldots \times 2 \times 1$. Similarly, $7! = 7 \times 6 \times \ldots \times 1$, and each factor from the 7! in the denominator cancels against the same factor in 10! in the numerator. That leaves $10 \times 9 \times 8$ divided by $3! = 3 \times 2 \times 1$. Therefore, we are left with

$$\frac{10 \times 9 \times 8}{3 \times 2} = 10 \times 3 \times 4 = 120.$$

21. **(C)** 40 ounces

Convert all the measures to the same unit, ounces in this case. A half-gallon = 2 quarts = 2×2 pints = 4×16 ounces, for a total of 64 ounces. The cup of milk used for cooking is 8 ounces (1 pint = 2 cups = 16 ounces; dividing by 2, $\frac{1}{2}$ pint = 1 cup = 8 ounces).

$$64 - 2 \times 8 - 8 = 64 - 24 = 40.$$

22. **(B)** 34 ounces

You have to find an equation relating ounces and liters. The table can be used as in the previous question to convert a larger unit (gallons in this case) into ounces, so that you can equate the number of liters and the number of ounces in a gallon.

1 gallon = 4 quarts = 4×2 pints = 8 pints = 8×16 ounces = 128 ounces.

Therefore, 128 ounces = 3.785 liters, and 1 liter is $128 \div 3.785$ ounces. Instead of performing long division to work out the answer, notice that the result has to be between $128 \div 4$ and $128 \div 3$. Use these, which are easier to calculate, to make an inequality around the answer, x.

$$128 \div 4 = 32 < x < 128 \div 3 = 42\tfrac{2}{3}.$$

Only Choice B lies in this range.

23. **(B)** $790.60

The woman has paid $396 a year for three years, so she has spent $3 \times \$396 = \$1,188$ for insurance. The insurance company paid her $\$2,278.60 - \$300 = \$1,978.60$. The difference is

$$\begin{array}{r} 1,976.60 \\ -1,188.00 \\ \hline 790.60 \end{array}$$

24. **(C)** $\frac{1}{2}$

The white bars of the bar chart show the number of days of unhealthful air in Los Angeles. This bar is usually above 160; in 2006 it was about 180 (you can guess this by comparing the part of the bar above 160 with the scale on the left side). A year has 365 days, so that $\frac{1}{4}$ of a year is about 91 days, $\frac{1}{3}$ is about 122 days, $\frac{1}{2}$ is about 182 days, and $\frac{1}{10}$ is about 36 days. The closest fraction for Los Angeles is Choice C, $\frac{1}{2}$.

25. **(D)** Sacramento Valley

Of the four regions in the chart, the one with the shortest bars, every year, is the one on the right. Comparing against the legend on the bottom right of the chart, we see that black represents San Diego, white is for Los Angeles, and medium gray is the South Central Coast. The rightmost bars stand for the Sacramento Valley, Choice D.

26. **(B)** 2 : 1

The inscribed square has its four corners on the circle, and the center of the square (where the diagonals cross) must be the center of the circle. The circumscribed square will have the centers of each side touching the circle, and again the square will be centered on the circle. Therefore, the diameter of the circle is a diagonal for the inside square and the same length as a side of the outside square. In other words the larger square has a side $\sqrt{2}$ times the side of the smaller square. The area of the larger square is then $\sqrt{2} \times \sqrt{2} = 2$ times the area of the smaller one.

27. **(B)** $0.83

Nancy collected $30 (6 × $5), so the amount to be divided among the contributors is that minus $25. $5 ÷ 6 can be done directly by long division, but it is simpler to multiply each answer in turn by 6 to check which one is best. Trying A gives 6 × $0.57 = $3.42; for B, 6 × $0.83 = 4.98; for C, 6 × $0.87 = $5.22; and for D the result will be even larger. Answer B is closest.

28. **(B)** $9\frac{1}{4}$

Use the common denominator (8ths) to express all three lengths:

$$1\tfrac{3}{8} + 2\tfrac{3}{8} + 5\tfrac{1}{2} = (1+2+5) + (\tfrac{3}{8} + \tfrac{3}{8} + \tfrac{4}{8}) =$$

$$8 + \tfrac{10}{8} = 9\tfrac{2}{8}$$

Reduce the $\frac{2}{8}$ fraction to $\frac{1}{4}$; the sum is $9\frac{1}{4}$.

29. **(A)** February

You are looking for a month in which the actual expense is more than (exceeds) the budgeted amount of $125.

A. February. She paid $126.25, which is *more* than the budget.

This must be the answer to the question, and you don't need to go on to check the other choices.

30. **(C)** $223.93

Martha's total expenses for April were:

$121.16	for rent
62.35	for food
36.22	for clothes
+4.20	for phone
$223.93	total

31. **(C)** 1995

All other years except 1995 have a percent CPI increase of more than 2%. This may be a bit hard to tell at a glance—to be sure, use a piece of paper (like the answer sheet), and move it over the graph from top to bottom, parallel with the edges of the graph. When only a single point remains visible, look down at the labels and check that the closest tick mark is the one for 1995.

32. **(D)** Irregular variation between 1% and 6%

The inflation rate on this graph starts at about 3%, rises to near 6%, drops back again below 3%, rises again to 6%, then drops below 2% before rising back up again. That's a fairly complex pattern. Choice A (increase, decrease, increase) is correct up to 1990, but that is less than half of the graph. Choices B and C are clearly wrong. The graph doesn't begin with a decrease or with a level section and a decrease. Choice D is not explicit about where the increases or decreases are, but it is true for the full course of the graph. All values are in the range between 1% and 6%, and the variation has no simple, regular pattern.

33. **(A)** 4 times

The low point for inflation was in 1995 at a value close to 1.5%; the highest points appear to be in 1990 or 2000 at or just above 6% (with 1984 close to 6% as well). These values are close enough to select the correct choice from those given. You can divide 6 by 1.5 to calculate 4, or just notice that doubling 1.5% gives 3% (too small!) and doubling again gives 6%.

34. **(B)** 30

There are two different rates at which the girls wash the cars: Kathy washes four cars per hour (it takes her 15 minutes, $\frac{1}{4}$ hour, to wash a car) and the others each wash three cars per hour (20 minutes is $\frac{20}{60} = \frac{1}{3}$ hour). At Kathy's rate, she can wash $4N$ cars in N hours. Emily and Nancy can each wash $3N$ cars in N hours. The total number of cars in three hours is $4 \times 3 + 3 \times 3 + 3 \times 3 =$

$12 + 9 + 9 = 12 + 18 = 30$. You could also solve this by simplifying the algebraic expression before multiplying by the three hours:

Total cars $= 4N + 3N + 3N = (4 + 3 + 3)N$ $= 10N$

For $N = 3$, this gives a total of 30.

35. **(A)** $y = 2 - x/3$

The equations given as possible choices are all in "slope-intercept" form, where the constant coefficient is the y-value where the line intercepts (crosses) the y-axis, and the coefficient of x is the slope of the line. In this case, the line crosses the y-axis at 2, and slopes downwards to cross the x-axis at 6. Thus, the slope is $-2/6$, or $-1/3$. Choices A and B both have y-intercept 2, but B has the wrong slope ($1/3$).

36. **(B)** $5,010

The car lost (50% + 20%) of its original value in the two years, or 70% altogether. Its value at the end of the two years is 100% − 70% = 30% of the original value, that is:

$16,700 \times 0.3 = 1,670 \times 3 = 5,010$

37. **(C)** 88

The average number of tickets that he sells per hour is the total number of tickets sold divided by the total number of hours. That is, 528 tickets ÷ 6 hours.

```
      88 tickets per hour
  6)528
    48
    ‾‾
    48
    48
```

38. **(B)** 10

Look for the pattern in the number arrangement. Each row begins with 1, then goes on to the number of its line (3 is in the third line, *etc.*). In fact, each number is the sum of the numbers above it in the previous row. But you do not need to solve this puzzle completely to get the answer; the rows show a pattern of increase and decrease from left to center and from center to the right side. The second half of the row will be the same as the first half in reverse, that is, 10, then

5, then 1. That is, the next number after 1, 5, and 10 will be Choice B, 10.

39. **(C)** $9,420

The woman takes out a loan for $96,000 minus the down payment of $17,500; that is, her loan is for $96,000 − $17,500 = $78,500. She must pay 12% of this amount in interest the first year. To find 12% of an amount, multiply the amount by 12%, which is the same as 0.12:

```
  $ 78,500
      ×.12
  1 570 00
  7 850 0
  $9,420.00
```

40. **(A)** The length of the longest side of the triangle

No information is given about the size of the triangle; it could be microscopically small or very large. There is no data from which the length of any side could be found. Hence, Choice A certainly meets the terms of the question—the length of the longest side *cannot* be determined. To confirm that this is the correct answer, you should also consider each of the other choices.

B. The size of the largest angle of the triangle. Since two angles are given (75° and 45°), the third can be calculated (180° minus the sum of the other two). It turns out to be 60° (180 − 120).

C. Which angle of the triangle is the largest. Since you can calculate the third angle, and the largest side is opposite the largest angle (and the smallest side is opposite the smallest angle—draw some pictures of triangles with large and small angles if this is not familiar), you can conclude that the 75° angle on the lower left is the largest.

D. Which side of the triangle is the largest. As in the reasoning about Choice C, the largest side is opposite the largest angle (and the smallest side is opposite the smallest angle). Therefore, you can conclude that the largest side of the triangle is side b, opposite the 75° angle.

Note: You do *not* need to do the calculations, or make any guesses about the answers that might turn up for Choices B, C, or D—all that matters is understanding that there is a method to get the answer if it's wanted.

41. **(A)** June 1

The man wants to save $900 in installments of $150, making his last deposit on November 1 in order to have the whole $900 tax payment on November 15. He must make six deposits altogether because $150 goes into $900 exactly 6 times $(900 \div 150 = \frac{90}{15} = 6)$. If he always makes the deposit on the first of the month and skips none of the deposits, he can figure out when to start by counting backwards from November 1 for six deposits:

(6) November 1
(5) October 1
(4) September 1
(3) August 1
(2) July 1
(1) June 1

The first deposit should be on June 1 (Choice A).

42. **(A)** $6.90

If the man pays $15 down and makes 3 monthly payments of $7.95 each, he will pay a total of $15 + (3 × $7.95) for the watch:

$$\begin{array}{r} \$\ 7.95 \\ \times\ \ \ 3 \\ \hline \$23.85 \end{array}$$

$$\$23.85 + \$15\ \text{down} = \$\ 3\overset{7}{8}.\overset{1}{8}5\ \text{total}$$
$$-31.95\ \text{(cash)}$$
$$\overline{\$\ \ 6.90}$$

If he pays cash ($31.95), he will save the difference.

43. **(B)** $269.70

To calculate the supermarket's profit of 1.5% on sales of $17,980, it is easiest to find 1% of the total sales and then find half of that 1% ($\frac{1}{2}$ of 1% = 0.5%) and add the two amounts together. It is also easy to find 1% of an amount—just shift the decimal point over two places to the left. 1% of $17,980 = $179.80.

Half of this is:

$$\begin{array}{r} \$\ 89.90 \\ 2\overline{)\$179.80} \\ \underline{16} \\ 19 \\ \underline{18} \\ 18 \\ \underline{18} \\ \end{array}$$

Adding the two values together:

1.0%	$179.80
+0.5%	+89.90
1.5%	$269.70

44. **(A)** 11 inches

If the handyman cut the board into three *equal* pieces, each piece would be 12 inches long (since a yard is 36 inches and $\frac{1}{3}$ of 36 inches = 12 inches). But one piece has to be an inch shorter and the third piece an inch longer than the second piece; if we "borrow" the extra inch for the third piece from the first piece, everything comes out right: the first piece is 1 inch shorter than the average, the second piece is just the average length, and the third piece is 1 inch longer than the average. 11 inches + 12 inches + 13 inches add up to 36 inches or 1 yard.

You can also do this as an equation, which you solve to find the length of the first piece; use the letter L to stand for the length of the first piece. The second piece is 1 inch longer than this, so its length is $L + 1$; and the third piece is 1 inch longer than the second, so its length is $L + 1 + 1 = L + 2$. We still don't know what L is, but we find out by adding all the lengths to make up 1 yard. $L + (L + 1) + (L + 2) = 36$. Adding the Ls together, we get $(3 \times L) + 1 + 2 = 36$ or $(3 \times L) + 3 = 36$. Subtract 3 from both sides: $3 \times L = 33$, and finally divide both sides by 3 to get

$$\frac{3 \times L}{3} = \frac{33}{3} = 11.$$

Therefore, the length of the first piece is 11 inches.

45. **(B)** 28

The number of boys is six times the number of girls, and the total enrollment is 196. Adding the boys and girls together we get # girls + # boys = 196. But # boys = 6 × # girls, so we have # girls + 6 × # girls = 196 or 7 × # girls = 196. Therefore the number of girls is 196 divided by 7: $7\overline{)196}$ $\,^{28}$

46. **(B)** $87.66

The man is unmarried; so he is unlikely to make use of the plans for "Member & Spouse" or "Member & Children" or "Member, Spouse, & Children." The premium for the "Member Only" program for someone aged 58 is in the row marked 50–59; that is, $87.66, Choice B.

47. **(C)** $89.58

The insurance rate for a 28-year-old wife is less than that for a 43-year-old husband. Since both are eligible, by taking out the insurance in the wife's name, they are arranging that she is the member, and her husband then becomes insured as the member's spouse. Therefore, they will find the premium in the second column ("Member & Spouse") and in the first row because the wife is less than 35 years old. This place in the table shows that their premium will be $89.58.

48. **(C)** $39.14

When the wife turns 35, the premium goes up from $89.58 to $128.72. The increase is:

$$\begin{array}{r} \$128.72 \\ -89.58 \\ \hline \$\ 39.14 \end{array}$$

49. **(C)** $1,399.68

In the two weeks, she works 2 × 30 = 60 regular hours, at the rate of $21.60 per hour, plus eight hours (three the first week, five the next) at the reduced rate. For the regular hours, she gets 60 × 21.60 = 6 × 216 = $1,296. Since she gets paid at the reduced rate for the extra eight hours, you can elimi-nate Choices A and B at this stage; only C or D could be correct. You could figure out exactly what she makes for the extra eight hours, but you can also estimate this as follows: 60% of $21.60 is somewhat more than half, say roughly $12 per hour. Then the eight hours are worth approximately 8 × $12 = $96. The correct answer, therefore, should be about $100 more than the $1,296 for her regular 60 hours, giving Choice C.

For the exact calculation, find 60% of $21.60

$$\begin{array}{r} 21.6 \\ \times 0.6 \\ \hline 12.96 \end{array}$$

Then, her pay for the extra hours is

$$\begin{array}{r} 12.96 \\ \times\ \ \ 8 \\ \hline 103.68 \end{array}$$

and her total pay is $1,296.00 + $103.68 = $1,399.68.

50. **(C)** Houston

A winning percentage of 45% means that fewer than half the games were won. From this, you can eliminate Choices A and B (Los Angeles won more than they lost; San Diego, the same number won and lost). 45% is not very much less than 50%, so Houston with ten wins should have a percentage not too far from San Diego's 50%. Check this by doing the division; if it isn't close to 45%, you can then try the remaining choice. It helps to reduce 10/22 to lowest terms, 5/11, to make the division easier:

$$\begin{array}{r} 0.45\ldots \\ 11\overline{)5.00\ldots} \\ 4\ 4 \\ \hline 60 \\ 55 \\ \hline \end{array}$$

The Basics of Writing

The Language Subtest of the CHSPE essentially tests your writing skills. Your first task is to write a persuasive short essay. If you have not had to do much writing in high school or if you have received poor grades on the written work you have handed in, you may be worried about how well you will do on this part of the test. Relax. If you can talk coherently, you can write coherently. The trick is to involve yourself in what you write.

WHAT THE EXAMINERS LOOK FOR

The examiners at California Proficiency Testing are looking for someone who can communicate ideas. Basically, your essay tells the examiners whether you are able to put your thoughts on paper and get across a point to a friendly audience. The examiners don't expect perfection from you—they expect proficiency.

What is proficiency? Fundamentally, it is a combination of four elements:

1. **Fluency.** Fluency is smoothness and ease in communicating. In this case, it is your ability to set down a given number of words on paper within a limited period of time. If you freeze on essay examinations, writing only a sentence or two when whole paragraphs are called for, then you need to practice letting your words and ideas *flow*.

2. **Organization.** Organization is coherent arrangement. In this case, it is your ability to arrange your thoughts in order, following a clear game plan. If you jump from subject to subject within a single paragraph, if you leave out critical elements, or if you never manage to state exactly what you mean, then you need to practice outlining your position before you express it in paragraph form.

3. **Technical English.** Technical English is the part of English most students hate—grammar, spelling, punctuation, word usage. In this case, it is your ability to produce grammatically correct sentences in standard written English. If your English compositions come back to you with the abbreviations "frag" (fragment) or "agr" (agreement) or "sp" (spelling) scribbled in the margins, then you need to practice reading your papers to catch any technical mistakes.

4. **Completeness.** Completeness means just that. The essay topic may include several questions. The examiners want you to answer every one of them. If you don't, you may lose up to half of the twelve points you could earn on the essay.

If you are taking all three sections of the CHSPE on the same day, you should allow yourself about 1½ hours for the Language Subtest: approximately half an hour for the essay and one hour for the multiple-choice portion that follows.

How can you write an essay in just 30 minutes? Read the following section to learn tactics that work when you must write under time pressure.

HOW TO WRITE AN ESSAY IN 30 MINUTES

Minute One—Analyze

Look at the essay question. What is it asking you to do? Is it asking you to explain the reasons for an opinion of yours? Is it asking you to take a stand on a particular issue? If you are being asked to argue for or against something, you may have an immediate gut reaction to what you're being asked. Pay attention to how you feel. If your immediate reaction is "Of course!" or "Never!" ask yourself why you feel that way.

See whether you can spot any key word or short phrase in the question that triggers your reaction. For example, consider the following essay question:

Write a brief essay explaining why you believe young persons should or should not be required to wear school uniforms.

What word or phrase triggers your reaction? "School uniforms."

Minutes Two to Three—Brainstorm

Write down the key word or phrase you spotted in the question. Circle it. Now write down other words and phrases that you associate with this key word or phrase. What words come to your mind, for example, when you think of school uniforms? Neutral words like *plaid, pleated skirts, blazers*? Negative words like *tacky, parochial, ugly, miserable, conformist, polyester*? Positive words like *noncompetitive, equal for everyone, no pressure, inexpensive*? Words like *soldiers, prisoners, police, guns*? Whether or not you ever had to wear a school uniform, you have some mental associations with the idea of uniforms and with wearing uniforms in school. By brainstorming, or clustering, as this process is sometimes called, you can tap these associations, call up the wealth of *ideas you already have*, and forget any worries you may have had about having nothing to say.

Note, by the way, in the illustration below, the many other words and phrases that branch off from the central phrase, "school uniforms." When you brainstorm, your mind leads you in innumerable directions, hinting at the whole range of what you already know about the subject at hand. If you feel like it, draw lines and arrows linking the various words and phrases to your key phrase. Don't worry about setting these words and phrases in any particular order. Just play with them, jotting them down and doodling around them—a sense of where you are going will emerge.

You have plenty to say. You have gut reactions to all sorts of questions. Let the brainstorming process tap the knowledge and feelings that lie within you.

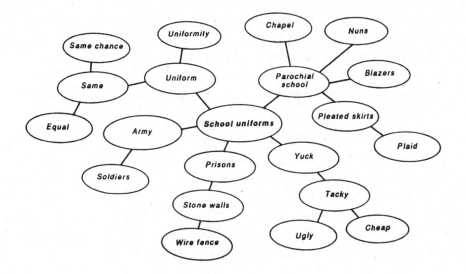

Minutes Four to Five—Define Your Position

After you have been brainstorming for a minute or so, something inside you is going to say "Now"—*now* I know what I'm going to write. Trust that inner sense. You know where you are going—now put it into words.

Look over your "map" or record of your mental associations and see what patterns have emerged. Just what is it that you have to say? Are you *for* school uniforms? Are you *against* them? Are your feelings *mixed*? What you are doing is coming up with a statement of your position—words to express your initial gut reaction—a *thesis sentence* for your essay.

> Thesis 1: I believe students should be required to wear uniforms in school because wearing school uniforms lessens peer pressure and promotes social equality.

> Thesis 2: I believe students should not be required to wear uniforms in school because school uniforms are unattractive outfits which no one likes.

> Thesis 3: Although I was miserable wearing a uniform in elementary school, I still believe young people should be required to wear uniforms in school.

Here are three possible thesis sentences, one for, one against, one mixed. Note how their main clauses start: *I believe, I believe, I still believe*. In your opening sentence, *state your point*. Don't wait. The examiners want to see whether you can express your ideas clearly. Make your point clear to them from the start.

In a sense, the test-makers give you your opening sentence. All you have to do is take the question and rephrase it. This does not take much work. Remember, your job is to prove your writing competence, not demonstrate your literary style. You do not need to open your essay with a quotation ("Henry Thoreau warns us, 'Beware of all enterprises that require new clothes.'") or with a statement designed to startle your reader ("My school uniform hates me."). You simply need to state your thesis. In doing so, however, you must exercise some caution: you must limit your thesis to something you can handle in a couple of hundred words.

The one problem with brainstorming is that you may wind up feeling that you have too much to say. Your job is not to write *Everything You Ever Wanted to Know about School Uniforms (But Were Afraid to Ask)*. It is to write one or two pages and make a single clear point. Avoid starting with open-ended statements like "School uniforms are ugly" or "Everybody should wear uniforms." These are weak thesis statements—they are too broad to help you focus on the topic and too vague to show why you hold the opinion that you have.

In writing your thesis statement, limit yourself. State your point—and be ready to support it with reasons.

Minutes Six to Eight—Outline

Now take a minute to organize what you are going to say in outline form. In a sense, your thesis sentence sets up everything else you have to say. It you have a clear thesis, the essay almost writes itself.

See how each of the thesis sentences just discussed sets up the essay, in each case requiring a slightly different outline.

Outline 1

I. Introduction—statement of your thesis
   I believe students should be required to wear uniforms in school because wearing school uniforms lessens peer pressure and promotes social equality.
II. Reasons
   A. Lessens Peer Pressure
      1. "Clothes wars"
      2. Pressure to keep up with Joneses
   B. Promotes Social Equality
      1. Rich and poor wear same clothes
      2. Clothes don't make the person
III. Conclusion—restatement of your thesis
   To promote a spirit of equality among young people and to free them from pressures inspired by the fashion industry, students should be required to wear uniforms while they attend school.

Outline 2

I. Introduction—statement of your thesis
   I believe students should not be required to wear uniforms in school because school uniforms are unattractive outfits that no one likes.
II. Description of School Uniform
   A. Unbecoming Colors
   B. Unflattering Cut
   C. Mediocre Materials
III. Conclusion—restatement of your thesis
   Young or old, nobody likes to wear unbecoming clothing. Young people should not be forced to wear unattractive uniforms that they heartily dislike.

Outline 3

I. Introduction—statement of your thesis
   Although I was miserable wearing a uniform in elementary school, I still believe young people should be required to wear uniforms in school.
II. Elementary School Experience
III. Reasons for Change of Opinion
IV. Conclusion—restatement of your thesis
   Being required to wear a school uniform distressed me in elementary school. Looking back, however, I can see it helped me as well. Thus, I believe that school uniforms are beneficial and that wearing them should be required.

Minutes Nine to Twenty-four—Write

You have 15 minutes to write your essay. You have your opening, your outline, and your conclusion all in mind. Devote this time to putting down your thoughts, writing approximately a page and a half. Try to write neatly, but don't worry so much about neatness that you wind up clenching your pencil for dear life. Just leave yourself room in the margins and know that there's no problem if you cross out or erase.

Minute Twenty-five—Read

Expert writers often test their work by reading it aloud. In the exam room, you cannot read out loud. However, when you read your essay silently, take your time and listen with your inner ear to how it sounds. Read to get a sense of your essay's logic and of its rhythm. Does one sentence flow smoothly into the next? Would they flow more smoothly if you were to add a transition word or phrase (*therefore*, *however*, *nevertheless*, *in contrast*, *similarly*)? Do the sentences follow a logical order? Is any key idea or example missing? Does any sentence seem out of place? How would things sound if you cut out that awkward sentence or inserted that transition word?

Minute Twenty-six—React

Take this minute to act on your response to hearing your essay. If it sounded to you as if a transition word was needed, insert it. If it sounded to you as if a sentence should be cut, delete it. If it sounded to you as if a sentence was out of place, move it. Trust your inner ear, but do not attempt to do too much. You know your basic outline for the essay is good. You have neither the need nor the time to attempt a total revision.

Minute Twenty-seven—Reword

Look over your vocabulary in your essay. In your concern to get your thoughts on paper, have you limited yourself to an overly simple vocabulary? Have you used one word over and over again, never substituting a synonym? Try upgrading your vocabulary. Replace one word in the essay with a synonym—*detest* or *loathe* in place of *hate* in the sentence *Students hate school uniforms*, for example. Substitute a somewhat more specific adjective or adverb for a vague one—*gentle* or *considerate* in place of *nice*; *extremely* unflattering in place of *really* unflattering. Again, do not attempt to do too much. Change only one or two words. Replace them with stronger words *whose meanings you are sure you know*.

Minute Twenty-eight—Rescan

Think of yourself as an editor. You need to have an eye for errors that damage your text. Take a minute to look over your essay for problems in spelling and grammar. From your English classes you should have an idea of particular words and grammatical constructions that have proved troublesome to you in the past. See whether you can spot any of these words or constructions in your essay. Correct those errors that you find.

Minute Twenty-nine—Reread

Now that you have looked over your essay like an editor, give yourself one final opportunity to hear your words again. Reread the composition to yourself, making sure that the changes you have made have not harmed the flow of your text.

Minute Thirty—Relax

You have just completed a basic essay. Now it is time to regroup your forces and relax before you go on to the next section of the test. Take a deep breath. Admire your essay. If you feel you have to do *something*, spend the time erasing stray marks on your paper or rewriting words that are hard to read. Do nothing major; at this point, you have earned a break.

DEVELOPING YOUR ESSAY WRITING SKILLS

You have just read about the process of writing a 30-minute essay. Now you should be ready to try writing a 30-minute essay of your own. Find a quiet corner where you will be undisturbed for the full 30 minutes—no phone calls, no Lady Gaga playing in the background, no Twitter breaks. You want to approximate exam conditions as closely as you can. In this practice session, however, you do get a choice of essay topics. Do not feel you have to write on all these topics. They are here to give you a wide choice and to make you aware of the range of topics on the CHSPE.

In the weeks to come, try writing on several of these topics. If you can, show your completed essays to a teacher or to a friend who does well in English. Get feedback on the organization of your essays, as well as on your technical mistakes. Make a check list of words you misspell. To write well is a valuable skill—the time you spend improving your ability as a writer will pay off, not only on the CHSPE, but throughout your adult life.

Argumentative Essay Topics

1. Many students today object to mandatory exercise and fitness classes. Write an essay explaining why you believe high school students should or should not be required to take physical education classes.
2. Write a short essay explaining why you believe young persons should or should not move away from home as soon as they are able to support themselves.
3. Write a short essay giving your opinion whether the speed limit should or should not be set at 55 miles per hour.
4. Write a short essay explaining why you believe young persons enrolled in school should or should not be limited to one hour of television viewing per day.
5. Write a short essay discussing why you believe students should or should not be allowed to bring cell phones to school.
6. Many young people are involved in hobbies or pastimes, such as photography or playing Angry Birds. Discuss a particular hobby or pastime with which you are acquainted, telling why you find it beneficial or harmful to participants.
7. Write a short essay explaining why you believe young people should or should not work part time while attending high school.
8. The automobile insurance industry considers teenage drivers risky clients and requires them to pay high rates. Write a short essay explaining why you believe teenage drivers are safer or less safe than elderly drivers are.
9. Write a short essay giving your opinion as to whether the drinking age should or should not be lowered in California.
10. Write a short essay explaining why you believe fraternities and sororities should or should not be permitted in high school.

ADVANCED OUTLINING

If you have been having trouble structuring your essays, you may find it helpful to consider the following typical ways in which essays are arranged. An essay may be arranged in one of several ways:

1. It may be arranged in **chronological order**—an order following a time sequence.
2. It may be arranged as a **comparison** or a **contrast**.
3. It may be arranged according to an **ascending or descending order of importance**.
4. It may be arranged to show a pattern of **cause and effect**.

Chronological order organizes details in the order in which they have happened, are happening, or should happen (will happen).

> On the first day God created light, and there was morning and evening on that day.
> On the second day God created the firmament.
> On the third day. . . .

This order is useful in telling a story or describing a process. Notice the sorts of words used to clarify transitions in a chronological paragraph: *first, second, third, fourth; in the beginning, next, then, after that; finally, last, in the end*. You want to use some of these transitional words to help your reader see the time sequence clearly.

When you **compare** two objects, you are trying to point out ways in which they resemble one another. When you **contrast** two objects, you are trying to point out ways in which they differ from one another. Transitional words useful in comparisons are *similarly, likewise, in like manner, in the same way, correspondingly*. Transitional words useful in contrasts are *however, but, in contrast, on the other hand, on the contrary, nevertheless*.

An **ascending order of importance** starts with the least important item in a series and works its way up to the most important. A **descending order of importance** starts with the most important item and works its way down to the least important. Both orders are useful in presenting an argument. In either case, you use transitional words like *first, second, third, fourth; most important, of the greatest importance, somewhat less important, significantly*.

Cause-and-effect order is particularly useful when you are trying to explain something. For example, if you were asked to write about the main reason for the decrease of interest in reading in America, you might write as follows:

> The invention of television has caused Americans to lose interest in reading. In the early days of television, few programs were available. People still had time to read. As television became more and more widespread, however, more hours of programming were available each day. *In consequence*, people who were attracted to the new medium

found themselves with less time in which to read. They *therefore* read less and *as a result* spent less time developing their basic reading skills. *Consequently*, they never had enough practice to become truly skilled readers; reading, which had been a source of pleasure to previous generations, was just plain hard work to these television fans.

In addition to the italicized transitional words in the preceding paragraph, useful transitional words for cause-and-effect paragraphs are *because, thus, inasmuch as, hence, it follows that you should*.

Select an appropriate order for your composition. Use transitional words to provide continuity.

THE LANGUAGE SUBTEST: MULTIPLE-CHOICE QUESTIONS

To pass the Language Subtest of the CHSPE, not only do you have to write a competent essay, but you also have to answer correctly most of the 48 multiple-choice questions that follow. As you have already seen in your self-assessment test, these multiple-choice questions test you on different aspects of writing. Some test your knowledge of simple grammar, punctuation, and capitalization. Others test your sense of what makes a good, clear sentence. Still others test your understanding of how to organize paragraphs and polish rough drafts of compositions.

GENERAL GRAMMAR REVIEW

If you have trouble spotting grammatical and other technical errors in your essays, you may find it helpful to work your way through some basic grammatical review. The next part of this chapter presents the essentials of grammar and usage, describes common problems, and outlines the effects of punctuation marks on the meaning and structure of a sentence. Work through the sections in order. To understand how to avoid common problems in grammar and word use, you need to know the technical grammatical terms used in the discussion.

If you already know and understand standard grammatical terms like *participle* and *dependent clause*, feel free to skip to page 126 and tackle the common problems in grammar and usage that you'll find there.

- **Nouns** are words that name or designate persons, places, things, states, or qualities. *Harry Potter, Diagonal Alley, book*, and *justice* are examples of nouns.
- **Pronouns** are words used in place of nouns. *He, we, them, who, which, this, what, each, everyone*, and *myself* are examples of pronouns.
- **Verbs** are words or phrases that express action or state of being. *Eat, enchant, believe, feel*, and *seem* are examples of verbs.
- **Adjectives** are words that serve as modifiers of nouns. *Famous, magical, tall*, and *enchanted* are examples of adjectives.

- **Adverbs** are words that modify verbs, adjectives, or other adverbs. *Too, very, happily,* and *quietly* are examples of adverbs.
- **Prepositions** are words used with nouns or pronouns to form phrases. *From, with, between, of,* and *to* are examples of prepositions.
- **Conjunctions** are words that serve to connect words, phrases, and clauses. *And, but, when,* and *because* are examples of conjunctions.
- **Articles** are the words *the, a,* and *an.* These words serve to identify as a noun the word that they modify.
- **Interjections** are grammatically independent words or expressions. *Alas, wow,* and *oh my* are examples of interjections.

NOUNS

Nouns change in form to indicate number and case. *Number* refers to the distinction between singular and plural; *case* refers to the way in which a noun is related to other elements in the sentence.

Number

Nouns are either singular or plural. To form the plural of a noun:

- Add *s* to the singular.

  girl / girls   house / houses

- Add *es* when the noun ends in *s, x, z, ch,* or *sh.*

  dish / dishes   church / churches

- Add *s* when the noun ends in *o* preceded by a vowel.

  folio / folios   trio / trios

- Add *es* when the noun ends in *o* preceded by a consonant.

  tomato / tomatoes   potato / potatoes

  (Exceptions to this rule: *contraltos, pianos, provisos, dynamos, Eskimos, sopranos.*)

- Add *s* to nouns ending in *f* or *fe* after changing these letters to *ve.*

  knife / knives   shelf / shelves

  (Exceptions to this rule: *chiefs, dwarfs, griefs, reefs, roofs, safes.*)

- Add *s* to nouns ending in *y* preceded by a vowel.

  boy / boys   valley / valleys

- Add *es* to nouns ending in *y* preceded by a consonant and change the *y* to *i.*

  baby / babies   story / stories

- Add *s* to the important part of a hyphenated word.

  brother-in-law / brothers-in-law   passer-by / passers-by

- Add *s* or *es* to proper nouns.

  Frank / Frank<u>s</u>   Smith / Smith<u>s</u>
  Jones / Jones<u>es</u>   Charles / Charles<u>es</u>

  (Note that the apostrophe (') is not used.)

- Add *s* or *es* to either the title or the proper noun when both are mentioned.

  Doctor Brown / Doctor<u>s</u> Brown or Doctor Brown<u>s</u>
  Miss Smith / Miss<u>es</u> Smith or Miss Smith<u>s</u>

- Add *'s* to form the plural of letters, numerals and symbols.

  e / e<u>'s</u>   9 / 9<u>'s</u>
  etc. / etc.<u>'s</u>   & / &<u>'s</u>

- Change to a different form in the following cases:

  foot / feet   tooth / teeth
  goose / geese   woman / women
  louse / lice   child / children
  man / men   ox / oxen

- Retain the foreign form with some words of foreign origin.

  alumna / alumnae   focus / foci
  alumnus / alumni   genus / genera
  analysis / analyses   hypothesis / hypotheses
  antithesis / antitheses   larva / larvae
  bacillus / bacilli   matrix / matrices
  bacterium / bacteria   monsieur / messieurs
  basis / bases   oasis / oases
  crisis / crises   parenthesis / parentheses
  criterion / criteria   thesis / theses
  erratum / errata   trousseau / trousseaux

Case

Nouns also change in form to show possession. The possessive case of nouns is formed in the following manner:

1. If the noun ends in *s*, add an apostrophe (').

2. If the noun does not end in *s*, add an apostrophe (') and an *s*.

   The <u>doctor's</u> office (The office of the doctor)
   The <u>doctors'</u> office (The office of two or more doctors)

   The <u>girl's</u> books (The books of one girl)
   The <u>girls'</u> books (The books of two or more girls)

Note

The correct formation or spelling of plurals is *not* directly tested on the CHSPE. However, you will need to be able to recognize singular and plural noun forms in order to spot certain grammatical errors.

Note that in nouns of one syllable ending in *s*, either the apostrophe or the apostrophe and an *s* may be used.

James' hat and James's hat are both correct.

A noun preceding a gerund should be in the possessive case. (A gerund is a verb form—a verbal—that is used as a noun: Slicing raw onions made him cry.)

Incorrect: The teacher complained about John talking.

Correct: The teacher complained about John's talking.

Questions involving the possessive case *definitely* show up on the CHSPE.

PRONOUNS

Pronouns are classified as *personal, relative, interrogative, demonstrative, indefinite,* or *reflexive.*

Personal Pronouns

Personal pronouns indicate the person speaking, the person spoken to, or the person spoken about. They change to indicate case and number. In the third person, they also indicate gender. *He* is the masculine pronoun, *she* is the feminine pronoun, and *it* is the neuter or common gender pronoun.

THE FIRST PERSON
(The person speaking or writing)

Case	Singular	Plural
Subjective	I	we
Possessive	my, mine	our, ours
Objective	me	us

THE SECOND PERSON
(The person spoken or written to)

Case	Singular	Plural
Subjective	you	you
Possessive	your, yours	your, yours
Objective	you	you

THE THIRD PERSON
(The person, place, or thing spoken or written about)

Case	Singular	Plural
Third Person Masculine		
Subjective	he	they
Possessive	his	their, theirs
Objective	him	them
Third Person Feminine		
Subjective	she	they
Possessive	her, hers	their, theirs
Objective	her	them
Third Person Neuter		
Subjective	it	they
Possessive	its	their, theirs
Objective	it	them

Relative Pronouns

The **relative pronouns** are *who*, *which*, and *that*. They are used to relate a word in an independent clause (see the section on clauses later in this chapter) to a dependent clause. *Who* is used to refer to persons, *which* to things, and *that* to both persons and things. Like the personal pronouns, *who* has different forms according to case:

Case	Singular	Plural
Subjective	who	who
Possessive	whose	whose
Objective	whom	whom

Interrogative Pronouns

The **interrogative pronouns** are *who*, *which*, and *what*. They are used to ask questions. *Which* and *what* do not change according to case. *Who* follows the forms listed under "Relative Pronouns."

Demonstrative Pronouns

The **demonstrative pronouns** are *this*, *that*, *these*, and *those*. They serve to point out people, places, and things. The plural of *this* is *these*; the plural of *that* is *those*.

Indefinite Pronouns

The **indefinite pronouns** include *all, anyone, each, either, everyone, somebody, someone, whatever, whoever*. The objective case of *whoever* is *whomever*; all the other indefinite pronouns have the same form in the nominative and objective cases. The possessive case of any indefinite pronoun is formed by adding *'s*: *everyone's, somebody's*.

Reflexive Pronouns

Reflexive pronouns refer back to the subject of the sentence.

Harry Potter saw *himself* in the mirror.

They often are used to intensify or emphasize a noun or pronoun.

Harry Potter *himself* could not have cast a better spell.

Person	Singular	Plural
First	myself	ourselves
Second	yourself	yourselves
Third	himself	themselves
	herself	themselves

Some Problems Involving Pronouns

The major grammatical problems concerning pronouns involve agreement and case. These are discussed in the following section.

A reflexive pronoun should not be used without the noun or pronoun to which it refers.

Incorrect: <u>Herself</u> led Harry to rescue Sirius.
Correct: <u>Hermione herself</u> led Harry to rescue Sirius.

Like nouns, a pronoun preceding a gerund should be in the possessive case.

Incorrect: She objected to <u>me</u> going out too late.
Correct: She objected to <u>my</u> going out too late.

VERBS

Conjugation of Verbs

Verbs change their forms to indicate person, number, tense, mood, and voice. The various changes involved are indicated when the verb is *conjugated*. In order to conjugate a verb, you must know its *principal parts*.

> **Principal Parts of** *to talk*
> Infinitive: *to talk*
> Present tense: *talk*
> Present participle: *talking*
> Past tense: *talked*
> Past participle: *talked*

CONJUGATION OF THE REGULAR VERB *TO CARRY*
(principal parts: carry, carried, carried)

Indicative Mood—Active Voice

Present Tense

Singular	*Plural*
I carry	We carry
You carry	You carry
He, she, it carries	They carry

Past Tense

Singular	*Plural*
I carried	We carried
You carried	You carried
He, she, it carried	They carried

Future Tense

Singular	*Plural*
I shall (will) carry*	We shall (will) carry*
You will carry	You will carry
He, she, it will carry	They will carry

Present Perfect Tense

Singular	*Plural*
I have carried	We have carried
You have carried	You have carried
He, she, it has carried	They have carried

Past Perfect Tense

Singular	*Plural*
I had carried	We had carried
You had carried	You had carried
He, she, it had carried	They had carried

Future Perfect Tense

Singular	*Plural*
I shall (will) have carried*	We shall (will) have carried*
You will have carried	You will have carried
He, she, it will have carried	They will have carried

* Some old-fashioned grammarians assert that only the auxiliary verb *shall* is correct in the first person when simple future or future perfect meaning is intended. Most modern writers and grammarians do not accept this distinction, however. For your purposes, *I will* is equally correct.

CONJUGATION OF THE REGULAR VERB *TO CARRY*
(principal parts: carry, carried, carried)

Indicative Mood—Passive Voice

Present Tense

Singular
I am carried
You are carried
He, she, it is carried

Plural
We are carried
You are carried
They are carried

Past Tense

Singular
I was carried
You were carried
He, she, it was carried

Plural
We were carried
You were carried
They were carried

Future Tense

Singular
I shall (will) be carried*
You will be carried
He, she, it will be carried

Plural
We shall (will) be carried*
You will be carried
They will be carried

Present Perfect Tense

Singular
I have been carried
You have been carried
He, she, it has been carried

Plural
We have been carried
You have been carried
They have been carried

Past Perfect Tense

Singular
I had been carried
You had been carried
He, she, it had been carried

Plural
We had been carried
You had been carried
They had been carried

Future Perfect Tense

Singular
I shall (will) have been carried*
You will have been carried
He, she, it will have been carried

Plural
We shall (will) have been carried*
You will have been carried
They will have been carried

---

*When the principal parts of a verb are listed, the infinitive and the present participle are often omitted.

CONJUGATION OF THE REGULAR VERB *TO CARRY*
(principal parts: carry, carried, carried)

Subjunctive Mood—Active Voice

Present Tense

Singular	*Plural*
If I, you, he carry	If we, you, they carry

Past Tense

Singular	*Plural*
If I, you, he carried	If we, you, they carried

Subjunctive Mood—Passive Voice

Present Tense

Singular	*Plural*
If I, you, he be carried	If we, you, they be carried

Past Tense

Singular	*Plural*
If I, you, he were carried	If we, you, they were carried

Imperative Mood—Present Tense

Carry!

Note that most verbs form the past and past participle forms by adding *ed* to the present tense. Verbs ending in *y* preceded by a consonant (like *carry*) change the *y* to *i* before adding *ed*. Verbs ending in *e* (like *raise*) add *d* only.

Verbs that do not follow these rules are called *irregular*. The principal parts of the most common irregular verbs follow; when two or more forms are given, the first form is preferred.

PRINCIPAL PARTS OF IRREGULAR VERBS

Present Tense	Past Tense	Past Participle
arise	arose	arisen
awake	awoke, awaked	awaked, awoke, awoken
bear	bore	borne, born
beat	beat	beaten, beat
befall	befell	befallen
begin	began	begun
bend	bent	bent
bid (command)	bade	bidden
bid (make an offer)	bid	bid
bind	bound	bound
blow	blew	blown
break	broke	broken
bring	brought	brought
broadcast	broadcast, broadcasted	broadcast, broadcasted
build	built	built
burst	burst	burst
buy	bought	bought
cast	cast	cast
catch	caught	caught
choose	chose	chosen
cling	clung	clung
come	came	come
creep	crept	crept
deal	dealt	dealt
dive	dived, dove	dived
do	did	done
draw	drew	drawn
drink	drank	drunk
drive	drove	driven
eat	ate	eaten
fall	fell	fallen
feed	fed	fed
feel	felt	felt
fight	fought	fought
find	found	found
flee	fled	fled
fling	flung	flung
fly	flew	flown
forbear	forbore	forborne
forbid	forbade, forbad	forbidden
forget	forgot	forgotten, forgot
forgive	forgave	forgiven
forsake	forsook	forsaken
freeze	froze	frozen
get	got	got, gotten
give	gave	given
go	went	gone
grow	grew	grown
hang (an object)	hung	hung
hang (a person)	hanged	hanged

PRINCIPAL PARTS OF IRREGULAR VERBS (continued)

Present Tense	Past Tense	Past Participle
have	had	had
hit	hit	hit
hold	held	held
kneel	knelt, kneeled	knelt, kneeled
know	knew	known
lay	laid	laid
lead	led	led
leave	left	left
lend	lent	lent
lie	lay	lain
lose	lost	lost
make	made	made
meet	met	met
put	put	put
read	read	read
ring	rang	rung
rise	rose	risen
run	ran	run
see	saw	seen
seek	sought	sought
sell	sold	sold
send	sent	sent
set	set	set
shine	shone	shone
shrink	shrank, shrunk	shrunk, shrunken
sing	sang	sung
sink	sank	sunk
sit	sat	sat
slay	slew	slain
sleep	slept	slept
slide	slid	slid
sling	slung	slung
slink	slunk	slunk
speak	spoke	spoken
spring	sprang, sprung	sprung
steal	stole	stolen
stick	stuck	stuck
sting	stung	stung
stride	strode	stridden
strike	struck	struck
swear	swore	sworn
sweat	sweat, sweated	sweated, sweat
sweep	swept	swept
swim	swam	swum
swing	swung	swung
take	took	taken
teach	taught	taught
tear	tore	torn
telecast	telecast, telecasted	telecast, telecasted
tell	told	told

PRINCIPAL PARTS OF IRREGULAR VERBS (continued)

Present Tense	Past Tense	Past Participle
think	thought	thought
throw	threw	thrown
wake	waked, woke	waked, woken, woke
wear	wore	worn
weep	wept	wept
win	won	won
wind	wound	wound
work	worked, wrought	worked, wrought
wring	wrung	wrung
write	wrote	written

How the Verb Tenses Are Used

In addition to the six tenses listed in the typical conjugation shown before (of the verb to *carry*), there are *progressive* and *intensive* forms for some of the tenses. These will be discussed as we consider the uses of each tense.

PRESENT TENSE

The **present tense** indicates that the action or state of being defined by the verb is occurring at the time of speaking or writing.

> I <u>plan</u> to vote for Harry Potter.

The present tense is used to state a general rule.

> Honesty <u>is</u> the best policy.

The present tense is used to refer to artistic works of the past or to artists of the past whose work is still in existence.

> Walt Disney <u>is</u> one of Hollywood's most famous film makers.

The present tense is used to tell the story of a fictional work.

> In *Gone with the Wind*, Rhett Butler finally <u>realizes</u> that Scarlett O'Hara <u>is</u> unworthy of his love.

The progressive form of the present tense (a combination of the present tense of the verb *to be* and the present participle) indicates prolonged action or state of being.

> I <u>am thinking</u> about the future.
> You <u>are flirting</u> with disaster.
> He <u>is courting</u> Hermione.
> We <u>are planning</u> a trip to Hogwarts Academy.
> They <u>are being</u> stubborn.

The intensive form of the present tense (a combination of the verb *to do* and the infinitive) creates emphasis.

> He <u>does care</u>.
> We <u>do intend</u> to stay.

PAST TENSE

The **past tense** is used to indicate that an event occurred in a specific time in the past and that the event is completed.

> I <u>lived</u> in New York in 1979.
> I <u>lived</u> in that house for six years. (I no longer live there.)

The progressive form of the past tense combines the past tense of *to be* and the present participle. It indicates prolonged past action or state of being.

> I, he, she, it <u>was playing Quidditch</u>.
> We, you, they <u>were going</u>.

The intensive form of the past tense combines the past tense of *to do* and the infinitive. It creates emphasis.

> I <u>did know</u> the answer to the question.

FUTURE TENSE

The **future tense** makes a statement about a future event. Additionally, the simple future uses *shall* in the first person and *will* in the second and third persons.

> I, <u>we shall go</u>.
> You, he, <u>they will go</u>.

To show determination, promise, or command, *will* is used in the first person and *shall* in the second and third persons.

> <u>I will catch</u> this bill on Friday.
> You, he, <u>they shall obey</u> Lord Voldemort or suffer the consequences.

However, most contemporary grammarians accept the use of *shall* and *will* interchangeably in the future tense.

The progressive form of the future tense combines the future tense of *to be* and the present participle.

> <u>I shall be wearing</u> a white jacket.
> <u>He will be going</u> to the ball with Hermione.

PERFECT TENSES

The **present perfect tense** combines the present tense of *to have* and the past participle.

> I <u>have gone</u>.
> He has <u>swallowed</u> the potion.

Whereas the past tense refers to a definite time in the past, the present perfect tense indicates that the event is "perfected" or completed at the present time.

The present perfect tense is also used to indicate that the event began in the past and is continuing into the present.

> He <u>has attended</u> Hogwarts Academy for three years. (He is still attending Hogwarts.)

The progressive form of the present perfect tense combines the present perfect tense of *to be* and the present participle.

> He <u>has been complaining</u> about a pain in his forehead for some time.

The **past perfect tense** is formed by combining the past participle of the verb and the past tense of the verb *to have*. It describes an event which was completely perfected at a definite time in the past. Its major use is to indicate that one event occurred before another in the past.

> By the time Professor Snape arrived, the boys <u>had extinguished</u> the blaze. (The fire was put out before Professor Snape came.)

The progressive form of the past perfect tense is formed by combining the present participle of the verb and the past perfect tense of *to be*.

> I <u>had been holding</u> this package for you for three weeks.

The **future perfect tense** is formed by combining the past participle of the verb and the future tense of the verb *to have*. It indicates that a future event will be completed before a definite time in the future.

> By one in the afternoon, Hagrid <u>will have finished</u> his lunch and <u>will have returned</u> to the forest.

The progressive form of the future perfect tense is formed by combining the present participle of the verb and the future perfect tense of *to be*.

> They <u>will have been swimming</u> all afternoon.

Kinds of Verbs

Transitive verbs are verbs that require an object. The object is the receiver of the action.

> He hit the boy. (The object <u>boy</u> has been hit.)
> I received a letter. (The object <u>letter</u> has been received.)

Intransitive verbs do not require an object.

> She <u>is walking</u>.

Linking verbs are intransitive verbs that connect the subject to a noun, pronoun, or adjective. The most common linking verb is *to be*.

> Professor Snape <u>is</u> the teacher.
> It <u>is</u> I.

(In these two sentences, <u>teacher</u> and <u>I</u> are called **predicate nominatives**.)

> The man <u>is</u> rich.
> The actress <u>is</u> beautiful.

(<u>Rich</u> and <u>beautiful</u> are **predicate adjectives**.)

Predicate nominatives and predicate adjectives are normally called predicate complements because they complete the thought of the linking verb. The predicate nominative represents the same person or thing as the subject of the verb *to be* and is in the nominative case.

> He is the <u>teacher</u>.
> The teacher is <u>he</u>.

The predicate adjective is connected to the subject by the linking verb. The description, the *lame horse*, becomes a statement or sentence when the linking verb is used as follows:

> The horse <u>is lame</u>.

The other linking verbs are *appear*, *become*, *feel*, *get*, *grow*, *look*, *seem*, *smell*, *sound*, and *taste*. These verbs should be followed by predicate adjectives.

> This <u>tastes</u> good.
> I <u>feel</u> sad.
> This <u>sounds</u> too loud.
> I <u>became</u> ill.

Be careful to distinguish between transitive and intransitive verbs. Words like *lie* and *lay*, *sit* and *set*, *rise* and *raise* often give students trouble.

- *Lie* is an intransitive verb, meaning "to rest or recline." Its principal parts are *lie, lay, lain*. *Lay* is transitive and means "to place down." Its principal parts are *lay, laid, laid*.

  Incorrect: I <u>lay</u> the book on the table.
  Correct: I <u>laid</u> the book on the table.

  Incorrect: Because I am tired, I am going to <u>lay</u> down.
  Correct: Because I am tired, I am going to <u>lie</u> down.

- *Sit* is intransitive. Its principal parts are *sit, sat, sat. Set* may be either transitive or intransitive. Its principal parts are *set, set, set.*

  Incorrect: I am going to <u>sit</u> this tripod on the floor.
  Correct: I am going to <u>set</u> this tripod on the floor (Transitive).
  Correct: The sun is going to <u>set</u> at 5:42 P.M. (Intransitive).

- *Rise*, meaning "to come up," is intransitive. Its principal parts are *rise, rose, risen. Raise*, meaning "to lift up," is transitive. Its principal parts are *raise, raised, raised.*

  Incorrect: The delta lowlands were in danger of being flooded when the sea <u>raised</u> by three feet.
  Correct: The delta lowlands were in danger of being flooded when the sea <u>rose</u> by three feet.

Voice and Mood

Voice is a characteristic of transitive verbs. In the **active voice**, the subject is the doer of the action stated by the verb, and the object of the verb is the receiver of the action.

Harry Potter caught the Golden Snitch. (<u>Harry Potter</u> is doing the catching and the <u>Golden Snitch</u> is being caught.)

In the **passive voice**, the receiver of the action is the subject. The doer of the action may be identified by using a phrase beginning with *by*.

The Golden Snitch was caught.
The <u>Golden Snitch</u> was caught <u>by Harry Potter</u>.

Some writers prefer the active voice and object to the use of the passive. However, both voices have their virtues and neither should be regarded as incorrect.

It is inadvisable to switch from one voice to the other in the same sentence.

Undesirable: Harry Potter <u>raced</u> toward the wall and the Golden Snitch <u>was caught</u>.
Preferable: Harry Potter <u>raced</u> toward the wall and <u>caught</u> the Golden Snitch.

Mood is used to indicate the intentions of the writer.

The **indicative mood** makes a statement or asks a question.

I <u>wrote</u> you a letter.
When <u>did</u> you <u>mail</u> it?

The **imperative mood** commands, directs, or requests.

<u>Go</u> home!
<u>Make</u> a left turn at the willow tree.
Please <u>talk</u> more slowly.

The **subjunctive mood** is used when the writer desires to express a wish or a condition contrary to fact.

> I wish I <u>were</u> able to go with you.
> (I am not able to go.)

> If he <u>were</u> less of a bore, people would invite him to dinner more frequently.
> (He is a bore.)

It is also used after a verb which expresses a command or a request.

> The headmaster has ordered that all trips to the village <u>be</u> deferred.
> Hermione demanded that Ron <u>leave</u> immediately.

Verbals

The infinitive, present participle, and past participle are called non-finite verbs, or **verbals**. These forms of the verb cannot function as verbs without an auxiliary word or words.

> *Running* is not a verb.
> *Am running, have been running, shall be running* are verbs.
> *Broken* is not a verb.
> *Is broken, had been broken, may be broken* are verbs.

The **infinitive** (the verb preceded by *to*) is used chiefly as a noun. Occasionally, it may serve as an adjective or an adverb.

> Harry wants <u>to go</u> to Hogwarts. (<u>To go</u> to Hogwarts is the object of <u>wants</u>. It serves as a noun.)
> I have miles <u>to go</u> before I sleep. (<u>To go</u> modifies <u>miles</u>. It serves as an adjective.)
> <u>To be honest</u>, we almost lost the battle. (<u>To be honest</u> modifies the rest of the sentence. It serves as an adverb.)

The **present participle** usually serves as an adjective.

> <u>Flying</u> wizards
> <u>Singing</u> waiters
> <u>Dancing</u> waters

(In each case, the participle modifies the noun it precedes.)

> <u>Writing on the blackboard</u>, the professor presented his arguments in favor of his thesis. (<u>Writing on the blackboard</u> is a <u>participial phrase</u> modifying <u>professor</u>.)

The present participle may also serve as a noun. When it does so, it is called a **gerund**.

> <u>Jogging</u> is good exercise.
> <u>Dieting</u> to lose weight requires discipline.

A noun or pronoun preceding a gerund should be in the possessive case.

Harry's talking to Ron annoyed the teacher.
We were frightened by his disappearing.

The **past participle** serves as an adjective.

Broken bones
Fallen towers
Pained expressions

ADJECTIVES

Adjectives are words that limit or describe nouns and pronouns.

Three wizards
The fourth quarter

(Three and fourth limit the words they precede.)

A pretty girl (Pretty describes the word it precedes.)
A daring young man (Daring is a participle used as an adjective, and describes man; young describes man.)

Adjectives usually precede the word they limit or describe. However, for emphasis the adjective may follow the word it modifies.

One nation, indivisible

Adjectives are often formed from nouns by adding suffixes such as *-al, -ish, -ly,* and *-ous.*

Noun	Adjective
magic	magical
girl	girlish
wizard	wizardly
joy	joyous

Predicate adjectives are adjectives that follow the linking verbs *be, appear, become, feel, get, grow, look, seem, smell, sound,* and *taste.* These adjectives follow the verb and refer to its subject.

The sorceror is tall. (A tall sorceror)
The witch looks beautiful. (A beautiful witch)

Adjectives are inflected; that is, they change form to indicate degree of comparison: positive, comparative, or superlative. The **positive degree** indicates the basic form without reference to any other object. The **comparative degree** is used to compare two objects. The **superlative degree** is used to compare three or more objects. Usually, *er* or *r* is added to the positive to form the comparative degree, *est* or *st* to form the superlative. Some adjectives of two syllables and all adjectives longer than two syllables use *more* (or *less*) to form the comparative degree and *most* (or *least*) to form the superlative.

Positive	Comparative	Superlative
tall	taller	tallest
pretty	prettier	prettiest
handsome	more handsome	most handsome
expensive	less expensive	least expensive

A few adjectives have irregular comparative and superlative forms. These include:

Positive	Comparative	Superlative
good	better	best
bad	worse	worst
ill	worse	worst

ADVERBS

Adverbs are words that modify verbs, adjectives, or other adverbs.

He spoke <u>sincerely</u>. (Sincerely modifies <u>spoke</u>.)
<u>Almost</u> any person can afford this kind of vacation. (<u>Almost</u> modifies the adjective <u>any</u>.)
He spoke <u>very</u> sincerely. (<u>Very</u> modifies the adverb <u>sincerely</u>.)

Most adverbs end in *ly* (*angrily, stupidly, honestly*). However, some adjectives also end in *ly* (*manly, womanly, holy, saintly*). Some commonly used words have the same form for the adjective and the adverb. These include *early, far, fast, hard, high, late, little, loud, quick, right, slow,* and *well.*

Adjective	Adverb
The *early* bird	He left *early.*
A *far* cry	You have gone too *far.*
He is a *fast* worker.	Don't go so *fast.*
This is *hard* to do.	She slapped him *hard.*
A *high* voice	Put it *high* on the agenda.
A *late* bloomer	He arrived *late.*
Men of *little* faith	She is a *little* late.
A *loud* explosion	He spoke *loud.*
A *quick* step	Think *quick.*
The *right* decision	Do it *right.*
A *slow* worker	Drive *slow.*
All is *well.*	She was *well* prepared.

Adverbs, like adjectives, change form to show comparison. The comparative degree uses the word *more* (or *less*); the superlative degree, the word *most* (or *least*). *Badly* and *well* have irregular comparative forms.

Positive	Comparative	Superlative
quickly	more quickly	most quickly
rapidly	less rapidly	least rapidly
badly	worse	worst
well	better	best

PREPOSITIONS

Prepositions are words that combine with nouns, pronouns, and noun substantives to form phrases that act as adverbs, adjectives, or nouns.

I arrived <u>at ten o'clock</u>. (Adverbial phrase)
The man <u>with the broken arm</u> stumbled. (Adjective phrase)
The shout came from <u>outside the castle</u>. (Noun phrase acting as object of *from*)

The most common prepositions are:

about	behind	during	on	to
above	below	except	out	touching
after	beneath	excepting	over	toward
against	beside	for	past	under
along	besides	from	round	underneath
amid	between	in	save	up
among	beyond	into	since	with
around	but	notwithstanding	through	within
at	by	of	throughout	without
before	down	off	till	

Some verbs call for the use of specific prepositions. See the list of Idiomatic Expressions on page 158.

CONJUNCTIONS

Conjunctions are connecting words that join words, phrases, and clauses. There are two kinds of conjunctions:

Coordinating conjunctions connect words, phrases, and clauses of equal rank. They are *and*, *but*, *or*, *nor*, *for*, *whereas*, and *yet*. Pairs of words like *either . . . or*, *neither . . . nor*, *both . . . and*, *not only . . . but also* are a special kind of coordinating conjunction called *correlative conjunctions*.

Subordinating conjunctions connect dependent clauses to independent clauses. Some of the more common subordinating conjunctions are *although*, *as*, *because*, *if*, *since*, *so*, *than*, *though*, *till*, *unless*, *until*, *whether*, and *while*. Also, when the relative pronouns *who*, *which*, *that* introduce a dependent clause, they act as subordinating conjunctions.

> Independent and dependent clauses are discussed in the section on Sentence Sense (see the bottom of this page).

ARTICLES

The three most frequently used adjectives—*a*, *an*, and *the*—are called **articles**. The *definite article* is *the*. The *indefinite articles* are *a* and *an*. *A* is used before a word beginning with a consonant sound. *An* is used before a word beginning with a vowel sound.

A bright light
An auspicious beginning
An ABC of magic
A humble beginning (the *h* sound is pronounced)
An hour ago (the *h* sound is omitted)

INTERJECTIONS

Interjections are words that express emotion and have no grammatical relation to the other words in the sentence.

Alas, I am disconsolate.
Wow! This is awesome!
Eureka! I have found it.

SENTENCE SENSE

The ability to write complete, error-free sentences is the sign of a student who has mastered standard written English. If you do not write in complete sentences, it is likely that you will wind up receiving poor grades on your essays.

A **sentence** may be defined as a group of words that contains a subject and a predicate, expresses a complete thought, and ends with a period (.), a question mark (?), or an exclamation point (!).

The sentence must contain a finite verb that makes the statement or asks the question.

The young wizards fought a battle.
Halt!
Where are you going?
The students have gone home.

I have been thinking about your offer.
Why have you been making this accusation?
Who will take Dumbledore's place?

(The verbs in the preceding sentences are *fought*, *halt*, *are going*, *have gone*, *have been thinking*, *have been making*, and *will take*.)

The forms of the verb that are not finite are the *infinitive*, the *participle*, and the *gerund*. These three forms cannot act as finite verbs.

CLAUSES

A **clause** is a group of words containing a subject and a verb. There are two kinds of clauses:

Main clauses (also called **principal** or **independent clauses**): A main clause does not modify anything; it can stand alone as a sentence.

I went to the headmaster's study.
I failed my herbology test.

A sentence containing one main clause is called a *simple sentence*.

A sentence containing two or more main clauses is called a *compound sentence*. The clauses must be connected by a coordinating conjunction or by a semicolon (;).

I went to the headmaster's study and I overheard him talking to Professor Snape.
You must pass this test, or you will be suspended from the Quidditch team.
Four boys played tennis; the rest went swimming.

Subordinate clauses (also called **dependent clauses**): A subordinate clause cannot stand alone; to be a good sentence, it must always accompany a main clause. A sentence containing a main clause and one or more subordinate clauses is called a *complex sentence*. If the subordinate clause modifies a noun or pronoun, it is called an *adjective clause*. If it modifies a verb, it is an *adverb clause* or an *adverbial clause*. A clause that acts as the subject or the object of a verb or as the object of a preposition is called a *noun clause*.

The book that is on the table belongs to my sister. (The clause <u>that is on the table</u> is an adjective clause because it modifies the noun <u>book</u>.)

She quit school because she had to go to work. (The clause <u>because she had to go to work</u> is an adverbial clause because it modifies the verb <u>quit</u>.)

I asked what the teacher did. (<u>What the teacher did</u> is a noun clause because it is the object of the verb <u>asked</u>.)

Give this medal to whoever comes in first. (<u>Whoever comes in first</u> is a noun clause because it is the object of the preposition <u>to</u>.)

PHRASES

A **phrase** is a group of words that lacks a subject and a predicate and acts as a unit. A phrase cannot serve as a complete sentence. These are the common types of phrases:

Prepositional phrases are introduced by a preposition and act as adjectives or adverbs.

> This is an overt act of war. (Of war is an adjective phrase modifying act.)
> Please come at 10:00 A.M. (At 10:00 A.M. is an adverbial phrase modifying come.)

Participial phrases are introduced by a participle and are used as adjectives to modify nouns and pronouns.

> Fighting his way through tacklers, he crossed the goal line. (Fighting his way through tacklers is a present participial phrase modifying the pronoun he.)

> Sung by this gifted artist, the words were especially stirring. (Sung by this gifted artist is a past participial phrase modifying the noun words.)

Gerund phrases are introduced by a gerund and are used as nouns.

> Smoking cigarettes is harmful to one's health. (Smoking cigarettes is a gerund phrase used as the subject of the verb is.)

Infinitive phrases are introduced by the infinitive form of the verb, usually preceded by *to*. They are used as nouns, adjectives, and adverbs.

> To win a decisive victory is our goal. (To win a decisive victory is an infinitive phrase used as the subject of the verb is.)

> I have a dress to alter. (To alter is an infinitive modifying the noun dress.)

> The ice is too soft to skate on. (To skate on is an infinitive modifying the adjective soft.)

Grammarians disagree about the interpretation of sentences like *I want him to buy a suit*. Some regard *him to buy a suit* as an infinitive clause with *him* the subject of the infinitive *to buy*. Others regard *him* as the object of the verb *want* and *to buy a suit* as an infinitive phrase acting as an objective complement. No matter how the sentence is interpreted, *him* is correct.

PUNCTUATION FOR SENTENCE SENSE

Errors in punctuation are noticeable: they stand out. When you write, it will help you to understand the effects of various punctuation marks on the meaning and structure of a sentence. In this section, we will review the most commonly used punctuation marks and illustrate the ways they should be used.

END PUNCTUATION

The Period (.)

1. The period is used to indicate the end of a declarative or imperative sentence.

   I am going home.
   Go home.

2. The period is used after initials and abbreviations.

   Mr. J. C. Smith
   John Rose, M.D.

3. The period is *not* used after contractions, initials of governmental agencies, chemical symbols, or radio and television call letters.

can't	HCL	didn't	Sn
IRS	WNBC	FBI	KPIX

4. A series of three periods is used to indicate the fact that material has been omitted from a quotation.

   We, the People of the United States, In Order to form a more perfect union, . . . do ordain and establish this Constitution for the United States of America.

The Question Mark (?)

1. The question mark is used after a direct question.

   Who is going with you?

2. The question mark should *not* be used when questions appear in indirect discourse.

   He asked whether you would go with him.

3. The question mark should *not* be used when a polite or formal request is made.

   Will you please come with me.

4. The question mark should *not* be used when the question is purely rhetorical (that is, asked only for effect, with no answer expected).

   That's very good, don't you think.

MIDDLE PUNCTUATION

The Comma (,)

1. The comma is used to set off nouns when you directly address someone.

   Mr. Smith, please answer this question.
   Tom, come here.

2. The comma is used to set off words or phrases that identify or explain nouns.

   Mr. Brown, our newly elected sheriff, has promised to enforce the law vigorously.
   Dr. Alexander, my instructor, has written several authoritative books on this topic.

3. The comma is used to set off items in a series.

   I bought milk, eggs, apples, and bread at the store.
   Maine, Vermont, New Hampshire, Massachusetts, Rhode Island, and Connecticut are the states that make up New England.
   The river tumbles down lofty mountains, cuts through miles of prairie land, and finally empties into the Atlantic Ocean.

4. The comma is used to separate the clauses of a compound sentence connected by a coordinating conjunction.

   The bill to reduce taxes was introduced by Congressman Jones, and it was referred to the House Ways and Means Committee for consideration. (Note that the omission of the conjunction <u>and</u> would result in a run-on sentence.)

5. The comma is used to set off long introductory phrases and clauses that precede the main clause.

   In a conciliatory speech to the striking employees, Mr. Brown agreed to meet with their leaders and to consider their complaints.
   Because I was ignorant of the facts in this matter, I was unable to reach a decision.

6. The comma is used to set off unimportant (or **nonrestrictive**) phrases and clauses in a sentence.

   My brother, who is a physician, has invited me to spend Christmas week with him.

7. The comma is used to set off parenthetical words like *first, therefore, however,* and *moreover,* from the rest of the sentence.

   I am, therefore, going to sue you in small claims court.
   More than two inches of rain fell last week; however, this was not enough to fill our reservoirs.

8. The comma is used to set off contrasting, interdependent expressions.

   The bigger they are, the harder they fall.

9. The comma is used to separate adjectives that could be connected by *and*.

   He spoke in a kind, soothing voice.

10. In sentences containing direct quotations, the comma is used to separate introductory words from quoted words.

    Mary said, "I hope you will understand my reasons for doing this to you."

11. The comma may be used to indicate omitted words whose repetition is understood.

    Tall and short are antonyms; rapid and swift, synonyms.

12. The comma is used to separate items in dates, addresses, and geographical names.

    January 5, 1981
    Detroit, Michigan
    My address is 5225 East 28 Street, Brooklyn, New York.

13. The comma is used to follow the salutation in a friendly letter.

    Dear Mary,

14. The comma follows the complimentary close in business and friendly letters.

    Yours sincerely,
    Truly yours,

The Semicolon (;)

1. The semicolon is used as a substitute for the comma followed by *and* that connects two independent clauses in a compound sentence.

   Mary won first prize in the contest, and John came in second.
   Mary won first prize in the contest; John came in second.

2. The semicolon is used before *namely*, *for instance*, and *for example* when they introduce a list.

   Four students were chosen to act as a committee; namely, John, Henry, Frank, and William.

3. When the words *however*, *nevertheless*, *furthermore*, *moreover*, and *therefore* are used to connect two independent clauses, they should be preceded by a semicolon.

   He worked diligently for the award; however, he did not receive it.

4. The semicolon is used to separate items in a list when the items themselves contain commas.

Among the contributors to the book were Roy O. Billett, Boston University; Lawrence D. Brennan, New York University; Allan Danzig, Lafayette College; and Mario Pei, Columbia University.

The Colon (:)

1. The colon is used to introduce a list, especially after the words *following* and *as follows*.

On this tour, you will visit the following countries: England, France, Spain, Italy, Greece, and Israel.

2. The colon is used after the salutation in business letters.

Dear Sir:
Dear Dr. Brown:
To Whom It May Concern:

3. The colon is used when time is indicated in figures.

Please meet me at 3:30 P.M.

4. The colon is used to indicate ratios.

2:5 :: 6:15

Quotation Marks (" ")

1. Quotation marks are used to indicate the exact words of a speaker or writer. The introductory words are separated from the quotation by a comma or commas.

Patrick Henry said, "Give me liberty or give me death."
"Give me liberty," Patrick Henry said, "or give me death."
"Give me liberty or give me death," Patrick Henry said.

2. When quotation marks are used, the capitalization of the original quotation should be retained.

"I have always wanted," John said, "to ride a ten-speed bike." (And small t is used because to was not capitalized in the statement being quoted.)

3. If the quotation is a question, the question mark should appear inside the quotation marks.

John asked, "When does the party start?"
"When does the party start?" John asked.

COMMON PROBLEMS IN GRAMMAR AND USAGE

The next section of this chapter introduces you to common problems in grammar and usage that you are likely to encounter on the test. This section includes many practice exercises. If you have difficulty handling these exercises or still have trouble with the grammatical terms involved, go back to the previous grammar and punctuation review sections. Review them. These should provide you with the grammatical background you need to do well on the multiple-choice portions of the subtest.

Common Problems in Grammar

SENTENCE FRAGMENTS

A **sentence fragment** occurs when a phrase or a dependent clause is incorrectly used as a sentence. Examples of sentence fragments and ways of correcting them follow:

1. When he walked into the room.
2. Apologizing for his behavior.
3. To discuss the problem amicably.
4. In our discussion of the problem.
5. Or yield to their demands.

In Example 1, we have a dependent clause used as a sentence. To correct, either remove the subordinating conjunction *when* or add an independent clause.

He walked into the room.
When he walked into the room, we yelled "Surprise."

In Example 2, we have a participial or gerund phrase used as a sentence. To correct, either change the phrase to a subject and a verb or add an independent clause.

He apologized for his behavior.
Apologizing for his behavior, he tried to atone for the embarrassment he had caused.

In Example 3, we have an infinitive phrase. To change this phrase to a complete sentence, either change the infinitive to a finite verb and add a subject, or add a subject and verb that will make a complete thought.

We discussed the problem amicably.
We want to discuss the problem amicably.

In Example 4, we have a prepositional phrase. To correct this fragmentary sentence, add an independent clause to which it can relate.

We failed to consider the public's reaction in our discussion of the problem.

In Example 5, we have part of a compound predicate. To correct this, combine it with the other part of the compound predicate in a single complete sentence.

<u>We must fight this aggressive act</u> or yield to their demands.

Practice

Correct the next two sentence fragments, following the methods of correction shown for Example 1.

When she gave birth to her baby.

_____

_____

Although I like ice cream.

_____

_____

Correct the next two sentence fragments, following the correction patterns shown for Example 2.

Substituting for the starting pitcher.

_____

_____

Expecting to go to the party.

_____

_____

Correct the next two sentence fragments, following the correction patterns shown for Example 3.

To remodel the kitchen completely.

_____

_____

To apologize to his father.

_____

_____

Correct the next two sentence fragments, following the correction pattern shown for Example 4.

In our enthusiasm for the team's victory.

_____

_____

At the conclusion of the history lesson.

_____

_____

Correct the final two sentence fragments, following the correction pattern shown for Example 5.

Or pay a cleaning deposit.

_____

_____

And save our money for a new car.

_____

_____

RUN-ON SENTENCES

The **run-on sentence** has been given many different names by grammarians, including the comma fault sentence or comma splice sentence, and the fused sentence.

> The jurors examined the evidence, they found the defendant guilty.
> (Comma fault sentence)
> It is very cloudy I think it is going to rain. (Fused sentence)

The **comma fault** or **comma splice** sentence may be defined as a sentence in which two independent clauses are improperly connected by a comma. The first example given is an illustration of the comma fault sentence. The **fused sentence** consists of two sentences that run together without any distinguishing punctuation. The second example illustrates this kind of error.

Any of four methods may be used to correct run-on sentences:

1. Use a period at the end of the first independent clause instead of a comma. Begin the second independent clause with a capital letter.

   The jurors examined the evidence. They found the defendant guilty.
   It is very cloudy. I think it is going to rain.

2. Connect the two independent clauses by using a coordinating conjunction.

The jurors examined the <u>evidence, and</u> they found the defendant guilty.
It is very <u>cloudy, and</u> I think it is going to rain.

3. Use a semicolon between two main clauses not connected by a coordinating conjunction.

The jurors examined the <u>evidence; they</u> found the defendant guilty.
It is very <u>cloudy; I</u> think it is going to rain.

4. Use a subordinating conjunction to make one of the independent clauses dependent on the other.

<u>When</u> the jurors examined the evidence, they found the defendant guilty.
<u>Because</u> it is very cloudy, I think it is going to rain.

Practice

Correct each of the following run-on sentences, using all four of the methods just shown.

The organist played the wedding march, the bride came down the aisle.

1. _____

_____

2. _____

_____

3. _____

_____

4. _____

_____

It is getting very late I had better go to bed.

1. _____

_____

2. _____

_____

3. _____

_____

4. _____

_____

(It is important to master method 4; if you are able to combine independent clauses in this way, you will be able to vary sentence structure and add interest to your paragraphs.)

PROBLEMS WITH AGREEMENT

Problems with agreement generally involve a violation of one of the two basic rules governing agreement.

> **Rule I:** A verb and its subject must agree in person and number. A singular verb must have a singular subject; a plural verb must have a plural subject.

If you examine the conjugation of the verb *to carry* on pages 105–107, you will observe that this rule applies only to the present and present perfect tenses. The other tenses use the same form for each of the three persons and with both singular and plural subjects. Therefore, an error in agreement cannot occur in any tense other than the present or present perfect tense, with the exception of the verb *to be*. The past tense of *to be* is:

Person	Singular	Plural
First	I was	We were
Second	You were	You were
Third	He, she, it was	They were

Rule I concerning agreement is simple and easy to remember. However, you should note the following:

1. The verb does *not* agree with the modifier of the subject or with a parenthetical expression introduced by *as well as, with, together with*, or a similar phrase.

   The father of the children is going to work. (The subject of the singular verb <u>is going</u> is the singular noun <u>father</u>. <u>Children</u> is part of the prepositional phrase <u>of the children</u>, which modifies <u>father</u>.)

   The pupils as well as the teacher are going to the zoo. (The subject of the plural verb <u>are going</u> is the plural noun <u>pupils</u>. <u>Teacher</u> is part of the parenthetical expression <u>as well as the teacher</u>. This parenthetical expression is <u>not</u> the subject.)

2. A plural verb is used with a compound subject (two or more nouns or pronouns connected by *and*).

   <u>John and his friends are going</u> camping.

   <u>John and Mary are planning</u> a party.

   However, when the compound subject can be considered as a single unit or entity, regard it as singular and follow it with a singular verb.

   "<u>Jack and Jill" is</u> a popular nursery rhyme.

   <u>Bacon and eggs is</u> one of the most popular breakfast dishes in America.

3. Collective nouns like *team, committee, jury, gang, class, army,* and so on are usually regarded as singular nouns.

   The <u>team is practicing</u> for the big game.

   The Revolutionary <u>Army was</u> at Valley Forge.

   When a collective noun is used to refer to the *individual members* of the group, it is considered a plural noun.

   The <u>jury were</u> unable to reach a verdict. (The individual jurors could not come to a decision.)

4. The words *billiards, economics, linguistics, mathematics, measles, mumps, news,* and *physics,* are considered singular nouns.

   <u>Billiards is</u> a game of skill.

   <u>Mathematics is</u> my most difficult subject.

5. The words *barracks, glasses, insignia, odds, pliers, scissors, tactics, tongs, trousers,* and *wages* are considered plural nouns.

   These <u>barracks have been</u> empty for some time.

   My <u>glasses are fogged</u>; I cannot see clearly.

6. The words *acoustics, ethics, gymnastics, politics,* and *statistics* are singular when they refer to specific fields of study or activity. They are plural at all other times.

   <u>Ethics is</u> part of our Humanities program.

   His <u>ethics are</u> questionable. (He is a liar and a cheat.)

7. Names of organizations and titles of books and shows are singular.

   <u>*The Canterbury Tales* was written</u> by Chaucer.

   <u>The United States</u> now <u>has</u> a national debt that exceeds ten trillion dollars.

8. In a sentence beginning with *there* or *here*, the subject of the verb *follows* the verb in the sentence.

   There are many reasons for his failure. (<u>Reasons</u> is the subject of the plural verb <u>are</u>.)

   Here is my suggestion. (<u>Suggestion</u> is the subject of the singular verb <u>is</u>.)

9. The words *anybody, anyone, each, either, every, everyone, everybody, neither, nobody, no one,* and *someone* are regarded as singular and require a singular verb.

   <u>Anyone</u> who likes candy <u>is</u> welcome to have some.

   <u>Each</u> of the songs he sang <u>was</u> memorable.

   <u>Either</u> of the two choices <u>is</u> satisfactory.

   <u>Nobody</u> in her classes <u>likes</u> her.

   <u>No one is going.</u>

   <u>Someone</u> in this group <u>is</u> a liar.

10. The words *few, many,* and *several* are regarded as plural and require a plural verb.

    <u>Many are called</u>, but <u>few are chosen</u>.

    <u>Several have</u> already <u>been disqualified</u> by the lawyers.

11. The expressions *the number* and *the variety* are regarded as singular and require a singular verb.

    <u>The number</u> of people able to meet in this room <u>is limited</u> by the Fire Department.

    <u>The variety</u> of food presented at this buffet <u>is</u> awesome.

12. The expressions *a number* and *a variety* are regarded as plural and require a plural verb.

    <u>A number</u> of new cases of malaria <u>have been reported</u> to the Health Department.

    <u>A variety</u> of disturbances in the neighborhood <u>have alarmed</u> the home-owners.

13. *Either* and *neither* are regarded as singular (see item 9). However, when *either* or *neither* is coupled with *or* or *nor*, a different rule applies. In these sentences, the verb agrees with the noun or pronoun that follows the word *or* or *nor*.

    Either Mary <u>or John is</u> eligible.

    Either Mary <u>or her sisters are mistaken</u>.

Neither Harry <u>nor you are</u> eligible.

Neither you <u>nor I was invited</u>.

14. When using the verb *to be*, be sure to make the verb agree with the subject and not with the predicate complement.

Our greatest <u>problem is</u> excessive taxes.

Excessive <u>taxes are</u> our greatest problem.

Practice

Correct each of the following errors in agreement based on the examples just shown.

1. The leader of the apes are swinging through the trees.

   _____

   _____

   The child as well as the parents are affected by a divorce.

   _____

   _____

2. Lassie and her pups is chasing rabbits.

   _____

   _____

   "Frankie and Johnny" are a love song.

   _____

   _____

3. The committee are meeting on Tuesday.

   _____

   _____

   The Latin class are studying Caesar.

   _____

   _____

4. Mumps are a dangerous disease.

   _____

   _____

Economics are a complete mystery to me.

_____

_____

5. My trousers is wrinkled; I need the iron.

_____

_____

His tactics was too outmoded for modern warfare.

_____

_____

6. Statistics are a field worth studying.

_____

_____

Their statistics is incorrect.

_____

_____

7. *Star Wars* were directed by George Lucas.

_____

_____

Pacific Gas & Electricity have sent me a bill.

_____

_____

8. Here is my answers to the question.

_____

_____

9. No one of the counselors are able to advise you.

_____

_____

Neither of the clerks want to wait on him.

_____

_____

Everybody from our office are going to the party.

_____

_____

10. Several of the class has handed in the exercise.

_____

_____

Many is unemployed, but few is getting unemployment insurance.

_____

_____

11. The variety of grammatical errors possible are countless.

_____

_____

The number of students taking the test are increasing.

_____

_____

12. A number of bad riots has troubled the city.

_____

_____

A variety of attempts to remedy the situation was made.

_____

_____

13. Either the mayor or the city manager are in charge.

_____

_____

Either the teacher or his students is correct.

_____

_____

Neither David nor you is welcome.

_____

_____

Neither you nor I were elected.

_____

_____

14. A storekeeper's greatest worry are bad checks.

_____

_____

Bad checks is a storekeeper's greatest worry.

_____

_____

> **Rule II:** A pronoun must agree with its antecedent in person, number, and gender. (The antecedent is the noun or pronoun to which the pronoun refers.)
>
> The detectives arrested <u>Mrs. Brown</u> as <u>she</u> entered the building. (The antecedent <u>Mrs. Brown</u> is a third person singular feminine noun; <u>she</u> is the third person singular feminine pronoun.)

Rule II concerning agreement is also easy to remember. However, watch out for these potentially troublesome points:

1. When the antecedent is an indefinite singular pronoun (*any, anybody, anyone, each, either, every, everybody, everyone, nobody, no one, somebody,* or *someone*), the pronoun should be singular.

   <u>Everybody</u> on the ship went to <u>his</u> cabin to get <u>his</u> life jacket.

   <u>Neither</u> of the girls is writing <u>her</u> thesis.

2. When the antecedent is compound (two or more nouns or pronouns connected by *and*), the pronoun should be plural.

   <u>Mary and Jane</u> like <u>their</u> new school.

3. When the antecedent is part of an *either . . . or* or *neither . . . nor* statement, the pronoun should agree with the nearer antecedent.

   Either John or <u>Henry</u> will invite Mary to <u>his</u> home. (<u>Henry</u> is closer to <u>his</u>.)

   Neither the seller nor the <u>buyers</u> have submitted <u>their</u> final offers. (<u>Buyers</u> is closer to <u>their</u>.)

   Neither the buyers nor the <u>seller</u> has submitted <u>his</u> final offer. (<u>Seller</u> is closer to <u>his</u>.)

Note: In some sentences, Rules I and II are combined.

John is one of the boys who (is, are) trying out for the team. (In this sentence, the antecedent of <u>who</u> is <u>boys</u>, a third person plural noun. The verb should be <u>are</u> because <u>are</u> is the third person plural verb.)

Practice

Correct each of the following errors in agreement based on the examples just shown.

1. Everybody in the class went to their desk to get their essay.

_____

_____

Neither of the teachers is correcting their tests.

_____

_____

2. Bob and Sue remodeled her new home.

_____

_____

3. Either John or Tom will donate their ball to the team.

_____

_____

Neither the students nor the teacher has picked up their tickets to the concert.

_____

_____

PROBLEMS WITH CASE

Nouns and pronouns have three cases: subjective, possessive, and objective.

The **subjective case** indicates that the noun or pronoun is being used as the subject of a verb, or as a word used to identify or explain the subject, or as a predicate nominative.

<u>John</u> is the batter. (<u>John</u> is in the subjective case, since it is the subject of the verb <u>is</u>.)

<u>Jane</u>, my younger <u>sister</u>, attends elementary school. (The noun <u>sister</u> is in the subjective case because it serves to identify <u>Jane</u>, the subject of the verb <u>attends</u>. It has been placed beside the noun <u>Jane</u> to help explain who Jane is.)

Mrs. Brown is the <u>teacher</u>. (<u>Teacher</u> is the predicate nominative of the verb <u>is</u>.)

The culprit is <u>he</u>. (<u>He</u> is the predicate nominative of the verb <u>is</u>.)

The **possessive case** indicates possession. Something or someone belongs to someone or something else.

I broke <u>Mary's</u> doll.

John did not do <u>his</u> homework.

The **objective case** indicates that the noun or pronoun is the object (receives the action) of a transitive verb, a verbal, or a preposition.

John hit <u>her</u>. (<u>Her</u> is the object of the verb <u>hit</u>.)

Practicing the <u>violin</u> can be boring at times. (<u>Violin</u> is the object of the participle <u>practicing</u>.)

Please come with <u>me</u>. (<u>Me</u> is the object of the preposition <u>with</u>.)

Some special rules concerning case:

1. The subject of an infinitive is in the objective case.

   I want <u>him</u> to go. (<u>Him</u> is the subject of the infinitive <u>to go</u>.)

   I told <u>her</u> to stop talking. (<u>Her</u> is the subject of the infinitive <u>to stop</u>.)

2. The predicate nominative of the infinitive *to be* is in the objective case.

   I want the leader to be <u>him</u>. (<u>Him</u> is the predicate complement of the infinitive <u>to be</u>.)

3. Nouns and pronouns used as parts of the compound subject of a verb are in the subjective case.

   <u>Mary</u> and <u>he</u> are going to the party. (The two parts of the compound subject, <u>Mary</u> and <u>he</u>, are both in the subjective case.)

   <u>John</u> and <u>we</u> are friends. (<u>John</u> and <u>we</u>, the two parts of the compound subject of the verb <u>are</u>, are both in the subjective case.)

4. Nouns and pronouns used as parts of the compound object of a verb, a verbal, or a preposition are in the objective case.

   I met <u>Mary</u> and <u>him</u> at the party. (<u>Mary</u> and <u>him</u> are the objects of the verb <u>met</u>.)

   Seeing <u>Mary</u> and <u>him</u> at the party was a treat. (<u>Mary</u> and <u>him</u> are the objects of the gerund <u>seeing</u>.)

   Take the food to <u>him</u> and <u>her</u>. (<u>Him</u> and <u>her</u> are objects of the preposition <u>to</u>.)

5. A noun or pronoun immediately preceding a gerund is in the possessive case.

   John's talking during the lesson was rude. (John's immediately precedes the gerund talking.)

   John was afraid that his speaking in class would be reported to his father. (His immediately precedes the gerund speaking.)

6. In sentences using the conjunctions *as* or *than* to make comparisons, the clause following *as* or *than* is often cut short. Such clauses are called **elliptical clauses**. In these sentences, the case of the noun or pronouns following the conjunction is based on its use in the elliptical clause.

   Mary is as tall as he. (The complete sentence is Mary is as tall as he is tall. The subjective case is used because he is the subject of the verb is.)

   The twins are older than I. (The complete sentence is The twins are older than I am old. The subjective case is used because I is the subject of the verb am.)

7. The case of the relative pronouns *who*, *whoever*, and *whosoever* is determined by their use in the clause in which they belong.

   Whom are you talking to? (The objective case is used because whom is the object of the preposition to.)

   Whom did you take them to be? (The objective case is used because whom is the predicate complement of the infinitive to be.)

   Give this book to whomever it belongs. (The objective case is used because whomever is the object of the preposition to.)

   Give this award to whoever has earned it. (The subjective case is used because whoever is the subject of the verb has earned. In this sentence, the object of the preposition to is the noun clause whoever has earned it.)

Practice

Correct each of the following errors in case based on the examples just shown.

1. He asked she to go dancing.

   _____

2. I want the leading lady to be she.

   _____

3. Alice and him are going to get married.

   _____

Judy and me are roommates.

_____

4. I saw she and Stan at the restaurant.

_____

Give the ice cream to Vicki and I.

_____

5. Toby leaving work early left us short-handed.

_____

6. John is as bright as me.

_____

Susan is brighter than me.

_____

7. Who is he speaking to?

_____

Who did you think them to be?

_____

Give this coat to whoever it fits.

_____

Give this kitten to whomever wants it.

_____

PROBLEMS WITH REFERENCE OF PRONOUNS

Since pronouns are words used in place of nouns, the nouns they refer to should be clear to the reader or speaker. Vagueness or ambiguity can be avoided by observing the following rules:

   1. The pronoun should refer to only one word or group of words. The technical term for this word or word group is the antecedent.

   Vague: The captain asked him to polish his boots. (Whose boots are to be polished?)

   Clear: The captain said, "Polish your boots."

   Clear: The captain said, "Polish my boots."

2. The antecedent of the pronoun should be a single noun and not a general statement. The pronouns most often affected by this rule are *it*, *this*, *that*, and *which*.

   Vague: The ship was pitching and tossing in the heavy seas, and <u>it</u> made me seasick. (<u>It</u> refers to the entire clause that precedes the pronoun.)

   Clear: The pitching and tossing of the ship in the heavy seas made me seasick. (Combine the two clauses in order to eliminate the pronoun.)

   Clear: The ship was pitching and tossing in the heavy seas, and <u>this motion</u> made me seasick. (Replace the vague pronoun with a noun preceded by <u>this,</u> <u>that,</u> or <u>which</u>.)

   Vague: When the teacher walked into the room, the students were shouting, <u>which</u> made her very angry. (<u>Which</u> refers to the entire clause rather than to a single noun.)

   Clear: When the teacher walked into the room, the students' shouting angered her.

   Clear: When the teacher walked into the room, the students were shouting. This lack of control angered her. (A sentence has been substituted for the vague pronoun.)

3. The antecedent of the pronoun should be explicitly stated, not merely implied in the sentence.

   Vague: My accountant has been taking classes at law school, but he does not intend to become one. (<u>One what?</u>)

   Clear: My accountant has been taking classes at law school, but he does not intend to become a lawyer.

Practice

Correct each of the following errors in pronoun reference based on the examples just shown.

1. The hostess asked her to finish her dessert.

_____

_____

2. The cafeteria was filthy, and it made me lose my appetite.

_____

_____

3. My son has been studying the violin, but he doesn't want to be one.

_____

_____

PROBLEMS INVOLVING VERBS

Sequence of Tenses

In this section, we will discuss five errors in tense that can occur when two or more verbs are used in the same sentence. The following are examples of these errors:

1. When I called him, he doesn't answer the phone.
2. At the present time, I attended John Adams High School for two years.
3. Our attorney already presented our proposition to the Planning Commission by the time I arrived.
4. I hoped to have won first prize in the contest.
5. We had ought to pay our respects.

In Example 1, we have one verb in the past tense and another in the present tense. Since the actions described by both verbs have occurred or are occurring at the same time, the tenses of the two verbs should be the same:

When I <u>called</u> him, he <u>didn't answer</u> the phone. (Both verbs are in the past tense.)

When I <u>call</u> him, he <u>doesn't answer</u> the phone. (Both verbs are in the present tense.)

Example 2 confuses the use of the past and present perfect tenses. As stated in the section on Verbs in this chapter, the past tense should be used to indicate action completed in the past. The present perfect tense should be used to indicate action begun in the past and carried into the present. The phrase *At the present time* indicates that the speaker is still attending high school. Therefore, the present perfect tense is required:

At the present time, I <u>have attended</u> John Adams High School for two years.

Example 3 exemplifies the need for the past perfect tense. Two events are mentioned in this sentence. To differentiate between the time when the attorney spoke and the time when the speaker arrived, the past perfect tense should be used for the event that occurred first:

Our attorney <u>had</u> already <u>presented</u> our proposition to the Planning Commission by the time I <u>arrived</u>.

Example 4 is an example of the use of the present and the perfect infinitive. The tense of the infinitive is determined by its relation to the principal verb. At the time specified by the principal verb, *hoped*, the speaker was still expecting *to win*. Therefore, the correct form of the sentence is:

I <u>hoped to win</u> first prize in the contest.

Example 5 uses the expression *had ought*, which is never acceptable. *Ought* is what we call a defective auxiliary verb. We call it defective because it has no other form. Thus the present and past tenses of *ought* are *ought*. The correct form of Example 5 is:

We <u>ought</u> to pay our respects.

Practice

Correct each of the following errors in tense based on the examples just shown.

1. When I asked her, she doesn't come to my party.

_____

_____

2. At the present time, I studied French for three years.

_____

_____

3. The life guard already performed artificial respiration by the time the ambulance got there.

_____

_____

4. I wanted to have found a new job.

_____

_____

5. We had ought to do our homework.

_____

_____

Mood

As noted earlier, verbs are conjugated in three moods: indicative, imperative, and subjunctive. Because the subjunctive mood is the least used, many students are not aware of the uses of the subjunctive:

1. The subjunctive mood is used to state a wish or a condition contrary to fact.

I wish this party <u>were</u> over. (The party is <u>not</u> over.)

If I <u>were</u> king, I would lower taxes. (I am <u>not</u> king.)

If he <u>had been elected</u>, he would have served his full term. (He was <u>not</u> elected.)

2. The subjunctive mood is also used after a verb that expresses a command or a request.

I insist that he <u>pay</u> me today. (<u>Pay</u> is in the subjunctive mood.)

I ask that this discussion <u>be postponed</u>. (<u>Be postponed</u> is in the subjunctive mood.)

3. The most common error involving the subjunctive is the following:

If he <u>would have known</u> about the side effects of this medicine, he would not have prescribed it for his patients.

The expression *would have known* in the subordinate clause is incorrect. The subjunctive should be used:

If he <u>had known</u> about the side effects of this medicine, he would not have prescribed it for his patients.

Practice

Correct each of the following errors in mood based on the illustrations just shown.

1. If I was President, I would end unemployment.

_____

_____

I wish this Rolls Royce was inexpensive.

_____

_____

2. I insist that she gives up marijuana now.

_____

_____

3. If I would have heard about the radar trap, I would not have driven so fast on the highway.

_____

_____

TIP

Avoid Errors in Your Essay

1. Stick to one tense. (Give your opinion using the present tense.) (Write a summary in the past tense.)

2. Use the active voice.

Voice

In the active voice, the subject of the verb is the doer of the action. In the passive voice, the subject of the verb is the receiver of the action.

Active Voice: The linebacker <u>intercepted</u> the pass.

Passive Voice: The pass <u>was intercepted</u> by the linebacker.

Switching from one voice to the other within a sentence is regarded as an error in style and should be avoided.

Poor: He <u>likes</u> to play chess and playing bridge <u>is</u> also <u>enjoyed</u> by him.

Better: He <u>likes</u> to play chess and he also <u>enjoys</u> playing bridge.

PROBLEMS INVOLVING MODIFIERS

Unclear Placement of Modifiers

In general, adjectives, adverbs, adjective phrases, adverbial phrases, adjective clauses, and adverbial clauses should be placed close to the word they modify. If these modifiers are separated from the word they modify, confusion may result. Here are some specific rules to apply:

1. The adverbs *only, almost, even, ever, just, merely,* and *scarcely* should be placed next to the word they modify.

   Ambiguous: I <u>almost</u> ate the whole cake. (Did the speaker eat any of the cake?)

   Clear: I ate <u>almost</u> the whole cake.

   Ambiguous: This house <u>only</u> cost $142,000.

   Clear: <u>Only</u> this house cost $142,000. (One house was sold at this price.)

   Clear: This house cost <u>only</u> $142,000. (The price mentioned is considered low.)

2. Phrases should be placed close to the word they modify.

   Unclear: The advertisement stated that a table was wanted by an elderly gentleman <u>with wooden legs</u>. (It is obvious that the advertisement was not written to reveal that the gentleman's legs had been amputated.)

   Clear: The advertisement stated that a table <u>with wooden legs</u> was wanted by an elderly gentleman.

3. Adjective clauses should be placed near the words they modify.

   Misplaced: I bought groceries at the Safeway store <u>that cost $29.47</u>.

   Clear: I bought groceries <u>that cost $29.47</u> at the Safeway store.

4. Words that may modify either a preceding or a following word are called **squinting modifiers**. In order to correct the ambiguity, move the modifier so that its relationship to only one word is clear.

   Squinting: He said that if we refused to leave <u>in two minutes</u> he would call the police.

   Clear: He said that he would call the police if we refused to leave in <u>two minutes</u>.

   Clear: He said that he would call the police <u>in two minutes</u> if we refused to leave.

   Squinting: We agreed <u>on Tuesday</u> to visit him.

   Clear: <u>On Tuesday</u>, we agreed to visit him.

   Clear: We agreed to visit him <u>on Tuesday.</u>

Practice

Clear up the following ambiguous sentences, using the preceding examples as models.

1. I almost drank all the milk.

_____

_____

This station wagon only seats five passengers.

_____

_____

2. The report mentioned that a man was wanted for murder with a wooden leg.

_____

_____

3. I found a roast at the supermarket that was big enough for eight.

_____

_____

4. We promised Mother on Sunday to go to church.

_____

_____

Dangling Modifiers

When modifying phrases or clauses precede the main clause of the sentence, good usage requires that they come directly before the subject of the main clause and clearly refer to the subject. Phrases and clauses that do not meet these requirements are called **dangling modifiers**. They seem to refer to a wrong word or group of words in the sentence, often with humorous or misleading results.

EXAMPLE 1

Dangling participle: Walking through Central Park, the Metropolitan Museum of Art was seen. (Is the museum walking?)

Corrected: Walking through Central Park, the tourists saw the Metropolitan Museum of Art. (The participle <u>walking</u> immediately precedes the subject of the main clause <u>tourists</u>.)

EXAMPLE 2

Dangling gerund phrase: Upon hearing the report that a bomb had been placed in the auditorium, the building was cleared. (Who heard the report?)

Corrected: Upon hearing the report that a bomb had been placed in the auditorium, the police cleared the building.

EXAMPLE 3

Dangling infinitive phrase: To make a soufflé, eggs must be broken. (Do eggs make a soufflé?)

Corrected: To make a soufflé, you must break some eggs.

EXAMPLE 4

Dangling elliptical construction: When about to graduate from elementary school, the teacher talked about the problems and joys of junior high school. (Is the teacher graduating?)

Corrected: When we were about to graduate from elementary school, the teacher talked about the problems and joys of junior high school.

Practice

Correct the following dangling modifiers according to the corrections shown in the preceding examples.

1. Driving along the Monterey Peninsula, the cypress trees were beautiful.

_____

_____

2. On reading the report that cockroaches had been found in the school cafeteria, the kitchen was fumigated.

_____

_____

3. To repair a flat tire, the car must be jacked up.

_____

_____

4. When about to get married for the fourth time, the minister talked to the divorcee about the holiness of marriage.

_____

_____

PROBLEMS WITH PARALLEL STRUCTURE

Balance in a sentence is obtained when two or more similar ideas are presented in **parallel form**. A noun is matched with a noun, an active verb with an active verb, an adjective with an adjective, a phrase with a phrase. A lack of parallelism weakens the sentence.

EXAMPLE 1

Not parallel: We are studying mathematics, French, and how to write creatively.

Parallel: We are studying mathematics, French, and creative writing. (All the objects of the verb <u>are studying</u> are nouns.)

EXAMPLE 2

Not parallel: He told the students to register in his course, to study for the examination, and that they should take the test at the end of January.

Parallel: He told the students to register in his course, to study for the examination, and to take the test at the end of January. (The parallel elements are all infinitives.)

EXAMPLE 3

Not parallel: The children ate all the candy and the birthday cake was devoured. (The use of the active voice in the first clause and the passive voice in the second clause creates a lack of parallelism.)

Parallel: The children ate all the candy and devoured the birthday cake. (The change in voice has been eliminated. The two verbs <u>ate</u> and <u>devoured</u> are both in the active voice.)

Practice

Based on the corrections shown in the preceding examples, correct the following unbalanced sentences to provide the parallel structure they lack.

1. The minister preached about sin, judgment, and how we needed to repent.

_____

_____

2. She told her husband to mow the lawn, to take out the trash, and that he should do the laundry.

_____

_____

3. The husband took out the trash, and the lawn was mowed.

_____

_____

Common Problems in Usage

WORDS OFTEN MISUSED OR CONFUSED

Errors in **diction**—that is, choice of words—often occur in student essays. Here are some of the most common diction errors to watch for.

accept/except. These two words are often confused. *Accept* means to receive; *except*, when used as a verb, means to preclude or exclude. *Except* may also be used as a preposition or a conjunction.

I will <u>accept</u> the award in his absence.

He <u>was excepted</u> from receiving the award because of his record of excessive lateness.

We all received awards <u>except</u> Tom.

affect/effect. *Affect* is a verb meaning (1) to act upon or influence, and (2) to feign or assume. *Effect*, as a verb, means to cause or bring about; as a noun, *effect* means result.

His poor attendance <u>affected</u> his grade.

To cover his embarrassment, he <u>affected</u> an air of nonchalance.

As he assumed office, the newly elected governor promised to <u>effect</u> many needed reforms in the tax structure.

What will be the <u>effect</u> of all this discussion?

aggravate. *Aggravate* means to worsen. It should not be used as a synonym for *annoy* or *irritate*.

You will <u>aggravate</u> your condition if you try to lift heavy weights so soon after your operation.

The teacher was <u>irritated</u> [not <u>aggravated</u>] by the whispering in the room.

ain't. *Ain't* is nonstandard English and should be avoided.

all the farther/all the faster. These are colloquial and regional expressions and so are considered inappropriate in standard English. Use *as far as* or *as fast as* instead.

already/all ready. These expressions are frequently confused. *Already* means previously; *all ready* means completely prepared.

I had <u>already</u> written to him.

The students felt that they were <u>all ready</u> for the examination.

alright. *All right* should be used instead of the misspelling *alright*.

altogether/all together. *All together* means as a group. *Altogether* means entirely, completely.

The teacher waited until the students were <u>all together</u> in the hall before she dismissed them.

There is <u>altogether</u> too much noise in the room.

among/between. *Among* is used when more than two persons or things are being discussed; *between*, when only two persons or things are involved.

The loot was divided <u>among</u> the three robbers.

This is <u>between</u> you and me.

amount/number. *Amount* should be used when referring to mass, bulk, or quantity. *Number* should be used when the quantity can be counted.

I have a large <u>amount</u> of work to do.

A large <u>number</u> of books were destroyed in the fire.

and etc. The *and* is unnecessary. Just write *etc.*

being as/being that. These phrases are nonstandard and should be avoided. Use *since* or *that*.

beside/besides. These words are often confused. *Beside* means alongside of; *besides* means in addition to.

Park your car <u>beside</u> mine.

Who will be at the party <u>besides</u> Mary and John?

between. See *among*.

but what. This phrase should be avoided. Use *that* instead.

Wrong: I cannot believe <u>but what</u> he will not come.

Better: I cannot believe <u>that</u> he will not come.

can't hardly. This phrase is a double negative that borders on the illiterate. Use *can hardly*.

continual/continuous. These words are used interchangeably by many writers; however, the careful stylist should make the distinction between the two words. *Continual* refers to a sequence that is steady but interrupted from time to time. A child's crying is *continual* because he or she does stop crying from time to time to catch his or her breath or to eat or sleep. *Continuous* refers to a passage of time or space that continues uninterruptedly. The roar of the surf at the beach is *continuous*.

could of. This phrase is nonstandard. Use *could have*.

different from/different than. Contemporary usage accepts both forms; however, *different from* remains the preferred choice.

effect. See *affect*.

except. See *accept*.

farther/further. *Farther* should be used when discussing physical or spatial distances; *further*, when discussing quantities.

We have six miles <u>farther</u> to go.

<u>Further</u> discussion will be futile.

fewer/less. *Fewer* should be used with things that can be counted; *less*, with things that are not counted but measured in other ways.

There are <u>fewer</u> pupils in this class than in the other group. (Note that you can count pupils—one pupil, two pupils, and so on.)

You should devote <u>less</u> attention to athletics and more to your studies.

former/latter. Use *former* and *latter* only when you are discussing a series of two. *Former* refers to the first item of the series and *latter* to the second. If you discuss a series of three or more, use *first* and *last*.

Both Judy and Charles are qualified for the position, but I will vote for the <u>former</u>.

Sam, Bob, and Harry invited Mary to the dance, but she decided to go with the <u>first</u>.

further. See *farther*.

had of. This phrase is nonstandard. Use *had*.

hanged/hung. Both words are the past participle of the verb *hang*. However, *hanged* should be used when the execution of a person is being discussed; *hung* when the suspension of an object is discussed.

The convicted murderer was scheduled to be <u>hanged</u> at noon.

When the abstract painting was first exhibited, very few noticed that it had been <u>hung</u> upside down.

healthful/healthy. These two words should not be confused. *Healthful* describes things or conditions that provide health. *Healthy* means in a state of health.

You should eat <u>healthful</u> foods like fresh vegetables, instead of the candy you have just bought.

To be <u>healthy</u>, you need good food, fresh air and sunshine, and plenty of sleep.

imply/infer. These are not synonyms. *Imply* means to suggest or indicate. *Infer* means to draw a conclusion.

Your statement <u>implies</u> that you are convinced of his guilt.

Do not <u>infer</u> from my action in this matter that I will always be this lenient.

in back of. Avoid this expression. Use *behind* in its place.

irregardless. This is nonstandard. Use *regardless* instead.

kind of/sort of. These phrases should not be used as adverbs. Use words like *quite*, *rather*, or *somewhat* instead.

Undesirable: I was <u>kind of</u> annoyed by her statement.

Preferable: I was <u>quite</u> annoyed by her statement.

last/latter. See *former*.

lay/lie. *Lay*, a transitive verb, means to place; *lie*, an intransitive verb, means to rest or recline. One way of determining whether to use *lay* or *lie* is to examine the sentence. If the verb has an object, use the correct form of *lay*. If the verb has no object, use *lie*.

He *laid* the book on the table. (<u>Book</u> is the object of the verb. The past tense of <u>lay</u> is correct.)

He <u>has lain</u> motionless for an hour. (The verb has no object. The present perfect tense of <u>lie</u> is correct.)

learn/teach. *Learn* means to get knowledge; *teach*, to impart information or knowledge.

I <u>learned</u> my lesson.

She <u>taught</u> me a valuable lesson.

leave/let. *Leave* means to depart; *let*, to permit.

Incorrect: <u>Leave</u> me go.

Correct: <u>Let</u> me go.

less. See *fewer*.

liable/likely. *Likely* is an expression of probability. *Liable* adds a sense of possible harm or misfortune.

> Incorrect: He is <u>liable</u> to hear you.

> Correct: He is <u>likely</u> to hear you.

> Incorrect: The boy is <u>likely</u> to fall and hurt himself.

> Correct: The boy is <u>liable</u> to fall and hurt himself.

lie. See *lay*.

mad/angry. These are not synonyms. Mad means *insane*.

number. See *amount*.

of. Don't substitute *of* for *have* in the expressions *could have*, *should have*, *must have*, and so on.

off of. The *of* is superfluous and should be deleted.

> Incorrect: I fell <u>off of</u> the ladder.

> Correct: I fell <u>off</u> the ladder.

prefer. This verb should not be followed by *than*. Use *to*, *before*, or *above* instead.

> Incorrect: I prefer chocolate <u>than</u> vanilla.

> Correct: I prefer chocolate <u>to</u> vanilla.

principal/principle. *Principal*, meaning chief, is mainly an adjective. *Principle*, meaning a rule or basic law, is a noun (e.g., a Scientific Principle). In a few cases, *principal* is used as a noun because the noun it once modified has been dropped.

> <u>principal</u> of a school (Originally, the <u>principal</u> teacher.)

> <u>principal</u> in a bank (Originally, the <u>principal</u> sum.)

> a <u>principal</u> in a transaction (Originally, the <u>principal</u> person.)

raise/rise *Raise* is a transitive verb (takes an object); *rise* is intransitive.

> Incorrect: They <u>are rising</u> the prices.

> Correct: They <u>are raising</u> the prices.

> Incorrect: The sun <u>will raise</u> at 6:22 A.M.

> Correct: The sun <u>will rise</u> at 6:22 A.M.

real. This word is an adjective and should not be used as an adverb.

> Incorrect: This is a <u>real</u> good story.

> Correct: This is a <u>really</u> [or <u>very</u>] good story.

the reason is because. This expression is ungrammatical. The copulative verb *is* should be followed by a noun clause; *because* introduces an adverbial clause.

> Incorrect: <u>The reason</u> I was late <u>is because</u> there was a traffic jam.

> Correct: <u>The reason</u> I was late <u>is that</u> there was a traffic jam.

same. Do not use *same* as a pronoun. Use *it, them, this, that* in its place.

> Incorrect: I have received your letter of inquiry; I will answer <u>same</u> as soon as possible.

> Correct: I have received your letter of inquiry; I will answer <u>it</u> as soon as possible.

sort of. See *kind of.*

teach. See *learn.*

try and. This phrase should be avoided. Use *try to* in its place.

> Incorrect: I will <u>try and</u> find your book.

> Correct: I will <u>try to</u> find your book.

unique. This adjective should not be qualified by *more, most, less,* or *least.*
> Incorrect: This was a <u>most unique</u> experience.
> Correct: This was a <u>unique</u> experience.

Practice

Some, but not all, of the following sentences contain errors in diction. Underline the errors and correct the sentences, following the models in the previous section. (Corrections for the sentences containing errors follow the exercise.)

1. Stevie Wonder is the most unique singer I know.

_____

_____

2. He is a real exciting performer.

_____

_____

3. I cannot believe but what he will not have a new hit record every year.

_____

_____

4. He performs in clubs, concert halls, theaters, etc.

_____

_____

5. He is all together the finest singer I have ever seen.

_____

_____

6. I want to be in the audience when he excepts his award.

_____

_____

7. He already has won many awards for his music.

_____

_____

8. If he made less records, I would be unhappy.

_____

_____

9. I can't hardly wait until his next record comes out.

_____

_____

10. When a Stevie Wonder record comes out. I try and buy it right away.

_____

_____

11. People are liable to remember his music for a hundred years.

_____

_____

12. What singers do you admire besides Stevie Wonder and Elvis?

_____

_____

13. Stevie and Elvis are both great, but I prefer the former to the latter.

_____

_____

14. I would of gone to Stevie's last concert, but I didn't have the money.

_____

_____

15. Stevie Wonder's private life is kind of interesting.

_____

_____

16. He takes care of himself and only eats healthful foods.

_____

_____

17. He has strong moral principles.

_____

_____

18. He has not let his fame affect him badly.

_____

_____

19. The amount of fans he has is huge, but he nonetheless remains a simple, modest man.

_____

_____

20. In my book, he is alright.

_____

_____

21. Between you and me, I think he's wonderful.

_____

_____

22. I get really aggravated when someone criticizes him.

_____

_____

23. The reason I get angry is because his critics are wrong.

_____

_____

24. They will learn a great deal if they listen to him.

_____

_____

25. You can infer from everything I have said that I am a confirmed Stevie Wonder fan.

_____

_____

Answers

The following sentences contain errors in diction: 1, 2, 3, 5, 6, 8, 9, 10, 11, 14, 15, 19, 20, 22, 23. Suggested corrections are:

1. . . . the most unusual singer I know (*or* . . . a unique singer).
2. . . . a highly exciting performer. (You may also omit the adverb *highly*.)
3. I cannot believe that he . . .
5. He is altogether the finest . . .
6. . . . when he accepts . . .
8. If he made fewer records . . .
9. I can hardly wait . . .
10. . . . I try to buy it . . .
11. People are likely to . . .
14. I would have gone . . .
15. . . . life is somewhat interesting (*or* quite interesting, *or* rather interesting).
19. The number of fans he has . . .
20. . . . he is all right.
22. I get really angry . . . (*or* I get really irritated . . . . Even better, drop the adverb *really*: I get angry . . .)
23. The reason I get angry is that his critics . . . . (Better: I get angry because his critics . . . .)

IDIOMATIC EXPRESSIONS

An idiom is a form of expression peculiar to a particular language. Occasionally, idioms seem to break grammatical rules; however, the common use of these expressions has made them acceptable. Some of the most common idioms in English involve prepositions. The following list indicates which preposition is idiomatically correct to use after each word:

accede to	desire for	observant of
accuse of	desirous of	partial to
addicted to	desist from	peculiar to
adhere to	different from	preview of
agreeable to	disagree with	prior to
amazement at	disdain for	prone to
appetite for	dissent from	revel in
appreciation of	distaste for	separate from
aside from	enveloped in	suspect of
associate with	expert in	tamper with
blame for	frugal of	try to
capable of	hint at	void of
characterized by	implicit in	weary of
compatible with	negligent of	willing to
conversant with	oblivious to	

The Basics of Reading

CHAPTER 2

HOW TO INTERPRET READING MATERIALS

General Reading

General reading is the reading you do in the course of your daily life. It may be the reading you do on the job or it may be the reading you do in the evening and on weekends to find out more about the things that interest you—cooking, computers, travel, etc. For this, you read Wikipedia articles, online magazines, and relevant blogs. You also consult books that deal with subjects in which you are interested.

This part of the examination tests your ability to read popular articles that deal with everyday topics. *What are the skills you will need to master?*

1. **You read to find the main idea of the selection.** You find it in a variety of places. It may be stated directly in the first sentence (easy to find). It may be stated in the final sentence to which the others build up (a bit harder to find). It may have to be discovered within the passage (most difficult). An example of this (note the underscored words) may be found in the following paragraph:

   > Several students were seriously injured in football games last Saturday. The week before, several more were hospitalized. <u>Football has become a dangerous sport.</u> The piling up of players in a scrimmage often leads to serious injury. Perhaps some rule changes would lessen the number who are hurt.

   You may also find that the main idea is not expressed at all, but can only be inferred from the selection as a whole.

   > The plane landed at 4 P.M. As the door opened, the crowd burst into a long, noisy demonstration. The waiting mob surged against the police guard lines. Women were screaming. Teenagers were yelling for autographs or souvenirs. The visitor smiled and waved at his fans.

   The main idea of the paragraph is not expressed, but it is clear that some popular hero, movie, or rock star is being welcomed enthusiastically at the airport.

> *To find the main idea of a passage,* ask yourself any or all of these questions:
>
> 1. What is the *main idea* of the passage? (Why did the author write it?)
> 2. What is the *topic sentence* of the paragraph or paragraphs (the sentence that the other sentences build on or flow from)?
> 3. What *title* would I give this selection?

2. **You read to find the details that explain or develop the main idea.** How do you do this? You must determine how the writer develops the main idea. He may give examples to illustrate that idea, or he may give reasons why the statement which is the main idea is true. Or he may give arguments for or against a position stated as the main idea. The writer may define a complex term and give a number of qualities of a complicated belief (such as democracy). He may also classify a number of objects within a larger category. Finally, he may compare two ideas or objects (show how they are similar) or contrast them (show how they are different).

   In the paragraph immediately above, you can see that the sentence "You must determine how the writer develops the main idea" *is* the main idea. Six ways in which the writer can develop the main idea follow. These are the details that actually develop the main idea of the paragraph.

> *To find the main details of a passage,* the questions to ask yourself are these:
>
> 1. What examples illustrate the main point?
> 2. What reasons or proof support the main idea?
> 3. What arguments are presented for or against the main idea?
> 4. What specific qualities are offered about the idea or subject being defined?
> 5. What classifications is a larger group broken down into?
> 6. What are the similarities and differences between two ideas or subjects being compared or contrasted?

3. **You read to make inferences by putting together ideas which are expressed to arrive at other ideas which are not.** In other words, you draw conclusions from the information presented by the author. You do this by locating relevant details and determining their relationships (time sequence, place sequence, cause and effect).

   How do you do this? You can put one fact together with a second to arrive at a third which is not stated. You can apply a given fact to a different situation. You can predict an outcome based on the facts given.

> ***To make inferences from a passage, ask yourself*** the following questions:
>
> **1.** From the facts presented, what conclusions can I draw?
> **2.** What is being suggested, in addition to what is being stated?
> **3.** What will be the effect of something which is described?
> **4.** What will happen next (after what is being described)?
> **5.** What applications does the principle or idea presented have?

Let's try to apply these skills to representative passages you will encounter in the general reading part of the test.

ILLUSTRATION

Camping

Family camping has been described as the "biggest single growth industry in the booming travel/leisure market." Camping ranges from backpacking to living in rolling homes with complete creature comforts. It is both an end in itself and a magic carpet to a wide variety of other forms of outdoor recreation.

Camping was once a June to September activity for the young and hardy. Today, it is a year-round fascination for big and small families, retired couples, the affluent, and the budget watchers, as nearly 800 manufacturers provide a camping rig to fit every pocketbook and camping need.

During the 1960's, the number of camping vehicles produced each year—travel trailers, camping trailers, truck campers, and motor homes—grew from less than 100,000 units to nearly half a million.

Until the 1960's, most campgrounds were owned and operated at public expense. For up to 10 months of each year the campground "ranger" may have been an area's only human resident. Today, nearly two-thirds of the nation's 15,000 campgrounds (800,000 campsites) are commercially operated and many include such conveniences as laundromats, supervised recreation programs, and babysitting services.

1. The article stresses the

    (1) role of the campground "ranger"
    (2) cost of camping
    (3) commercialization of camping
    (4) benefits of camping
    (5) growth of camping

1. ① ② ③ ④ ⑤

2. A major change in camping, mentioned in the passage, has involved the

    (1) length of the camping season
    (2) kinds of vehicles produced
    (3) role of the campground "ranger"
    (4) increase of publicly operated campgrounds
    (5) wide variety in recreation provided   **2.** ① ② ③ ④ ⑤

3. It can be inferred from the passage that the LEAST luxurious form of camping is

    (1) backpacking
    (2) travel trailers
    (3) camping trailers
    (4) truck campers
    (5) motor homes   **3.** ① ② ③ ④ ⑤

ANSWERS

1. **5**   2. **1**   3. **1**

ANSWER ANALYSIS

1. **(5)** This question asks you to find the main idea of the passage. The first sentence of paragraph 1, the topic sentence, establishes the theme of growth—growth in appeal of camping to all kinds of people, growth in the number of camping vehicles, etc.

2. **(1)** Question 2 requires the location of an important detail. The key phrase is "mentioned in the passage." Since the second paragraph states that camping was once a June to September activity but is now a year-round event, Choice 1 is correct. There is no mention in the passage of a change in the kinds of vehicles produced, Choice 2. Nor is there a discussion of the role of the campground "ranger," Choice 3; the increase of publicly operated campgrounds, Choice 4; or a change in the variety of recreation available, Choice 5. Length of the camping season is the only change specifically mentioned.

3. **(1)** This question requires you to make an inference from the information in the passage. The second sentence in paragraph 1 refers to the range of camping—from backpacking to the "creature comforts" of rolling homes. From this, it can be inferred that backpacking is the least luxurious form of camping.

Practice

Directions: Read each of the following selections carefully. After each selection there are questions to be answered or statements to be completed. Select the best answer. Then blacken the appropriate space in the answer column to the right.

Life insurance is a way to provide immediate financial protection for the loss of income through the death of the breadwinner. Once children are expected, the need arises for life insurance. Life insurance is usually purchased to cover the cost of the funeral and the expenses of the last illness, as well as to provide income for the survivors.

In planning for this type of financial protection be sure to consider all resources the survivors will have to use (earning ability as well as financial), the amount of income that will meet necessities, and finally the cost of such a program. Concentrate insurance dollars on the breadwinner and buy the type of insurance that will give the most protection for the cost.

A savings account is the second leg of the stool for a savings program. It is here where a family keeps the money that it may need immediately or plans to use within the near future.

Life insurance, savings accounts, and Government bonds have fixed value. They lose buying power during inflationary periods. However, they should form the basis of a family's savings program.

Some family finance professionals strongly suggest that a family should have 2 to 6 months' income reserved for emergencies.

After this is accomplished, a family is ready to consider other types of investments.

In times of inflation, your home may be one of the best protections against inflation. Of course, home ownership is not for everyone, and all homes do not appreciate. Some lose value. In the sequence of selecting investments, a home is often chosen after life insurance and savings accounts.

Common stock, variable annuities, and real estate—either in a growth area or rental property—are the best investments for protection against inflation. These are the ones that can appreciate, but of course you must select them carefully.

1. The person most concerned about inflation should turn for protection to

    (1) life insurance
    (2) savings accounts
    (3) government bonds
    (4) corporate bonds
    (5) real estate

1. ① ② ③ ④ ⑤

2. The author gives first priority in planning family financial protection to

    (1) savings
    (2) life insurance
    (3) a home
    (4) common stock
    (5) variable annuities

2. ① ② ③ ④ ⑤

3. It can be inferred that the best financial protection for a family is

    (1) life insurance
    (2) fixed value investments
    (3) an emergency reserve
    (4) fixed and variable value investments
    (5) home ownership

3. ① ② ③ ④ ⑤

The new feminism will have two effects: an increased awareness of women's decision-making role within the family and society, and a drive on the part of women for more personal satisfaction through greater independence, self-expression, and personal achievement.

Many women will rediscover their personal autonomy and satisfaction in the wife-mother role in the family. This role will take on greater economic significance as society begins to place dollar value on family functions such as caring for children and providing services for family members.

The woman's contribution to the family will become increasingly important and complex because of the information she needs for decision making and the knowledge that the productivity and health of family members depends upon the quality of choices she makes.

The changing role of women assumes a corresponding change for men in attitudes and role identity. A more equal sharing of the decision making and more equal division of labor in the family are obvious changes. The male as authority figure and head of household may disappear. Children, as well as women, will become more directly involved in family decision making, will share the growing equality of the family, and will have a less dependent relationship with their parents.

4. The changing role in women will result in

    (1) abandonment of the wife-mother role
    (2) simpler contributions by the woman to the family
    (3) greater importance to the male
    (4) decreased monetary significance of the woman's contribution
    (5) increased equality of all family members

4. ① ② ③ ④ ⑤

5. The changing role of the male will result in

      (1) greater independence
      (2) less labor in the family
      (3) stability in male role identity
      (4) increased economic importance to the family
      (5) greater self-expression   **5.** ① ② ③ ④ ⑤

6. The new feminism will give many women all of
the following EXCEPT

      (1) greater personal achievement
      (2) increased economic importance
      (3) greater decision-making power in the family
      (4) greater control over the children
      (5) greater self-expression   **6.** ① ② ③ ④ ⑤

7. The women will assume all of the following roles,
according to the passage, EXCEPT

      (1) decision-maker
      (2) wife-mother
      (3) services-provider
      (4) authority figure
      (5) raiser of children   **7.** ① ② ③ ④ ⑤

You can become a more competent consumer when you consciously follow management and economic principles as you select, maintain, and use goods and services. These principles apply, regardless of what you purchase, but are especially important when the cost is large.

- *Plan what to buy*. Each decision to buy means that you do not have that money for something else. Fit purchases into the family's spending plan. Anticipate and set aside money for large future purchases.
- *Decide where and when to shop*. Buy from reputable dealers. Learn merchandising practices and use them to your advantage. Example: Dealers may give a greater discount on an automobile during the off-season.
- *Know how to buy*. Get information on cost, quality, grades, guarantees, annual percentage interest rate (if item is to be financed), and expected performance. Make price and feature comparison (especially on expensive items).

- *Be a responsible consumer.* Know about and use laws and regulations that protect consumers. Understand consumer rights and assume consumer responsibilities.
- *Develop family business skills.* Maintain a good credit record. Understand contracts and other legal business forms. Develop a workable system for family business papers, spending, income tax records, etc.

8. The best title for this selection is

    (1) "Do's for the Consumer"
    (2) "The Responsible Consumer"
    (3) "Principles for the Consumer"
    (4) "The Competent Consumer"
    (5) "The Knowledgeable Consumer" **8.** ① ② ③ ④ ⑤

9. Comparison shopping is most important, according to the passage, when you

    (1) have a family spending plan
    (2) shop in the off-season
    (3) buy on credit
    (4) learn merchandising practices
    (5) buy a costly item **9.** ① ② ③ ④ ⑤

10. An example of a family business skill, according to the passage, is a(an)

    (1) family spending plan
    (2) off-season purchase
    (3) feature comparison
    (4) consumer protection law
    (5) good credit record **10.** ① ② ③ ④ ⑤

11. All of the following kinds of information should be obtained according to the article EXCEPT

    (1) merchandising practices
    (2) consumer laws and regulations
    (3) consumer rights and responsibilities
    (4) income tax records
    (5) interest rates on financial items **11.** ① ② ③ ④ ⑤

The more sophisticated and advanced our culture becomes, the more we seem to need the relaxation of growing our own plants.

Gardening can be an easygoing hobby, a scientific pursuit, an opportunity for exercise and fresh air, a serious source of food to help balance the family budget, a means of expression in art and beauty, an applied experiment in green plant growth, or all of these things together.

You may be a city dweller whose yearning for green plants is satisfied by minigardens in the house or patio, a shut-in who can enjoy container grown plants, a homeowner in the suburbs whose garden is a basement, or someone in the wide open spaces who is letting loose his or her yearning for creativity.

Gardening has no bounds, no space limitations, no requirements that cannot be met readily in today's world. Not really needed are power tools, large areas of sunshine-bathed land, or even a strong back. A gardener is not restricted by any age limitations, training requirements, or any social background from doing "his thing." And many physically handicapped persons can garden.

12. The author's attitude toward gardening is

    (1) cautious
    (2) pessimistic
    (3) enthusiastic
    (4) irrational
    (5) impractical   **12.** ① ② ③ ④ ⑤

13. All of the following are made possible by gardening according to the passage EXCEPT

    (1) relaxation
    (2) exercise
    (3) experimentation
    (4) artistic expression
    (5) hard work   **13.** ① ② ③ ④ ⑤

14. Gardening is restricted by

    (1) age
    (2) availability of land
    (3) training
    (4) social class
    (5) no limitation at all   **14.** ① ② ③ ④ ⑤

15. All of the following are mentioned as possible places for a garden EXCEPT a

    (1) backyard
    (2) patio
    (3) container
    (4) wide open space
    (5) house   **15.** ① ② ③ ④ ⑤

    Accidents are the major cause of death for all young people under 35 and the fourth most frequent cause of death for all age groups in this country—fourth only to heart disease, cancer, and stroke. Each year some 115,000 Americans are killed in accidents, over 400,000 are permanently crippled, and at least 11 million are disabled for a day or longer.

    Each year about 55,000 of our fellow citizens lose their lives and 2 million suffer disabling injuries in traffic accidents. Over 14,000 die and 2.3 million are seriously maimed in accidents at work. And 28,000 deaths and over 4 million serious injuries result from accidents in the home.

    Statistically, by far the most common types of home accidents are falls. Each year over 10,500 Americans meet death in this way, within the four walls of their home, or in yards around the house. Nine out of 10 of the victims are over 65, but people of all ages experience serious injuries as a result of home falls. It is impossible to estimate how many injuries result from falls, but they must run into the millions.

16. The most frequent cause of death for all age groups in this country is

    (1) accidents
    (2) heart disease
    (3) cancer
    (4) stroke
    (5) falls   **16.** ① ② ③ ④ ⑤

17. Falls most frequently result in death for

    (1) children
    (2) adults under 35
    (3) all age groups
    (4) adults over 65
    (5) factory workers   **17.** ① ② ③ ④ ⑤

18. The most frequent cause of death in accidents is

    (1) traffic accidents
    (2) accidents at work
    (3) accidents in the home
    (4) falls at home
    (5) falls in yards around the house   **18.** ① ② ③ ④ ⑤

19. Most serious injuries result from

    (1) traffic accidents
    (2) accidents at work
    (3) accidents in the home
    (4) falls in the home
    (5) falls in yards around the house   **19.** ① ② ③ ④ ⑤

20. People who are maimed are

    (1) under 35
    (2) over 65
    (3) victims of falls
    (4) crippled
    (5) killed   **20.** ① ② ③ ④ ⑤

ANSWERS

1. **5**	6. **4**	11. **4**	16. **2**
2. **2**	7. **4**	12. **3**	17. **4**
3. **4**	8. **3**	13. **5**	18. **1**
4. **5**	9. **5**	14. **5**	19. **3**
5. **1**	10. **5**	15. **1**	20. **4**

Practical Reading

Practical reading is primarily for purposes of information. *In the home*, you follow a recipe or read the label on a bottle of aspirin. You read a house plan or charts and tables dealing with storing food in a freezer. You read the warranty for an appliance you buy. You consult Craigslist when you look for a job. You read an advertisement from a bank offering different kinds of accounts. *On the road*, you read a train schedule or a road map.

We shall provide practice in all of these kinds of practical reading. *But what skills are required?* The skills are as varied as the different kinds of reading you are called upon to do. Here are some examples:

   1. **Recipe.** You need to know how to follow instructions *in the order* in which they are given, using a basic cooking vocabulary.

2. **Drug label.** You must *locate essential details* as to dosage and dangers of misuse.
3. **Charts and tables.** You have to move up and down and back and forth to *locate* either *numbers* or numbers in their relationship to others.
4. **Advertisements.** You sometimes have to *know special abbreviations* when reading classified (or want) ads; you will have to *sort out* facts you need from all the *irrelevant material* presented.
5. **Maps.** In road maps, you have to *read symbols* indicating various locations and the distances between them.
6. **Train and bus schedules.** These are similar to charts and tables, but you must deal with time and a set of code letters or numbers that refer you to footnotes.
7. **Warranties.** You've heard of the expression "read the small print." Well, warranties are similar to contracts in that they constitute an agreement between the manufacturer and the user. You have to determine what you are offered by the manufacturer and under what conditions.

These are only some of the more common examples of practical reading, but they are similar to many others. Following directions in making bookends in a shop does not require different skills from those in following a recipe. Charts, tables, and maps are encountered in social studies.

Let us turn to three typical kinds of practical reading: reading a drug label, reading a recipe, and reading a bank newspaper advertisement.

ILLUSTRATION 1

ASPIRIN
TABLETS
(Analgesic)
5 grains each

   For relief of minor headaches and neuralgia. Adults: 1 to 2 tablets with water every 3 or 4 hours, 5 to 6 times daily as required. Children 10–16 years: 1 tablet; 6–10 years; $\frac{1}{2}$ tablet; 3–6 years: $\frac{1}{4}$ tablet. For children under 3 years of age, consult your physician. Indicated dosage for children may be repeated every 3 hours, but not more than 3 times in one day unless prescribed by the child's physician.

CAUTION: If pain persists or recurs, be sure to consult a physician.
WARNING: KEEP THIS AND ALL DRUGS OUT OF REACH OF CHILDREN.
IN CASE OF ACCIDENTAL OVERDOSE, SEEK PROFESSIONAL ASSISTANCE OR CONTACT A POISON CONTROL CENTER IMMEDIATELY.

1. The maximum dosage for adults in any 24-hour period is

    (1) 4 tablets
    (2) 6 tablets
    (3) 8 tablets
    (4) 10 tablets
    (5) 12 tablets   **1.** ① ② ③ ④ ⑤

2. According to the warning on the label, in case of an overdose, one should consider the symptoms to be the same as

    (1) the effects of a normal dosage of any
          other medicine
    (2) the effects of a normal dosage of aspirin
    (3) poisoning
    (4) a child's ailment
    (5) a minor headache or neuralgia   **2.** ① ② ③ ④ ⑤

3. From the words after CAUTION, it can be inferred that the meaning of *analgesic* is

    (1) painkiller
    (2) digestive
    (3) analytic
    (4) dangerous
    (5) headache   **3.** ① ② ③ ④ ⑤

ANSWERS

1. **5**   2. **3**   3. **1**

ANSWER ANALYSIS

1. **(5)** If, according to the instructions on the label, an adult takes the maximum dosage of 2 tablets every 3 or 4 hours for a maximum of 6 times daily, he or she will consume a total of 12 tablets.

2. **(3)** The instructions following the word WARNING suggest contacting a poison control center immediately or seeking professional assistance. This is the procedure followed in the event of poisoning.

3. **(1)** The words "CAUTION: If pain persists . . ." lead to the inference that aspirin is used to kill pain. *Analgesic*, therefore, means painkiller.

ILLUSTRATION 2

NUT BREAD

4 cups flour	2 cups milk
4 tsp. baking powder	3 eggs separated
1 tsp. salt	1 cup broken nuts
$1\frac{1}{2}$ cups sugar	

Mix flour, baking powder, salt and sugar; add milk, egg yolks and nuts; fold in stiffly beaten egg whites. Pour into bread pan and let rise 30 minutes. Bake about 45 minutes in slow oven.

1. Before beginning to bake the nut bread, one must do all of the following EXCEPT

    (1) use a tablespoon
    (2) separate the egg white from the egg yolk
    (3) beat the egg white
    (4) break nuts
    (5) have a bread pan and a mixing bowl on hand   **1.** ① ② ③ ④ ⑤

2. The correct order of actions required to make the nut bread is

    (1) mix, add, pour, let rise, bake, fold
    (2) mix, add, let rise, bake, pour, fold
    (3) mix, add, fold, pour, let rise, bake
    (4) mix, add, bake, let rise, fold, pour
    (5) mix, add, pour, fold, let rise, bake   **2.** ① ② ③ ④ ⑤

3. Preparing the nut bread requires approximately

    (1) 30 minutes
    (2) 45 minutes
    (3) 1 hour
    (4) 1 hour and 15 minutes
    (5) 2 hours   **3.** ① ② ③ ④ ⑤

ANSWERS

1. **1**   2. **3**   3. **4**

ANSWER ANALYSIS

1. **(1)** To arrive at this answer, one must make inferences from the steps indicated in the recipe and also apply a general knowledge of the abbreviations for teaspoon and tablespoon. If you must pour the mixture into a bread pan, the bread pan must be on hand, and if you have to mix the flour and baking powder, a mixing bowl is necessary. The only thing not needed from the choices given is a tablespoon.

2. **(3)** According to the recipe, the correct order for the six steps to make nut bread is: mix, add, fold, pour, let rise, and bake.

3. **(4)** According to the recipe, the rising time for the bread is 30 minutes and baking time is 45 minutes—a total of 1 hour and 15 minutes. Allowing time for mixing the ingredients, the approximate time might be 15 minutes more. Choices 1, 2, and 3 are all below the minimum 1 hour and 15 minute figure. Choice 5, 2 hours, is too long. The closest approximate time is 1 hour and 15 minutes, Choice 4.

ILLUSTRATION 3

8.17% effective annual yield on	**7.75%** a year	Time Deposit Savings Account 6 to 7 year term Minimum Deposit $1,000
7.90% effective annual yield on	**7.50%** a year	Time Deposit Savings Account 4 to 6 year terms Minimum Deposit $1,000
7.08% effective annual yield on	**6.75%** a year	Time Deposit Savings Account $2\frac{1}{2}$ to 4 year terms Minimum Deposit $500
6.81% effective annual yield on	**6.50%** a year	Time Deposit Savings Account 1 to $2\frac{1}{2}$ year terms Minimum Deposit $500
5.47% annual yield on	**5.25%** per year	Daily Dividend—Grace Day dividend Savings Accounts

Put your money in our "Daily Dividend" account and take it out any time you like without losing a single day's earned dividends. We currently pay 5.25% from day of deposit to day of withdrawal compounded daily (as long as $5 remains to the end of the quarter).

OR

Deposit any amount before the 10th of any month in a Regular Grace Day Account and your dividends start from the 1st. Leave your money in, and daily compounding at the current 5.25% dividend rate adds up to an annual return of 5.47%.

On all accounts, interest/dividends are compounded daily and credited quarterly. To earn annual yields shown, interest/dividends must remain on deposit for a full year.

Withdrawals on time deposit accounts permitted before maturity, but Federal Deposit Insurance Corporation regulations require that a substantial penalty be imposed (i.e., that interest be reduced to regular savings account rate on amount withdrawn and three months' interest be forfeited).

1. To gain the maximum interest allowed, you must be prepared to deposit

    (1) $500 for $2\frac{1}{2}$ years
    (2) $1,000 for 4 years
    (3) $1,000 for 6 years
    (4) $500 for 4 years
    (5) $1,000 for 1 year   **1.** ① ② ③ ④ ⑤

2. If you deposit and withdraw money frequently, it is best for you to use a

    (1) Daily Dividend Account
    (2) Grace Day Account
    (3) Time Deposit Savings Account
    (4) Time Deposit Savings Account for 4 years
    (5) Time Deposit Savings Account for 7 years   **2.** ① ② ③ ④ ⑤

3. According to the chart in the advertisement, what is the maximum interest that can be earned if you have $100 to save and do not need the money for a year?

    (1) 5.25%
    (2) 5.47%
    (3) 6.50%
    (4) 6.81%
    (5) 7.08%   **3.** ① ② ③ ④ ⑤

ANSWERS

1. **3**   2. **1**   3. **2**

ANSWER ANALYSIS

1. **(3)** This question deals with the maximum interest for the smallest deposit allowable for that amount of interest. According to the ad, a minimum deposit of $1,000 for six years, Choice 3, will earn the highest possible yield, an effective annual yield of 8.17%.

2. **(1)** According to the ad, in a Daily Dividend Account, you may deposit or withdraw money any time you like without losing a single day's earned dividends.

3. **(2)** All annual yields higher than 5.47%, Choice 2, require $500 or $1,000 minimum deposits. Choice 1, 5.25%, is wrong because it doesn't represent the highest amount of interest that can be earned.

Practice

Directions: Each of the statements or questions based on the materials below is followed by five suggested answers or completions. In each instance, choose the one that best completes the statement or answers the question. Mark the frame in the answer column whose number corresponds to the answer you have selected.

Refer to the following directions on a can of liquid plastic clear gloss to answer the next four questions.

Keep contents away from heat and open flame.

Avoid prolonged contact with skin and breathing of vapors or spray mist.

Do not take internally.

Close container after each use.

Use only with adequate ventilation.

KEEP OUT OF REACH OF CHILDREN

Directions for Use

Be sure surface is absolutely dry, free from all wax, grease, and dirt. Sand with fine sandpaper and wipe off dust. Use LIQUIPLAST Liquid Plastic unthinned straight out of the can. If thinning is desired, use mineral spirits.

UNFINISHED WOOD SURFACES: Apply LIQUIPLAST directly to the unfinished wood. When using paste fillers, remove excess paste from the surface before finishing. When using LIQUIPLAST Liquid Plastic as a sealer, sand before recoating to get the best finish.

LACQUERED, VARNISHED, OR STAINED SURFACES: Sand to remove surface imperfections and sheen from the previous coatings. Do not use LIQUIPLAST Liquid Plastic over shellac, lacquer sanding sealers, or fillers and stains containing stearates.

Under normal use, a three-coat application of LIQUIPLAST will wear well. Under conditions of severe wear, more coats may be necessary. Sand lightly between coats to eliminate sheen and allow fresh LIQUIPLAST to adhere.

Use paint thinner to clean brushes.

---

1. The minimum number of coats of LIQUIPLAST recommended for normal conditions of wear is

(1) one coat
(2) two coats
(3) three coats
(4) four coats
(5) five coats

1. ① ② ③ ④ ⑤

2. According to the warning on the label, you should NOT

(1) close the container after each use.
(2) apply LIQUIPLAST in a tightly sealed room
(3) mix LIQUIPLAST with mineral spirits
(4) use LIQUIPLAST out of the reach of children
(5) sand LIQUIPLAST to remove sheen

2. ① ② ③ ④ ⑤

3. From the directions about sanding between coats, it can be inferred that sheen

(1) is a condition of severe wear
(2) is a stain containing stearates
(3) must be used unthinned from the can
(4) may hinder the adhesion of LIQUIPLAST
(5) may be increased by light sanding

3. ① ② ③ ④ ⑤

4. LIQUIPLAST should NOT be

(1) used unthinned straight out of the can
(2) used to seal unfinished wood surfaces
(3) used over lacquer sanding sealers
(4) mixed with mineral spirits
(5) used over paste fillers

4. ① ② ③ ④ ⑤

Refer to the following recipe to answer the next four questions.

PEANUT BUTTER COOKIES

$\frac{1}{4}$ c. butter $1\frac{1}{2}$c. all-purpose flour

$\frac{7}{8}$c. peanut butter $\frac{1}{2}$tsp. baking soda

$\frac{1}{2}$c. brown sugar $\frac{1}{2}$tsp. baking powder

$\frac{1}{2}$c. white sugar $\frac{1}{4}$ tsp. salt

2 small eggs

Blend the softened butter with the peanut butter. Cream the sugars with the peanut butter mixture. Add the eggs and mix thoroughly. Sift the flour. Then resift it with the rest of the dry ingredients. Mix and knead the dry ingredients into the peanut butter mixture. Shape the dough with your fingers into small balls and place them (not too close together) on an ungreased baking sheet. Using a fork dipped into flour, press the balls flat in a crisscross pattern. Bake at 375°F for 10–15 minutes. Watch the cookies carefully, as they brown quickly at the end of the baking period. Yield: 3–4 dozen cookies.

Note: For a cookie that tastes less "peanutty," reduce the amount of peanut butter and substitute an equal amount of butter.

---

5. The remaining dry ingredients to be sifted with the flour are

(1) baking soda, baking powder, and salt
(2) baking soda, baking powder, brown sugar, and salt
(3) baking powder, brown sugar, white sugar, and salt
(4) baking powder, baking soda, brown sugar, white sugar, and salt
(5) baking soda, brown sugar, white sugar, and salt   **5.** ① ② ③ ④ ⑤

6. The eggs are to be added to the peanut butter mixture

(1) after the flour
(2) before the sugars are creamed
(3) after kneading is completed
(4) after the sugars are combined with the butter and peanut butter
(5) using a fork dipped in flour as a mixing tool   **6.** ① ② ③ ④ ⑤

7. The greatest single ingredient in this recipe is

    (1) flour
    (2) sugars (both kinds)
    (3) butter
    (4) peanut butter
    (5) baking powder
                                         7. ① ② ③ ④ ⑤

8. To reduce the nutty taste of these cookies, the recipe advises you to

    (1) increase the amount of flour
    (2) bake the cookies for only ten minutes
    (3) substitute one egg for some of the peanut butter
    (4) replace some peanut butter with an equal
         quantity of butter
    (5) press the cookies flat in a crisscross pattern   **8.** ① ② ③ ④ ⑤

Refer to the following chart to answer the next three questions.

SOURCES OF IRON	
Meat, Fish, & Poultry	**Milligrams**
Most poultry, lamb, fish (raw), 4 oz.	1.5
Sardine & shrimp (canned), 3 oz.	2.5
Beef & pork (raw), 4 oz.	2.8
Beef heart (raw), 4 oz.	4.5
Beans: red, white, or lima (canned), 1 cup	5.0
Beef liver (raw), 4 oz.	7.2
Pork liver (raw), 4 oz.	22.0
Breads & Cereals	
Bread, 1 slice	0.5
Cereal (cooked), 1 cup	1.0
Fruit & Vegetables	
Peas (cooked), $\frac{1}{2}$ cup	1.5
Lima beans (cooked), $\frac{1}{2}$ cup	2.0
Spinach (cooked), $\frac{1}{2}$ cup	2.0
Prune juice, $\frac{1}{2}$ cup	5.0
Other Foods	
Brown sugar, 2 tablespoons	1.0
Molasses, 2 tablespoons	1.8
Chocolate (bitter), 1 oz.	1.9
Cocoa, 4 tablespoons	3.3

9. Which of the following contains the greatest amount of iron?

    (1) Three ounces of shrimp
    (2) Four ounces of spinach
    (3) Two ounces of bitter chocolate
    (4) Eight ounces of raw lamb
    (5) Four tablespoons of cocoa   **9.** ① ② ③ ④ ⑤

10. Which of the following statements are true?

    I. An ounce of canned beans contains more iron than an ounce of bitter chocolate.
    II. Cooked spinach contains more iron than cooked lima beans do.
    III. Beef heart is a better source of iron than beef liver is.

    (1) Statements I and II only
    (2) Statements I and III only
    (3) Statements II and III only
    (4) All of the statements
    (5) None of the statements   **10.** ① ② ③ ④ ⑤

11. Men between the ages of 18 and 75 years need 10 milligrams of iron per day. Which of the following food combinations would supply a twenty-year-old with his day's requirement of iron?

    (1) 2 slices of bread, 8 ounces of beef steak, and $\frac{1}{2}$ cup of peas
    (2) 1 cup of cooked cereal, 2 tablespoons of brown sugar, 4 ounces of beef heart, and $\frac{1}{2}$ cup of spinach
    (3) 2 slices of bread, $\frac{1}{2}$ cup of peas, and 4 ounces of beef liver
    (4) 1 cup of cooked cereal, 4 tablespoons of cocoa, $\frac{1}{2}$ cup of prune juice, and 3 ounces of shrimp
    (5) 2 ounces of bitter chocolate, $\frac{1}{2}$ cup of cooked lima beans, 4 ounces of pork, and 1 slice of bread   **11.** ① ② ③ ④ ⑤

Refer to the following chart to answer the next four questions.

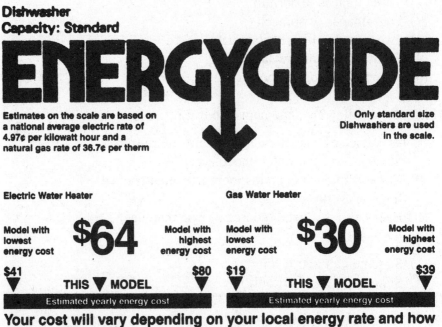

Ask your salesperson or local utility for the energy rate (cost per kilowatt hour or therm) in your area, and for estimated costs if you have a propane or oil water heater.

12. The national average natural gas rate is

(1) 3.67 ¢ per kilowatt hour
(2) 4.97 ¢ per kilowatt hour
(3) 36.7 ¢ per therm
(4) 49.7 ¢ per therm
(5) between $19 and $39

12. ① ② ③ ④ ⑤

13. We may infer that the standard sources of energy
for dishwashers are

    (1) oil and propane
    (2) electricity and oil
    (3) electricity and propane
    (4) propane and gas
    (5) gas and electricity

13. ① ② ③ ④ ⑤

14. If you run eight loads in your dishwasher per
week and the cost per therm is 30¢, your estimated
annual cost of running your dishwasher is

    (1) $23
    (2) $27
    (3) $32
    (4) $52
    (5) $78

14. ① ② ③ ④ ⑤

15. Which of the following statements are true?

    I. Electric rates are measured in terms of
      kilowatt hours.
    II. Heating water with gas costs more than heating
       water with electricity.
    III. The U.S. government conducts standard tests
        of dishwasher models.

    (1) Statements I and II only
    (2) Statements I and III only
    (3) Statements II and III only
    (4) All of the statements
    (5) None of the statements

15. ① ② ③ ④ ⑤

Refer to the following recommendations to answer the next three questions.

HOW TO THAW A TURKEY

First, when do you want to cook your fresh frozen turkey?

Cook it immediately?
1. Remove wrap. Place frozen turkey on rack in shallow roasting pan.
2. Cook for 1 hour in preheated 325°F oven.
3. Take turkey from oven and remove neck and giblets from body cavity and wishbone area.
4. Immediately return turkey to oven and cook until done.

Later today?
1. Leave in original wrap.
2. Thaw in running water or water that is changed frequently.

Thawing Time
5–9 pounds	3–4 hours
Over 9 pounds	4–7 hours

3. Cook or refrigerate thawed turkey immediately.

Cook it tomorrow?
1. Leave in original wrap.
2. Place frozen turkey in brown paper bag or wrap in 2–3 layers of newspaper.

Thawing Time
Under 12 pounds	10–18 hours
Over 12 pounds	18–30 hours

3. Check turkey often during last hours of thawing and refrigerate immediately if completely thawed.

Cook it day after tomorrow?
1. Leave in original wrap and place on tray or drip pan.
2. Thaw in refrigerator. (Turkeys over 12 pounds may take up to 3 days.)

These suggestions were released by the Poultry and Egg National Board.

16. The fastest way to thaw a fresh frozen turkey is to

    (1) place it in a brown paper bag
    (2) refrigerate it on a drip pan
    (3) check it often during thawing
    (4) put it in running water
    (5) heat it in a 325° oven for one hour   **16.** ① ② ③ ④ ⑤

17. What is the longest a 20-pound turkey may take to thaw in the refrigerator?

    (1) 3–4 hours
    (2) 4–7 hours
    (3) 10–18 hours
    (4) 18–30 hours
    (5) Up to 3 days   **17.** ① ② ③ ④ ⑤

18. Before heating a fresh frozen turkey, you must be sure to

    (1) refrigerate it
    (2) thaw it
    (3) remove its original wrap
    (4) wrap it in 2–3 layers of newspaper
    (5) allow it to stand at room temperature   **18.** ① ② ③ ④ ⑤

Refer to the following provisions on a residential rental agreement to answer the following two questions.

RESIDENTIAL RENTAL AGREEMENT
(Month-to-Month Tenancy)

Upon not less than 24 hours' advance notice, Tenant shall make the demised premises available during normal business hours to Landlord or his authorized agent or representative, for the purpose of entering (*a*) to make necessary agreed repairs, decorations, alterations or improvements or to supply necessary or agreed services, and (*b*) to show the premises to prospective or actual purchasers, mortgagees, tenants, workmen or contractors. In an emergency, Landlord, his agent or authorized representative may enter the premises at any time without securing prior permission from Tenant for the purpose of making corrections or repairs to alleviate such emergency.

19. According to the residential agreement, the Landlord can enter the Tenant's apartment with less than 24 hours' notice

  (1) to show the unit to prospective buyers
  (2) to redecorate the premises
  (3) to deal with an emergency
  (4) only after normal business hours
  (5) with an agent or authorized representative

  19. ① ② ③ ④ ⑤

20. Which of the following statements are false?

  I. Landlord has no right to show the premises to a future tenant while the current tenant resides there.
  II. The tenant normally must have more than 24 hours' notice before the Landlord enters the premises.
  III. Landlords must secure prior permission from the tenant to enter the premises in an emergency.

  (1) Statements I and II only
  (2) Statements I and III only
  (3) Statements II and III only
  (4) All of the statements
  (5) None of the statements

  20. ① ② ③ ④ ⑤

ANSWERS

1. **3**	6. **4**	11. **4**	16. **5**
2. **2**	7. **1**	12. **3**	17. **5**
3. **4**	8. **4**	13. **5**	18. **3**
4. **3**	9. **3**	14. **2**	19. **3**
5. **1**	10. **5**	15. **2**	20. **2**

The Basics of Mathematics

INTERPRETING MATH PROBLEMS

I t is helpful to use a systematic method of solving mathematics problems. You can use the following steps in almost all cases.

> 1. Read the problem carefully.
> 2. Collect the information that is given in the problem.
> 3. Decide upon what must be found.
> 4. Develop a plan to solve the problem.
> 5. Use your plan as a guide to complete the solution of the problem.
> 6. Check your answer.

The following examples will show you how to use this systematic method.

Arithmetic Problem Example

1. **Read the problem carefully.** Mr. Bates bought a jacket and a shirt at a sale where all items were reduced 25% below the marked price. If the marked price of the jacket was $80 and the marked price of the shirt was $16, how much did Mr. Bates save by buying at the sale?

2. **Collect the information that is given in the problem.**

	Marked Price	Discount Percent
Jacket	$80	25%
Shirt	$16	25%

3. **Decide upon what must be found.** Find the amount of money saved.

4. **Develop a plan to solve the problem.** Find the amount of savings on the jacket. Then find the amount of savings on the shirt. Finally, add the two savings.

5. **Use your plan as a guide to complete the solution of the problem.**
   Savings on jacket = 25% of 80 = $\frac{1}{4}$ of 80 = $20
   Savings on shirt = 25% of 16 = $\frac{1}{4}$ of 16 = $4
   Total savings was 20 + 4 = $24.

6. **Check your answer.**
   Total of the two marked prices = 80 + 16 = $96
   Savings of 25% of marked prices = $\frac{1}{4}$ of 96 = $24

Algebra Problem Example

1. **Read the problem carefully.** A father is 15 years more than twice the age of his daughter. If the sum of the ages of the father and daughter is 48 years, what is the age of the daughter?

2. **Collect the information that is given in the problem.**
   Age of father = twice age of daughter + 15
   Age of father + age of daughter = 48

3. **Decide upon what must be found.** We must find the age of the daughter.

4. **Develop a plan to solve the problem.** Set up an equation using the given facts. Then solve the equation.

5. **Use your plan as a guide to complete the solution of the problem.**
   Let n = age of daughter
   And $2n + 15$ = age of father.

$$age\ of\ daughter + age\ of\ father = 48$$
$$n + 2n + 15 = 48$$
$$3n + 15 = 48$$
$$3n + 15 - 15 = 48 - 15$$
$$3n = 33$$
$$n = 33/3$$
$$n = 11$$

The daughter's age is 11 years.

6. **Check your answer.**

$$Age\ of\ daughter = 11$$
$$Age\ of\ father = 2 \times 11 + 15 = 22 + 15 = 37$$
$$Age\ of\ father + age\ of\ daughter$$
$$37 \quad + \quad 11 \quad = 48$$

Geometry Problem Example

1. **Read the problem carefully.** A room is 22 feet long, 14 feet wide, and 9 feet high. If the walls and ceiling of the room are to be painted, how many square feet must be covered by paint?

2. **Collect the information that is given in the problem.** Sometimes, it is helpful to draw a diagram to collect information. In this case, we have

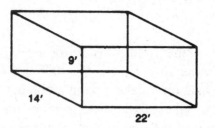

3. **Decide upon what must be found.** We must find the sum of the areas of the front and back, the two sides, and the ceiling of the room.

4. **Develop a plan to solve the problem.** Here again, diagrams are helpful. Front and back of room.

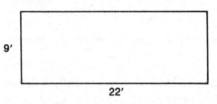

Sides of room.

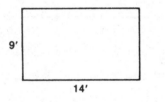

Ceiling of room.

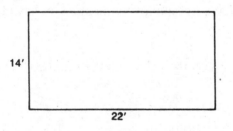

5. **Use your plan as a guide to complete the solution of the problem.**

$$
\begin{aligned}
\text{Area of front} &= 9 \times 22 = 198 \text{ square feet} \\
\text{Area of back} &= 9 \times 22 = 198 \text{ square feet} \\
\text{Area of side} &= 9 \times 14 = 126 \text{ square feet} \\
\text{Area of second side} &= 9 \times 14 = 126 \text{ square feet} \\
+\ \text{Area of ceiling} &= 14 \times 22 = 308 \text{ square feet} \\
\textit{Total Area} &= 956 \text{ square feet}
\end{aligned}
$$

6. **Check your answer.** In this case, the best method of checking is to go over your work carefully.

I. ARITHMETIC

I. A. The Number Line

A-1

It is often useful to pair numbers and collections (or sets) of numbers with points on a line, called the **number line**. Here is how this is done.

Draw a straight line and, on it, take a point and label it 0. This starting point is called the **origin**. Next, take a point to the right of the zero-point and label it 1, as follows. The arrows on the line indicate that the line extends infinitely in either direction.

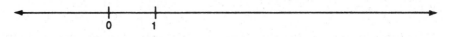

Now, use the distance between 0 and 1 as a unit and mark off the next few counting numbers, as follows.

The number that is paired with a point is called the **coordinate** of that point. For example, the coordinate of point *A* on the number line below is 2.

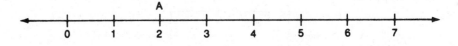

Practice

Directions: Solve the following problems and blacken the space at the right under the number which corresponds to the one you have selected as the correct answer.

1. The number paired with the origin on the number line is

    (1) 1   (4) 5
    (2) 0   (5) 3
    (3) 2   **1.** ① ② ③ ④ ⑤

2. The coordinate of a point is a(n)

    (1) number   (4) line
    (2) point   (5) arrow
    (3) letter   **2.** ① ② ③ ④ ⑤

3. The collection (or set) of numbers whose graph is shown below is

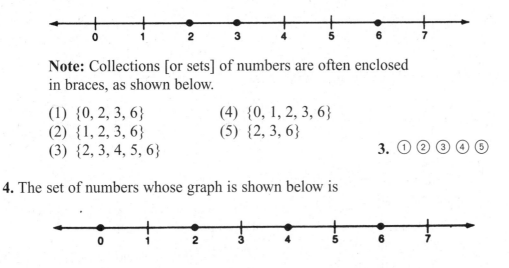

Note: Collections [or sets] of numbers are often enclosed in braces, as shown below.

(1) {0, 2, 3, 6}   (4) {0, 1, 2, 3, 6}
(2) {1, 2, 3, 6}   (5) {2, 3, 6}
(3) {2, 3, 4, 5, 6}

3. ① ② ③ ④ ⑤

4. The set of numbers whose graph is shown below is

(1) {0, 1, 2, 4}   (4) {0, 1, 2, 4, 6}
(2) {0, 2, 4, 6}   (5) {0, 1, 2, 3, 6}
(3) {1, 2, 4, 6}

4. ① ② ③ ④ ⑤

Answers

1. **2**   2. **1**   3. **5**   4. **2**

I. B. Factors and Prime Numbers

B-1

When we divide 12 by 4, the result is 3. We say that 4 and 3 are *factors* of 12. In the same way, 5 and 4 are factors of 20.

An **even number** is a number that has 2 as a factor. Examples of even numbers are 2, 4, 6, 8, 10, 12, . . .

An **odd number** is a number that does not have 2 as a factor. Examples of odd numbers are 1, 3, 5, 7, 9, 11, . . .

A **prime number** is a number that has only itself and 1 as factors. The numeral 1 is not a prime number. Examples of prime numbers are 2, 3, 5, 7, 11, . . .

Practice

Directions: Blacken the space at the right under the number which corresponds to the one you have selected as the correct answer.

1. A factor of 15 is

(1) 4   (4) 10
(2) 6   (5) 9
(3) 5

1. ① ② ③ ④ ⑤

2. The next greater even number than 20 is

(1) 21   (4) 25
(2) 24   (5) 22
(3) 30

2. ① ② ③ ④ ⑤

3. An example of a prime number is

(1) 6   (4) 10
(2) 1   (5) 39
(3) 17

3. ① ② ③ ④ ⑤

4. When an odd number and an even number are added, the sum is a(an)

(1) odd number   (4) factor
(2) prime number   (5) coordinate
(3) even number

4. ① ② ③ ④ ⑤

5. A factor of every even number is

(1) 3   (4) 2
(2) 4   (5) 7
(3) 6

5. ① ② ③ ④ ⑤

6. The next prime number in the series of prime numbers 7, 11, 13, 17 is

(1) 18   (4) 20
(2) 23   (5) 21
(3) 19

6. ① ② ③ ④ ⑤

Answers

1. **3**   2. **5**   3. **3**   4. **1**   5. **4**   6. **3**

I. C. Whole Numbers

C-1

The process of division involves some ideas which should be recalled.

When we divide 18 by 3, we have $18 \div 3 = 6$. In this case, 18 is called the **dividend**, 3 is called the **divisor**, and 6 is called the **quotient**.

When we divide 27 by 4, we have $27 \div 4 = 6\frac{3}{4}$. In this case, 27 is the dividend, 4 is the divisor, 6 is the quotient, and 3 is called the **remainder**.

If you wish to check the answer to a division example, multiply the divisor by the quotient and add the remainder to obtain the dividend.

EXAMPLE

Divide 897 by 36, and check the result.

$$
\begin{array}{r}
24 \rightarrow \text{quotient} \\
\text{divisor} \leftarrow 36\overline{)897} \rightarrow \text{dividend} \\
\underline{72} \\
177 \\
\underline{144} \\
33 \rightarrow \text{remainder}
\end{array}
$$

CHECK:

$$36 \times 24 + 33$$
$$= 864 + 33$$
$$= 897$$

Practice

Addition

	1.	2.	3.	4.
	307	49	1769	$685.17
	58	26	3205	48.09
	129	7	467	103.15
	984	38	5108	234.68
	+236	+92	+2073	+580.80

Subtraction

5. From 805, take 196 _____
6. Subtract 69 from 204 _____
7. Find the difference between 817 and 349 _____
8. Subtract 107 from 315 _____

Find the Products.

9. 4327   **10.** 3092   **11.** 283   **12.** 409
  39   45   97   307

Divide and Check Your Results.

13. Divide 986 by 29 _____
14. Divide 29,040 by 48 _____
15. Divide 1,035 by 37 _____
16. Divide 47,039 by 126 _____

Answers

1. **1,714**	5. **609**	9. **168,753**	13. **34**
2. **212**	6. **135**	10. **139,140**	14. **605**
3. **12,622**	7. **468**	11. **27,451**	15. **27 36/37**
4. **$1,651.89**	8. **208**	12. **125,563**	16. **373 41/126**

I. D. Rational Numbers

D-1

A number obtained when a counting number or 0 is divided by a counting number is called a **rational number**. For example, $\frac{2}{3}$, $\frac{9}{7}$, and $\frac{5}{1}$ (or 5), are rational numbers. Zero is also a rational number since 0 may be written as $\frac{0}{6}$.

A **fraction** is a form in which a rational number may be written. That is, $\frac{2}{3}$ is a rational number in fractional form. But 4 is a rational number which is not in fractional form. A fraction is a form which has a numerator and a denominator. For example, in the fraction $\frac{4}{5}$, 4 is the numerator and 5 is the denominator. Every rational number has fractional forms. For example, the rational number 5 has the fractional forms $\frac{5}{1}$, $\frac{10}{2}$, etc.

All counting numbers and 0 are rational numbers. Rational numbers may be located on the number line, as shown below.

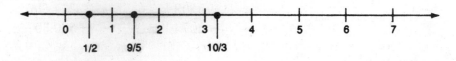

I. E. Fractions

E-1

In counting, we need only whole numbers. However, when we measure, we frequently have parts, and we need fractions. For example, consider the circle shown. The circle is divided into four equal parts, and each part is $\frac{1}{4}$ of the circle. Since the shaded portion contains three of these parts, we say that the shaded portion is $\frac{3}{4}$ of the circle. In this case, the denominator (4) tells us that the circle is divided into four equal parts. The numerator (3) tells us that we are considering 3 of these parts. In this section, you will obtain some practice in understanding the meaning of fraction.

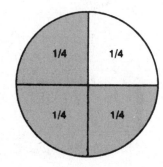

EXAMPLE

A baseball team won 37 games and lost 15 games. What fractional part of the games played did the team win?

The required fraction is

$$\frac{\text{number of games won}}{\text{total number of games played}} = \frac{37}{37+15} = \frac{37}{52}$$

EXAMPLE

A certain school has an enrollment of 500 students. Of these students, X are girls. What fractional part of the enrollment consists of boys?

Since the total enrollment is 500 and X students are girls, the number of boys is obtained by subtracting the number X from 500. Thus, the number of boys enrolled in the school is $500 - X$. The required fraction is

$$\frac{\text{number of boys}}{\text{total enrollment}} = \frac{500 - X}{500}$$

Practice

Directions: Solve the following problems and blacken the space at the right under the number which corresponds to the one you have selected as the correct answer.

1. The Star Movie Theater has 650 seats. At one performance 67 seats were not occupied. What fractional part of the theater seats were occupied?

    (1) 67/650   (4) 67/717
    (2) 583/650   (5) 583/717
    (3) 67/588   **1.** ① ② ③ ④ ⑤

2. Mr. Davis parked his car at 2:45 P.M. in a one-hour parking zone. If he drove away at 3:08 P.M., during what fractional part of an hour was his car parked?

    (1) 63/100   (4) 8/60
    (2) 53/60   (5) 23/60
    (3) 45/60   **2.** ① ② ③ ④ ⑤

3. Mr. Barnes spent a dollars for a jacket and $40 for a pair of slacks. What fractional part of the money spent was spent for the jacket?

    (1) $\dfrac{a}{40}$ (4) $\dfrac{a}{a+40}$

    (2) $\dfrac{40}{a}$ (5) $\dfrac{a+40}{a}$

    (3) $\dfrac{40}{a+40}$ **3.** ① ② ③ ④ ⑤

4. Mr. Stern planned to drive a distance of x miles. After driving 120 miles, Mr. Stern stopped for gas. What fractional part of the trip had Mr. Stern covered when he stopped?

(1) $\dfrac{x}{120}$

(2) $\dfrac{120}{x}$

(3) $\dfrac{x}{x+120}$

(4) $\dfrac{120}{x+120}$

(5) $\dfrac{x+120}{x}$

4. ① ② ③ ④ ⑤

5. On a test taken by 80 students, y students failed. What fractional part of the students passed the test?

(1) $\dfrac{80-y}{80}$

(2) $\dfrac{y}{80}$

(3) $\dfrac{80}{y}$

(4) $\dfrac{y-80}{80}$

(5) $\dfrac{80}{80-y}$

5. ① ② ③ ④ ⑤

6. A dealer bought a shipment of 150 suits. Of these, 67 were blue, 39 were brown, and the rest were gray. What fractional part of the shipment was made up of gray suits?

(1) $\dfrac{67}{150}$

(2) $\dfrac{106}{150}$

(3) $\dfrac{39}{150}$

(4) $\dfrac{44}{150}$

(5) $\dfrac{83}{150}$

6. ① ② ③ ④ ⑤

7. A carpenter cut strips x inches wide from a board 16 inches wide. After he had cut 5 strips, what fractional part of the board was left? (Do not allow for waste.)

(1) $\dfrac{5x}{16}$

(2) $\dfrac{16-5x}{16}$

(3) $\dfrac{5}{16-x}$

(4) $\dfrac{5}{16x}$

(5) $\dfrac{5}{16}$

7. ① ② ③ ④ ⑤

8. A class has 35 students. If *y* pupils were absent, what fractional part of the class was present?

(1) $\dfrac{y}{35}$

(2) $\dfrac{35}{y}$

(3) $\dfrac{35-y}{35}$

(4) $\dfrac{y-35}{35}$

(5) $\dfrac{y}{35+y}$

8. ① ② ③ ④ ⑤

9. A family spent *a* dollars for food, *b* dollars for rent, and *c* dollars for all other expenses. What fractional part of the money spent was spent for food?

(1) $\dfrac{a+b+c}{a}$

(2) $\dfrac{a}{a+b+c}$

(3) $\dfrac{a}{a+b}$

(4) $\dfrac{b}{a+c}$

(5) $\dfrac{a+c}{a+b+c}$

9. ① ② ③ ④ ⑤

10. An electrical contractor used 6 men on a job. The men worked 5 days each at a salary of $45 per day. In addition, the contractor spent $687 for materials. What fractional part of the total cost of the job was spent for labor?

(1) $\dfrac{270}{957}$

(2) $\dfrac{225}{912}$

(3) $\dfrac{270}{2,037}$

(4) $\dfrac{495}{2,037}$

(5) $\dfrac{1,350}{2,037}$

10. ① ② ③ ④ ⑤

11. A table and four chairs cost $735. If the cost of each chair was *z* dollars, what fractional part of the total cost was spent for chairs?

(1) $\dfrac{z}{735}$

(2) $\dfrac{735}{z}$

(3) $\dfrac{4z}{735}$

(4) $\dfrac{735}{4z}$

(5) $\dfrac{735-4z}{4z}$

11. ① ② ③ ④ ⑤

12. A hockey team won 8 games, lost 3 games, and tied *x* games. What fractional part of the games played were won?

(1) $\dfrac{8}{11+x}$

(2) $\dfrac{8}{11}$

(3) $\dfrac{8+x}{11+x}$

(4) $\dfrac{8}{x+3}$

(5) $\dfrac{11}{11+x}$

12. ① ② ③ ④ ⑤

Answers

1. **2**	3. **4**	5. **1**	7. **2**	9. **2**	11. **3**
2. **5**	4. **2**	6. **4**	8. **3**	10. **5**	12. **1**

E-2

Operations with Fractions. In order to be able to work with fractions, you must know how to perform operations with fractions. We will first explain the meanings of "improper fraction" and "mixed number," and then show how to reduce a fraction to lowest terms.

An **improper fraction** is a fraction in which the numerator is equal to, or greater than, the denominator. For example, $\frac{7}{3}$ and $\frac{8}{5}$ are improper fractions.

A **mixed number** consists of the sum of a whole number and a fraction. For example, $1\frac{1}{2}$ and $7\frac{3}{5}$ are mixed numbers.

In working with fractions, we will frequently use the multiplication property of 1. That is, when a number is multiplied by 1, the value of the number remains unchanged.

E-3

Changing an Improper Fraction to a Mixed Number. It is sometimes necessary to change an improper fraction to a mixed number.

EXAMPLE

Change $\frac{17}{5}$ to a mixed number.

$$\frac{17}{5}=\frac{2+15}{5}=\frac{2}{5}+\frac{15}{5}=3\frac{2}{5}$$

You may obtain the same result by dividing the numerator 17 by the denominator 5.

$$5\overline{)17}\quad 3\frac{2}{5}$$

E-4

Changing a Mixed Number to an Improper Fraction.

EXAMPLE

Change $2\frac{3}{7}$ to an improper fraction.

$$2\frac{3}{7} = 2 + \frac{3}{7}$$

$$2 = \frac{14}{7}$$

$$2\frac{3}{7} = \frac{14}{7} + \frac{3}{7} = \frac{17}{7}$$

The same result may be obtained by multiplying the whole number 2 by the denominator 7, and adding 3, to obtain the numerator. The denominator is unchanged.

$$2\frac{3}{7} = 2 \times 7 + 3 = 17 \rightarrow \text{numerator}$$

$$2\frac{3}{7} = \frac{17}{7}$$

E-5

Reducing a Fraction to Lowest Terms. You may use the multiplication property of 1 to reduce a fraction to lowest terms.

EXAMPLE

Reduce $\frac{21}{28}$ to lowest terms.

$$\frac{21}{28} = \frac{3 \times 7}{4 \times 7} = \frac{3}{4} \times \frac{7}{7} = \frac{3}{4} \times 1 = \frac{3}{4}$$

The same result may be obtained by dividing the numerator and the denominator of the fraction by the same number, 7.

$$\frac{21}{28} = \frac{21 \div 7}{28 \div 7} = \frac{3}{4}$$

Practice

Change the following improper fractions to mixed numbers.

1. $\frac{8}{5}$ 3. $\frac{22}{7}$ 5. $\frac{17}{3}$ 7. $\frac{29}{4}$

2. $\frac{9}{8}$ 4. $\frac{26}{9}$ 6. $\frac{11}{10}$ 8. $\frac{17}{8}$

Change the following mixed numbers to improper fractions.

9. $1\frac{2}{3}$ 11. $2\frac{7}{10}$ 13. $3\frac{1}{2}$ 15. $6\frac{1}{4}$

10. $5\frac{3}{7}$ 12. $3\frac{5}{7}$ 14. $4\frac{5}{8}$ 16. $8\frac{3}{4}$

Reduce the following fractions to lowest terms.

17. $\frac{4}{6}$ 19. $\frac{12}{32}$ 21. $\frac{6}{12}$ 23. $\frac{42}{63}$

18. $\frac{16}{18}$ 20. $\frac{36}{64}$ 22. $\frac{15}{20}$ 24. $\frac{76}{114}$

Answers

1. $1\frac{3}{5}$ 7. $7\frac{1}{4}$ 13. $\frac{7}{2}$ 19. $\frac{3}{8}$

2. $1\frac{1}{8}$ 8. $2\frac{1}{8}$ 14. $\frac{37}{8}$ 20. $\frac{9}{16}$

3. $3\frac{1}{7}$ 9. $\frac{5}{3}$ 15. $\frac{25}{4}$ 21. $\frac{1}{2}$

4. $2\frac{8}{9}$ 10. $\frac{38}{7}$ 16. $\frac{35}{4}$ 22. $\frac{3}{4}$

5. $5\frac{2}{3}$ 11. $\frac{27}{10}$ 17. $\frac{2}{3}$ 23. $\frac{2}{3}$

6. $1\frac{1}{10}$ 12. $\frac{26}{7}$ 18. $\frac{8}{9}$ 24. $\frac{2}{3}$

E-6

Multiplying Fractions. To multiply two or more fractions, multiply the numerators to obtain the numerator of the product. Then, multiply the denominators to obtain the denominator of the product.

EXAMPLE

Multiply $\frac{4}{7}$ by $\frac{3}{5}$.

$$\frac{4}{7} \times \frac{3}{5} = \frac{4 \times 3}{7 \times 5} = \frac{12}{35}$$

Sometimes, the process of multiplying fractions may be simplified by reducing to lowest terms before performing the multiplication.

EXAMPLE

Multiply $\frac{8}{15}$ by $\frac{5}{12}$.

$$\frac{8}{15} \times \frac{5}{12}$$

Since 8 and 12 can both be divided by 4, the result can be simplified by performing this division before multiplying. Similarly, 5 and 15 can both be divided by 5.

$$\frac{\overset{2}{\cancel{8}}}{\underset{3}{\cancel{15}}} \times \frac{\overset{1}{\cancel{5}}}{\underset{3}{\cancel{12}}} = \frac{2 \times 1}{3 \times 3} = \frac{2}{9}$$

If you are required to multiply a whole number by a fraction, you may write the whole number in fractional form with denominator 1 and proceed as before.

EXAMPLE

Multiply 12 by $\frac{5}{9}$.

$$12 \times \frac{5}{9} = \frac{12}{1} \times \frac{5}{9} = \frac{\overset{4}{\cancel{12}}}{1} \times \frac{5}{\underset{3}{\cancel{9}}} = \frac{4 \times 5}{1 \times 3} = \frac{20}{3}$$

If you are required to multiply two mixed numbers, you can convert the mixed numbers to improper fractions and proceed as before.

EXAMPLE

Multiply $3\frac{2}{3}$ by $1\frac{1}{5}$.

$$3\frac{2}{3} = \frac{11}{3} \quad \text{and} \quad 1\frac{1}{5} = \frac{6}{5}$$

$$\frac{11}{3} \times \frac{6}{5} = \frac{11}{\underset{1}{\cancel{3}}} \times \frac{\overset{2}{\cancel{6}}}{5} = \frac{11 \times 2}{1 \times 5} = \frac{22}{5}$$

Practice

Perform the following multiplications.

1. $\frac{2}{3} \times \frac{5}{7}$

2. $\frac{1}{4} \times \frac{3}{10}$

3. $\frac{1}{6} \times \frac{4}{5}$

4. $\frac{3}{8} \times \frac{5}{12}$

5. $15 \times \frac{2}{3}$

6. $\frac{5}{6} \times \frac{9}{10}$

7. $12 \times \frac{5}{6}$

8. $\frac{5}{8} \times 24$

9. $3 \times 2\frac{2}{5}$

10. $8 \times 1\frac{3}{4}$

11. $2 \times 3\frac{5}{6}$

12. $1\frac{1}{3} \times 2\frac{1}{2}$

13. $1\frac{5}{8} \times 3\frac{1}{3}$

14. $2\frac{3}{4} \times 3\frac{1}{5}$

15. $4\frac{1}{8} \times 3\frac{1}{3}$

Answers

1. $\frac{10}{21}$ 5. **10**   9. $\frac{36}{5}$ 13. $\frac{65}{12}$

2. $\frac{3}{40}$ 6. $\frac{3}{4}$ 10. **14**   14. $\frac{44}{5}$

3. $\frac{2}{15}$ 7. **10**   11. $\frac{23}{3}$ 15. $\frac{55}{4}$

4. $\frac{5}{32}$ 8. **15**   12. $\frac{10}{3}$

E-7

Dividing Fractions. Suppose we wish to divide $\frac{2}{5}$ by $\frac{3}{4}$. We may write this operation as $\dfrac{\frac{2}{5}}{\frac{3}{4}}$. Recall that you may multiply the numerator and denominator of a fraction by the same number. Notice what happens when you multiply the numerator and denominator of the above fraction by $\frac{4}{3}$:

$$\frac{\frac{2}{5}\times\frac{4}{3}}{\frac{3}{4}\times\frac{4}{3}}=\frac{\frac{2\times4}{5\times3}}{\frac{3\times4}{4\times3}}=\frac{\frac{8}{15}}{1}=\frac{8}{15}$$

Note that the final result was obtained by multiplying the dividend by the divisor inverted, $\frac{4}{3}$. This is a method for dividing one fraction by another fraction: **To divide one fraction by another fraction**, invert the divisor and multiply the resulting fractions.

EXAMPLE

Divide $\frac{2}{3}$ by $\frac{5}{6}$.

$$\frac{2}{3}\div\frac{5}{6}=\frac{2}{3}\times\frac{6}{5}=\frac{2}{{}_1\cancel{3}}\times\frac{\cancel{6}^2}{5}=\frac{4}{5}$$

EXAMPLE

Divide 8 by $\frac{6}{7}$. We write 8 in fractional form, as $\frac{8}{1}$, and proceed as before:

$$8\div\frac{6}{7}=\frac{8}{1}\times\frac{7}{6}=\frac{{}^4\cancel{8}}{1}\times\frac{7}{\cancel{6}_3}=\frac{28}{3}$$

EXAMPLE

Divide $3\frac{3}{5}$ by $2\frac{1}{10}$.

$$3\frac{3}{5} = \frac{18}{5}, \text{ and } 2\frac{1}{10} = \frac{21}{10}$$

$$\frac{18}{5} \div \frac{21}{10} = \frac{18}{5} \times \frac{10}{21} = \frac{\overset{6}{\cancel{18}}}{\cancel{5}} \times \frac{\overset{2}{\cancel{10}}}{\cancel{21}_7} = \frac{12}{7}$$

Practice

Perform the following divisions.

1. $\frac{1}{3} \div \frac{1}{2}$ **5.** $\frac{7}{8} \div \frac{9}{16}$ **9.** $\frac{5}{6} \div 1\frac{1}{4}$ **13.** $3\frac{1}{3} \div 4\frac{1}{6}$

2. $\frac{2}{7} \div \frac{2}{3}$ **6.** $5 \div \frac{1}{2}$ **10.** $\frac{7}{8} \div 5\frac{1}{4}$ **14.** $3\frac{3}{4} \div 2\frac{2}{9}$

3. $\frac{3}{4} \div \frac{5}{8}$ **7.** $4 \div \frac{2}{5}$ **11.** $2\frac{2}{5} \div 3\frac{3}{10}$ **15.** $5\frac{5}{6} \div 2\frac{5}{8}$

4. $\frac{7}{10} \div \frac{1}{5}$ **8.** $1\frac{1}{8} \div \frac{9}{20}$ **12.** $2\frac{3}{4} \div 3\frac{1}{7}$

Answers

1. $\frac{2}{3}$ 5. $\frac{14}{9}$ 9. $\frac{2}{3}$ 13. $\frac{4}{5}$

2. $\frac{3}{7}$ 6. **10**   10. $\frac{1}{6}$ 14. $\frac{27}{16}$

3. $\frac{6}{5}$ 7. **10**   11. $\frac{8}{11}$ 15. $\frac{20}{9}$

4. $\frac{7}{2}$ 8. $\frac{5}{2}$ 12. $\frac{7}{8}$

E-8

Adding Fractions. Two fractions may be added directly if they have the same denominator. For example,

$$\frac{1}{5} + \frac{2}{5} = \frac{1+2}{5} = \frac{3}{5}$$

The diagram below shows why this is true.

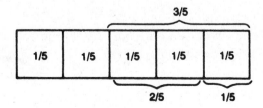

Next, consider the addition of two fractions with different denominators. Add $\frac{1}{2}$ and $\frac{1}{3}$, using the diagram below to help.

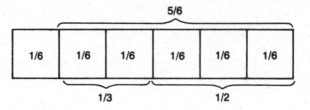

We see that $\frac{1}{2} + \frac{1}{3} = \frac{5}{6}$. Now, let us see how we may obtain the same result without the use of a diagram. Actually, we convert both $\frac{1}{2}$ and $\frac{1}{3}$ to equivalent fractions whose denominators are 6, by using the multiplication property of 1.

$$\frac{1}{2} = \frac{1}{2} \times \frac{3}{3} = \frac{3}{6}$$

$$\frac{1}{3} = \frac{1}{3} \times \frac{2}{2} = \frac{2}{6}$$

Therefore,

$$\frac{2}{6} + \frac{3}{6} = \frac{2+3}{6} = \frac{5}{6}$$

The denominator 6, which was used above, is called the **least common denominator**, or the **L.C.D.** for short. It is the smallest number into which each of the denominators of the fractions to be added can be divided evenly. For example, if we wish to add $\frac{3}{10}$ and $\frac{8}{15}$, the L.C.D. is 30 because 30 is the smallest number into which 10 and 15 may be divided evenly. Since finding the L.C.D. is most important, we will get some practice in this process.

We may use sets of multiples to find the L.C.D. Study the following examples:

EXAMPLE

Find the L.C.D. used in adding the fractions $\frac{2}{3}$ and $\frac{5}{7}$.

First, write the sets of multiples of the denominators of the two fractions:

The set of multiples of 3 is (3, 6, 9, 12, 15, 18, 21, 24, 27, . . .)
The set of multiples of 7 is (7, 14, 21, . . .)
The first number which is a multiple of both the denominators, 3 and 7, is the L.C.D. In this case, the L.C.D. is 21.

EXAMPLE

Find the L.C.D. used in adding the fractions $\frac{3}{8}$ and $\frac{7}{10}$.

The set of multiples of 8 is (8, 16, 24, 32, 40, 48, 56, . . .)
The set of multiples of 10 is (10, 20, 30, 40, . . .)
The *L.C.D.* is 40.

Practice

In each case, find the L.C.D.

1. $\frac{2}{3} + \frac{1}{4}$ **5.** $\frac{3}{4} + \frac{7}{18}$ **9.** $\frac{1}{3} + \frac{2}{11}$ **13.** $\frac{3}{10} + \frac{7}{15}$

2. $\frac{1}{6} + \frac{1}{3}$ **6.** $\frac{1}{5} + \frac{7}{10}$ **10.** $\frac{2}{7} + \frac{1}{4}$ **14.** $\frac{5}{6} + \frac{1}{10}$

3. $\frac{5}{6} + \frac{3}{8}$ **7.** $\frac{1}{4} + \frac{5}{6}$ **11.** $\frac{1}{4} + \frac{5}{8}$ **15.** $\frac{7}{10} + \frac{1}{12}$

4. $\frac{1}{9} + \frac{1}{6}$ **8.** $\frac{5}{9} + \frac{1}{12}$ **12.** $\frac{3}{8} + \frac{1}{12}$

Answers

1. **12**	5. **36**	9. **33**	13. **30**
2. **6**	6. **10**	10. **28**	14. **30**
3. **24**	7. **12**	11. **8**	15. **60**
4. **18**	8. **36**	12. **24**	

E-9

Adding Fractions with Unlike Denominators. We are now ready to get some practice in adding fractions with unlike denominators.

EXAMPLE

Add $\frac{7}{8}$ and $\frac{5}{6}$.

The L.C.D. is 24.

$$\frac{7}{8} = \frac{7}{8} \times \frac{3}{3} = \frac{21}{24}$$

$$\frac{5}{6} = \frac{5}{6} \times \frac{4}{4} = \frac{20}{24}$$

$$\frac{21+20}{24} = \frac{41}{24} \text{ or } 1\frac{17}{24}$$

In adding mixed numbers, add the whole numbers and the fractions separately and then combine the results.

EXAMPLE

Add $3\frac{5}{6}$ and $2\frac{3}{4}$.

The L.C.D. is 12.

$$\frac{5}{6} = \frac{5}{6} \times \frac{2}{2} = \frac{10}{12}$$

$$\frac{3}{4} = \frac{3}{4} \times \frac{3}{3} = \frac{9}{12}$$

$$\frac{10+9}{12} = \frac{19}{12}$$

The result is $5\frac{19}{12}$, which can be written as $5 + 1 + \frac{7}{12}$, or $6\frac{7}{12}$.

Practice

Add the following:

1. $\frac{1}{12} + \frac{5}{12}$ 6. $\frac{2}{9} + \frac{2}{3}$ 11. $2\frac{3}{8} + 3\frac{1}{2}$ 16. $\frac{1}{2} + \frac{1}{3} + \frac{1}{4}$

2. $\frac{3}{10} + \frac{1}{2}$ 7. $\frac{3}{10} + \frac{1}{5}$ 12. $2\frac{7}{10} + \frac{1}{6}$ 17. $\frac{2}{3} + \frac{1}{4} + \frac{5}{6}$

3. $\frac{7}{8} + \frac{2}{3}$ 8. $\frac{5}{6} + \frac{3}{8}$ 13. $4\frac{1}{3} + 2\frac{2}{5}$ 18. $\frac{3}{5} + \frac{1}{8} + \frac{7}{10}$

4. $\frac{5}{6} + \frac{1}{3}$ 9. $\frac{3}{7} + \frac{1}{2}$ 14. $1\frac{5}{6} + 2\frac{1}{2}$

5. $\frac{3}{4} + \frac{1}{6}$ 10. $1\frac{4}{9} + \frac{5}{6}$ 15. $2\frac{5}{12} + 3\frac{1}{9}$

Answers

1. $\frac{6}{12} = \frac{1}{2}$ 6. $\frac{8}{9}$ 11. $5\frac{7}{8}$ 16. $\frac{13}{12} = 1\frac{1}{12}$

2. $\frac{8}{10} = \frac{4}{5}$ 7. $\frac{5}{10} = \frac{1}{2}$ 12. $2\frac{26}{30} = 2\frac{13}{15}$ 17. $\frac{21}{12} = 1\frac{3}{4}$

3. $\frac{37}{24} = 1\frac{13}{24}$ 8. $\frac{29}{24} = 1\frac{5}{24}$ 13. $6\frac{11}{15}$ 18. $\frac{57}{40} = 1\frac{17}{40}$

4. $\frac{7}{6} = 1\frac{1}{6}$ 9. $\frac{13}{14}$ 14. $4\frac{1}{3}$

5. $\frac{11}{12}$ 10. $2\frac{5}{18}$ 15. $5\frac{19}{36}$

E-10

Subtracting Fractions. To subtract fractions which have the same denominator, subtract the numerators and retain the denominator.

EXAMPLE

From $\frac{6}{7}$, subtract $\frac{2}{7}$.

$$\frac{6}{7} - \frac{2}{7} = \frac{6-2}{7} = \frac{4}{7}$$

To subtract denominators which have unlike denominators, first find the L.C.D., next convert the fractions to equivalent fractions which have the same denominator, and then perform the subtraction (as in the last example).

EXAMPLE

From $\frac{8}{9}$, subtract $\frac{1}{6}$.

The L.C.D. is 18.

$$\frac{8}{9} = \frac{8}{9} \times \frac{2}{2} = \frac{16}{18}$$

$$\frac{1}{6} = \frac{1}{6} \times \frac{3}{3} = \frac{3}{18}$$

$$\text{Difference} = \frac{13}{18}$$

When mixed numbers are involved in subtraction, it is sometimes necessary to borrow, as in this example.

EXAMPLE

From $4\frac{1}{8}$, subtract $1\frac{5}{12}$.

The L.C.D. is 24.

$$4\frac{1}{8} = 4\frac{3}{24}$$

$$1\frac{5}{12} = 1\frac{10}{24}$$

Since we cannot subtract $\frac{10}{24}$ from $\frac{3}{24}$, we write $4\frac{3}{24}$ as

$$3 + 1 + \frac{3}{24} = 3 + \frac{24}{24} + \frac{3}{24} = 3\frac{27}{24}$$

$$3\frac{27}{24}$$

$$-1\frac{10}{24}$$

$$\text{Difference} = 2\frac{17}{24}$$

Practice

Perform the following subtractions:

1. $\frac{5}{9} - \frac{1}{9}$ 5. $\frac{5}{6} - \frac{1}{4}$ 9. $\frac{4}{5} - \frac{2}{3}$ 13. $4\frac{5}{6} - 2\frac{3}{4}$

2. $\frac{11}{12} - \frac{7}{12}$ 6. $\frac{7}{10} - \frac{3}{5}$ 10. $\frac{8}{9} - \frac{5}{6}$ 14. $3\frac{1}{8} - 1\frac{1}{4}$

3. $\frac{2}{3} - \frac{1}{6}$ 7. $\frac{5}{8} - \frac{1}{6}$ 11. $\frac{9}{10} - \frac{5}{6}$ 15. $5\frac{4}{9} - 2\frac{5}{6}$

4. $\frac{3}{4} - \frac{1}{3}$ 8. $\frac{2}{3} - \frac{1}{2}$ 12. $3\frac{1}{2} - 1\frac{1}{3}$

Answers

1. $\frac{4}{9}$ 5. $\frac{7}{12}$ 9. $\frac{2}{15}$ 13. $2\frac{1}{12}$

2. $\frac{4}{12} = \frac{1}{3}$ 6. $\frac{1}{10}$ 10. $\frac{1}{18}$ 14. $1\frac{7}{8}$

3. $\frac{3}{6} = \frac{1}{2}$ 7. $\frac{11}{24}$ 11. $\frac{2}{30} = \frac{1}{15}$ 15. $2\frac{11}{18}$

4. $\frac{5}{12}$ 8. $\frac{1}{6}$ 12. $2\frac{1}{6}$

E-11

Problems Involving Fractions. In general, there are three types of problems involving fractions:

1. To find a number that is a fractional part of a number.

EXAMPLE

A dealer sold 70 television sets one month. If $\frac{2}{5}$ of the sets were color sets, how many color sets were sold?

The word *of* indicates that we are to multiply 70 by $\frac{2}{5}$.

$$\frac{70}{1} \times \frac{2}{5} = \frac{70^{14}}{1} \times \frac{2}{5_1} = 28$$

The dealer sold 28 color television sets.

2. To find what fractional part one number is of another.

> ### EXAMPLE
>
> A hotel has 70 guest rooms. Of these, 15 are single rooms. What fractional part of the total number of rooms are the single rooms?
>
> We form a fraction as follows:
>
> $$\frac{\text{number of single rooms}}{\text{total number of rooms}} = \frac{15}{70}, \text{ or } \frac{3}{14}$$

3. To find a number when a fractional part of the number is known.

> ### EXAMPLE
>
> In a town election, only $\frac{2}{3}$ of the registered voters cast ballots. If there were 1,620 cast, how many registered voters were there?
>
> $\frac{2}{3}$ of the registered voters = 1,620.
>
> $\frac{1}{3}$ of the registered voters = $\frac{1,620}{2} = 810.$
>
> Then, $\frac{3}{3}$ or the total number of registered voters = 810 × 3 = 2,430.
> There were 2,430 registered voters.

Practice

Directions: Solve the following problems and blacken the space at the right under the number which corresponds to the one you have selected as the correct answer.

1. The Globe Theater has 600 seats. At one showing, $\frac{4}{5}$ of the seats were taken. How many seats were taken?

   (1) 400
   (2) 420
   (3) 450
   (4) 480
   (5) 750

   1. ① ② ③ ④ ⑤

2. At a sale, Mr. Morse bought a suit for $96. This was $\frac{3}{4}$ of the regular price of the suit. The regular price of the suit was

   (1) $72
   (2) $128
   (3) $120
   (4) $125
   (5) $80

   2. ① ② ③ ④ ⑤

3. An oil tank holds 640 gallons. When the tank is $\frac{3}{8}$ full, the number of gallons of oil in the tank is

    (1) 240   (4) 400

    (2) 320   (5) 450

    (3) 350   **3.** ① ② ③ ④ ⑤

4. A football team scored 35 points in a game. If the team scored 21 points in the first half, the fractional part of the total scored in the second half was

    (1) $\frac{3}{5}$ (4) $\frac{2}{5}$

    (2) $\frac{7}{12}$ (5) $\frac{3}{7}$

    (3) $\frac{1}{5}$ **4.** ① ② ③ ④ ⑤

5. The Star Company employs 17 engineers. If this is $\frac{1}{3}$ of the total work force, the number of employees of the Star Company is

    (1) 20   (4) 23

    (2) 41   (5) 51

    (3) 47   **5.** ① ② ③ ④ ⑤

6. The Mills family saves n dollars per year. The number of dollars saved in 5 months is

    (1) $5n$ (4) $n + 5$

    (2) $\frac{5}{12}n$ (5) $\frac{5}{12}$

    (3) $12n$ **6.** ① ② ③ ④ ⑤

7. A plane contains 5 times as many second class seats as first class seats. The fractional part of second class seats on the plane is

    (1) $\frac{1}{6}$ (4) $\frac{3}{5}$

    (2) $\frac{1}{5}$ (5) $\frac{1}{3}$

    (3) $\frac{5}{6}$ **7.** ① ② ③ ④ ⑤

8. A baseball player hit 90 singles in one season. If this was $\frac{3}{5}$ of his total number of hits, the number of hits the player made that season was

    (1) 54   (4) 144

    (2) 150   (5) 154

    (3) 540   **8.** ① ② ③ ④ ⑤

9. During a sale on radio sets, $\frac{1}{4}$ of the stock was sold the first day. The next day, $\frac{2}{3}$ of the remaining sets were sold. The fractional part of the total stock sold during the second day was

    (1) $\frac{2}{3}$
    (2) $\frac{1}{4}$
    (3) $\frac{1}{6}$
    (4) $\frac{1}{2}$
    (5) $\frac{1}{12}$

    9. ① ② ③ ④ ⑤

10. It takes a man n hours to complete a job. The fractional part of the job that he can complete in 3 hours is

    (1) $3n$
    (2) $\frac{3}{n}$
    (3) $\frac{n}{3}$
    (4) $3 + n$
    (5) $\frac{1}{n+3}$

    10. ① ② ③ ④ ⑤

11. The regular price for hats is x dollars each. If they are reduced by $\frac{1}{5}$ of the regular price, the new price is

    (1) $\frac{1}{5}x$
    (2) $x + \frac{1}{5}$
    (3) $\frac{4}{5}x$
    (4) $x - \frac{1}{5}$
    (5) $5x$

    11. ① ② ③ ④ ⑤

12. On a motor trip Mr. Anderson covers $\frac{3}{8}$ of the distance during the first day by driving 300 miles. The total distance to be covered by Mr. Anderson is

    (1) 624 miles
    (2) 640 miles
    (3) 720 miles
    (4) 750 miles
    (5) 800 miles

    12. ① ② ③ ④ ⑤

13. The Palmer Shoe Company received a shipment of 288 pairs of shoes composed equally of black and brown shoes. If 36 pairs of the brown shoes are returned and replaced by pairs of black shoes, the fractional part of the shipment consisting of black shoes is

    (1) $\frac{3}{8}$
    (2) $\frac{5}{8}$
    (3) $\frac{7}{12}$
    (4) $\frac{1}{8}$
    (5) $\frac{3}{4}$

    13. ① ② ③ ④ ⑤

14. An auditorium contains 540 seats and is $\frac{4}{9}$ filled. The number of seats left unfilled is

    (1) 240
    (2) 60
    (3) 120
    (4) 200
    (5) 300

    14. ① ② ③ ④ ⑤

15. At a dance, x boys and y girls attended. Of the total attendance, the fraction which represents the number of boys is

(1) $\dfrac{x}{y}$

(2) $\dfrac{y}{x}$

(3) $\dfrac{y}{x+y}$

(4) $\dfrac{x}{x+y}$

(5) $\dfrac{x+y}{x}$

15. ① ② ③ ④ ⑤

16. Mr. Adams paid $\frac{1}{4}$ of his total monthly income for rent. If Mr. Adams earned y dollars per month, the number of dollars remaining after he paid his rent was

(1) $\frac{1}{4}y$

(2) $y + 4$

(3) $\frac{3}{4}y$

(4) $12y$

(5) $3y$

16. ① ② ③ ④ ⑤

17. Mr. Benson is on a diet. For breakfast and lunch he consumed $\frac{4}{9}$ of his allowable number of calories. If he still had 1,000 calories left for the day, his daily allowance in calories was

(1) 1,500

(2) 1,800

(3) 1,200

(4) 2,250

(5) $444\frac{4}{9}$

17. ① ② ③ ④ ⑤

18. In his will, Mr. Mason left $\frac{1}{2}$ of his estate to his wife, $\frac{1}{3}$ to his daughter, and the balance, consisting of \$12,000, to his son. The value of Mr. Mason's estate was

(1) \$24,000

(2) \$60,000

(3) \$14,400

(4) \$65,000

(5) \$72,000

18. ① ② ③ ④ ⑤

19. An oil tank is $\frac{3}{10}$ full. It takes 420 gallons more to fill the tank. The number of gallons the tank holds is

(1) 600

(2) 480

(3) 840

(4) 1,260

(5) 1,000

19. ① ② ③ ④ ⑤

20. A family spends $\frac{1}{4}$ of its income for rent and $\frac{1}{5}$ for food. The fractional part of its income left is

(1) $\frac{9}{20}$

(2) $\frac{19}{20}$

(3) $\frac{11}{20}$

(4) $\frac{4}{5}$

(5) $\frac{8}{9}$

20. ① ② ③ ④ ⑤

Answers

1. **4**	6. **2**	11. **3**	16. **3**
2. **3**	7. **3**	12. **5**	17. **2**
3. **1**	8. **2**	13. **2**	18. **5**
4. **4**	9. **4**	14. **5**	19. **1**
5. **5**	10. **2**	15. **4**	20. **3**

E-12

Arranging Fractions in Order. We know that $\frac{1}{2}$ and $\frac{3}{6}$ are equivalent fractions. This fact can be checked as follows:

$$\frac{1}{2} \diagdown\diagup \frac{3}{6}$$

$$1 \times 6 = 2 \times 3$$

We know that $\frac{3}{4}$ is greater than $\frac{2}{5}$. This fact can be checked as follows:

$$\frac{3}{4} \diagdown\diagup \frac{2}{5}$$

3×5 is greater than 4×2. The symbol $>$ means is *greater than*. Thus, we may write $\frac{3}{4} > \frac{2}{5}$ because $15 > 8$.

We know that $\frac{3}{7}$ is less than $\frac{5}{6}$. This fact can be checked as follows:

$$\frac{3}{7} \diagdown\diagup \frac{5}{6}$$

3×6 is less than 7×5. The symbol $<$ means *is less than*. Thus, we may write $\frac{3}{7} < \frac{5}{6}$ because $18 < 35$.

Practice

In each case, use the symbol =, >, or < to show the relationship between the given fractions.

1. $\frac{3}{4}$ $\frac{7}{10}$ 5. $\frac{4}{9}$ $\frac{7}{15}$ 9. $\frac{21}{28}$ $\frac{24}{32}$ 13. $\frac{15}{35}$ $\frac{12}{28}$

2. $\frac{6}{9}$ $\frac{40}{60}$ 6. $\frac{12}{20}$ $\frac{3}{5}$ 10. $\frac{8}{13}$ $\frac{5}{8}$ 14. $\frac{6}{13}$ $\frac{11}{20}$

3. $\frac{2}{3}$ $\frac{11}{16}$ 7. $\frac{7}{11}$ $\frac{13}{19}$ 11. $\frac{5}{16}$ $\frac{10}{31}$ 15. $\frac{9}{17}$ $\frac{5}{7}$

4. $\frac{5}{8}$ $\frac{4}{7}$ 8. $\frac{7}{9}$ $\frac{15}{17}$ 12. $\frac{4}{11}$ $\frac{8}{21}$

Answers

1. $\frac{3}{4} > \frac{7}{10}$ 5. $\frac{4}{9} < \frac{7}{15}$ 9. $\frac{21}{28} = \frac{24}{32}$ 13. $\frac{15}{35} = \frac{12}{28}$

2. $\frac{6}{9} = \frac{40}{60}$ 6. $\frac{12}{20} = \frac{3}{5}$ 10. $\frac{8}{13} < \frac{5}{8}$ 14. $\frac{6}{13} < \frac{11}{20}$

3. $\frac{2}{3} < \frac{11}{16}$ 7. $\frac{7}{11} < \frac{13}{19}$ 11. $\frac{5}{16} < \frac{10}{31}$ 15. $\frac{9}{17} < \frac{2}{7}$

4. $\frac{5}{8} > \frac{4}{7}$ 8. $\frac{7}{9} < \frac{15}{17}$ 12. $\frac{4}{11} < \frac{8}{21}$

I. F. Decimals

F-1

A **decimal fraction**, or **decimal**, is a fraction in which the denominator is not written. The denominator is a power of 10; the denominator may be 10, 100, 1,000, etc., and is shown by the way the decimal is written. For example,

Written as common fractions	Written as decimals
$\frac{3}{10}$	0.3
$\frac{19}{100}$	0.19
$\frac{7}{100}$	0.07
$\frac{163}{1,000}$	0.163

If a number consists of a whole number and a fraction, the whole number is written first and is then followed by the decimal. For example,

$$8\frac{3}{10} = 8.3$$

$$9\frac{7}{100} = 9.07$$

Note: The value of a decimal is *not* changed by annexing zeros to the right of the decimal. For example,

$$\frac{1}{2} = 0.5 = 0.50 = 0.500 = 0.5000$$

One reason for the use of decimals is that they are convenient to write and to work with. For example, it is more convenient to add decimals than to add fractions: in adding decimals you don't need to find common denominators.

F-2

Addition of Decimals. Mrs. Gordon bought the following items at a supermarket: bread, $0.53; steak, $4.70; tomato juice, $0.60; fish, $2.20. When she checked the total cost she arranged her work as follows:

$$\begin{array}{r} \$0.53 \\ 4.70 \\ 0.60 \\ +2.20 \\ \hline \$8.03 \end{array}$$

You can see that she followed this rule:

TIP

In adding decimals, always put the decimal points under each other.

F-3

Subtraction of Decimals. In subtracting decimals we follow the same rule.

EXAMPLE

Subtract 9.73 from 15.58.

$$\begin{array}{r} 15.58 \\ -9.73 \\ \hline 5.85 \end{array}$$

F-4

Multiplication of Decimals. Mr. Burns figured that it cost him about 9.8 cents per mile for the expense of driving his car. He drives 286 miles to work and back each week. How much does it cost him to do this?

In order to obtain the result we must multiply 286 by 9.8 cents. Note that in this multiplication we write 9.8 cents as $0.098. Before we actually multiply we can see that the answer should be roughly in the neighborhood of $28: 9.8¢ is almost one-tenth of a dollar, and $\frac{1}{10}$ of 286 is slightly more than 28.

$$
\begin{array}{r}
286 \\
\times \$0.098 \\
\hline
2288 \\
2574 \\
\hline
\$28.028
\end{array}
$$

Do you agree that the answer should be $28.028, or $28.03 to the nearest cent?

This example illustrates the following rule:

In multiplying decimals the number of decimal places in the product is the sum of the number of decimal places in the numbers being multiplied.

EXAMPLES

0.02 (2 decimal places)	1.02 (2 decimal places)
×0.3 (1 decimal place)	×0.004 (3 decimal places)
0.006 (3 decimal places)	0.00408 (5 decimal places)

F-5

Division of Decimals. Consider the division $\frac{8.46}{0.2}$. Since we may multiply the numerator and denominator of a fraction by the same number without changing the value of the fraction, we may multiply the numerator and denominator of this fraction by 10 to obtain

$$
\frac{8.46}{0.2} = \frac{84.6}{2}
$$

This is often written as

$$
0.2. \overline{)8.4.6} \quad \text{or} \quad 2 \overline{)84.6}^{\,42.3}
$$

The result is 42.3.

In dividing decimals, multiply both the divisor and the dividend by whatever power of 10 (10, 100, 1,000, etc.) that is necessary to make the divisor a whole number, and then proceed with the division. The decimal point in the quotient is always in the same place as in the new dividend.

EXAMPLES

| 6.93 ÷ .3 | 35.75 ÷ 0.05 | 0.08136 ÷ 0.006 |

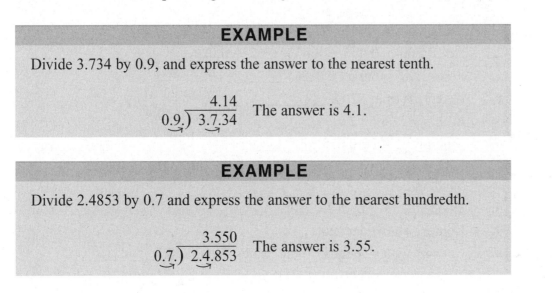

Sometimes, there is a remainder and you are told to find the answer to the nearest tenth, nearest hundredth, etc. In such cases, carry out the division to one more place than is called for. *Regarding remainders*—If the digit just to the right of the desired decimal place is 5 or greater, add 1 to the desired decimal place number. Otherwise, drop the digit to the right of the desired decimal place.

EXAMPLE

Divide 3.734 by 0.9, and express the answer to the nearest tenth.

$$0.9\overline{)\,3.7.34}$$ with quotient 4.14 The answer is 4.1.

EXAMPLE

Divide 2.4853 by 0.7 and express the answer to the nearest hundredth.

$$0.7\overline{)\,2.4.853}$$ with quotient 3.550 The answer is 3.55.

F-6

Conversion of Fractions to Decimals. It is sometimes necessary to change a fraction to a decimal. To do this, we divide the numerator by the denominator, placing zeros after the decimal point in the numerator when they are needed.

EXAMPLE

Change $\frac{3}{8}$ to a decimal.

$$8\overline{)\,3.000}$$ with quotient 0.375

$$\frac{3}{8} = 0.375$$

EXAMPLE

Change $\frac{5}{12}$ to a decimal.

$$\begin{array}{r} 0.4166\frac{2}{3} \\ 12\overline{)5.0000} \end{array}$$

To the nearest tenth, $\frac{5}{12} = 0.4$.
To the nearest hundredth, $\frac{5}{12} = 0.42$.
To the nearest thousandth, $\frac{5}{12} = 0.417$.

Practice

1. Add $38.52 + 7.09 + 92.78 + 0.84.$ _____

2. Add $2.806 + 0.935 + 4.037 + 65 + 0.029.$ _____

3. From 1.907 subtract $0.023.$ _____

4. Take 3.79 from $12.82.$ _____

5. Multiply 5.68 by $2.9.$ _____

6. Multiply 3.14 by $0.015.$ _____

7. Divide 1.6357 by 0.37 and express the result to the nearest hundredth. _____

8. Divide 0.32277 by $5.3.$ _____

9. Convert $\frac{17}{20}$ to a decimal. _____

10. Convert $\frac{8}{15}$ to a decimal to the nearest hundredth. _____

Answers

1. **139.23**	4. **9.03**	7. **4.42**	10. **0.53**
2. **72.807**	5. **16.472**	8. **0.0609**	
3. **1.884**	6. **0.04710**	9. **0.85**	

I. G. Percent

G-1

We have seen that rational numbers may be expressed as fractions or as decimals. A rational number may also be expressed as a percent. In this section, we will learn how to work with percents.

On a motor trip of 100 miles, 73 miles were on parkway. If we wish to indicate the part of the trip taken on a parkway, we may say that $\frac{73}{100}$ of the trip was on a parkway. Another way of stating the same fact is to say that 0.73 of the trip was taken on a parkway. A third way to express the same idea is to say that 73% of the trip was taken on a parkway. *Percent is just another way of writing a fraction in which the denominator is 100.* The % sign is used instead of writing the denominator 100. In short, 73% means $\frac{73}{100}$ or 0.73. It is a simple matter to change a percent to a fraction or to a decimal.

EXAMPLE

Change 45%   (*a*) to a decimal.
$$45\% = 0.45$$
(*b*) to a fraction.
$$45\% = \frac{45}{100}, \text{ or } \frac{9}{20}$$

EXAMPLE

Change 0.37 to a percent.

$$0.37 = \frac{37}{100} = 37\%$$

Change 0.025 to a percent.

$$0.025 = \frac{2.5}{100} = 2.5\% \text{ or } 2\frac{1}{2}\%$$

Change $\frac{3}{4}$ to a percent.

We first change $\frac{3}{4}$ to a decimal and then to a percent.

$$\begin{array}{r} 0.75 \\ 4{\overline{)3.00}} \end{array}$$

$$\frac{3}{4} = 0.75 = 75\%$$

Change $\frac{5}{19}$ to a decimal and then to a percent.

$$\begin{array}{r} 0.26 \\ 19{\overline{)5.00}} \\ 3\,8 \\ \hline 1\,20 \\ 1\,14 \\ \hline 6 \end{array}$$

$$\frac{5}{19} = 0.26\frac{6}{19} = 26\frac{6}{19}\%$$

Practice

Fill in the following blanks:

	Fraction	Decimal	Percent
1.	$\frac{1}{2}$		
2.		0.35	
3.			36%
4.	$\frac{3}{7}$		
5.		0.24	
6.			$4\frac{1}{2}\%$
7.	$\frac{5}{9}$		
8.		$0.37\frac{1}{2}$	
9.			$83\frac{1}{3}$
10.	$1\frac{1}{5}$		

Answers

	Fraction	Decimal	Percent
1.	$\frac{1}{2}$	0.50	50%
2.	$\frac{35}{100} = \frac{7}{20}$	0.35	35%
3.	$\frac{36}{100} = \frac{9}{25}$	0.36	36%
4.	$\frac{3}{7}$	$0.42\frac{6}{7}$	$42\frac{6}{7}\%$
5.	$\frac{6}{25}$	0.24	24%
6.	$\frac{4\frac{1}{2}}{100} = \frac{9}{200}$	$0.04\frac{1}{2} = .045$	$4\frac{1}{2}\%$
7.	$\frac{5}{9}$	$0.55\frac{5}{9}$	$55\frac{5}{9}\%$
8.	$\frac{37\frac{1}{2}}{100} = \frac{75}{200} = \frac{3}{8}$	$0.37\frac{1}{2}$	$37\frac{1}{2}\%$
9.	$\frac{83\frac{1}{3}}{100} = \frac{250}{300} = \frac{5}{6}$	$0.83\frac{1}{3}$	$83\frac{1}{3}\%$
10.	$1\frac{1}{5}$	1.2	120%

Certain fractions and their equivalent percents are used frequently.
Helpful Equivalents to Memorize

$\frac{1}{2} = 50\%$	$\frac{3}{4} = 75\%$	$\frac{4}{5} = 80\%$	$\frac{3}{8} = 37\frac{1}{2}\%$
$\frac{1}{3} = 33\frac{1}{3}\%$	$\frac{1}{5} = 20\%$	$\frac{1}{6} = 16\frac{2}{3}\%$	$\frac{5}{8} = 62\frac{1}{2}\%$
$\frac{2}{3} = 66\frac{2}{3}\%$	$\frac{2}{5} = 40\%$	$\frac{5}{6} = 83\frac{1}{3}\%$	$\frac{7}{8} = 87\frac{1}{2}\%$
$\frac{1}{4} = 25\%$	$\frac{3}{5} = 60\%$	$\frac{1}{8} = 12\frac{1}{2}\%$	

G-2

Problems on Percents. Since percents are fractions in another form, problems involving percents are similar to problems involving fractions.

1. To find a percent of a given number.

EXAMPLE

In a factory, 4,775 machine parts were manufactured. When these were tested, 4% of them were found to be defective. How many machine parts were defective?

In this case, the word *of* indicates that we are to multiply 4,775 by 4%. Since 4% = 0.04, we have

$$
\begin{array}{rl}
4775 & \text{parts manufactured} \\
\times\ .04 & \text{percent defective} \\
\hline
191.00 & \text{number of defective parts}
\end{array}
$$

191 machine parts were defective.

2. To find what percent one number is of another.

EXAMPLE

During the season, a professional basketball player tried 108 foul shots, and made 81 of them. What percent of the shots tried were made?

We form a fraction as follows:

$$\frac{\text{number of shots made}}{\text{total number of shots tried}} = \frac{81}{108}$$

This fraction may be expressed as a percent by changing $\frac{81}{108}$ to a decimal and then to a percent:

$$
\begin{array}{r}
0.75 \\
108\overline{)\ 81.00} \\
\underline{75\ 6} \\
5\ 40 \\
\underline{5\ 40}
\end{array}
$$

$$\frac{81}{108} = 0.75 = 75\%$$

The player made 75% of his shots.

3. To find a number when a percent of it is given.

EXAMPLE

A businessman decided to spend 16% of his expense budget for advertising. If he spent \$2,400, what was his total expense?

We know that 16%, or $\frac{16}{100}$, of his expenses amounted to \$2,400.

$$\frac{16}{100} \text{ of expense} = 2,400$$

$$\frac{1}{100} \text{ of expense} = \frac{2,400}{16} = 150$$

$$\text{then } \frac{100}{100} \text{ or total expense} = 150 \times 100 = \$15,000.$$

Practice

Directions: Solve the following problems and blacken the space at the right under the number which corresponds to the one you have selected as the correct answer.

1. Of \$500 spent by the Jones family one month, \$150 was spent for clothing. The percent spent for clothing was

    (1) $33\frac{1}{3}\%$ (4) 12%

    (2) 40%   (5) 20%

    (3) 30%   **1.** ① ② ③ ④ ⑤

2. Mr. Frank bought a jacket for $48 and a pair of slacks for $12.50. If there was a sales tax of 3% added to his bill, the amount of the tax was

    (1) $18   (4) $0.18
    (2) $1.82   (5) $0.36
    (3) $0.63   **2.** ① ② ③ ④ ⑤

3. A TV dealer made 20% of his annual sales during the month before Christmas. If he sold 130 sets during this month, the number of sets he sold during the year was

    (1) 650   (4) 520
    (2) 260   (5) 390
    (3) 1,300   **3.** ① ② ③ ④ ⑤

4. Of 600 students in a high school graduating class, 85% plan to go on to college. The number of students planning to go on to college is

    (1) 5,100   (4) 500
    (2) 51   (5) 510
    (3) 540   **4.** ① ② ③ ④ ⑤

5. A motorist planned a trip covering 720 miles. After he had covered 600 miles, what percent of the trip was completed?

    (1) 80%   (4) $16\frac{2}{3}\%$
    (2) $83\frac{1}{3}\%$ (5) 85%
    (3) 60%   **5.** ① ② ③ ④ ⑤

6. A school library contained 3,200 books. Of these, 48% were books of fiction. The number of books of fiction that the library contained was

    (1) 1,200   (4) 1,380
    (2) 1,208   (5) 1,300
    (3) 1,536   **6.** ① ② ③ ④ ⑤

7. A homeowner figured that 60% of his expenses were taxes. If his tax bill was $900, the total expense of running his house was

    (1) $540   (4) $1,500
    (2) $5,400   (5) $2,000
    (3) $1,800   **7.** ① ② ③ ④ ⑤

8. The value of a new car decreases 35% during the first year. Mr. Ames paid $6,000 for a new car. The value of the car at the end of the first year was

(1) $2,100   (4) $4,200
(2) $3,100   (5) $3,900
(3) $4,000

8. ① ② ③ ④ ⑤

9. In a large housing development there are 1,250 apartments. Of these, 250 were three-room apartments. The percent of three-room apartments in the development is

(1) $16\frac{2}{3}\%$ (4) 24%
(2) 25%   (5) 30%
(3) 20%

9. ① ② ③ ④ ⑤

10. Mrs. Breen bought a dining room suite for $800. She agreed to pay 25% down and the rest in installments. Her down payment was

(1) $400   (4) $100
(2) $200   (5) $250
(3) $150

10. ① ② ③ ④ ⑤

11. An oil tank contains 560 gallons. After 210 gallons of oil were used, the percent of oil left in the tank was

(1) $37\frac{1}{2}\%$ (4) $62\frac{1}{2}\%$
(2) 40%   (5) 58%
(3) 60%

11. ① ② ③ ④ ⑤

12. When Mrs. Green had paid $600 for her fur coat, she had paid 40% of the total cost. The total cost of her fur coat was

(1) $1,000   (4) $2,400
(2) $1,200   (5) $1,800
(3) $1,500

12. ① ② ③ ④ ⑤

13. Mrs. Miller received a bill for electricity for $24.50. She was allowed a discount of 2% for early payment. If Mrs. Miller paid promptly her payment was

(1) $0.49   (4) $24.01
(2) $19.60   (5) $4.90
(3) $24.45

13. ① ② ③ ④ ⑤

14. A table usually sells for $72. Because it was slightly shopworn, it sold for $60. The percent of reduction was

    (1) 20%   (4) 30%

    (2) $16\frac{2}{3}$%   (5) $12\frac{1}{2}$%

    (3) 80%   **14.** ① ② ③ ④ ⑤

15. The sales tax on a lawn mower was $4.80. If the tax rate is 4%, the selling price of the mower was

    (1) $19.20   (4) $120

    (2) $192   (5) $115.20

    (3) $124.80   **15.** ① ② ③ ④ ⑤

16. A bookstore sold 800 copies of a popular cookbook at $5 each. If the dealer made a profit of 40% on each sale, his total profit on the sale of the cookbooks was

    (1) $160   (4) $1,200

    (2) $960   (5) $1,600

    (3) $240   **16.** ① ② ③ ④ ⑤

17. At an evening performance, $83\frac{1}{3}$% of the seats in a movie house were occupied. If 500 people attended this performance, the seating capacity of the movie house was

    (1) 600   (4) 650

    (2) 500   (5) 750

    (3) 583   **17.** ① ② ③ ④ ⑤

18. A food store made sales of $9,000 during one week. If 5% of the sales amount was profit, the profit for the week was

    (1) $45   (4) $544.42

    (2) $4,500   (5) $434.42

    (3) $450   **18.** ① ② ③ ④ ⑤

19. The Blue Sox baseball team won 56 games and lost 28 games. The percent of the games won by the Blue Sox was

    (1) 50%   (4) 40%

    (2) $66\frac{2}{3}$%   (5) 36%

    (3) $33\frac{1}{3}$%   **19.** ① ② ③ ④ ⑤

20. The Star Motel had 60 rooms occupied one night. This was 80% of the total number of rooms. The total number of rooms in the motel was

(1) 80 (4) 75
(2) 48 (5) 100
(3) 140

20. ① ② ③ ④ ⑤

Answers

1. **3**	6. **3**	11. **4**	16. **5**
2. **2**	7. **4**	12. **3**	17. **1**
3. **1**	8. **5**	13. **4**	18. **3**
4. **5**	9. **3**	14. **2**	19. **2**
5. **2**	10. **2**	15. **4**	20. **4**

G-3

Business Applications of Percentage. Manufacturers will frequently suggest a price for which an article is to be sold. This is called the **list price**. Dealers will sometimes reduce the price in order to meet competition. The amount by which the price is reduced is called the **discount**. And the reduced price is called the **net price**, or **selling price**.

EXAMPLE

In a department store, a chair was marked as follows: "List Price $45. For sale at $31.50." What was the rate of discount?

The discount was $45.00 − $31.50 = $13.50. To find the rate of discount, we use the fraction.

$$\frac{\text{Discount}}{\text{List Price}} = \frac{13.50}{45.00}$$

$$= \frac{135}{450}$$

$$= \frac{3}{10}$$

$$= 30\%$$

The rate of discount was 30%.

Practice

Directions: Solve the following problems and blacken the space at the right under the number which corresponds to the one you have selected as the correct answer.

1. The list price of a coat was $120. Mr. Barr bought the coat at a discount of 10%. The net price of the coat was

    (1) $132   (4) $118
    (2) $12   (5) $100
    (3) $108   **1.** ① ② ③ ④ ⑤

2. A men's store advertises a shirt that usually sells for $16.00 at a special price of $12.00. The rate of discount is

    (1) $33\frac{1}{3}$%   (4) 40%
    (2) 25%   (5) 35%
    (3) 20%   **2.** ① ② ③ ④ ⑤

3. A radio set is sold at a discount of $12\frac{1}{2}$%. If the discount amounts to $6, the list price of the radio set is

    (1) $42   (4) $50
    (2) $45   (5) $48
    (3) $54   **3.** ① ② ③ ④ ⑤

4. An electric toaster has a list price of $21. If it is sold at a discount of $33\frac{1}{3}$% the net price is

    (1) $7   (4) $25
    (2) $28   (5) $16
    (3) $14   **4.** ① ② ③ ④ ⑤

5. The net price of a watch was $40 after a discount of 20%. The list price of the watch was

    (1) $50   (4) $35.20
    (2) $30   (5) $45
    (3) $48   **5.** ① ② ③ ④ ⑤

Answers

1. **3**   2. **2**   3. **5**   4. **3**   5. **1**

Sometimes a manufacturer will allow a **trade discount** and an additional discount on top of the trade discount. Two or more discounts are called **successive discounts**.

EXAMPLE

Mr. Boyd bought a table from a dealer. The list price was $180, and he was allowed a discount of 15%. In addition, he received a 2% discount for payment within 10 days. How much did Mr. Boyd pay for the table?

$$
\begin{array}{ll}
\$180 & \text{list price} \\
\times 0.15 & \text{rate of discount} \\
\hline
900 & \\
180 & \\
\hline
\$27.00 & \text{amount of discount}
\end{array}
$$

$$
\begin{array}{ll}
\$180.00 & \text{list price} \\
-27.00 & \text{amount of discount} \\
\hline
\$153.00 & \text{cost price}
\end{array}
$$

When we compute the second discount, we base it on the price after the first discount is taken off.

$$
\begin{array}{ll}
\$153 & \text{cost price} \\
\times 0.02 & \text{rate of discount} \\
\hline
\$3.06 & \text{discount for early payment}
\end{array}
$$

$$
\begin{array}{ll}
\$153.00 & \text{cost price} \\
-3.06 & \text{discount for early payment} \\
\hline
\$149.94 & \text{actual payment}
\end{array}
$$

Practice

Directions: Solve the following problems and blacken the space at the right under the number which corresponds to the one you have selected as the correct answer.

1. Mr. Mack bought a television set. The list price was $400. He was allowed successive discounts of 10% and 5%. How much did Mr. Mack actually pay for the television?

   (1) $340   (4) $342
   (2) $350   (5) $324
   (3) $352

   1. ① ② ③ ④ ⑤

2. Mr. Drew bought a shipment of books. The list price of the books was $180. If Mr. Drew was allowed discounts of 15% and 5%, how much did he actually pay for the books?

(1) $153
(2) $171
(3) $144

(4) $150
(5) $145.35

2. ① ② ③ ④ ⑤

3. On a purchase of $500, how much is saved by taking discounts of 20% and 10%, rather than discounts of 10% and 15%?

(1) $40
(2) $23.50
(3) $22.50

(4) $32.50
(5) $35

3. ① ② ③ ④ ⑤

4. Mr. Benson bought a boat which had a list price of $120. He was allowed a $12\frac{1}{2}$% discount and an additional 2% discount for cash. How much did Mr. Benson pay for the boat?

(1) $102.90
(2) $103.90
(3) $112.90

(4) $98.90
(5) $105

4. ① ② ③ ④ ⑤

Answers

1. **4**   2. **5**   3. **3**   4. **1**

When a businessman decides upon the price at which to sell an article, he must consider a number of items. First, the cost of the article is noted. Then the businessman must consider such items as rent, sales help salaries, and other expenses. This is called **overhead**. Any amount left over after taking account of cost and overhead is the **profit**. Thus, we have

Selling Price = Cost + Overhead + Profit

EXAMPLE

One week the Town Shoe Shop's sales amounted to $1,590. The merchandise sold cost $820, and the overhead was 20% of the sales. What was the profit?

$$20\% = 0.20$$
The overhead was $1,590 \times 0.20 = \$318$.

To obtain the profit, we must subtract the sum of the cost and the overhead from the selling price.

$820	cost of merchandise
+318	overhead
$1,138	cost + overhead
$1,590	selling price
−1,138	cost + overhead
$ 452	profit

The profit was $452.

Practice

Directions: Solve the following problems and blacken the space at the right under the number which corresponds to the one you have selected as the correct answer.

1. The cost of a chair is $68. The overhead is $10, and the profit is $18. The selling price is

   (1) $77.50   (4) $96
   (2) $86.50   (5) $92
   (3) $95   **1.** ① ② ③ ④ ⑤

2. A merchant buys lawn mowers at $43.50. He sells them at retail for $75. If his overhead is 12% of the selling price, his profit was

   (1) $9   (4) $61.50
   (2) $22.50   (5) $31.50
   (3) $23.50   **2.** ① ② ③ ④ ⑤

3. A merchant bought a shipment of cameras at a cost of $1,600 and sold the shipment for $2,500. If his profit was 25% of the cost of the shipment, his overhead expenses were

   (1) $900   (4) $500

   (2) $400   (5) $4,100

   (3) $650   **3.** ① ② ③ ④ ⑤

4. Raincoats cost a dealer $25 each. He plans to sell the raincoats at a profit of 30% on the cost. If his overhead on each sale is $2, the selling price of the raincoats is

   (1) $32.50   (4) $7.50

   (2) $30.50   (5) $35.10

   (3) $34.50   **4.** ① ② ③ ④ ⑤

5. The receipts of the Village Cafeteria for one week was $4,250. The cost of the merchandise sold was $1,560 and the overhead was 34% of the receipts. The profit was

   (1) $3,005   (4) $1,545

   (2) $1,245   (5) $1,255

   (3) $1,445   **5.** ① ② ③ ④ ⑤

Answers

1. **4**   2. **2**   3. **4**   4. **3**   5. **2**

We are often interested in finding the percent of increase or decrease.

EXAMPLE

The price of a bus ride was increased from $1.20 to $1.35. What was the percent of increase?

$1.35   new fare

−1.20   original fare

$0.15   increase in fare

To find the percent of increase we form the following fraction

$$\frac{0.15}{1.20} \quad \frac{\text{increase in fare}}{\text{original fare}}$$

We now change this fraction to a percent, as follows

$$\frac{0.15}{1.20} = \frac{15}{120} = \frac{3}{24} = \frac{1}{8}$$

$$8\overline{)1.000}^{\,0.125}$$

The percent of increase was $12\frac{1}{2}\%$.

EXAMPLE

During the past ten years the population of a small town decreased from 1,250 to 1,000. What was the percent of decrease?

1,250	original population
−1,000	population after decrease
250	actual decrease

To find the percent of decrease we form the following fraction

$$\frac{250}{1,250} \quad \frac{\text{actual decrease}}{\text{original population}}$$

We now change this fraction to a percent, as follows

$$1,250\overline{)250.00}^{\,0.20}$$
$$\underline{250\ 0}$$
$$0$$

The percent of decrease was 20%.

Sometimes we have occasion to work with percents greater than 100%.

EXAMPLE

The profit of the X Corporation this year was 108% of its profit last year. If its profit last year was $250,000, what was its profit this year?

$250,000	profit last year
1.08	percent this year

20000 00
250000 0
$270,000.00·

Its profit this year was $270,000.

EXAMPLE

Mr. Fowler bought some stock at $40 per share. Three years later Mr. Fowler sold the stock at $90 per share. What percent of profit did Mr. Fowler make?

$90   selling price of stock per share
−40   cost of stock per share
$50   profit per share

$$\frac{50}{40} \quad \frac{\text{profit per share}}{\text{original cost per share}}$$

$$
\begin{array}{r}
1.25 \\
40\overline{)50.00} \\
\underline{40} \\
100 \\
\underline{80} \\
200 \\
\underline{200}
\end{array}
$$

Mr. Fowler made a profit of 125%.

Practice

Directions: Solve the following problems and blacken the space at the right under the number which corresponds to the one you have selected as the correct answer:

1. A man bought a house for $40,000. Eight years later he sold the house for $64,000. What percent of profit did he make?

    (1) 40%   (4) 60%
    (2) $37\frac{1}{2}$%   (5) 75%
    (3) 50%

1. ① ② ③ ④ ⑤

2. During a sale an overcoat was reduced from $120 to $102. What was the percent of reduction?

    (1) 18%   (4) 12%
    (2) 15%   (5) 16%
    (3) 50%

2. ① ② ③ ④ ⑤

3. A dealer sold a watch at 130% of his cost. If the sale price was $39, how much did the watch cost the dealer?

(1) $5.70
(2) $11.70
(3) $16.50

(4) $30
(5) $89.70

3. ① ② ③ ④ ⑤

4. The price of a pound of coffee increased from $1.40 to $3.50. What was the percent of increase?

(1) 250%
(2) 150%
(3) 125%

(4) 140%
(5) 200%

4. ① ② ③ ④ ⑤

5. Mr. Thorne's salary was $210 per week. He received a promotion and his salary rose to $375 per week. The percent of increase of his salary, to the nearest percent, is

(1) 79%
(2) 80%
(3) 78%

(4) 179%
(5) 178%

5. ① ② ③ ④ ⑤

6. $137\frac{1}{2}\%$ of what number is 55?

(1) 50
(2) 39
(3) 40

(4) 45
(5) 42

6. ① ② ③ ④ ⑤

Answers

1. **4**   2. **2**   3. **4**   4. **2**   5. **1**   6. **3**

I. H. Insurance

H-1

The amount of money paid for insurance is called the **premium**. It is usually paid annually. On many types of insurance the premium rate is stated as so many dollars per $100 or per $1,000 of insurance bought.

There are several types of life insurance sold. The ordinary life policy provides that the person buying the insurance continues to pay a premium for many years to come although dividends may reduce the premium as time goes on. The twenty-payment life policy provides that the person insured will pay the premium over a period of 20 years. The endowment policy provides that a person will pay premiums for a stated number of years. At the end of the period, he or she will receive a lump sum. During the period of the policy, he or she is protected by insurance. The rates are determined by the insurance company and given to the agent in tabular form. For example, the following figures are a portion of such a table.

Age in Years	Ordinary Life Premium per $1,000 of Insurance	Twenty-Payment Life Premium per $1,000 of Insurance	Endowment Premium per $1,000 of Insurance
20	$17.50	$23.40	$26.50
25	19.75	25.60	29.10
30	22.60	29.80	34.40
35	25.40	34.75	38.50
40	30.20	40.50	43.10

EXAMPLE

At the age of 30, a man buys a twenty-payment life policy for $7,500. What is his annual premium?

The table indicates that at age 30 the rate is $29.80 per $1,000. In 7,500 there are 7.5 thousands. His annual premium is 7.5 × $29.80 = $223.50.

Practice

Directions: Solve the following problems and blacken the space at the right under the number which corresponds to the one you have selected as the correct answer.

1. The annual premium rate on $6,500 worth of an ordinary life insurance policy is $28.24 per $1,000. The annual premium is

    (1) $18.35   (4) $1,835.50
    (2) $173.55   (5) $184.55
    (3) $183.56   **1.** ① ② ③ ④ ⑤

2. A house is insured against fire for 70% of its value. If the house has a value of $48,000 and the premium rate is $2.30 per $1,000, the annual premium is

    (1) $772.80   (4) $77.08
    (2) $77.28   (5) $75.08
    (3) $75.28   **2.** ① ② ③ ④ ⑤

3. A car is insured for fire and theft for $5,700. If the annual premium rate is $1.04 per $100, the annual premium is

(1) $59.28   (4) $60.32
(2) $79.80   (5) $79.28
(3) $58.24

3. ① ② ③ ④ ⑤

4. The annual premium rate for a twenty-payment life policy is $36.40 per $1,000. The total amount paid in premiums over a twenty-year period for a $6,500 policy is

(1) $236.60   (4) $6,532
(2) $573.20   (5) $4,732
(3) $4,532

4. ① ② ③ ④ ⑤

5. The annual premium on a fire insurance policy for $12,000 is $22.80. The premium rate per $100 is

(1) $1.90   (4) $37.46
(2) $3.74   (5) $0.29
(3) $0.19

5. ① ② ③ ④ ⑤

Answers

1. **3**   2. **2**   3. **1**   4. **5**   5. **3**

I. I. Investments

I-1

The most common form of investment is the placement of money in a savings bank where it draws interest. In order to compute interest, we use the following formula.

$$\boxed{\text{Interest} = \text{Principal} \times \text{Rate} \times \text{Time}}$$

which is often written

$$I = P \times R \times T, \text{ or } I = PRT$$

The principal is the amount invested, the annual rate is the percent of the principal given to the investor each year, and the time is stated in years.

EXAMPLE

What is the interest on $1,200 at $4\frac{1}{2}$% for 9 months?

$$I = PRT$$

In this case,
$$\begin{cases} P = 1{,}200 \\ R = \dfrac{4\frac{1}{2}}{100} \\ T = \dfrac{9}{12} \text{ or } \dfrac{3}{4} \end{cases}$$

Therefore, $\qquad I = 1{,}200 \times \dfrac{4\frac{1}{2}}{100} \times \dfrac{3}{4}$

Then, if you multiply the numerator and the denominator of

$$\frac{4\frac{1}{2}}{100} \text{ by 2, you have } \frac{9}{200}.$$

$$I = 1{,}200 \times \frac{9}{200} \times \frac{3}{4}$$

$$I = \overset{3}{\cancel{1{,}200}} \times \frac{9}{\underset{1}{\cancel{200}}} \times \frac{3}{\underset{2}{\cancel{4}}} = \frac{81}{2} \text{ or } 40\frac{1}{2}$$

The interest is $40.50. If the interest is added to the principal we have the **amount**. In this case, the amount is $1,200 + $40.50, or $1,240.50.

Many banks **compound interest** every three months. That is, they add the interest to the principal at the end of three months. Then they compute interest for the next three months on an increased principal. This computation is made from tables. Interest that is not compounded is called **simple interest**.

A corporation is owned by stockholders who own **shares of stock**. Many such shares are traded on a stock exchange and are listed in the newspapers with current prices. For example,

American Telephone—63
United States Steel—$48\frac{1}{2}$

Stocks such as these pay dividends based upon the earnings of the company.

A corporation may borrow money by selling **bonds** to the public. Bonds carry a fixed rate of interest and are issued for a certain number of years. At the **maturity date** of the bond the corporation pays back the borrowed amount to the bondholder. Thus, a shareholder is a part owner of a company but a bondholder is a creditor.

EXAMPLE

Mr. Black owns 45 shares of stock in Company A. The stock pays an annual dividend of $1.60 per share. How much does Mr. Black receive in dividends per year?

To obtain the amount of dividends we multiply 45 by $1.60.

$$45 \times 1.60 = \$72.00$$

Mr. Black receives $72 in dividends.

EXAMPLE

Mr. Glenn owns six $1,000 bonds that pay $8\frac{1}{2}$% interest each year. How much does Mr. Glenn receive in interest each year?

This is a problem in computing simple interest. The principal is $6 \times \$1,000$ or $6,000, the rate is $8\frac{1}{2}$% and the period is 1 year.

$$\text{Interest} = 6,000 \times \frac{8\frac{1}{2}}{100} \times 1$$

$$= 6,000 \times \frac{17}{200} \times 1$$

$$= \overset{30}{6,000} \times \frac{17}{200_1} \times 1 = 510$$

Mr. Glenn receives $510 in interest.

Practice

Directions: Solve the following problems and blacken the space at the right under the number which corresponds to the one you have selected as the correct answer.

1. Simple interest on $2,400 at $4\frac{1}{2}$% for 3 years is

    (1) $288   (4) $324

    (2) $32.40   (5) $314

    (3) $3,240   **1.** ① ② ③ ④ ⑤

2. Mr. Payne borrowed $5,200 from a friend for 1 year and 3 months. He agreed to pay $5\frac{1}{2}$% simple interest on the loan. The amount of money that he paid back at the end of the loan period was

    (1) $5,553.50   (4) $4,842.50

    (2) $357.50   (5) $5,000

    (3) $5,557.50   **2.** ① ② ③ ④ ⑤

3. Mrs. Holden kept $3,800 in a savings bank for 9 months at 5% simple interest. The interest on her money was

    (1) $142.50   (4) $1.43

    (2) $285   (5) $1,425

    (3) $3,942.50   **3.** ① ② ③ ④ ⑤

4. Mrs. Moss bought 80 shares of X Corporation at $28\frac{3}{4}$ and sold the shares a year later at $31\frac{1}{2}$. Her profit, before paying commission, was

    (1) $22   (4) $180

    (2) $220   (5) $242

    (3) $140   **4.** ① ② ③ ④ ⑤

5. Mr. Kern owns 120 shares of Y Corporation. The corporation declared a dividend of $1.35 per share. The amount Mr. Kern received in dividends was

    (1) $16.20   (4) $162

    (2) $121.35   (5) $1,620

    (3) $135   **5.** ① ② ③ ④ ⑤

6. Mr. Cooper owns 280 shares of Z Corporation. The corporation pays a quarterly dividend of $0.35 per share. The amount Mr. Cooper receives in dividends for the year is

    (1) $98   (4) $196

    (2) $9.80   (5) $280

    (3) $392   **6.** ① ② ③ ④ ⑤

7. Mrs. Ross owns eight $1,000 bonds that pay $8\frac{1}{2}\%$ interest each year. The amount of interest Mrs. Ross receives each year is

    (1) $645   (4) $640

    (2) $680   (5) $85

    (3) $68   **7.** ① ② ③ ④ ⑤

8. Mr. Dolan borrows $960 at $7\frac{1}{2}\%$ for 3 months. The total amount that he will have to repay is

    (1) $1,032   (4) $978

    (2) $942   (5) $967.50

    (3) $1,140   **8.** ① ② ③ ④ ⑤

Answers

1. **4**   2. **3**   3. **1**   4. **2**   5. **4**   6. **3**   7. **2**   8. **4**

I. J. Taxation

J-1

We ordinarily pay many kinds of taxes. In this section we will consider the more common types of taxes.

Many states in the United States have a **sales tax** on articles bought at retail. This may be 3%, 4%, 5% or a higher percent of the retail price of an article.

EXAMPLE

Mrs. Horn buys a small rug for $39.95. If she has to pay a sales tax of 3%, what is the total cost of the rug?

$$3\% \text{ of } \$39.95 = 0.03 \times \$39.95 = \$1.1985$$

In a case such as this the amount of tax is rounded off to the nearest penny. In this case, the tax is $1.20. Mrs. Horn must pay $39.95 + $1.20, or $41.15.

A homeowner must pay a **real estate tax**. This tax is based upon the assessed valuation of the home. The assessed valuation of a home is determined by town or city authorities. The tax rate may be expressed as a percent or in the form "$4.70 per $100." In many localities, there is a separate school tax which is also based on the assessed valuation of the home.

EXAMPLE

Mr. Martin's home is assessed at $43,500. His realty tax is $3.89 per $100, and his school tax is $1.09 per $100. What is Mr. Martin's total tax on his home?

We note that there are 435 hundreds in $43,500 since 43,500 = 435 × 100.

$$\text{The realty tax is } 435 \times 3.89 = \$1,692.15$$
$$\text{The school tax is } 435 \times 1.09 = \ +474.15$$

Total tax $2,166.30

The federal government and most state governments levy an **income tax**. Every person or business with an income above a certain minimum amount must file a tax return. The tax is based upon taxable income which is obtained after certain allowable deductions are taken off the gross income. For federal income taxes and some state income taxes, employers are required to withhold part of a worker's wages. Employers are also required to deduct a certain amount for social security taxes. After all deductions are made, the amount the employee gets is called "take-home pay."

EXAMPLE

Mr. Dean's weekly salary is $285. Each week his employer deducts 5.9% of his salary for social security. He also deducts $15.70 for his federal withholding tax. What is Mr. Dean's weekly take-home pay?

5.9% of $285 = $16.82
Total deductions = $16.82 + $15.70 = $32.52
Mr. Dean's take-home pay is $285 − $32.52 = $252.48.

EXAMPLE

Mr. Stark earns $16,400 per year. In paying his tax, he has allowable deductions of $3,750. On his state tax he pays 2% on the first $3,000 of taxable income, 3% on the next $3,000 of taxable income and 4% on the balance of his income. What is his state tax?

Mr. Stark's taxable income:
$$\begin{array}{ll} \$16,400 & \text{(Gross income)} \\ \underline{-3,750} & \text{(Allowable deductions)} \\ \$12,650 & \text{(Taxable income)} \end{array}$$

Tax on first $3,000:
$$\begin{array}{l} \$3,000 \\ \underline{\times 0.02} \\ \$\quad 60 \end{array}$$

Tax on next $3,000:
$$\begin{array}{l} \$3,000 \\ \underline{\times 0.03} \\ \$\quad 90 \end{array}$$

Balance:
$$\begin{array}{ll} \$12,650 & \\ \underline{-6,000} & \text{(Taxed income)} \\ \$\ 6,650 & \end{array}$$

Tax on $6,650:
$$\begin{array}{l} \$6,650 \\ \underline{\times 0.04} \\ \$\ 266 \end{array}$$

Total Tax =
$$\begin{array}{l} \$60 \\ 90 \\ \underline{+266} \\ \$416 \end{array}$$

Practice

Directions: Solve the following problems and blacken the space at the right under the number which corresponds to the one you have selected as the correct answer.

1. Mr. Minor buys an overcoat for $137.50. If he must pay a sales tax of 3%, the total cost of the coat is

   (1) $178.80   (4) $133.37
   (2) $141.63   (5) $141.03
   (3) $137.92   **1.** ① ② ③ ④ ⑤

2. On a purchase of a table for $64, Mrs. Morton paid a sales tax of $2.56. The rate of sales tax was

   (1) 3%   (4) $2\frac{1}{2}$%
   (2) $3\frac{1}{2}$% (5) 4%
   (3) 2%   **2.** ① ② ③ ④ ⑤

3. Mr. Powell's home is assessed at $36,500. The realty tax rate is $3.97 per $100. Mr. Powell's realty tax is

   (1) $144.91   (4) $14,490.50
   (2) $1,439.05   (5) $145
   (3) $1,449.05   **3.** ① ② ③ ④ ⑤

4. Mrs. Olson bought a house for $32,000. It was assessed at 80% of her purchase price. If the school tax is $1.93 per $100, Mrs. Olson's school tax was

   (1) $494.08   (4) $49.41
   (2) $617.60   (5) $515.28
   (3) $61.76   **4.** ① ② ③ ④ ⑤

5. Mr. Emerson sets aside $80 per month to cover his realty and school taxes. His home is assessed at $29,400. His realty tax is $3.14 per $100, and his school tax is $1.19 per $100. The amount he must add at the end of the year to cover both taxes is

   (1) $303.02   (4) $313.02
   (2) $213.02   (5) $473.02
   (3) $31.32   **5.** ① ② ③ ④ ⑤

6. Mrs. Howe has a gross income of $9,800 per year. Her deductions amount to $3,650. She pays state income taxes at the rate of 2% on the first $1,000 of taxable income, 3% on the next $2,000 of taxable income and 4% on the balance. Her total tax is

    (1) $146   (4) $140

    (2) $126   (5) $137.50

    (3) $206   **6.** ① ② ③ ④ ⑤

7. Mr. Robinson earns $235 per week. Each week his employer deducts 5.9% of his salary for social security. He also deducts $14.85 for his federal withholding tax. Mr. Robinson's weekly take-home pay is

    (1) $221.13   (4) $249.85

    (2) $206.28   (5) $205.28

    (3) $210.15   **7.** ① ② ③ ④ ⑤

8. Mrs. Tobin's taxable income is $8,900. On this, she must pay 2% on the first $3,000, 3% on the next $3,000, and 4% on the balance for state income tax. During the year her employer had withheld $4.50 per week. To settle her tax bill at the end of the year, Mrs. Tobin had to pay an additional

    (1) $32   (4) $226

    (2) $31   (5) $225

    (3) $59   **8.** ① ② ③ ④ ⑤

Answers

1. **2**   2. **5**   3. **3**   4. **1**   5. **4**   6. **3**   7. **2**   8. **1**

II. ALGEBRA

II. A. Fundamentals

A-1

As we have seen earlier, we frequently use letters to represent numbers in algebra. For example, in the formula

$$I = P \times R \times T$$

I represents interest, *P* represents principal, *R* represents rate, and *T* represents time.

This is done because it enables us to solve many kinds of problems. That is, *P* may be \$5,000 in one problem and \$786 in another problem. In indicating multiplication in arithmetic we also use the $\times$ sign. For example, 5×6. In indicating multiplication in algebra, three methods are used:

1. Use the multiplication symbol. For example, $P \times R$.
2. Use a raised dot. For example, $P \cdot R$.
3. Place the numbers and letters next to each other. For example, $7a$ means $7 \times a$ or $7 \cdot a$; bc means $b \times c$ or $b \cdot c$.

For other operations we use the same symbols as are used in arithmetic. In order to use algebra effectively, you must learn how to translate from ordinary language into symbols and letters.

EXAMPLE

John is x years old. How old will he be 7 years from now?

$$x + 7$$

EXAMPLE

An apple costs a cents. What is the cost of 6 apples?

($6 \times a$, or $6 \cdot a$, or $6a$ [$6a$ is preferred])

EXAMPLE

Alice weighed y pounds a year ago. Since then she has lost 9 pounds. What is her present weight?

$$y - 9$$

EXAMPLE

Take a number z. Increase it by 2. Multiply the result by 6.

$6(z + 2)$. Notice that the number represented by $(z + 2)$ is to be multiplied by 6. The answer might also be written $(z + 2)6$.

Practice

Directions: Solve the following problems and blacken the space at the right under the number which corresponds to the one you have selected as the correct answer.

1. A sweater costs \$18. The cost of c sweaters is

    (1) $18 + c$ (4) $18c$

    (2) $18 \div c$ (5) $c - 18$

    (3) $c \div 18$ **1.** ① ② ③ ④ ⑤

2. Fred is x years old. Bill is 4 years younger. Bill's age is

    (1) $x + 4$ (4) $4x$

    (2) $x - 4$ (5) $4x - 4$

    (3) $4 - x$ **2.** ① ② ③ ④ ⑤

3. A car travels y miles per hour. The distance covered by the car in z hours is

    (1) $y + z$ (4) $y \div z$

    (2) $y - z$ (5) $z \div y$

    (3) yz **3.** ① ② ③ ④ ⑤

4. Bob had \$15 and spent x dollars. The amount he had left was

    (1) $x - 15$ (4) $x \div 15$

    (2) $15x$ (5) $15 - x$

    (3) $15 \div x$ **4.** ① ② ③ ④ ⑤

5. If 12 eggs cost a cents, the cost of one egg is

    (1) $12a$ (4) $12 + a$

    (2) $12/a$ (5) $a - 12$

    (3) $a/12$ **5.** ① ② ③ ④ ⑤

6. Paul bought 3 ties at x dollars each. The change that he received in dollars from a \$20 bill was

    (1) $3x$ (4) $20 - 3x$

    (2) $20 + 3x$ (5) $3x \div 20$

    (3) $3x - 20$ **6.** ① ② ③ ④ ⑤

7. Mr. Barry bought a suit for y dollars. The sales tax rate on the purchase was 3%. The sales tax was

    (1) $0.03y$ (4) $y \div 3$

    (2) $3y$ (5) $y + 0.03y$

    (3) $0.03 + y$ **7.** ① ② ③ ④ ⑤

8. Bill had *y* dollars. He bought *a* articles at *b* dollars each. The number of dollars Bill had left was

(1) $ab - y$ (4) y/ab

(2) $ab + y$ (5) aby

(3) $y - ab$ **8.** ① ② ③ ④ ⑤

Answers

1. **4**   2. **2**   3. **3**   4. **5**   5. **3**   6. **4**   7. **1**   8. **3**

II. B. Exponents and Evaluations

B-1

There are times when we wish to multiply a number by itself. Of course, if we wish to multiply 7 by itself, we can write 7 × 7. However, in modern science where we may have occasion to multiply a number by itself many times, it becomes awkward to write such numbers as 7 × 7 × 7 × 7 × 7 × 7 × 7 × 7 × 7. Instead, we use a shortcut and write the product of nine sevens as 7^9. In this case, 9 is known as an exponent and 7 is called the base.

EXAMPLES

6^3 means $6 \times 6 \times 6$.

a^5 means $a \times a \times a \times a \times a$.

$3b^4$ menas $3 \times b \times b \times b \times b$.

We often wish to find the numerical value of an algebraic expression when we know the numerical value assigned to each letter of the expression. The following examples show how this is done.

EXAMPLE

Find the numerical value of $5x + 3y - 7z$ when $x = 6$, $y = 4$, and $z = 1$.

$$5x + 3y - 7z = (5 \cdot 6) + (3 \cdot 4) - (7 \cdot 1)$$
$$= 30 + 12 - 7$$
$$= 35$$

EXAMPLE

Find the value of $4a^3 - 2b + 9c^2$ when $a = 5$, $b = 3$, and $c = 2$.

$$4a^3 - 2b + 9c^2 = (4 \cdot 5^3) - (2 \cdot 3) + (9 \cdot 2^2)$$
$$= (4 \cdot 125) - (6) + (9 \cdot 4)$$
$$= (500) - (6) + (36)$$
$$= 530$$

EXAMPLE

Find the value of $5(x^3 - 2y^2)$ when $x = 4$ and $y = 3$.

$$5(x^3 - 2y^2) = 5(4^3 - 2 \cdot 3^2) = 5(64 - 18)$$
$$= 5 \cdot 46$$
$$= 230$$

Practice

Directions: Solve the following problems and blacken the space at the right under the number which corresponds to the one you have selected as the correct answer.

In the following examples, $x = 5$, $y = 4$, $z = 3$, $a = 2$, and $b = 1$.

1. The value of $2x^3 + 3y$ is

    (1) 112   (4) 262

    (2) 32   (5) 98

    (3) 47   **1.** ① ② ③ ④ ⑤

2. The value of $3x + 5a - 7b$ is

    (1) 18   (4) 20

    (2) 17   (5) 37

    (3) 15   **2.** ① ② ③ ④ ⑤

3. The value of $3ab + x^2y$ is

    (1) 9   (4) 15

    (2) 32   (5) 106

    (3) 11   **3.** ① ② ③ ④ ⑤

4. The value of $2x^2 - y^2 + 5ab$ is

(1) 54   (4) 92
(2) 94   (5) 78
(3) 44

4. ① ② ③ ④ ⑤

5. The value of $3x^2y^3z$ is

(1) 8,100   (4) 900
(2) 14,400   (5) 1,800
(3) 96

5. ① ② ③ ④ ⑤

6. The value of $\dfrac{y^2}{a^2}$ is

(1) 8   (4) 4
(2) 2   (5) 36
(3) 16

6. ① ② ③ ④ ⑤

7. The value of $\dfrac{a^3}{y} + 2xz$ is

(1) 23   (4) 32
(2) 31   (5) 54
(3) 9

7. ① ② ③ ④ ⑤

8. The value of $\dfrac{4x^2}{5a} + 3y^2 - z^3$ is

(1) 21   (4) 46
(2) 29   (5) 31
(3) 32

8. ① ② ③ ④ ⑤

Answers

1. **4** 2. **1** 3. **5** 4. **3** 5. **2** 6. **4** 7. **4** 8. **5**

II. C. Formulas

C-1

Mr. Wells had a garden 60 feet long and 40 feet wide. He wished to fence in the garden. How many feet of fencing did he need?

We can see that Mr. Wells needed two lengths of 60 feet each and two widths of 40 feet each.

Thus, he needed $(2 \times 60) + (2 \times 40)$, or $120 + 80 = 200$ feet.

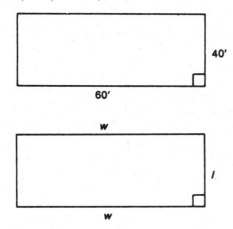

Now, suppose that we wish to find a formula to find the distance around the **rectangle** (called "the **perimeter**"). A rectangle is a figure having four sides and four right angles. If we represent the perimeter by P, the length by l, and the width by w,

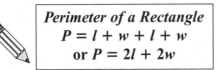

Perimeter of a Rectangle
$$P = l + w + l + w$$
$$\text{or } P = 2l + 2w$$

We can write this as $P = 2(l + w)$.
$P = 2l + 2w$, or $P = 2(l + w)$, is an example of a **formula** in mathematics.

EXAMPLE

The formula $C = 40 + 8(n - 3)$ gives the cost of borrowing a book from a circulating library. The minimum number of days is 3 and the minimum cost is 40 cents. In this formula, $C = $ cost, in cents, and $n = $ the number of days for which the book is borrowed. What is the cost of borrowing a book for 7 days?

$$C = 40 + 8(n - 3)$$
$$C = 40 + 8(7 - 3)$$
$$C = 40 + 8(4)$$
$$C = 40 + 32 = 72 \text{ cents}$$

Practice

Directions: Solve the following problems and blacken the space at the right under the number which corresponds to the one you have selected as the correct answer.

1. Mr. Dale wishes to fence in a rectangular lawn which is 60 feet long and 30 feet wide. He uses the formula $P = 2(l + w)$ to obtain the result. The perimeter, in feet, is

   (1) 90   (4) 180
   (2) 120   (5) 200
   (3) 150   **1.** ① ② ③ ④ ⑤

2. The formula $A = \dfrac{a+b+c}{3}$ is used to find the average

   (*A*) of three numbers *a*, *b*, and *c*. The average of 95, 119, and 104 is

   (1) 108   (4) $104\frac{2}{3}$
   (2) 106   (5) 110
   (3) 160   **2.** ① ② ③ ④ ⑤

3. The formula $C = 80 + 15(n - 4)$ is used to find the cost, *C*, of a taxi ride where *n* represents the number of $\frac{1}{4}$ miles of the ride. The cost of a taxi ride of $2\frac{3}{4}$ miles is

   (1) $0.95   (4) $1.85
   (2) $3   (5) $2
   (3) $1.65   **3.** ① ② ③ ④ ⑤

4. The formula $C = 72m + 32h$ is used to find the daily labor cost, in dollars, of a job in carpentry. The letter *m* represents the number of master carpenters; *h* represents the number of helpers. (Note that a master carpenter earns $72 per day and a helper earns $32 per day.) On a certain job, 6 master carpenters are used and 4 helpers are used. The daily labor cost is

   (1) $480   (4) $600
   (2) $550   (5) $560
   (3) $650   **4.** ① ② ③ ④ ⑤

5. The formula for the relationship between the length (L) and width (W) of a certain flag is $L = 1.8W$. A flag has a width of 5 feet. Its length is

(1) 2.3 feet   (4) 1.3 feet

(2) 9 feet   (5) 8 feet

(3) 90 feet

5. ① ② ③ ④ ⑤

6. The weight of an adult is given by the formula $W = \frac{11}{2}(h - 60) + 110$ where W = weight in pounds and h = height in inches. If Mr. Conrad is 68 inches tall, he should weigh, in pounds,

(1) 144   (4) 174

(2) 164   (5) 184

(3) 154

6. ① ② ③ ④ ⑤

Answers

1. **4**   2. **2**   3. **4**   4. **5**   5. **2**   6. **3**

II. D. Solving Equations

D-1

The ability to solve equations is important because it enables us to solve many different types of problems. In this section, you will learn how to solve some of the simpler kinds of equations. In a later section you will apply these skills in problem solving.

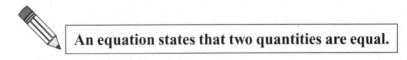 **An equation states that two quantities are equal.**

Consider the equation

$$3x + 2 = 20$$

This tells us that $3x + 2$ and 20 name the same number. If this is so, then x must represent the number 6 since

$$3 \times 6 + 2 = 20$$

And 6 is the only number which will replace x and make $3x + 2$ equal 20. The number 6, which makes the statement $3x + 2 = 20$ true, is called the **root of the equation** and is said to satisfy the equation, or to **balance** the equation.

Practice

Directions: Solve the following problems and blacken the space at the right under the number which corresponds to the one you have selected as the correct answer.

In each case, select the root of the equation.

1. $x + 2 = 9$

    (1) 5   (4) 3
    (2) 9   (5) 10
    (3) 7   **1.** ① ② ③ ④ ⑤

2. $x - 3 = 5$

    (1) 5   (4) 10
    (2) 3   (5) 8
    (3) 2   **2.** ① ② ③ ④ ⑤

3. $2x = 10$

    (1) 8   (4) $\frac{1}{5}$
    (2) 5   (5) 9
    (3) 20   **3.** ① ② ③ ④ ⑤

4. $\frac{x}{3} = 4$

    (1) 12   (4) 1
    (2) $\frac{4}{3}$ (5) 6
    (3) $\frac{3}{4}$ **4.** ① ② ③ ④ ⑤

5. $2x + 1 = 7$

    (1) 4   (4) 3
    (2) $3\frac{1}{2}$ (5) 6
    (3) 5   **5.** ① ② ③ ④ ⑤

6. $2x - 1 = 9$

    (1) 10   (4) 4
    (2) 8   (5) 3
    (3) 5   **6.** ① ② ③ ④ ⑤

7. $\frac{x}{2} + 3 = 7$

    (1) 4   (4) $2\frac{1}{2}$
    (2) 8   (5) 20
    (3) $1\frac{1}{2}$ **7.** ① ② ③ ④ ⑤

8. $\frac{x}{3} - 1 = 5$

    (1) 18   (4) 6
    (2) 12   (5) 15
    (3) 2

8. ① ② ③ ④ ⑤

9. $\frac{2x}{5} + 1 = 9$

    (1) 8   (4) 6
    (2) 50   (5) 4
    (3) 20

9. ① ② ③ ④ ⑤

10. $\frac{3x}{4} - 2 = 1$

    (1) 5   (4) 4
    (2) 6   (5) 9
    (3) 12

10. ① ② ③ ④ ⑤

11. $2x + 3 = 10$

    (1) 4   (4) $7\frac{1}{2}$
    (2) $6\frac{1}{2}$ (5) 5
    (3) $3\frac{1}{2}$

11. ① ② ③ ④ ⑤

12. $3x - 4 = 6$

    (1) $3\frac{1}{3}$ (4) $3\frac{1}{2}$
    (2) $\frac{2}{3}$ (5) 7
    (3) 2

12. ① ② ③ ④ ⑤

Answers

1. **3**	3. **2**	5. **4**	7. **2**	9. **3**	11. **3**
2. **5**	4. **1**	6. **3**	8. **1**	10. **4**	12. **1**

We will now study **systematic methods of finding the root of an equation**.

Consider the equation $x + 2 = 5$. This tells us that a certain number added to 2 will give us the result of 5. We can see that $x = 3$. Now, how can we get from

$$x + 2 = 5$$
$$\text{to } x = 3?$$

To get from $x + 2$ to x, we need only to subtract 2 from $x + 2$. Thus, $x + 2 - 2 = x$. Since $x + 2$ and 5 name the same number, we may subtract the same number from $x + 2$ and from 5 to obtain equal results.

$$x + 2 - 2 = 5 - 2$$
$$\text{or } x = 3$$

Consider the equation $x - 1 = 5$. In order to obtain x on the left side of the equation, we add 1 to $x - 1$. Since $x - 1$ and 5 name the same number, we may add 1 to both $x - 1$ and 5 to obtain equal results.

$$x - 1 + 1 = 5 + 1$$
$$\text{or } x = 6$$

Consider the equation $2x = 12$. In order to obtain x on the left side of the equation we must divide $2x$ (twice x) by 2. Since $2x$ and 12 name the same number, we divide both $2x$ and 12 by 2 to obtain equal results.

$$2x = 12$$
$$\frac{2x}{2} = \frac{12}{2}$$
$$1x, \text{ or } x = 6$$

Consider the equation $\frac{y}{3} = 4$. In order to obtain y on the left side of the equation, we must multiply $\frac{y}{3}$, or $\frac{1}{3}$ of y, by 3. Since $\frac{y}{3}$ and 4 name the same number, we multiply both $\frac{y}{3}$ and 4 to obtain equal results.

$$\frac{y}{3} = 4$$

$$3 \times \frac{y}{3} = 3 \times 4$$
$$y = 12$$

To remember these procedures, note the following.

Methods of Finding the Root of an Equation

1. Subtract when there is a sum. For example, $x + 2 - 2 = 5 - 2$.

2. Add when there is a difference. For example, $x - 1 + 1 = 5 + 1$.

3. Divide when there is a product. For example, $\dfrac{2x}{2} = \dfrac{12}{2}$.

4. Multiply when there is a quotient. For example, $3 \times \dfrac{y}{3} = 3 \times 4$.

Practice

Solve the following equations:

1. $x + 1 = 3$, $x =$ ___

2. $x - 2 = 4$, $x =$ ___

3. $3x = 12$, $x =$ ___

4. $x/2 = 5$, $x =$ ___

5. $x + 5 = 7$, $x =$ ___

6. $x - 3 = 4$, $x =$ ___

7. $5x = 10$, $x =$ ___

8. $x/4 = 2$, $x =$ ___

9. $x + 2 = 9$, $x =$ ___

10. $5x = 15$, $x =$ ___

11. $x - 2 = 9$, $x =$ ___

12. $x + 4 = 7$, $x =$ ___

13. $x/5 = 2$, $x =$ ___

14. $3x = 18$, $x =$ ___

15. $x + 9 = 11$, $x =$ ___

16. $x - 1 = 5$, $x =$ ___

17. $3x = 21$, $x =$ ___

18. $x + 4 = 7$, $x =$ ___

19. $x/4 = 3$, $x =$ ___

20. $x - 5 = 11$, $x =$ ___

Answers

1. **2**	6. **7**	11. **11**	16. **6**
2. **6**	7. **2**	12. **3**	17. **7**
3. **4**	8. **8**	13. **10**	18. **3**
4. **10**	9. **7**	14. **6**	19. **12**
5. **2**	10. **3**	15. **2**	20. **16**

D-2

Solving More Difficult Equations. In order to solve interesting problems, it is necessary to be able to solve more difficult equations.

EXAMPLE

Solve the equation $5x + 2x = 28$.

Since $5x + 2x = 7x$, we have

$$7x = 28$$
$$x = \frac{28}{7}$$
$$x = 4$$

EXAMPLE

Solve the equation $\frac{2}{3}x = 16$.

In order to obtain x on the left side, we must multiply $\frac{2}{3}x$ by $\frac{3}{2}$. Since $\frac{2}{3}x$ and 16 name the same number, we multiply both $\frac{2}{3}x$ and 16 to obtain equal results.

$$\frac{\cancel{3}}{\cancel{2}} \cdot \frac{\cancel{2}}{\cancel{3}}x = \frac{3}{2} \cdot 16$$

$$x = 24$$

EXAMPLE

Solve the equation $2x + 3 = 15$.

$$2x + 3 = 15$$
$$2x + 3 - 3 = 15 - 3$$
$$2x = 12$$
$$\frac{2x}{2} = \frac{12}{2}$$
$$x = 6$$

EXAMPLE

Solve the equation $\frac{3}{5}x - 1 = 8$.

$$\frac{3}{5}x - 1 = 8$$

$$\frac{3}{5}x - 1 + 1 = 8 + 1$$

$$\frac{3}{5}x = 9$$

$$\frac{\cancel{5}}{\cancel{3}} \cdot \frac{\cancel{3}}{\cancel{5}}x = \frac{5}{3} \cdot 9$$

$$x = 15$$

Practice

Solve the following equations:

1. $2x + 3x = 40$, $x =$ _____

2. $\frac{2}{3}x = 12$, $x =$ _____

3. $4x - 1 = 27$, $x =$ _____

4. $x/5 + 4 = 6$, $x =$ _____

5. $3x - 5 = 16$, $x =$ _____

6. $3x + 7 = 37$, $x =$ _____

7. $4x - 2 = 22$, $x =$ _____

8. $x/2 - 3 = 5$, $x =$ _____

9. $2x + x + 5 = 17$, $x =$ _____

10. $\frac{4}{5}x + 2 = 30$, $x =$ _____

11. $\frac{2}{3}x + 5 = 7$, $x =$ _____

12. $5x - 2x + 4 = 31$, $x =$ _____

13. $x/7 + 5 = 6$, $x =$ _____

14. $3x + 2x + 1 = 21$, $x =$ _____

15. $2x + x - 3 = 12$, $x =$ _____

16. $\frac{3}{4}x - 7 = 8$, $x =$ _____

Answers

1. **8**
2. **18**
3. **7**
4. **10**

6. **10**
5. **7**
7. **6**
8. **16**

9. **4**
10. **35**
12. **9**
11. **3**

13. **7**
14. **4**
15. **5**
16. **20**

II. E. Solving Word Problems

E-1

We may use equations to solve problems stated in words, such as the following.

EXAMPLE

A plumber must cut a pipe 50 inches long into two pieces so that one piece will be 12 inches longer than the other piece. Find the length of each piece.

Let x = the length of one piece
And $x + 12$ = the length of the other piece.

Since the sum of the two pieces is 50 inches, we have

$$x + x + 12 = 50$$
$$2x + 12 = 50$$
$$2x + 12 - 12 = 50 - 12$$
$$2x = 38$$
$$\frac{2x}{2} = \frac{38}{2}$$
$$x = 19$$

One piece is 19 inches long and the other piece is 31 inches long.

EXAMPLE

Divide an estate of $46,000 among three sons so that the second son gets $6,000 more than the youngest, and the eldest son gets three times as much as the youngest.

Let x = amount the youngest son gets
And $x + 6,000$ = amount the second son gets
And $3x$ = amount the eldest son gets.

$$x + x + 6,000 + 3x = 46,000$$
$$5x + 6,000 = 46,000$$
$$5x + 6,000 - 6,000 = 46,000 - 6,000$$
$$5x = 40,000$$
$$\frac{5x}{5} = \frac{40,000}{5}$$
$$x = 8,000$$

The youngest son gets $8,000.
The second son gets $8,000 + $6,000 = $14,000.
The eldest son gets 3 × $8,000 = $24,000.

EXAMPLE

Eighteen coins, consisting of nickels and dimes, have a total value of $1.25. How many dimes are there?

Let x = the number of dimes
And $18 - x$ = the number of nickels.
$10x$ = the value of the dimes
$5(18 - x)$ = the value of the nickels

$$10x + 5(18 - x) = 125$$
$$10x + 90 - 5x = 125$$
$$5x + 90 = 125$$
$$5x + 90 - 90 = 125 - 90$$
$$5x = 35$$
$$\frac{5x}{5} = \frac{35}{5}$$
$$x = 7$$

There are 7 dimes.

EXAMPLE

A dealer has some candy worth 75 cents per pound, and some candy worth 55 cents per pound. He wishes to make a mixture of 80 pounds that will sell for 60 cents per pound. How many pounds of each type of candy should he use?

Let x = the number of pounds of 75-cent candy
And $80 - x$ = the number of pounds of 55-cent candy.
$75x$ = the value of the 75-cent candy
$55(80 - x)$ = the value of the 55-cent candy
80×60, or 4,800 cents = the value of the mixture

$$75x + 55(80 - x) = 4,800$$
$$75x + 4,400 - 55x = 4,800$$
$$20x + 4,400 = 4,800$$
$$20x + 4,400 - 4,400 = 4,800 - 4,400$$
$$20x = 400$$
$$\frac{20x}{20} = \frac{400}{20}$$
$$x = 20$$

The dealer uses 20 pounds of the 75-cent candy. The dealer uses $80 - 20$, or 60 pounds, of the 55-cent candy.

EXAMPLE

An investment of $12,500, part at 8% and part at 7%, earns a yearly income of $955. Find the amount invested at each rate.

Let x = the amount invested at 8%
And $12,500 - x$ = the amount invested at 7%.
$0.08x$ = the income on the 8% investment
$0.07(12,500 - x)$ = the income on the 7% investment

$$0.08x + 0.07(12,500 - x) = 955$$
$$0.08x + 875 - 0.07x = 955$$
$$0.01x + 875 = 955$$
$$0.01x + 875 - 875 = 955 - 875$$
$$0.01x = 80$$
$$\frac{1}{100}x = 80$$
$$100\left(\frac{1}{100}x\right) = 100 \times 80$$
$$x = 8,000$$

$8,000 was invested at 8%. $12,500 - $8,000 = $4,500 was invested at 7%.

EXAMPLE

Two cars start at the same time from two cities 480 miles apart and travel toward each other. One car averages 35 miles per hour, and the other car averages 45 miles per hour. In how many hours will the two cars meet?

Let x = the number of hours it takes the two cars to meet.
   In problems involving motion, it is convenient to collect our information in a box as shown below, with the formula Rate $\times$ Time = Distance.
   Since the sum of the two distances covered is 480 miles, we have

$$35x + 45x = 480$$
$$80x = 480$$
$$\frac{80x}{80} = \frac{480}{80}$$
$$x = 6$$

The cars will meet in 6 hours.

	RATE	$\times$ TIME	= DISTANCE
FIRST CAR	35	x	$35x$
SECOND CAR	45	x	$45x$

Practice

Solve the following problems:

1. Two partners in a business earn $60,000 one year. If the senior partner's share is 3 times that of the junior partner, what is the junior partner's share? _____

2. A wooden beam is 58 inches long. A carpenter must cut the beam so that the longer part is 8 inches longer than the shorter part. How long is the shorter part? _____

3. A certain kind of concrete contains five times as much gravel as cement. How many cubic feet of each of these materials will there be in 426 cubic feet of the concrete? _____

4. The length of a field is 3 times its width. If the perimeter (distance around the field) of the field is 312 feet, what is the width of the field? _____

5. A master carpenter earns $5 more per hour than his helper. Together they earn $119 for a 7-hour job. How much does the helper earn per hour?

   _____

6. A boy has $3.75 in nickels and dimes. If he has 6 more dimes than nickels, how many dimes does he have? _____

7. Mr. Dale asked his son to deposit $495 in the bank. There were exactly 70 bills, consisting of 10-dollar bills and 5-dollar bills. Find the number of 10-dollar bills he had to deposit. _____

8. The perimeter of a triangle is 27 inches. One side is 3 inches longer than the shortest side, and the longest side is twice the length of the shortest side. What is the length of the shorter side? _____

9. The sum of two numbers is 50. If the larger one is 5 more than twice the smaller number, what is the smaller number? _____

10. A dealer wishes to mix candy worth 90 cents per pound with candy worth 65 cents per pound in order to obtain 40 pounds of candy to be sold at 75 cents per pound. How many pounds of the 90-cent candy should be use?

    _____

11. Mr. Charles invests $20,000, part at 5% and the rest at 4%. If he obtains an annual income of $920, how much does he invest at each rate?

    _____

12. Tickets at a movie house cost $2 for adults and $1 for children. For a matinee performance, 800 tickets were sold, and the receipts were $1,150. How many adult tickets were sold? _____

13. At a sale, some radio sets were sold for $50 each and the rest for $35 each. If 175 sets were sold and the receipts were $7,250, how many $50 sets were sold? _____

14. Mr. Carter invested a sum of money at 4%. He invested a second sum, $400 more than the first sum, at 6%. If the total annual income was $184, how much did he invest at each rate? _____

15. In basketball, a foul basket counts 1 point and a field basket counts 2 points. A team scored 73 points, making 8 more field baskets than foul baskets. How many foul baskets did the team make? _____

16. A sofa was marked for sale at $270. This was a discount of 25% on the original sale price. What was the original sale price? _____

17. The sum of the ages of a father and son is 62. If the father is 11 years more than twice the age of the son, how old is the son? _____

18. A boy has $4.35 in nickels and dimes. If he has 12 more dimes than nickels, how many nickels does he have? _____

19. The perimeter of a rectangular field is 204 feet. If the length is 3 feet less than 4 times the width, what is the width of the field? _____

20. A dealer wishes to mix candy selling for $1.32 per pound with candy selling for $1.20 per pound to produce a mixture of 20 pounds that will sell for $1.29 per pound. How many pounds of $1.32 candy should he use? _____

21. Two cars start at the same time to travel toward each other from points 440 miles apart. If the first car averages 42 miles per hour and the second car averages 46 miles per hour, in how many hours will they meet? _____

22. Two trains start at the same time and travel in opposite directions. The first train averages 39 miles per hour and the second train averages 43 miles per hour. In how many hours are the trains 574 miles apart? _____

23. Two trains are 800 miles apart. They start at 9:00 A.M. traveling toward each other. One train travels at an average rate of 45 miles per hour and the other train travels at an average rate of 55 miles per hour. At what time do the trains meet? _____

24. Two motorboats start at the same time from the same place and travel in opposite directions. If their rates are 12 miles per hour and 16 miles per hour respectively, in how many hours will they be 140 miles apart? _____

Answers

1. **$15,000**	13. **75 sets**
2. **25 inches**	14. **$1,600 at 4%**
3. **71 cubic feet of cement**	**$2,000 at 5%**
355 cubic feet of gravel	15. **19**
4. **39 feet**	16. **$360**
5. **$6**	17. **17**
6. **27 dimes**	18. **21 nickels**
7. **29**	19. **21 feet**
8. **6 inches**	20. **15 pounds**
9. **15**	21. **5 hours**
10. **16 pounds**	22. **7 hours**
11. **$12,000 at 5%**	23. **5:00 P.M.**
$8,000 at 4%	24. **5 hours**
12. **350 adult tickets**	

II. F. Solving Inequalities

F-1

Recall that the symbol $>$ means is greater than and that the symbol $<$ means is less than. For example, $9 > 5$ and $3 < 8$.

An **inequality** is a statement in which two quantities are unequal. Consider the inequality

$$3x + 1 > 7$$

This tells us that $3x + 1$ names a number that is greater than 7. If this is so, then x must represent a number that is greater than 2. If $x = 2$, we have $3 \cdot 2 + 1 = 7$. When $x > 2$, $3x + 1 > 7$. For example, when $x = 5$, $3x + 1 = 16$. Thus, the solution of the inequality $3x + 1 > 7$ is $x > 2$. Note that the inequality $3x + 1 > 7$ has an infinite number of solutions. For example, some solutions are 2.1, 4, $5\frac{1}{2}$, 7, and 8.67 since the replacement of x by any of these numbers will make the inequality true.

Practice

Directions: In each case, select the number which is a solution of the given inequality.

1. $2x + 3 > 11$

    (1) 4   (4) 5

    (2) 1   (5) 3

    (3) $2\frac{1}{2}$

                                      1. ① ② ③ ④ ⑤

2. $3x - 1 > 5$

    (1) 1   (4) $1\frac{1}{2}$

    (2) 2   (5) 0

    (3) 6

                                        2. ① ② ③ ④ ⑤

3. $x + 2 < 7$

    (1) 6   (4) 3

    (2) 8   (5) 10

    (3) 5

                                        3. ① ② ③ ④ ⑤

4. $2x - 3 < 5$

    (1) 2   (4) 6

    (2) 5   (5) 4

    (3) 7

                                        4. ① ② ③ ④ ⑤

5. $5x + 2 > 17$

    (1) 1   (4) 2

    (2) 3   (5) 0

    (3) 4

                                        5. ① ② ③ ④ ⑤

6. $4x - 3 < 9$

    (1) 5   (4) 7

    (2) 2   (5) 9

    (3) 4

                                        6. ① ② ③ ④ ⑤

Answers

1. **4**   2. **3**   3. **4**   4. **1**   5. **3**   6. **2**

Systematic Methods of Solving Inequalities. Consider the inequality $x + 3 > 7$. This tells us that when certain numbers are added to 3, the result is greater than 7. We can see that x must be greater than 4, or $x > 4$. Now, how can we get from

$$x + 3 > 7$$

$$\text{to } x > 4?$$

To get from $x + 3$ to x we need only to subtract 3 from $x + 3$. Since subtracting the same quantity from both members of an inequality does not change the sense of the inequality, we may subtract 3 from 7 to get the result:

$$x + 3 - 3 > 7 - 3$$

$$x > 4$$

Consider the inequality $x - 2 < 4$. In order to obtain x on the left side, we add 2 to $x - 2$. Since adding the same quantity to both members of an inequality does not change the sense of the inequality, we may add 2 to 4 to obtain the result:

$$x - 2 + 2 < 4 + 2$$

$$x < 6$$

Consider the inequality $2x < 10$. In order to obtain x on the left side of the inequality, we must divide $2x$ by 2. Since dividing both members of an inequality by a positive number does not change the sense of the inequality, we may divide 10 by 2 to obtain the result:

$$\frac{2x}{2} < \frac{10}{2}$$

$$x < 5$$

Consider the inequality $\frac{y}{3} > 2$. In order to obtain y on the left side of the inequality, we must multiply $\frac{y}{3}$ by 3. Since multiplying both members of an inequality by a positive number does not change the sense of the inequality, we may multiply 2 by 3 to obtain the result:

$$3 \times \frac{y}{3} > 3 \times 2$$

$$y > 6$$

EXAMPLE

Solve the inequality $x + 5 > 7$.

$$x + 5 > 7$$
$$x + 5 - 5 > 7 - 5$$
$$x > 2$$

EXAMPLE

Solve the inequality $y - 1 < 4$.

$$y - 1 < 4$$
$$y - 1 + 1 < 4 + 1$$
$$y < 5$$

EXAMPLE

Solve the inequality $3x < 18$.

$$3x < 18$$
$$\frac{3x}{3} < \frac{18}{3}$$
$$x < 6$$

EXAMPLE

Solve the inequality $\frac{y}{4} > 2$.

$$\frac{y}{4} > 2$$
$$4 \times \frac{y}{4} > 4 \times 2$$
$$y > 8$$

Practice

Solve the following inequalities:

1. $x + 2 > 5, x >$ _____

2. $x - 3 > 1, x >$ _____

3. $2y < 8, y <$ _____

4. $y/2 > 6, y >$ _____

5. $y - 3 < 2, y <$ _____

6. $y/4 > 3, y >$ _____

7. $x - 5 > 2, x >$ _____

8. $2y < 12, y <$ _____

9. $y + 1 < 10, y <$ _____

10. $x - 3 < 4, x <$ _____

Answers

1. $x > 3$	3. $y < 4$	5. $y < 5$	7. $x > 7$	9. $y < 9$
2. $x > 4$	4. $y > 12$	6. $y > 12$	8. $y < 6$	10. $x < 7$

F-2

Solving More Difficult Inequalities.

EXAMPLE

Solve the inequality $2y + 3 > 11$.
$$2y + 3 - 3 > 11 - 3$$
$$2y > 8$$
$$\frac{2y}{2} > \frac{8}{2}$$
$$y > 4$$

EXAMPLE

Solve the inequality $\frac{y}{4} - 1 < 5$.

$$\frac{y}{4} - 1 < 5$$
$$\frac{y}{4} - 1 + 1 < 5 + 1$$
$$\frac{y}{4} < 6$$
$$4 \times \frac{y}{4} < 4 \times 6$$
$$y < 24$$

Practice

Solve the following inequalities:

1. $2x + 1 > 7, x >$ _____

5. $y/3 - 4 > 1, y >$ _____

2. $3y - 2 < 4, y <$ _____

6. $5y + 1 < 6, y <$ _____

3. $4x - 7 > 5, x >$ _____

7. $7y - 2 > 19, y >$ _____

4. $y/2 + 1 < 5, y <$ _____

8. $y/4 + 3 > 5, y >$ _____

Answers

1. $x > 3$ 3. $x > 3$ 5. $y > 15$ 7. $y > 3$
2. $y < 2$ 4. $y < 8$ 6. $y < 1$ 8. $y > 8$

II. G. Ratio and Proportion

G-1

We may compare two numbers by subtraction or by division. For example, Mr. Carson earns $48 per day, and Mr. Burns earns $36 per day. We may say that Mr. Carson earns $12 per day more than Mr. Burns. Or, we may say that the ratio of Mr. Carson's earnings per day to Mr. Burns' earnings per day is $\frac{48}{36}$. We may reduce $\frac{48}{36}$ to $\frac{4}{3}$, which indicates that Mr. Carson earns $1\frac{1}{3}$ times as much per day as Mr. Burns.

The comparison of the two pay rates may be written as $\frac{48}{36}$ or as $48 : 36$. In general, the ratio of a number a to a number b (b cannot be 0) is a/b, or $a : b$.

EXAMPLES

1. At a party there are 12 men and 8 women. What is the ratio of men to women? The ratio is $\frac{12}{8}$ or $12 : 8$. In simplest form, this is $\frac{3}{2}$, or $3 : 2$.

2. At the same party, what is the ratio of women to men?

The ratio is $\frac{8}{12}$ or $8 : 12$. In simplest form, this is $\frac{2}{3}$, or $2 : 3$.

3. At the same party, what is the ratio of men to the number of people at the party?

The ratio is $\frac{12}{20}$ or $12 : 20$. In simplest form, this is $\frac{3}{5}$, or $3 : 5$.

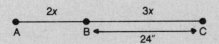

4. If $AB:BC = 2:3$ and if $BC = 24$ inches, what is the length of AB?

Let $AB = 2x$
And $BC = 3x$.

We know that

$$3x = 24$$
$$\frac{1}{3}(3x) = \frac{1}{3}(24)$$
$$x = 8$$

Since $x = 8$, $2x$ $(AB) = 2 \cdot 8 = 16$. Therefore, $AB = 16$ inches.

Consider the following problem: A baseball team wins 15 games out of 30 games played. If the team continues to win at the same rate, how many games will it win out of 40 games played?

Let n = number of games team will win in 40 games played.

The ratio of games won to games already played is $\frac{15}{30}$. Since the ratio of games won to games played is to remain the same, we may write this ratio as $n/40$. These ratios may also be written as $15:30$ and $n:40$.

We may now write the equation $\frac{15}{30} = n/40$. Such an equation, which tells us that one ratio is equal to another ratio, is called a *proportion*. Of course, in this case we know that $n = 20$, since the team wins $\frac{1}{2}$ of the games it plays.

Proportions have a very useful property which we will investigate. Consider the proportion

$$\frac{1}{3} = \frac{2}{6} \text{ or } 1:3 = 2:6$$

The two inside terms (3 and 2) are called the **means** of the proportion, and the two outside terms (1 and 6) are called the **extremes** of the proportion. Notice that if we multiply the two means, we obtain $3 \times 2 = 6$. Also, if we multiply the two extremes, we obtain $1 \times 6 = 6$. This illustrates the following property of proportions:

> *In a proportion, the product of the means is equal to the product of the extremes.*

This property is very useful in solving problems.

EXAMPLE

The ratio of alcohol to water in a certain type of antifreeze is $3:4$. If a tank contains 24 quarts of alcohol, how many quarts of water must be added to make the antifreeze mixture?

Let $x =$ the number of quarts needed.

$$\frac{\text{alcohol}}{\text{water}} \quad \frac{3}{4} = \frac{24}{x}$$

Now, we may use the property of proportions to find x.

$$3:4 = 24:x$$
$$3x = 4 \times 24$$
$$3x = 96$$
$$\frac{1}{3}(3x) = \frac{1}{3}(96)$$
$$x = 32 \text{ quarts of water}$$

Note: We may use the same property in the form

$$\frac{3}{4} \diagdown \frac{24}{x}$$
$$3x = 4 \times 24$$
$$3x = 96$$
$$x = 32$$

The following examples will indicate how we may use ratio and proportion to solve problems.

EXAMPLE

If 3 ties cost \$12.57, what is the cost of 5 ties at the same rate?

Let $y =$ the cost of 5 ties.
We form the proportion

$$3:12.57 = 5:x$$
$$\frac{3}{12.57} = \frac{5}{x}$$
$$3x = 5 \times 12.57 = 62.85$$
$$\frac{1}{3}(3x) = \frac{1}{3}(62.85)$$
$$x = \$20.95$$

5 ties cost \$20.95 at the same rate.

EXAMPLE

The scale on a map is 1 inch to 60 miles. If the distance between two cities is $2\frac{3}{4}$ inches on the map, what is the actual distance between the two cities?

Let $d =$ the actual distance between the cities.

$$1:60 = 2\frac{3}{4}:d$$

$$1 \times d = 60 \times 2\frac{3}{4}$$

$$d = 60 \times \frac{11}{4} = 165$$

The actual distance is 165 miles.

EXAMPLE

Two numbers are in the ratio $9:5$. Their difference is 28. Find the numbers.

Let $9x =$ the larger number
And $5x =$ the smaller number.

$$\text{Then } 9x - 5x = 28$$

$$4x = 28$$

$$\frac{1}{4}(4x) = \frac{1}{4}(28)$$

$$x = 7$$

The larger number is $9x$, or $9 \cdot 7 = 63$. The smaller number is $5x$, or $5 \cdot 7 = 35$.

EXAMPLE

The numerator and denominator of a fraction are in the ratio $3:7$. If 2 is added to both the numerator and the denominator, the ratio becomes $1:2$. Find the original fraction.

Let $3n$ = the numerator of the fraction
And $7n$ = the denominator of the fraction.

If we add 2 to both the numerator and the denominator, the numerator becomes $3n + 2$ and the denominator becomes $7n + 2$. Thus, we have

$$\frac{3n+2}{7n+2} = \frac{1}{2}$$
$$1(7n + 2) = 2(3n + 2)$$
$$7n + 2 = 6n + 4$$
$$7n + 2 - 2 = 6n + 2$$
$$7n - 6n = 6n - 6n + 2$$
$$n = 2$$

The original denominator was $3n$, or $3 \times 2 = 6$. The original numerator was $7n$, or $7 \times 2 = 14$. The original fraction was $\frac{6}{14}$.

Practice

Directions: Solve the following problems and blacken the space at the right under the number which corresponds to the one you have selected as the correct answer.

1. At a dance, the ratio of the number of boys to the number of girls is $4:3$. If there are 32 boys present, the number of girls present is

    (1) 36   (4) 24
    (2) 40   (5) 28
    (3) 20

    1. ① ② ③ ④ ⑤

2. John earned $150 one week and spent $120. The ratio of the amount John saved to the amount John spent is

    (1) $1:5$ (4) $4:5$
    (2) $1:4$ (5) $5:4$
    (3) $4:1$

    2. ① ② ③ ④ ⑤

3. On a trip, a motorist drove x miles on a local road and y miles on a parkway. The ratio of the number of miles driven on the parkway to the total number of miles driven was

(1) $\dfrac{y}{x}$

(4) $\dfrac{x}{x+y}$

(2) $\dfrac{x}{y}$

(5) $\dfrac{x+y}{y}$

(3) $\dfrac{y}{x+y}$

3. ① ② ③ ④ ⑤

4. The ratio of a father's age to his son's age is $9:2$. If the son's age is 12 years, the age of the father, in years, is

(1) 45   (4) 50
(2) 36   (5) 54
(3) 63

4. ① ② ③ ④ ⑤

5. On the line RS, $RT = 4$ and $RT:TS = 2:5$. The length of RS is

(1) 10   (4) 9
(2) 12   (5) 14
(3) 7

5. ① ② ③ ④ ⑤

6. A picture measures 2 inches by $1\frac{1}{2}$ inches. If the picture is enlarged so that the 2-inch dimension becomes 3 inches, the other dimension becomes

(1) $2\frac{1}{4}$ inches   (4) $1\frac{3}{4}$ inches
(2) $2\frac{1}{2}$ inches   (5) $3\frac{1}{4}$ inches
(3) 2 inches

6. ① ② ③ ④ ⑤

7. If 3 shirts cost \$23, the cost of a dozen shirts at the same rate is

(1) \$95   (4) \$92
(2) \$84   (5) \$98.50
(3) \$276

7. ① ② ③ ④ ⑤

8. On a map, the scale is 1 inch to 80 miles. The actual distance between two cities is 200 miles. The distance between the cities, on the map, is

    (1) 2 inches   (4) $3\frac{1}{2}$ inches

    (2) 3 inches   (5) 4 inches

    (3) $2\frac{1}{2}$ inches   **8.** ① ② ③ ④ ⑤

9. A certain recipe that will yield 4 portions calls for $1\frac{1}{2}$ ounces of sugar. If the recipe is used to yield 6 portions, then the amount of sugar needed is

    (1) $2\frac{1}{2}$ ounces   (4) 2 ounces

    (2) $2\frac{1}{4}$ ounces   (5) 3 ounces

    (3) $2\frac{3}{4}$ ounces   **9.** ① ② ③ ④ ⑤

10. A gallon of paint covers 240 square feet of surface. If a living room contains 906 square feet of paintable surface and a kitchen contains 334 square feet of surface, the number of gallons of paint needed for the living room and kitchen is

    (1) 6   (4) $5\frac{1}{2}$

    (2) $4\frac{1}{2}$ (5) $6\frac{1}{2}$

    (3) $5\frac{1}{6}$ **10.** ① ② ③ ④ ⑤

11. A recipe for hot chocolate calls for 2 ounces of chocolate, 4 cups of milk, and 4 tablespoons of sugar. If only 3 cups of milk are available, the number of ounces of chocolate to be used is

    (1) 3   (4) 6

    (2) $\frac{2}{3}$ (5) $\frac{3}{4}$

    (3) $1\frac{1}{2}$ **11.** ① ② ③ ④ ⑤

12. Mr. Ash finds that he spends $47.50 for gas for each 1,000 miles that he drives his car. One month he drives his car 1,800 miles. The amount he spends for gas during that month is

    (1) $855   (4) $85.50

    (2) $95   (5) $8.55

    (3) $82.50   **12.** ① ② ③ ④ ⑤

13. An artist finds that he obtains the most pleasing result when the ratio of the length of a painting to its width is $8:5$. If the length of a painting is 2 feet 8 inches, then its width should be

    (1) 2 feet   (4) 3 feet

    (2) 1 foot 8 inches   (5) 2 feet 5 inches

    (3) 2 feet 8 inches   **13.** ① ② ③ ④ ⑤

14. A recipe for chocolate fudge calls for $\frac{3}{4}$ cup of corn syrup and $\frac{1}{2}$ teaspoon of salt. If 1 cup of corn syrup is used, the number of teaspoons of salt to be used is

    (1) $\frac{2}{3}$ (4) $2\frac{2}{3}$

    (2) $1\frac{1}{3}$ (5) $\frac{3}{4}$

    (3) $\frac{3}{8}$ **14.** ① ② ③ ④ ⑤

15. It takes a train c hours to cover d miles. If the train travels k miles at the same rate, the number of hours it takes is

    (1) cdk (4) $\dfrac{ck}{d}$

    (2) $\dfrac{d}{ck}$ (5) $\dfrac{cd}{k}$

    (3) $\dfrac{dk}{c}$ **15.** ① ② ③ ④ ⑤

16. A man finds that he spends a total of y dollars per month for heating oil during 7 months of cold weather. If he wishes to prorate his cost over a 12-month period, the cost per month is

    (1) $\dfrac{12}{7y}$ (4) $\dfrac{7y}{12}$

    (2) $\dfrac{y}{12}$ (5) $84y$

    (3) $\dfrac{12y}{7}$ **16.** ① ② ③ ④ ⑤

17. A 25-acre field yields 375 bushels of wheat. How many acres should be planted to yield 525 bushels of wheat?

  (1) 33
  (2) 32
  (3) 45
  (4) 35
  (5) 75

  17. ① ② ③ ④ ⑤

18. A house which is assessed at \$30,000 is taxed \$1,170. At the same rate, the tax on a house which is assessed for \$40,000 is

  (1) \$992.50
  (2) \$156
  (3) \$1,560
  (4) \$2,340
  (5) \$1,360

  18. ① ② ③ ④ ⑤

19. A family consumes q quarts of milk each week. The number of quarts this family consumes in 10 days is

  (1) $\dfrac{7q}{10}$
  (2) $\dfrac{10q}{7}$
  (3) $\dfrac{70}{q}$
  (4) $\dfrac{10}{7q}$
  (5) $\dfrac{q}{70}$

  19. ① ② ③ ④ ⑤

20. In making a certain type of concrete, the ratio of cement to sand used is $1:4$. In making x barrels of this concrete, the number of barrels of cement used is

  (1) $\dfrac{x}{5}$
  (2) $\dfrac{x}{4}$
  (3) x
  (4) $4x$
  (5) $\dfrac{1}{5x}$

  20. ① ② ③ ④ ⑤

Answers

1. 4	6. 1	11. 3	16. 4
2. 2	7. 4	12. 4	17. 4
3. 3	8. 3	13. 2	18. 3
4. 5	9. 2	14. 1	19. 2
5. 5	10. 3	15. 4	20. 1

III. BASIC GRAPHS

Pictures or graphs are often used in reports, magazines, and newspapers to present a set of numerical facts. This enables the viewer to make comparisons and to draw quick conclusions. In this section, we will learn how to interpret pictographs, bar graphs, line graphs, circle graphs, and formula graphs.

This section gives only a basic introduction to simple graphing. Graphs are also used extensively for data analysis in science, economics, manufacturing, and other areas. Section VI of this chapter has an introduction to data analysis using somewhat more complex examples than the graphs in this section.

III. A. Pictographs

A-1

A **pictograph** is a graph in which objects are used to represent numbers.

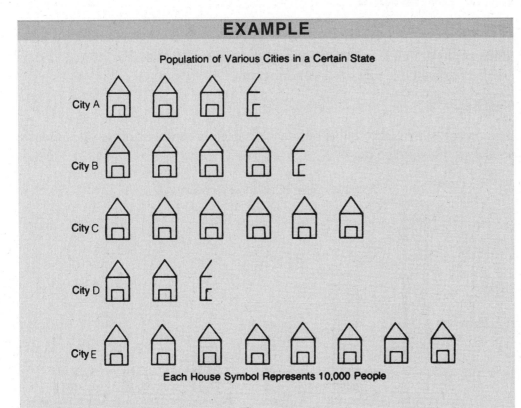

EXAMPLE

Population of Various Cities in a Certain State

Each House Symbol Represents 10,000 People

1. Which city has the largest population?

   City E

2. By how many people does the population of the largest city exceed the population of the next largest city?

   City E has 80,000 people.
   City C has 60,000 people.
   City E has 20,000 people more than City C.

3. What is the ratio of the population of City B to City C?

City B has a population of 45,000.
City C has a population of 60,000.
Ratio is 45,000 : 60,000.
This ratio can be simplified to 3 : 4.

4. If City D's population is increased by 40%, what will its population be?

City D has a population of 25,000. If the population is increased by 40%, we have 25,000 × 0.4 = 10,000 more people.
City D's population will become 35,000.

III. B. Bar Graphs

B-1

Bar graphs are used to show relationships in a set of quantities. Here, bars are used very much like pictures in a pictograph.

Practice

In a recent year, a large industrial concern used each dollar of its sales income as shown in the graph below.

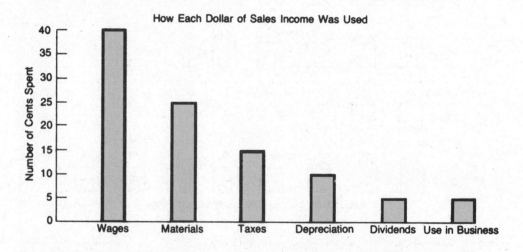

How Each Dollar of Sales Income Was Used

1. How many cents of each dollar of sales income did the company use to pay wages?

$0.40

2. How many more cents of each sales dollar were spent on wages than on materials?

$0.15

3. What percent of the sales dollar was spent for depreciation and dividends?

15%

4. The amount of money the company paid in taxes was how many times the amount of money it paid in dividends?

3 times

5. What percent of the sales dollar was spent on wages, materials, and taxes?

Wages, 40%
Materials, 25%
Taxes, 15%
Total, 80%

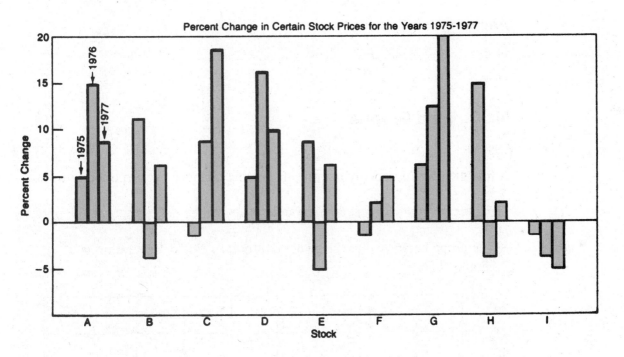

Percent Change in Certain Stock Prices for the Years 1975-1977

1. Which stock had the greatest percent increase in price during any year?

(1) B   (4) G
(2) H   (5) A
(3) D

1. ① ② ③ ④ ⑤

2. Which of the following pairs of stocks gained in price during each of the years 1975, 1976, and 1977?

(1) H and I   (4) C and G
(2) A and D   (5) F and I
(3) B and E

2. ① ② ③ ④ ⑤

3. Which stock had the smallest average percent change in the years 1975, 1976, and 1977?

    (1) I   (4) G

    (2) A   (5) H

    (3) C   **3.** ① ② ③ ④ ⑤

4. Which stock had the greatest percent decrease in price between two consecutive years?

    (1) B   (4) E

    (2) D   (5) A

    (3) F   **4.** ① ② ③ ④ ⑤

Answers

1. **4**   2. **2**   3. **1**   4. **4**

III. C. Line Graphs

C-1

A **line graph** is especially helpful in showing changes over a period of time.

EXAMPLE

The graph below shows the growth in motor vehicle registration in a certain state.

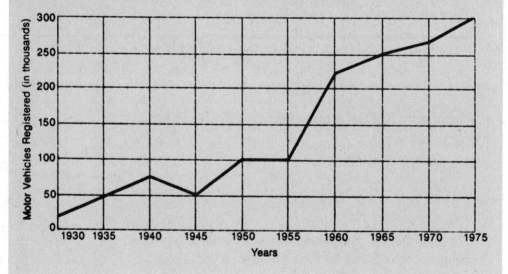

1. Approximately how many motor vehicles were registered in 1960?

   We cannot tell exactly from the graph, but a good estimate is 220,000.

2. Approximately how many times as many motor vehicles were registered in 1965 as in 1935?

   Registered in 1965—250,000
   Registered in 1935—50,000
   There were 5 times as many motor vehicles registered in 1965 as in 1935.

3. What percent of increase in registration took place between 1945 and 1975?

   Registered in 1945—50,000
   Registered in 1975—300,000
   Increase in registration—250,000

$$\text{Percent of increase} = \frac{\text{Increase}}{\text{Original}} = \frac{250,000}{50,000} = \frac{5}{1}, \text{ or } 500\%.$$

4. Between what two periods shown was the increase the greatest?

   Between 1955 and 1960. This is shown on the graph by the sharpest rise in the line.

5. Between what two periods shown was there no increase?

   Between 1950 and 1955. This is shown by the horizontal (or flat) line between 1950 and 1955.

III. D. Circle Graphs

D-1

A **circle graph** is used when a quantity is divided into parts, and we wish to make a comparison of the parts. Recall that a complete revolution is divided into 360°. Thus, if we wish to mark off one-quarter of the circle, the angle at the center must be $\frac{1}{4} \times 360°$, or 90°. For the same reason, a part of the circle with an angle at the center of 60° will be $\frac{60}{360}$, or $\frac{1}{6}$ of the circle.

EXAMPLE

The circle graph below shows how the wage earners in a certain city earned their living in a certain year.

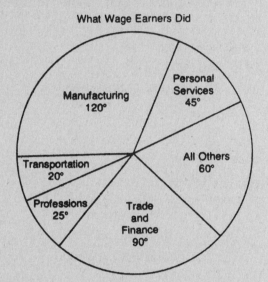

What Wage Earners Did

1. What fractional part of the labor force works in professions?

$$\frac{25}{360} = \frac{5}{72}$$

2. What fractional part of the labor force works in personal services?

$$\frac{45}{360} = \frac{1}{8}$$

3. If there were 180,000 workers in the city, how many are engaged in manufacturing?

The fractional part of the workers engaged in manufacturing was $\frac{120}{360} = \frac{1}{3}$.

$\frac{1}{3}$ of 180,000 = 60,000 workers engaged in manufacturing.

4. What is the ratio of the number of workers in transportation to the number of workers in personal services?

The ratio is 20:45, or more simply, 4:9.

5. What percent of the workers are in trade and finance?

The fractional part of the total number of workers in trade and finance is $\frac{90}{360} = \frac{1}{4}$. The fraction $\frac{1}{4}$, written as a percent, is 25%.

III. E. Formula Graphs

E-1

In working with a formula we may have occasion to obtain a number of bits of information. Instead of using the formula each time it may be easier to work from a graph of the formula (*formula graph*).

In most parts of Europe and in all scientific work, the scale used to measure temperature is the Celsius scale. In the United States, the Fahrenheit scale is still used but mention is frequently made of the Celsius scale. We sometimes find it necessary to convert from one scale to the other. The graph below shows how the scales are related.

In this case, the formula for the graph is the linear equation

Degrees Fahrenheit = 32 + 9/5 × Degrees Celsius

There is more information about linear equations in **Section V. E-3**.

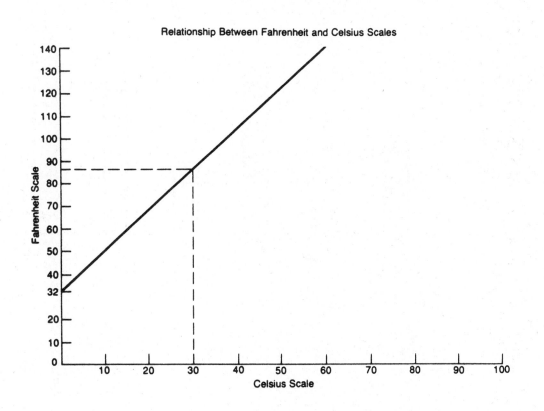

Relationship Between Fahrenheit and Celsius Scales

1. A weather report in Paris indicated that the temperature was 30° Celsius. What was the corresponding Fahrenheit temperature?

   Locate 30° on the Celsius scale (the horizontal scale). At this point draw a line so that it is perpendicular to the Celsius scale line (as shown in the diagram).
   You can read the corresponding Fahrenheit temperature by drawing a line perpendicular to the Fahrenheit scale line from the point where the first line cuts the graph. The answer is 86°.

2. What Celsius reading corresponds to a Fahrenheit reading of 77?

25°

3. During one day the temperature rose from 41° to 68° Fahrenheit. What was the corresponding rise in the temperature on the Celsius scale?

The Celsius temperature rose from 5° to 20°.

Practice

Directions: Blacken the space at the right under the number which corresponds to the one you have selected as the correct answer.

For questions 1–3: The bar graph below shows the average monthly rainfall, in inches, for the first 6 months of a year in a certain city.

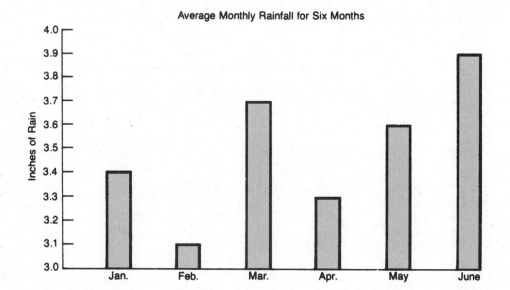

1. The month with the greatest rainfall was

   (1) February   (4) June
   (2) March   (5) January
   (3) May   **1.** ① ② ③ ④ ⑤

2. The total rainfall for the 6 months was

   (1) 10 inches   (4) 21 inches
   (2) 19 inches   (5) 18.5 inches
   (3) 19.6 inches   **2.** ① ② ③ ④ ⑤

3. The average monthly rainfall for the 6-month period was

(1) 3 inches

(4) $3\frac{5}{6}$ inches

(2) $3\frac{1}{2}$ inches

(5) $3\frac{1}{3}$ inches

(3) $3\frac{1}{6}$ inches

3. ① ② ③ ④ ⑤

For questions 4–6: The graph below shows the record of profits of the Beacon Co. for a period of 8 years.

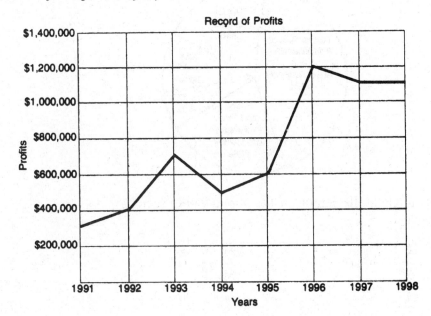

4. The profits of the Beacon Co. rose most sharply between the years

(1) 1992–1993

(4) 1993–1994

(2) 1995–1996

(5) 1991–1992

(3) 1996–1997

4. ① ② ③ ④ ⑤

5. The year when the profits of the Beacon Co. were about $700,000 was

(1) 1995

(4) 1993

(2) 1998

(5) 1996

(3) 1994

5. ① ② ③ ④ ⑤

6. The profits of the Beacon Co. dropped most sharply between the years

(1) 1997–1998

(4) 1991–1992

(2) 1994–1995

(5) 1996–1997

(3) 1993–1994

6. ① ② ③ ④ ⑤

For questions 7–10:

7. In a large city, the breakdown of the $30,000,000 raised by means of real estate taxes for all purposes, except schools, is shown in the graph. To raise this sum, the tax rate was set at $21.95 per $1,000 of assessed valuation.

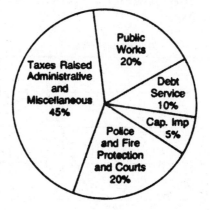

The angle at the center for the public works sector measures

    (1) 90°   (4) 80°
    (2) 72°   (5) 75°
    (3) 100°

7. ① ② ③ ④ ⑤

8. Mr. Mitchell's home is assessed at $18,000. His real estate tax bill is

    (1) $385.10   (4) $395.10
    (2) $394.10   (5) $375
    (3) $3,951

8. ① ② ③ ④ ⑤

9. The amount of money spent for public works is

    (1) $5,000,000   (4) $3,000,000
    (2) $1,500,000   (5) $2,500,000
    (3) $6,000,000

9. ① ② ③ ④ ⑤

10. The ratio of money spent for administrative and miscellaneous to the money spent for public works is

    (1) 9:4   (4) 5:9
    (2) 4:9   (5) 2:1
    (3) 9:5

10. ① ② ③ ④ ⑤

For questions 11–13:

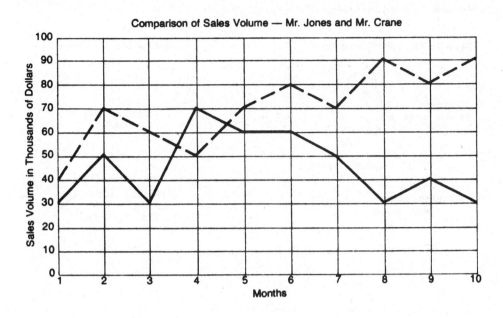

Comparison of Sales Volume — Mr. Jones and Mr. Crane

11. Mr. Jones and Mr. Crane are salesmen. They kept a record of their sales over a 10-month period. The solid line on the graph above represents Mr. Jones' volume of sales, and the broken line represents Mr. Crane's volume of sales.

   Mr. Jones' greatest sales volume for the 10-month period occurred in the month numbered

   (1) 3   (4) 6
   (2) 4   (5) 9
   (3) 7   **11.** ① ② ③ ④ ⑤

12. How much greater volume was Mr. Crane's best month over Mr. Jones' best month? (in thousands)

   (1) 10   (4) 90
   (2) 30   (5) 20
   (3) 50   **12.** ① ② ③ ④ ⑤

13. How much greater was Mr. Crane's average for the 10 months than Mr. Jones' average for this period? (in thousands)

   (1) 44   (4) 36
   (2) 70   (5) 16
   (3) 25   **13.** ① ② ③ ④ ⑤

For questions 14–17: The graphs below were published by the federal government to show where the tax dollar comes from and where it goes.

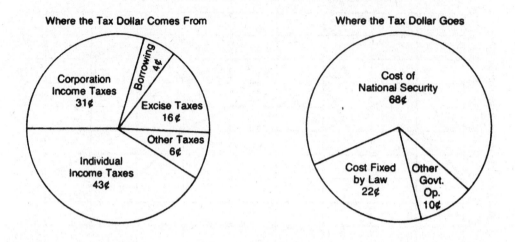

14. The percent spent on national security was

    (1) 78%   (4) 10%
    (2) 90%   (5) 32%
    (3) 68%   14. ① ② ③ ④ ⑤

15. By how much percent was the money obtained from individual income taxes greater than the money obtained from corporation income taxes?

    (1) 6%   (4) 31%
    (2) 12%   (5) 22%
    (3) 43%   15. ① ② ③ ④ ⑤

16. The angle at the center of the sector for cost of other government operations is

    (1) 10°   (4) 36°
    (2) 20°   (5) 80°
    (3) 40°   16. ① ② ③ ④ ⑤

17. The percent of income derived from both corporation income taxes and individual income taxes is

    (1) 84%   (4) 82%
    (2) 12%   (5) 74%
    (3) 75%   17. ① ② ③ ④ ⑤

Answers

1. **4**	6. **3**	11. **2**	16. **4**
2. **4**	7. **2**	12. **5**	17. **5**
3. **2**	8. **4**	13. **3**	
4. **2**	9. **3**	14. **3**	
5. **4**	10. **1**	15. **2**	

IV. MEASURES

IV. A. Length

A-1

> The most *common measures of length* are
>
> 12 inches = 1 foot 5,280 feet = 1 mile
> 3 feet = 1 yard 1,760 yards = 1 mile

EXAMPLE

A plumber has a pipe $\frac{3}{4}$ yard in length. If he cuts off a piece 23 inches long, how much pipe does he have left?

$$\frac{3}{4} \text{ yard} = \frac{3}{4} \times 36 = 27 \text{ inches}$$

The plumber has 4 inches of pipe left.

Practice

Directions: Blacken the space at the right under the number which corresponds to the one you have selected as the correct answer.

1. A plane flies at a height of 23,760 feet. In miles, this is

    (1) 4   (4) $4\frac{1}{2}$

    (2) $4\frac{2}{3}$ (5) $4\frac{3}{4}$

    (3) $4\frac{1}{4}$ **1.** ① ② ③ ④ ⑤

2. Mrs. Bryant buys 6 yards of linen. The number of towels 27 inches in length that she can cut is

    (1) 8   (4) 9

    (2) 6   (5) 15

    (3) 12   **2.** ① ② ③ ④ ⑤

3. A room is 18 feet long and 12 feet wide. The number of rubber tiles measuring 8 inches by 8 inches needed to cover the floor is

(1) 45　　　　　　　　(4) 286
(2) 27　　　　　　　　(5) 304
(3) 486　　　　　　　**3.** ① ② ③ ④ ⑤

4. A lecture room is 50 feet wide. On each side of the room, there is an aisle 40 inches wide. The number of seats, 20 inches wide, that can be fitted across the room is

(1) 20　　　　　　　　(4) 30
(2) 26　　　　　　　　(5) 35
(3) 40　　　　　　　**4.** ① ② ③ ④ ⑤

5. A long-distance race covers $6\frac{3}{4}$ miles. The number of yards covered is

(1) 10,560　　　　　　(4) 11,880
(2) 12,000　　　　　　(5) 14,350
(3) 11,000　　　　　**5.** ① ② ③ ④ ⑤

Answers

1. **4**　　2. **1**　　3. **3**　　4. **2**　　5. **4**

IV. B. Time

B-1

The most *common measures of time* are
| 60 seconds = 1 minute | 12 months = 1 year |
| 60 minutes = 1 hour | 365 days = 1 year |

EXAMPLE

A man works from 9:45 A.M. until 1:30 P.M. How many hours does he work?

From 9:45 A.M. to 10:00 A.M. is 15 minutes, or $\frac{1}{4}$ hour.
From 10:00 A.M. to 1:00 P.M. is 3 hours.
From 1:00 P.M. to 1:30 P.M. is 30 minutes, or $\frac{1}{2}$ hour.
The time the man worked is $\frac{1}{4} + 3 + \frac{1}{2} = 3\frac{3}{4}$ hours.

Practice

Directions: Blacken the space at the right under the number which corresponds to the one you have selected as the correct answer.

1. A man is paid $6.50 per hour. He works from 10:45 A.M. until 3:15 P.M. He earns

   (1) $30.50   (4) $27.75
   (2) $16.25   (5) $22.75
   (3) $29.25   **1.** ① ② ③ ④ ⑤

2. A bell rings every 45 minutes. The number of times the bell rings in 15 hours is

   (1) 18   (4) 12
   (2) 20   (5) 25
   (3) 11   **2.** ① ② ③ ④ ⑤

3. A man leaves New York on a plane at 10:40 A.M. bound for Los Angeles. If he gains 3 hours in time and the trip takes 5 hours and 50 minutes, he arrives in Los Angeles at

   (1) 1:30 P.M.   (4) 3:10 P.M.
   (2) 2:30 P.M.   (5) 2:50 P.M.
   (3) 3:30 P.M.   **3.** ① ② ③ ④ ⑤

4. In flight, a plane covers 1 mile in 10 seconds. At the same rate of speed, the number of miles the plane covers in 1 hour is

   (1) 100   (4) 300
   (2) 200   (5) 360
   (3) 720   **4.** ① ② ③ ④ ⑤

5. On March 5, a man borrows $900 from a bank for 90 days. He must repay the loan on

   (1) June 1   (4) June 8
   (2) June 5   (5) June 9
   (3) June 3   **5.** ① ② ③ ④ ⑤

Answers

1. **3**   2. **2**   3. **1**   4. **5**   5. **3**

IV. C. Weight

C-1

> The most *commonly used measures of weight* are
>
> 16 ounces = 1 pound   2,000 pounds = 1 ton

EXAMPLE

How many 2-ounce portions of candy can be obtained from a 10-pound box?

Since there are 16 ounces in 1 pound, each pound of candy will yield $\frac{16}{2}$ or 8 portions. Therefore, 10 pounds of candy will yield 8×10, or 80 portions.

Practice

Directions: Blacken the space at the right under the number which corresponds to the one you have selected as the correct answer.

1. Bread sells for $0.32 per pound. The cost of a bread weighing 3 pounds 6 ounces is

   (1) $0.98   (4) $0.78
   (2) $1.08   (5) $1.15
   (3) $1.12   **1.** ① ② ③ ④ ⑤

2. A 12-ounce package of cheese costs $0.69. What is the cost of one pound of the same cheese?

   (1) $0.78   (4) $0.92
   (2) $0.95   (5) $1.04
   (3) $0.96   **2.** ① ② ③ ④ ⑤

3. A shipment of coal weighs 9,500 pounds. What is the cost of the shipment if 1 ton of coal costs $26.40?

   (1) $125.40   (4) $104.55
   (2) $106.85   (5) $112.60
   (3) $110.70   **3.** ① ② ③ ④ ⑤

4. A certain cut of meat costs $1.18 per pound. What is the cost of this cut of meat weighing 1 pound 13 ounces?

(1) $2.05   (4) $1.92
(2) $1.98   (5) $2.14
(3) $2.20

4. ① ② ③ ④ ⑤

5. A truckload of steel bars weighs $3\frac{1}{4}$ tons. If each bar weighs 26 pounds, the number of bars on the truck is

(1) 25   (4) 250
(2) 2,500   (5) 270
(3) 240

5. ① ② ③ ④ ⑤

Answers

1. **2**   2. **4**   3. **1**   4. **5**   5. **4**

IV. D. Liquid Measure

D-1

> The most *commonly used liquid measures* are
> 16 fluid ounces = 1 pint   2 measuring cups = 1 pint
>   2 pints = 1 quart   4 quarts = 1 gallon

EXAMPLE

A snack bar sells half-pint bottles of milk at 15 cents a bottle. If 3 gallons of milk are sold one morning, how much money is taken in?

Since half-pint bottles sell for 15 cents, a full pint sells for 30 cents. Thus, one quart sells for 60 cents, and 1 gallon sells for $2.40. And, 3 gallons sell for 3 × $2.40 = $7.20.

Practice

Directions: Blacken the space at the right under the number which corresponds to the one you have selected as the correct answer.

1. The number of measuring cups of milk in a 5-gallon can is

(1) 40   (4) 100
(2) 60   (5) 160
(3) 80

1. ① ② ③ ④ ⑤

2. A can of orange juice contains 36 ounces. The number of pints of orange juice is

(1) 2   (4) $2\frac{1}{4}$
(2) $2\frac{1}{2}$ (5) 3
(3) $1\frac{1}{4}$ **2.** ① ② ③ ④ ⑤

3. A punch bowl contains $3\frac{1}{2}$ gallons of punch. The number of 4-ounce portions that can be obtained from the punch bowl is

(1) 102   (4) 115
(2) 112   (5) 156
(3) 204   **3.** ① ② ③ ④ ⑤

4. A restaurant cook uses 150 measuring cups of milk in one day. The cost of the milk at $0.40 per quart is

(1) $15   (4) $150
(2) $30   (5) $15.20
(3) $14.80   **4.** ① ② ③ ④ ⑤

5. The number of fluid ounces in 1 gallon is

(1) 64   (4) 96
(2) 48   (5) 128
(3) 100   **5.** ① ② ③ ④ ⑤

Answers

1. **3** 2. **4** 3. **2** 4. **1** 5. **5**

IV. E. Dry Measure

E-1

Such commodities as berries, apples, and potatoes are often sold by the quart or bushel.

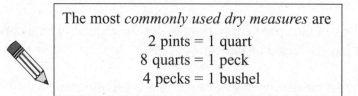

> The most *commonly used dry measures* are
>
> 2 pints = 1 quart
> 8 quarts = 1 peck
> 4 pecks = 1 bushel

EXAMPLE

A dealer received a shipment of 60 bags of apples, each bag containing 1 peck. If 1 bushel of the apples weighed 48 pounds and the dealer sold them at a price of 3 pounds for 85 cents, how much did he receive?

The dealer received 60 pecks of apples. This is $\frac{60}{4}$, or 15 bushels. Since each bushel weighed 48 pounds, the total weight of the shipment was 15×48, or 720 pounds.

At 3 pounds for 85 cents, the dealer received

$$\frac{720}{3} \times 0.85, \text{ or } 240 \times 0.85 = \$204.00$$

Practice

Directions: Blacken the space at the right under the number which corresponds to the one you have selected as the correct answer.

1. A storekeeper paid $5.60 for a bushel of potatoes. If 1 peck of potatoes weighs 15 pounds and the storekeeper sold the potatoes in 5-pound bags at $0.86 per bag, his profit on the deal was

   (1) $6.72 (4) $4.32
   (2) $4.52 (5) $10.02
   (3) $4.72

   1. ① ② ③ ④ ⑤

2. If a bushel of coal weighs 80 pounds and coal sells for $24 per ton, the cost of a bushel of coal is

   (1) $1 (4) $0.96
   (2) $0.98 (5) $1.02
   (3) $2

   2. ① ② ③ ④ ⑤

3. A fruiterer received a truckload of berries containing 15 bushels. If he sold the berries at $0.42 per pint, the amount he received for the berries was

   (1) $403.20 (4) $253.20
   (2) $201.60 (5) $25.32
   (3) $40.32

   3. ① ② ③ ④ ⑤

4. A fruiterer paid $19.20 for 2 bushels of apples. If he sold the apples for $3.60 per peck, his profit was

(1) $7.60

(2) $8.90

(3) $9

(4) $9.60

(5) $11.60

4. ① ② ③ ④ ⑤

Answers

1. **3**   2. **4**   3. **1**   4. **4**

IV. F. The Metric System

F-1

The metric system of measures is used in most scientific work and in all European countries. It is especially useful because its units are related by multiples of 10. In this section, we will consider the most frequently used metric measures. However, please be aware that memorization of the metric system is *not* necessary for the California High School Proficiency Examination. We are introducing this section so that you will not be surprised by metric references in various problems. *You need not know any metric equivalences for this examination.*

The important unit of length in the metric system is the **meter**. The meter is a little bigger than 1 yard. In fact,

1 meter = approximately 39.37 inches

The **kilometer**, or 1,000 meters, is used for measuring large distances, like the distance between two cities.

1 kilometer = approximately $\frac{5}{8}$ mile

The important unit of liquid measure in the metric system is the **liter**.

1 liter = approximately 1.1 liquid quarts

The basic unit of weight in the metric system is the **gram**. The gram is used extensively in the science laboratory. In practice, the **kilogram**, or 1,000 grams, is used extensively in weighing foods and other merchandise.

1 kilogram = approximately 2.2 pounds

To sum up, *the following metric equivalencies are important:*
1 meter = approximately 39.37 inches
1 kilometer = approximately $\frac{5}{8}$ mile
1 liter = approximately 1.1 liquid quarts
1 kilogram = approximately 2.2 pounds

EXAMPLE

In traveling on a European road, an American motorist notes that the speed limit is 70 kilometers per hour. Approximately how fast is this, in miles per hour?

Since 1 kilometer = approximately $\frac{5}{8}$ mile

$$\frac{5}{8} \times 70 = \frac{350}{8} = 43\frac{3}{4}$$

This is approximately $43\frac{3}{4}$ miles per hour.

Practice

Directions: Blacken the space at the right under the number which corresponds to the one you have selected as the correct answer.

1. A package from Europe is marked to contain $3\frac{1}{2}$ kilograms. In pounds, this is

(1) 77
(2) 770
(3) 7.7
(4) 6.6
(5) 14

1. ① ② ③ ④ ⑤

2. If you weigh 160 pounds, your weight in kilograms, to the nearest kilogram, is

(1) 72
(2) 73
(3) 352
(4) 35
(5) 70

2. ① ② ③ ④ ⑤

3. A motorist bought 50 liters of gasoline. The number of gallons bought, to the nearest gallon, is

(1) 14
(2) 13
(3) 11
(4) 12
(5) 15

3. ① ② ③ ④ ⑤

4. If a plane is flying at the rate of 760 kilometers per hour, its rate of speed in miles per hour is

    (1) 1,216   (4) 455

    (2) 1,200   (5) 475

    (3) 675   **4.** ① ② ③ ④ ⑤

5. A building lot, rectangular in shape, is 35 meters in length and 15 meters in width. Its perimeter, in feet, to the nearest foot, is

    (1) 3,937   (4) 984

    (2) 328   (5) 394

    (3) 109   **5.** ① ② ③ ④ ⑤

6. The distance between two European cities is 440 kilometers. At an average speed of 50 miles per hour, the number of hours it would take a motorist to cover this distance is

    (1) 5   (4) $5\frac{1}{2}$

    (2) $8\frac{4}{5}$ (5) 6

    (3) 10   **6.** ① ② ③ ④ ⑤

Answers

1. **3**   2. **2**   3. **1**   4. **5**   5. **2**   6. **4**

IV. G. Operations with Measures

G-1

It is often necessary to add, subtract, multiply, and divide with measures. The following examples indicate how this is done.

EXAMPLE

A woman bought a steak weighing 2 lb. 14 oz. and another steak weighing 3 lb. 6 oz. How many pounds of steak did she buy?

$$\begin{array}{r} 2\,\text{lb.}\ 14\,\text{oz.} \\ +\,3\,\text{lb.}\ 6\,\text{oz.} \\ \hline 5\,\text{lb.}\ 20\,\text{oz.} \end{array}$$

Since there are 16 ounces in 1 pound, we have

$$5\,\text{lb.}\ 20\,\text{oz.} = 5\,\text{lb.} + 1\,\text{lb.} + 4\,\text{oz.} = 6\,\text{lb.}\ 4\,\text{oz.}$$

EXAMPLE

A plumber had a piece of pipe 6 ft. 3 in. long. If he cut off a piece 2 ft. 7 in. in length, what was the length of the pipe that was left?

$$6\text{ ft. }3\text{ in. }=5\text{ ft. }+1\text{ ft. }+3\text{ in. }=5\text{ ft. }15\text{ in.}$$
$$\underline{-\ 2\text{ ft. }7\text{ in.}}$$
$$3\text{ ft. }8\text{ in.}$$

The piece of pipe that was left was 3 ft. 8 in.

EXAMPLE

A butcher cuts steaks, each of which weighs 1 lb. 9 oz. What is the weight of 5 such steaks?

$$1\text{ lb. }9\text{ oz.}$$
$$\underline{\times 5}$$
$$5\text{ lb. }45\text{ oz. }=5\text{ lb. }+32\text{ oz. }+13\text{ oz. }=7\text{ lb. }13\text{ oz.}$$

EXAMPLE

Mrs. Gordon buys a bolt of cloth 21 ft. 8 in. in length. She cuts the bolt into four equal pieces to make drapes. What is the length of each drape?

$$4\overline{)21\text{ ft. }8\text{ in.}}=4\overline{)20\text{ ft. }+1\text{ ft. }+8\text{ in.}}$$
$$=4\overline{)20\text{ ft. }20\text{ in.}}$$
$$=5\text{ ft. }5\text{ in.}$$

Each drape is 5 ft. 5 in.

Practice

Directions: Blacken the space at the right under the number which corresponds to the one you have selected as the correct answer.

1. A picture frame is 2 ft. 6 in. long and 1 ft. 8 in. wide. The perimeter of the frame is

    (1) 4 ft. 2 in.   (4) 8 ft.

    (2) 8 ft. 8 in.   (5) 8 ft. 4 in.

    (3) 8 ft. 6 in.   **1.** ① ② ③ ④ ⑤

2. A movie show lasts 2 hr. 15 min. A movie house has 5 such shows daily. The time consumed by the 5 shows is

    (1) 11 hrs.   (4) 12 hrs. 30 min
    (2) 11 hrs. 15 min.   (5) 12 hrs.
    (3) 10 hrs. 15 min.

2. ① ② ③ ④ ⑤

3. On a certain day the sun rises at 6:48 A.M. and sets at 7:03 P.M. The time from sunrise to sunset is

    (1) 12 hrs. 15 min.   (4) 12 hrs. 25 min
    (2) 12 hrs. 5 min.   (5) 10 hrs. 15 min.
    (3) 11 hrs. 45 min.

3. ① ② ③ ④ ⑤

4. If 6 cans of orange juice weigh 15 lb. 6 oz., the weight of 1 can of orange juice is

    (1) 2 lb. 6 oz.   (4) 2 lb. 9 oz.
    (2) 2 lb. 7 oz.   (5) 2 lb. 3 oz.
    (3) 2 lb. 1 oz.

4. ① ② ③ ④ ⑤

5. A jug contains 2 gallons, 3 quarts of milk. The number of 8 oz. glasses that can be filled from this jug is

    (1) 24   (4) 36
    (2) 32   (5) 40
    (3) 44

5. ① ② ③ ④ ⑤

6. A carpenter has a board 5 ft. 3 in. in length. He cuts off a piece 2 ft. 7 in. in length. The length of the piece that is left is

    (1) 3 ft. 6 in.   (4) 2 ft. 8 in.
    (2) 2 ft. 6 in.   (5) 2 ft. 5 in.
    (3) 2 ft. 3 in.

6. ① ② ③ ④ ⑤

7. A set of books weighs 7 lb. 10 oz. The weight of 4 such sets is

    (1) 28 lb. 4 oz.   (4) 29 lb. 10 oz.
    (2) 30 lb. 8 oz.   (5) 29 lb. 11 oz.
    (3) 29 lb. 8 oz.

7. ① ② ③ ④ ⑤

8. A store sold 6 gal. 2 qt. of ice cream on one day and 7 gal. 3 qt. the next day. The amount of ice cream sold on both days was

    (1) 15 gal. 2 qt.   (4) 15 gal. 1 qt.
    (2) 14 gal. 3 qt.   (5) 13 gal. 2 qt.
    (3) 14 gal. 1 qt.

8. ① ② ③ ④ ⑤

Answers

1. **5**   2. **2**   3. **1**   4. **4**   5. **3**   6. **4**   7. **2**   8. **3**

V. GEOMETRY

V. A. Lines and Angles

A-1

Geometry studies simple shapes that are often used as component parts of more complicated figures and structures. We saw isolated examples earlier in this chapter, in formulas for the perimeter of a rectangle and questions about ratio and proportion. The number line is an example of geometrical reasoning about numbers.

Lines are imagined as infinitely long and composed of a continuous set of points. In diagrams, only segments of a line are shown, sometimes with a few points distinguished by a dot to mark their position:

Dots or other markers for points are not meant to suggest that these points are bigger than any of the others; all points are dimensionless, with no height or width or depth. The line above is a straight line, meaning that if you imagined picking up a copy of it and moving that along the original, they would keep on matching no matter how far you moved the copy.

Two straight lines in the same plane (such as the surface of a piece of paper) are called **parallel** if they never intersect, however far they are imagined as extending in both directions. If they do intersect, they form **angles**:

In the diagram above, $L1$ and $L2$ are parallel; $L3$ and $L4$ intersect forming four angles (a, b, c, and d). Angles are measured by rotation; if you imagine keeping $L4$ fixed but rotating $L3$ counterclockwise around the point of intersection, $L3$ would coincide with $L4$ after rotating by c degrees. Angles a and b fit together along one side of straight line $L3$; their combined angle makes a rotation of 180°, also called a **straight angle**. That is, $a + b = 180°$. The sum of all four angles is one complete circle, 360°.

Notice that *b* and *c* also form a straight angle, as do *c* and *d*, and *d* and *a*. As a good first example of geometrical reasoning, we see

$$a + b = 180 = b + c;$$ therefore (cancelling *b*) $a = c$. Similarly, $b = d$.

Note: The **opposite angles** of intersecting lines are equal.

Pairs of angles that add up to 180° are known as **supplementary angles**; they needn't be adjacent angles lying along a line for this relationship to hold. The angles to the right are supplementary.

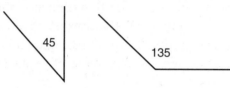

There is a special case of intersecting lines, where all four angles are equal; each angle must be 90° (each pair adds up to 180°, but since the two are equal, $r = 180/2°$). Angles of 90° are called **right angles**, and lines intersecting at right angles are described as **perpendicular**.

If a line intersects two parallel lines, there are several important relations among the angles that are formed:

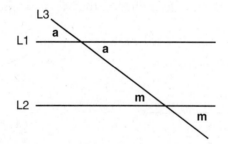

The opposite angles at the intersections are equal, as above. But if you could take the intersection of *L*1 and *L*3 and move it down and to the right, always keeping *L*1 parallel to *L*2, and moving *L*3 along its own length, you would get *L*1 eventually lying exactly on *L*2, and the two intersections will exactly coincide. That is, angle *a* = angle *m*. Similarly, the unmarked angles are also equal. The angles *a* and *m* are called **alternate interior angles**.

You don't need to know the terminology to answer any questions on the test, but this is one of the facts that will help you find correct answers when a geometry problem has parallel lines.

Reasoning that involves moving objects, or reflecting them in a mirror, or rotating them to discover that the objects coincide after these operations, is a basic tool of geometry. Figures, or parts of figures, that are the same after these operations are **symmetric**, and looking for symmetries is an important skill to develop for solving geometry problems.

Practice

Directions: Solve the following problems and blacken the space at the right under the number that corresponds to the one you have selected as the correct answer.

1. In this diagram, angle *s* equals

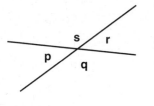

(1) *p*   (4) $90° - p$
(2) *q*   (5) $180° - q$
(3) *r*   **1.** ① ② ③ ④ ⑤

2. Which angle is supplementary to an angle of 36°?

(1) 54°   (4) 180°
(2) 90°   (5) 360°
(3) 144°   **2.** ① ② ③ ④ ⑤

3. In this diagram, $\angle a = \angle e = 30°$; $\angle c =$

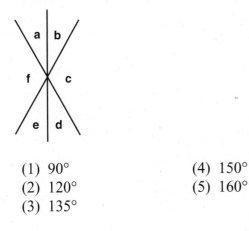

(1) 90°   (4) 150°
(2) 120°   (5) 160°
(3) 135°   **3.** ① ② ③ ④ ⑤

4. If line *L* is parallel to line *M* and ∠1 = 50°, ∠2 =

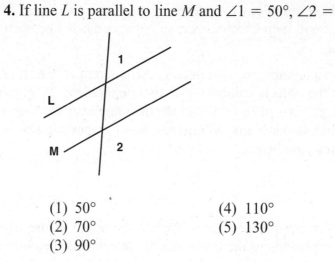

(1) 50°   (4) 110°
(2) 70°   (5) 130°
(3) 90°   **4.** ① ② ③ ④ ⑤

5. If line *V* is perpendicular to line *W*, how big is the angle *a* around their outside?

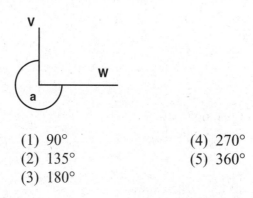

(1) 90°   (4) 270°
(2) 135°   (5) 360°
(3) 180°   **5.** ① ② ③ ④ ⑤

Answers

1. **2**   2. **3**   3. **2**   4. **5**   5. **4**

V. B. Figures Made of Straight Lines

B-1

When three or more lines in the same plane intersect each other, there is a central region with the lines as a boundary. The points of intersection are called **vertexes** (or **vertices**), and the line segments between vertexes are called **edges**. These points and line segments are emphasized in the diagram below:

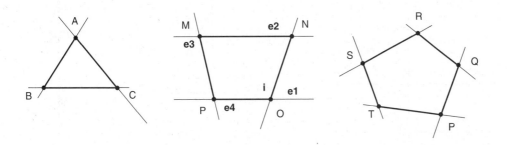

The figures are named from the number of edges (or angles; there is one angle for every edge): **triangles** have three edges and three angles, **quadrilaterals** have four, **pentagons** have five, etc. These names are derived from Latin or Greek words meaning three angles, four edges, and five angles, respectively.

There is an angle less than 180° on the inside of a plane figure like these, between any two successive edges. This is called an **interior angle**; the angle *i* between the edges *PO* and *ON* in the quadrilateral is an example of an interior angle. If you look at the extension of edge *PO* past the boundary of the quadrilateral, you see that the angle *e*1 is supplementary to *i*; it is called an **exterior angle** of the figure. The exterior angle is the amount you would have to turn (rotate) if you walked along edge *PO* and then along *ON*. If you make a complete circuit of the figure, you will have made four turns, totaling 360°. On a circuit of the pentagon, you'd make five turns, but again the total will be 360°. The sum of the exterior angles in a plane figure (like these, with all the interior angles less than 180°) is 360°. As a result of this, we get one of the most basic facts from plane geometry.

This follows because each interior angle and its exterior angle are supplementary. Each exterior angle is 180° minus the interior angle. In the triangle shown, use int(*A*) to stand for the interior angle at *A* and ext(*A*) for the exterior angle, and so on around the triangle, ext(*A*) = 180 − int(*A*), ext(*B*) = 180 − int(*B*), and ext(*C*) = 180 − int(*C*).

$$\text{ext}(A) + \text{ext}(B) + \text{ext}(C) = 360 =$$
$$180 - \text{int}(A) + 180 - \text{int}(B) + 180 - \text{int}(C).$$

Simplify this by adding int(*A*) + int(*B*) + int(*C*) to both sides, and subtracting 360.

TIP

The sum of the interior angles in a triangle is 180°.

A triangle with two sides equal is called **isosceles**; if all three sides are equal, it is **equilateral**. Isosceles triangles have an important property: the angles opposite the equal sides are equal. (You can see this from symmetry; imagine a vertical mirror going through the top vertex in the three triangles below, which are isosceles triangles placed with the third side horizontal. Each side will match the other in the mirror's reflection.) In an equilateral triangle, all the sides are equal; so all the angles are, too.

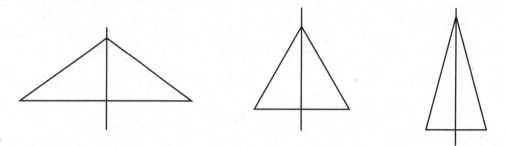

Note: The angles opposite the equal sides of an isosceles triangle are equal.

Note: An equilateral triangle has each of its angles equal to 60°.

These facts reflect a more general rule:

Note: In any triangle, the largest side is opposite the largest angle and the smallest side is opposite the smallest angle.

In figures with more than three sides, you can draw interior lines between a vertex and another vertex that is not immediately next to it. These lines are called **diagonals**. A quadrilateral has only two diagonals, and they intersect somewhere in the middle of the figure. By using diagonals, you can slice any multi-sided plane figure into triangles. This trick is sometimes useful in solving problems.

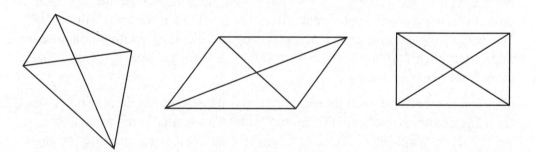

Some kinds of quadrilaterals are given special names from their distinctive properties. The most important of these are parallelograms, which have two sets of parallel lines as their opposite edges, and rectangles, in which all four angles are right angles. In the diagram above, the middle figure is a parallelogram and the one on the right is a rectangle. Rectangles are also parallelograms. In a rectangle, the diagonals are equal.

Practice

Directions: Solve the following problems and blacken the space at the right under the number that corresponds to the one you have selected as the correct answer.

1. What is the average size of an angle in any triangle?

    (1) 30°
    (2) 60°
    (3) 90°
    (4) 180°
    (5) Cannot be determined   **1.** ① ② ③ ④ ⑤

2. Triangle *ABC* has ∠*A* = 65°, and ∠*B* = 35°; ∠*C* is

    (1) 60°   (4) 90°
    (2) 70°   (5) 100°
    (3) 80°   **2.** ① ② ③ ④ ⑤

3. In triangle *PQR*, side *PQ* is equal to side *PR*.
   If ∠*P* = 48°, ∠*Q* =

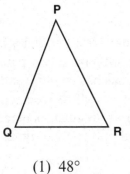

    (1) 48°   (4) 66°
    (2) 52°   (5) 90°
    (3) 60°   **3.** ① ② ③ ④ ⑤

4. In rectangle *EFGH*, diagonal *EG* = 5 feet.
   Diagonal *FH* is

    (1) 5 feet
    (2) 6 feet
    (3) 7 feet
    (4) 8 feet
    (5) Cannot be determined   **4.** ① ② ③ ④ ⑤

5. How many distinct diagonals can be drawn in pentagon *NOPQR*?

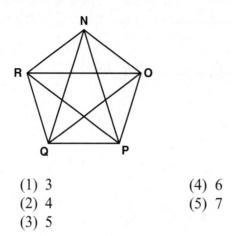

(1) 3 (4) 6
(2) 4 (5) 7
(3) 5

5. ① ② ③ ④ ⑤

Answers

1. **2**   2. **3**   3. **4**   4. **1**   5. **3**

B-2

Perimeter and Area

The **perimeter** of a plane figure is the total length of its sides. Parallelograms (and rectangles, which are a special case of parallelograms) have two pairs of equal sides, so their perimeter is $2(a + b)$ if one of the sides has length a and the adjacent side has length b. A **regular** figure is one that has all its sides equal. Equilateral triangles are regular figures, as are squares, regular pentagons, regular hexagons, etc. The perimeter of a regular n-sided polygon is n times the length of each side.

The **area** of a figure is a measure of its two-dimensional content. If you divide a rectangle 3 inches by 4 inches into squares 1-inch on a side, you can fit $3 \times 4 = 12$ such unit-squares into its interior. Its area is 12 square inches.

If you take a parallelogram and slice off the part that doesn't fit in a rectangle of the same height, and move that to the other side of the parallelogram, you get a rectangle.

TIP

The area of a rectangle is its width times its height $(A = w \times h)$.

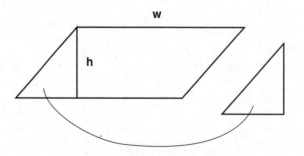

The measure of area remains unchanged by this, so the fact above generalizes to:

Any triangle can be put inside a parallelogram by reflecting it around one side as a diagonal for the parallelogram. The triangle is obviously one-half of the resulting parallelogram.

Note: The area of a parallelogram is its width times its height. All parallelograms with the same width and height have the same area ($A = w \times h$).

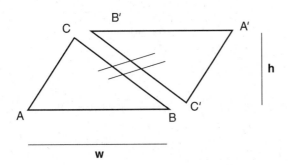

TIP

The area of a triangle is one-half its width times its height ($A = (w \times h)/2$).

Practice

Directions: Solve the following problems and blacken the space at the right under the number that corresponds to the one you have selected as the correct answer.

1. What is the perimeter of a parallelogram with one side 15 inches and one side 5 inches?

   (1) 10 inches   (4) 40 inches

   (2) 20 inches   (5) 50 inches

   (3) 30 inches

1. ① ② ③ ④ ⑤

2. The area of the figure in this diagram is

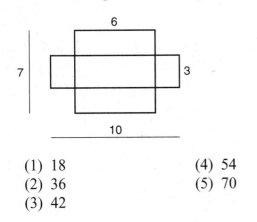

   (1) 18   (4) 54

   (2) 36   (5) 70

   (3) 42

2. ① ② ③ ④ ⑤

3. Rectangle *PQRS* shares a side with triangle *QST*. The area of △*QST* is

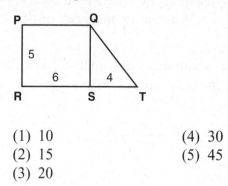

(1) 10   (4) 30
(2) 15   (5) 45
(3) 20

3. ① ② ③ ④ ⑤

4. Which triangle in the rectangle *ABCD* has the smallest area?

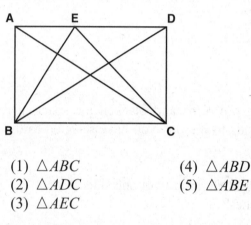

(1) △*ABC*   (4) △*ABD*
(2) △*ADC*   (5) △*ABE*
(3) △*AEC*

4. ① ② ③ ④ ⑤

5. The perimeter of a regular pentagon of side 8 inches is

(1) 24 inches
(2) 32 inches
(3) 40 inches
(4) 48 inches
(5) Cannot be determined from what is given

5. ① ② ③ ④ ⑤

Answers

1. **4**   2. **4**   3. **1**   4. **5**   5. **3**

B-3

Right Triangles

An important special case of triangles occurs when one of the angles is a right angle; since the sum of all three angles is 180°, when one of the angles is 90°, the others add up to 90°, so each of them must be less than 90°. (Angles whose sum is 90° are called **complementary angles**.) A right-angled triangle, or **right triangle**, is half of a rectangle. The longest side of the triangle, opposite the right angle, is called the **hypotenuse**; and the sides that form the right angle are called the **legs** of the right triangle. There is an extremely important relationship that holds for the sides of a right triangle; it is known as the Pythagorean Theorem.

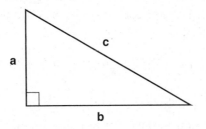

TIP

The square of the hypotenuse of a right triangle is equal to the sum of the squares of the legs (the other two sides). In the diagram (left), $c^2 = a^2 + b^2$. If you can only memorize *one* thing in geometry, *this* is the one to memorize!

You may be asked to figure out one side of a right triangle given two of the other sides. Sometimes, an approximate answer will be good enough, and you won't have to do complex calculations of squares and square roots (e.g., to find $a = \sqrt{(c^2 - b^2)}$). The most likely cases of right triangles you will see will not require this much work. Instead, they will use a few special cases. There are some right triangles that have "nice" sides:

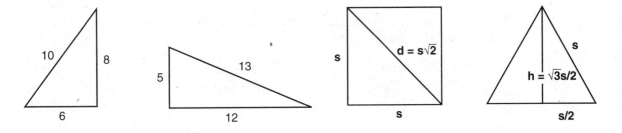

3-4-5 Triangle. $3^2 + 4^2 = 9 + 16 = 25 = 5^2$. Any triangle with sides of length 3, 4 and 5 (in any units) satisfies the Pythagorean Theorem, and the sides of length 3 and 4 are the legs, with the side of length 5 as the hypotenuse. You are very likely to see triangles that have sides of length 3, 4 and 5, or some small multiples of these values. Be on the lookout for 6-8-10 and 9-12-15 triangles as well as 3-4-5 triangles!

5-12-13 Triangle. $5^2 + 12^2 = 25 + 144 = 169 = 13^2$. This is another special case with simple whole number sides in a right triangle. Triangles with this ratio of the sides are less common on tests than 3-4-5 triangles, but be alert for them; here also you may see small multiples (10-24-26, for example). Reduce to lowest terms to see what you are dealing with.

Half-Square (or Isosceles Right Triangle). In a square of side *s*, the diagonal *d* is found from the Pythagorean rule to be: $d^2 = s^2 + s^2 = 2s^2$; $d = s\sqrt{2}$. Since the other angles of this triangle are equal, they must be 45°; and this triangle is also known as a 45° right triangle. It comes up often enough that you should memorize the relation of the hypotenuse to the sides (the relation of the diagonal of a square to its sides), namely $\sqrt{2} = 1.414\ldots$ For most problems, it is good enough to know that $\sqrt{2}$ is about 1.4.

Half-Equilateral (30-60-90) Triangle. Any isosceles triangle is made up of two right triangles, by drawing a line from the vertex between the equal side to its base (the third side). The most likely case of this to show up on tests uses the equilateral triangle. Splitting this in half gives a right triangle with angles of 30° and 60°. If the side of the equilateral triangle is *s*, the base is *s*/2, and the other leg of the triangle is given by

$$s^2 = (s/2)^2 + h^2$$

From this, $h^2 = s^2 - s^2/4 = 3s^2/4$, so $h = s\sqrt{3}/2$. Or, in other words, the height is $\sqrt{3}$ times the base (which is one-half the side of the equilateral triangle). $\sqrt{3} = 1.732\ldots$; again you can usually get by remembering that $\sqrt{3}$ is about 1.7.

Practice

Directions: Solve the following problems and blacken the space at the right under the number that corresponds to the one you have selected as the correct answer.

1. A right triangle has each of its short legs 6 inches long; its hypotenuse is about

    (1) 6.5 inches   (4) 9.5 inches
    (2) 7.5 inches   (5) 10.5 inches
    (3) 8.5 inches   **1.** ① ② ③ ④ ⑤

2. In △*LMN*, side *MN* is approximately

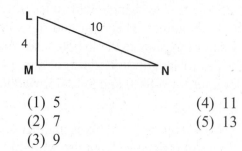

    (1) 5   (4) 11
    (2) 7   (5) 13
    (3) 9   **2.** ① ② ③ ④ ⑤

3. In △*PQR*, *RS* is perpendicular to *PQ*. Side *SQ* has length

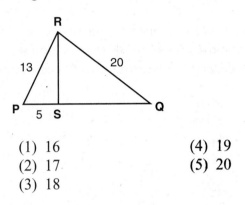

(1) 16
(2) 17
(3) 18
(4) 19
(5) 20

3. ① ② ③ ④ ⑤

4. The height of an equilateral triangle with side 20 feet is about

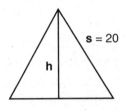

(1) 10 square feet
(2) 14 square feet
(3) 15 square feet
(4) 17 square feet
(5) 20 square feet

4. ① ② ③ ④ ⑤

5. An isosceles triangle has a base of 8 inches, and the equal sides are each 5 inches. The area of the triangle is

(1) 6 square inches
(2) 12 square inches
(3) 18 square inches
(4) 24 square inches
(5) 40 square inches

5. ① ② ③ ④ ⑤

Answers

1. **3**   2. **3**   3. **1**   4. **4**   5. **2**

V. C. Circles

C-1

In addition to plane figures made up of straight lines, geometry also studies figures with curved boundaries. The most important of these is a **circle**, a continuous set of points all at the same distance (the **radius**) from a **center** point.

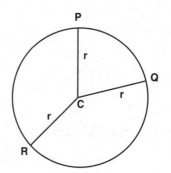

In this diagram, C is the center, and points P, Q and R are on the circle at radius r from the center at C. A line through the center from one side of a circle to the other is called a **diameter** of the circle; it is the largest line that can be drawn inside a circle. A diameter extends in both directions from the center of the circle to its boundary; so a diameter is exactly twice the length of a radius.

The perimeter of a circle (also called its **circumference**) always has the same ratio to its diameter. That ratio has a special name, π (pronounced "pie").

A slice of the circle, like the figure QCP with the curved arc from P to Q and the radial lines PC and QC, is called a **sector** of the circle. The arc PQ has the same ratio to the circumference that the angle PQC has to $360°$. If the angle is $80°$, then the length of PQ is $80/360 = 8/36 = 2/9$ (about 22%) of the circumference. The area of the sector is the same fraction of the area of the whole circle.

A plane figure is **inscribed** in a circle if all its vertexes lie on the circle; it is **circumscribed** around the circle if each edge just touches the circle (without cutting across the curve.) In the diagram below, the figures on the left and right are inscribed and the figure in the middle is circumscribed. If a square or other regular figure is inscribed in or circumscribed around a circle, its center (the intersection of its diagonals) will be the same point as the center of the circle.

TIP

The circumference (perimeter) of a circle is $C = \pi \times D = 2\pi \times r$.

TIP

The area of a circle is $A = \pi \times r^2$. A sector of a circle with angle n degrees at its center has area $(n/360) \times \pi \times r^2$.

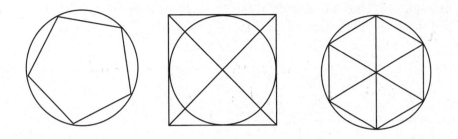

For inscribed and circumscribed squares, you should be able to figure out the relation between the radius or diameter of the circle and a side or a diagonal of the square. In the diagram above, for example, the side of the square is equal to the diameter (and, therefore, to twice the radius) of the circle. The regular hexagon case is also worth remembering; here, the hexagon divides into 6 equilateral triangles with all the sides equal to the radius of the circle.

If you are asked to compare the areas of some figure with a circle, use a sketch or your imagination to see if the circle can fit around or inside the figure. In the diagram above, the circle obviously has less area than the square and more area than the pentagon or hexagon, and you can conclude that without knowing any formulas for the areas.

Practice

Directions: Solve the following problems and blacken the space at the right under the number that corresponds to the one you have selected as the correct answer.

1. A circle has area 4π; its circumference is

   (1) π (4) 4

   (2) 2   (5) 4π

   (3) 2π **1.** ① ② ③ ④ ⑤

2. In this diagram, the rectangle is formed by joining the centers of the circles. The circles each have area π; the perimeter of the rectangle is

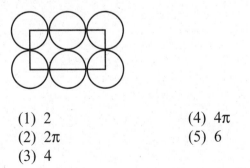

   (1) 2   (4) 4π

   (2) 2π (5) 6

   (3) 4   **2.** ① ② ③ ④ ⑤

3. Triangle *ABC* has a diameter of the circle as its base, and *AC = BC*. The area of *ABC* is

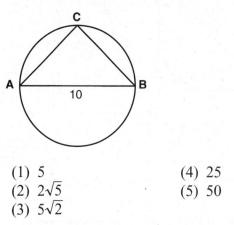

(1) 5
(2) $2\sqrt{5}$
(3) $5\sqrt{2}$

(4) 25
(5) 50

3. ① ② ③ ④ ⑤

4. A circle is inscribed in a square of side 10; what is the area inside the square but outside the circle?

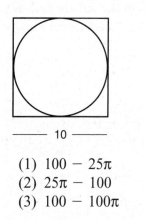

—— 10 ——

(1) $100 - 25\pi$
(2) $25\pi - 100$
(3) $100 - 100\pi$

(4) π
(5) $100 - 10\pi$

4. ① ② ③ ④ ⑤

5. A wheel is 4 feet in diameter; about how far does it travel in 12 revolutions?

(1) 100 feet
(2) 125 feet
(3) 150 feet

(4) 175 feet
(5) 200 feet

5. ① ② ③ ④ ⑤

Answers

1. **5**   2. **5**   3. **4**   4. **1**   5. **3**

V. D. Solid Figures and Volume

D-1

Geometry also studies figures that are not totally in one plane, but have depth as well as height and width. These figures are harder to deal with but are more like the ordinary objects around us in our three-dimensional world. You do not have to expect many questions about solid figures on the test, but you should know some basic facts about rectangular solids and about cylinders and spheres.

The simplest solid figures are rectangular solids; these are rectangles extruded (extended) from one plane into a perpendicular direction behind the surface of the original rectangle. Solid figures are usually sketched with their depth dimension hinted at by angling away from the straight up-and-down of a plane figure.

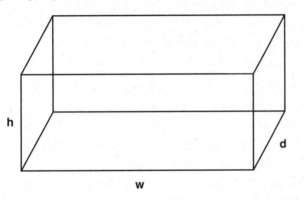

Just as we measure the area of a plane figure by filling it with unit squares (or fractions of unit squares), we measure the solid content (the **volume**) of a three-dimensional figure by filling it with unit cubes. If the rectangular solid above is 6 inches long, 4 inches high, and 3 inches deep, there will be $6 \times 4 \times 3 = 72$ cubes, each one 1 inch on a side, filling it. Its volume is 72 cubic inches.

Just as in the case of a parallelogram, a solid can be made up of parallel planes that are not at right angles to each other; however, the volume will still be $w \times h \times d$ if you measure each dimension along perpendicular axes rather than along the edges of the solid.

In general, if you know the area of a plane figure, and you extend it perpendicularly into the depth dimension, the volume will be the area of the figure times its depth. The most common example of this is a **cylinder**, which is just a circle extended into the third dimension. The volume of a cylinder is $V = \pi \times r^2 \times d$.

TIP

The volume of a rectangular solid is width $\times$ height $\times$ depth, $V = w \times h \times d$.

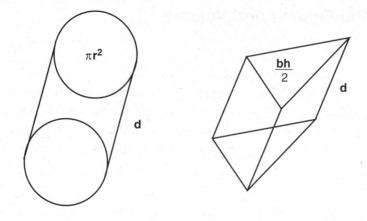

The solid on the right is a **triangular prism** (a triangle extended in depth). This figure has volume $V = b \times h \times d/2$, where b is the base of the triangle, h is its height, and d is the depth in the third dimension. This is just the area of the triangle ($\frac{1}{2}b \times h$) times the depth.

A *sphere* is a solid figure formed by rotating a circle around a diameter as an axis. It is just barely possible that you may need to know the volume of a sphere, which is $V = 4/3\pi \times r^3$. It is more likely that you will be asked to compare spheres with other solids such as cylinders and cubes. Like area problems involving circumscribed and inscribed figures, the key here is to see which figures fit inside the others. For example, a sphere of diameter 10 fits inside a cylinder with radius 5 and height 10.

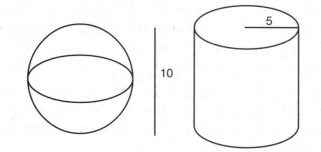

Practice

Directions: Solve the following problems and blacken the space at the right under the number that corresponds to the one you have selected as the correct answer.

1. A shipping box is 36 inches by 24 inches by 18 inches; how many cubic feet can it hold?

    (1) 8   (4) 12
    (2) 9   (5) 15
    (3) 10   **1.** ① ② ③ ④ ⑤

2. A cylinder has a diameter of 2 feet and a height of 10 feet. Its volume is approximately

    (1) $31.5\,\text{ft}^3$ (4) $94\,\text{ft}^3$
    (2) $40\,\text{ft}^3$ (5) $126\,\text{ft}^3$
    (3) $63\,\text{ft}^3$ **2.** ① ② ③ ④ ⑤

3. Which of the following is too big to fit in a box 2 feet by 2 feet by 3 feet?

    (1) a sphere of radius 1 foot
    (2) a cube of side 2 feet
    (3) a cylinder of radius 1 foot and height
        3 feet
    (4) a sphere of radius 2 feet
    (5) a cylinder of diameter 2 feet and height
        2 feet   **3.** ① ② ③ ④ ⑤

4. A sphere of diameter 6 inches holds

    (1) 25 cubic inches
    (2) 36 cubic inches
    (3) 25π cubic inches
    (4) 36π cubic inches
    (5) 1000 cubic inches   **4.** ① ② ③ ④ ⑤

Answers

1. **2**   2. **1**   3. **4**   4. **4**

V. E. Coordinate Geometry

E-1

The number line is a one-dimensional graph, with an imagined grid marking whole number positions. We can extend the graph into two dimensions by taking a horizontal number line and a vertical number line that intersects it at right angles, with the zero-point of both lines as the intersection. This point is called the **origin**, and the number lines are the *axes*. The horizontal *axis* is usually labeled *x*, and the vertical axis is labeled *y*.

The **position** of a point is given by writing a pair of numbers in parentheses, as (x,y), where you find *x* by locating the horizontal position of the point along the *x*-axis and *y* by its vertical position along the *y*-axis. On graph paper, with vertical and horizontal lines at every whole number on the axes, these values are easy to find (or to estimate) if the point is not exactly on these lines.

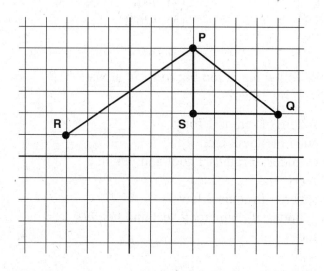

In this diagram, *P* is (3,5), *Q* is (7,2) and *R* is (−3,1).

Coordinate graphs like this are set up to allow right triangle calculations using the Pythagorean Theorem. For example, a line from *P* to *Q* is the hypotenuse of a right triangle where the legs are segments of coordinate grid lines, drawn a bit thicker in the diagram to emphasize them. The third vertex of this right triangle is at *S*, which has the coordinates (3,2). Similarly, *P* and *R* form a right triangle with a point one unit below *S* at coordinates (3,1). To find the distance from *P* to *Q*, notice that the leg *PS* has length 3 and the leg *SQ* has length 4. So you should recognize that *PQS* is a 3-4-5 right triangle, and so *PQ* has length 5. In general, use the Pythagorean Theorem:

$$RP^2 = 6^2 + 4^2 = 36 + 16 = 52; \text{ therefore } RP = \sqrt{52} = 2\sqrt{13}.$$

Note: The distance between points (x_1,y_1) and $(x_2,y_2) = \sqrt{(x_1-x_2)^2+(y_1-y_2)^2}$.

$(x_1 - x_2)$ is the horizontal part of the distance; $(y_2 - y_1)$ is the vertical part. These are the legs of the right triangle, and the distance is the hypotenuse of that triangle.

You can find the midpoint of the line between P and Q by going halfway in the x-direction (2 units) and halfway in the y-direction ($1\frac{1}{2}$ units). The coordinates can be found by averaging the original (x,y) coordinates:

Note: The midpoint of the line from (x_1,y_1) to $(x_2,y_2) = [\frac{1}{2}(x_1 + x_2), \frac{1}{2}(y_1 + y_2)]$.

E-2

Slope. The **slope** of a line is a measure of how steep it is. A horizontal line has slope 0, and a line that starts at the origin and goes through (1,1), (2,2), (3,3), etc., is going up in the y-direction exactly as rapidly as it covers horizontal distance in the x-direction. The definition is:

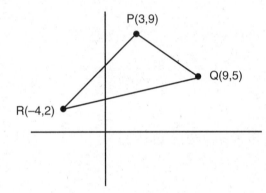

Note: The slope of the line from (x_1,y_1) to $(x_2,y_2) = (y_2 - y_1)/(x_2 - x_1)$.

Less formally, the slope is "rise" over "run," where "rise" means the change in vertical position and "run" means the change in horizontal position. Either the numerator or the denominator can be negative in this formula, and you must be careful to use the coordinates in the correct order (subtract the first point from the second; put another way, the change is what you have to add to the first point to get to the second one).

The line from R to Q has slope $(5 - 2)/[9 - (-4)] = 3/13$. It is rising gently, at a small fraction (slope $= 1$ means rising at a 45° angle from the horizontal; the angle here must be smaller than 45°). The line from P to Q has slope $(5 - 9)/(9 - 3) = -4/6 = -2/3$. The negative slope indicates that the line is dropping (negative rise) as it goes to the right. In a horizontal line, $(y_2 - y_1) = 0$, so the slope is 0; in a vertical line $(x_2 - x_1) = 0$, and division by it is undefined. You may think of it as "infinite"—as the angle of the line with the horizontal increases toward 90°, the slope gets larger and larger, without limit.

Practice

Directions: Solve the following problems and blacken the space at the right under the number that corresponds to the one you have selected as the correct answer.

1. The distance between the points (2,1) and (5,7) is

(1) 9   (4) $\sqrt{45}$

(2) $\sqrt{5}$ (5) $\sqrt{75}$

(3) $\sqrt{9}$ **1.** ① ② ③ ④ ⑤

2. A circle of radius 4 with its center at the origin passes through all of the following points *except*

(1) (−4,0)   (4) (4,0)

(2) (4,4)   (5) (0,−4)

(3) (0,4)   **2.** ① ② ③ ④ ⑤

3. The midpoint of the line from (−2,3) to (6,5) is

(1) (4,8)   (4) (3,3)

(2) (8,2)   (5) (0,0)

(3) (2,4)   **3.** ① ② ③ ④ ⑤

4. The slope of the line from (2,7) to (9,1) is

(1) −6/7   (4) 1

(2) 7/6   (5) 0

(3) 9/7   **4.** ① ② ③ ④ ⑤

5. The slope of the line through the points (2,−3) and (2,7) is

(1) 2   (4) 1

(2) −3/5   (5) undefined

(3) 5/3   **5.** ① ② ③ ④ ⑤

Answers

1. **4**   2. **2**   3. **3**   4. **1**   5. **5**

E-3

Linear Equations

Any algebraic expression using x and y variables in the form $ax + by = c$ is called a **linear equation**. If we have the slope of the line (call it m) and one point on the line, say $(x0, y0)$, then for any other point (x, y) we have

$$\frac{(y - y0)}{(x - x0)} = m, \text{ or } y = y0 + m(x - x0) = mx + (y0 - mx0).$$

The value $(y0 - mx0)$ has an interesting geometrical meaning; it is the value of y for this line when x is zero – in other words, the point where the line crosses the y-axis of the graph. This is also called the "y-intercept" for the line. Any linear equation can be rewritten to have this form; for example, $ax + by = c$ becomes $y = -ax/b + c/b$. Graphs with straight lines are usually written in this "slope-intercept" form. If the slope is positive, all points on the line to the right of the y-axis will be proportionally higher than the y-intercept; if the slope is negative, the points to the right of the y-axis will be proportionally lower than the y-intercept.

Similar to the y-intercept, the x-intercept of the line is the point where the line crosses the x-axis; that is, the point where the y-coordinate is zero. The x-intercept is also easy to calculate from the equation of the line:

For the line $y = mx + k$, at the x-intercept $y = 0$, and so $mx = -k$, so $x = -k/m$.

The x-intercept of this line is $(-k/m, 0)$.

EXAMPLE

Calculate the slope, the y-intercept, and the x-intercept of the line $y = x/2 - 5$.

The slope (the factor by which y changes with x) is the coefficient of x in this equation, namely 1/2. (For every two units x moves to the right, y moves up one unit.) The y-intercept (the point on the line where x is 0) is $(0, -5)$; just "plug in" 0 in the equation for the line to get the y value. For the x-intercept, substitute $y = 0$ to get

$$0 = x/2 - 5$$

Simplify this to $x/2 = 5$ and then multiply both sides by 2 to get $x = 10$. The x-intercept is $(10, 0)$.

These two points should give you a good picture of the line: it crosses the vertical axis 5 units below the origin, and rises fairly slowly to cross the horizontal axis 10 units to the right of the origin. The graph of the line looks like this:

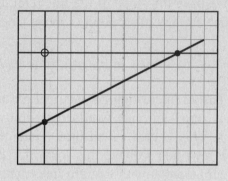

EXAMPLE

What is the equation of the line in the graph below?

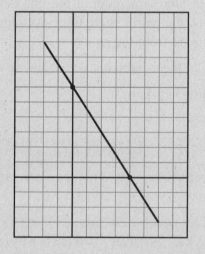

This line intercepts the *y*-axis at the point (0,6) and the *x*-axis at the point (4,0). That is, the line drops 6 units while moving 4 units to the right. That is, $(y1 - y0) = 0 - 6 = -6$, and $(x1 - x0) = 4 - 0 = 4$. The slope of the line is $-6/4 = -3/2$, and the value of *y* at the *y*-intercept is 6, so the equation of the line is:

$$y = \frac{-3}{2}x + 6$$

Practice

Directions: For each graph below, find the equation of the line represented by the graph. Assume each square on the graphs is 1 × 1.

1.

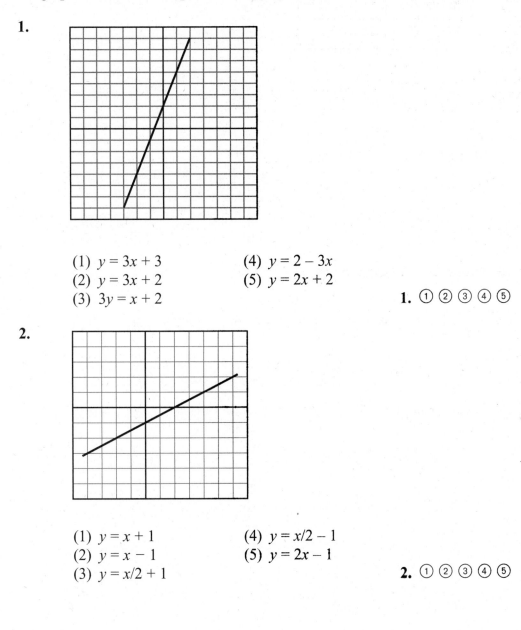

(1) $y = 3x + 3$ (4) $y = 2 - 3x$

(2) $y = 3x + 2$ (5) $y = 2x + 2$

(3) $3y = x + 2$

1. ① ② ③ ④ ⑤

2.

(1) $y = x + 1$ (4) $y = x/2 - 1$

(2) $y = x - 1$ (5) $y = 2x - 1$

(3) $y = x/2 + 1$

2. ① ② ③ ④ ⑤

3.

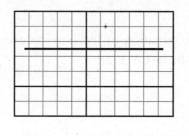

(1) $y = x + 2$ (4) $y = 2.5$

(2) $y = x + 2.5$ (5) $y = 3$

(3) $y = 2$

3. ① ② ③ ④ ⑤

4. What is the slope of the line $3y = 2 - 5x$?

(1) 2   (4) $y = 5/3$

(2) 5   (5) $y = -5/3$

(3) 3/5

4. ① ② ③ ④ ⑤

Answers

1. **2**   2. **3**   3. **4**   4. **5**

Summary of Important Facts from Geometry

$\pi = 3.14\ldots \sqrt{2} = 1.41\ldots \sqrt{3} = 1.73\ldots$

Intersecting Lines:

If two lines intersect, opposite angles are equal.

If a line intersects two parallel lines, alternate interior angles are equal.

Triangles:

The sum of the interior angles in a triangle is $180°$.

An equilateral triangle has each of its angles equal to $60°$.

The angles opposite the equal sides of an isosceles triangle are equal.

In any triangle, the largest side is opposite the largest angle and the smallest side is opposite the smallest angle.

Right Triangles:

In a right triangle, $c^2 = a^2 + b^2$ (Pythagorean Theorem).

Triangles with sides in the ratio $3:4:5$ are right triangles.

Triangles with sides in the ratio $5:12:13$ are right triangles.

A $45°$ right triangle (half-square) of side s has hypotenuse $s\sqrt{2}$.

A $30°$-$60°$-$90°$ triangle with short side s has height $s\sqrt{3}$.

Area and Volume:

Area of a rectangle or parallelogram with base b and height h,

$A = b \times h$.

Area of a square of side s, $A = s^2$.

Area of a triangle with base b and height h, $A = (b \times h)/2$.

Area of a circle of radius r, $A = \pi r^2$ (circumference $C = 2\pi r$).

Volume of a rectangular solid or parallelepiped with base b, height h and depth d, $V = b \times h \times d$.

Volume of a cube of side s, $V = s^3$.

Volume of a cylinder of radius r and height h, $V = \pi r^2 h$.

Volume of a sphere of radius r, $V = \pi r^3$.

Coordinate Geometry:

The distance between points (x_1, y_1) and $(x_2, y_2) =$

$\sqrt{(x_1 - x_2)^2 + (y_1 - y_2)^2}$.

The midpoint of the line from $(x_1 y_1)$ to $(x_2, y_2) =$
$[\frac{1}{2}(x_1 + x_2), \frac{1}{2}(y_1 + y_2)]$.

The slope of the line from (x_1, y_1) to $(x_2, y_2) = (y_2 - y_1)/(x_2 - x_1)$.

The slope-intercept form of a linear equation is:

$y = mx + b$

where m is the slope of the line, and b is the y-coordinate where the line intercepts the y-axis.

VI. DATA, GRAPHS, AND STATISTICS

Mathematical skills and reasoning, both with calculations and the kind of spatial thinking used in geometry, play a big part in "data analysis"—in science, engineering, economics, manufacturing, and other areas. Aspects of this kind of math frequently show up in the news, as the basis for arguments and discussion of public policy. Some basic ideas and practices are important in handling this kind of material.

VI. A. Scientific Notation

A-1

Orders of Magnitude

For most things in our everyday lives, the sizes and numbers of items have a fairly small range: tens or dozens of pens and pencils, maybe a hundred or so CDs, or a thousand songs on an MP3 player. Most sizes range from an eighth or sixteenth of an inch up to several yards (or from a few millimeters up to several meters). In science or technical fields like engineering, however, there are lots of very large or very small numbers: computer processors on a solid-state 22 nanometer process (a nanometer is one-billionth of a meter), galaxies like the Andromeda galaxy "near by" at 2.6 million light-years distance, and comprising about one trillion stars, billions of bacteria in a single gram of soil, etc. The most common way to write, and do calculations with, very large or small numbers is "scientific notation," using a decimal value between 1 and 10 followed by a power of 10 to give the *order of magnitude*. For example, the Andromeda galaxy's distance is 2.6×10^6 light years distant; Intel's "Ivy Bridge" CPU process die is 22×10^{-9} meters; the Pacific Ocean is 64.1 million square miles in area, or 6.41×10^7 miles^2.

Each factor of 10 increases (for positive exponents) or decreases (for negative ones) the order of magnitude.

EXAMPLE

The area of the state of California, 163,695 square miles, would be written in scientific notation as 1.63695×10^5 miles^2, or more likely would usually be rounded off to 1.6×10^5 or 1.64×10^5.

Note that you must "move the decimal point 5 places to the left" (starting from after the 5 at the end of this number, as written). Each move of the decimal point adds one to the exponent of 10.

The state of Rhode Island, at 1,545 square miles, would be 1.545×10^3 (or rounded to 1.5×10^3) miles^2. Here, the decimal point moves 3 places to the left. For numbers less than 1, each decimal place you move the point to the *right* is another *negative* power of 10.

Note that California's area is close to 100 (10^2) times as large as Rhode Island's; one way to say this is to observe (from the exponents of the power of 10 in the scientific notation) that the area of CA is "2 orders of magnitude" (*i.e.*, two powers of 10) larger than that of RI.

Practice

Directions: Convert each of these numbers in common notation into scientific notation. Note that some of the answers will be given as rounded-off values. What is important is the left-most digits (the "most significant" digits) and the exponent (the "order of magnitude").

1. 1,717,854

2. 0.004356

3. 123,456,789,012

4. 0.0000000075

Directions: Convert each of these numbers into "common notation" (no factors of 10^n).

5. 7.35×10^5

6. 2.92×10^{-4}

7. 1.2345×10^8

8. 8.1×10^{-2}

Answers

1. 1.2×10^6 2. 4.356×10^{-3} 3. 1.234×10^{11} 4. 7.5×10^{-9}

5. 735,000 6. 0.000292 7. 123,450,000 8. 0.081

A-2

Significant Digits

Measurements always have errors. Sometimes, it is just a matter of "rounding error," where you record the value to the closest mark on a scale. Sometimes (*e.g.,* when sampling and using averages), there are other sources of possible error. When you see a number like $n.nn \times 10^i$, you should usually assume that the last digit is rounded, and the actual value is just somewhere between ($n.nn - 0.005$) and ($n.nn + 0.005$). That is, the leftmost 3 digits are "meaningful," and anything beyond that is more noise than information. Scientific measurements typically omit any measured digits beyond (to the right) of those that analysis indicates are sufficiently above the "noise" level to be meaningful—that is, the *significant* digits.

EXAMPLE

Doing arithmetic on numbers in scientific notation can be a bit misleading about the significance of the digits. Suppose we multiply 2.8×10^4 by 7.9×10^{-3}. Mathematically, this works out to:

$$(2.8 \times 7.9) \times 10^4 \times 10^{-3} = 22.12 \times 10^{(4-3)} = 22.12 \times 10^1 = 2.212 \times 10^2$$

However, rounding error in the .8 of the first factor and the .9 of the second (or other sources of error) magnify the uncertainty in the answer. It is almost certain that the actual result does not have all four digits containing good information. As a very rough rule of thumb (actual data analysis is more complex than this, unfortunately!), the answer is not going to have *more* significant digits than either of the two factors. So, instead of writing four digits in the answer to the multiplication above, it is likely that using just two digits gives a "better" answer (in the sense of not suggesting a false precision): 2.2×10^2.

Practice

Directions: Perform the indicated arithmetic operations below and give the result in scientific notation, rounded to three significant digits.

1. $(1.23 \times 10^4) \times (3.10 \times 10^{-2})$

2. $2.35 \times 10^{-2} + 6.89 \times 10^{-3}$

3. $(7.65 \times 10^{12}) \div (1.50 \times 10^5)$

4. $6.37 \times 10^9 - 1.25 \times 10^5$

Answers

1. 3.81×10^2 **2.** 3.04×10^{-2} **3.** 5.10×10^7 **4.** 6.37×10^9

VI. B. Graphing Data—Scatter Plots

Algebra studies straight lines and quadratic graphs (for equations like $y = mx + b$, or $y = ax^2 + bx + c$), among others. Graphs like these express functions; for each value of x, there is a function or formula that determines the value of y. (We called such graphs formula graphs in Section III. E of this chapter.) With real-world data (in science, for example), we often do not know at the outset whether there is any simple relationship between two variables, or what the relationship might be. Graphs provide one "view" of the data that can help to answer questions about the relationships. Here is an example.

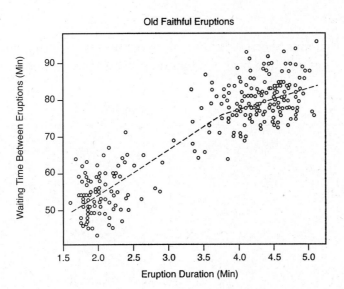

In this graph, each point represents one eruption of the Old Faithful Geyser in Yellowstone National Park; the *x* value is the length of time the eruption lasted, and the *y* value is the number of minutes between the previous eruption and the current one.

This is a scatter plot or scatter graph, often a useful tool for finding patterns in data. In this case, one interesting pattern is that there are two clusters of data points—one cluster around 2 minutes duration for the eruptions and a bit more than 50 minutes waiting time, and another around 4.5 minutes eruption time and 80 minutes waiting time. There are relatively few eruptions of 3 minutes duration, or at waits of about 70 minutes.

If you are at Old Faithful, and it has been over an hour since the last eruption, it looks like a pretty good bet that you will see a long one (4 minutes or so) within half an hour. The graph suggests a very rough general relationship, that the longer the wait, the longer the eruption will be. This is a relatively "weak" correlation, since the points are indeed "scattered" over a wide range; if all the points were more tightly clustered near the dotted line drawn in the graph, the relationship of wait time and eruption duration would be stronger.

Practice

Directions: Examine the two scatter plots below for patterns, and blacken the space to the right with the best description given in the questions below.

Graph A   Graph B

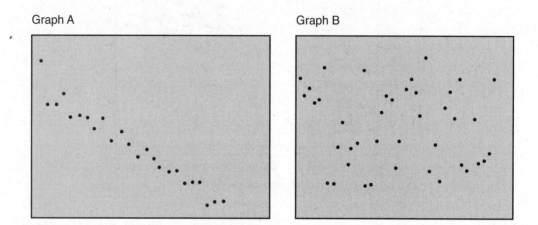

1. For Graph A,

      (1) as *x* increases, *y* increases
      (2) as *x* increases, *y* decreases
      (3) there is a cluster of points in the middle
          of the graph
      (4) there are two clusters of points in the graph
      (5) no pattern is present in this data   **1.** ① ② ③ ④ ⑤

2. For Graph B,

      (1) as *x* increases, *y* increases
      (2) as *x* increases, *y* decreases
      (3) there is a cluster of points in the middle
          of the graph
      (4) there are two clusters of points in the graph
      (5) no pattern is present in this data   **2.** ① ② ③ ④ ⑤

Answers

1. **2**   2. **5**

VI. C. Graphing Data—Histograms

When there is a limited set of values, and a lot of data, a variation of the pictograph or bar graph of Sections III. A and III. B, called a histogram is often used to give a visual overview of the data. For example, in digital cameras or photo processing software, the range of pixel brightness from darkest (0) to brightest (255) is often displayed in a histogram. Here is one example.

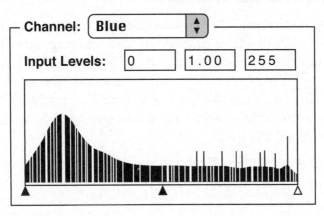

What this shows is vertical bars or lines at each pixel value 0–255, with the height proportional to the number of pixels having that value, which may be thousands of pixels in modern digital cameras. In this case, the dark blues (near the left side of the graph) have more pixels than comparable regions on the light blue side. The "peak" in the graph, about 1/8 of the way from the left side (so, at a pixel value of about 30–40) is called a mode (or modal value) of the distribution. If there were two peaks, the graph would be bi-modal.

Histograms can be given horizontally as well as vertically, and represented (as in a pictograph) with other graphic symbols than lines. For example, here is a table of the heights of a group of 50 ten-year old girls, rounded to the nearest inch:

Height	Number of girls
48	*
49	
50	***
51	***
52	***
53	***********
54	*********
55	********
56	******
57	*
58	**
59	*

Each * marks the height of one girl in the group. Doing this, instead of just writing the number of girls at each height, turns the table into a histogram. As for the photo histogram, this one also has a mode, in this case at 53 inches, and the values nearby are also generally higher than those at the extreme high and low values recorded.

VI. D. Mean, Median, and Mode

The **mode**, or modal value (the highest value in a set of data values), is one measure of the center of a table or graph of data. There are other measures, generally more useful for extended calculation or data analysis, namely the **mean** (the arithmetic average of the values) and the **median** (the value or values with an equal number of data points higher or lower). For certain kinds of data (like heights, or pixel values in a photo), the mode may be the easiest to spot—just look at the graph and there it is.

The mean is what people usually think of as the "average"; it is the sum of all the values divided by the number of data points. In the previous height example, it would be

$$(48 + 50 + 50 + 50 + 51 + 51 + 51 + \ldots + 57 + 58 + 58 + 59)/50 = 2692/50$$

or 5384/100 = 53.84 inches. Adding this many numbers can be difficult. One way to simplify the task is to keep a running total of the differences from the lowest value in the table; the mean of the data values is the lowest value plus the mean of the differences:

Height	Number	Diff.	Total
48	1	0	0
49	0	1	0
50	3	3×2	6
51	3	3×3	15
52	3	3×4	27
53	12	12×5	87
54	9	9×6	141
55	9	9×7	204
56	6	6×8	252
57	1	9	261
58	2	2×10	281
59	1	11	292

This adds up to $292/50 = 584/100 = 5.84$ as the mean difference from 48 inches, so the mean height is $48 + 5.84 = 53.84$, just as you would find if you did the full addition of all the height values. (Do not expect to have to do this much arithmetic on the test!)

Finally, the median is generally easier to find than the mean, and often equally or more useful. In the sample of 50 heights, we need to find the height that has 25 girls that height or lower and 25 girls that height or higher. To find this, just add up the number of asterisks (or the second column in the table we used for the mean calculation) until you reach 25. For 48 to 52 inches we get $1 + 3 + 3 + 3 = 10$ girls, at 53 inches there are 12 more to reach 22, and part way into the 54-inch group we pass 25. Notice that we do not get a perfect division into two groups of 25; in this case, there are 22 girls less than 54 inches tall and 19 more than 54 inches. Or you could express this as 31 girls $\leq$ 54 inches and $28 \geq 54$ inches. For simplicity, we usually just take whatever the data value is that has the "middle" data points (the 25th and 26th girls in this case, the third and fourth girls in the 54-inch group) and say the median height is 54 inches. What matters is that the exact division into two equal groups comes (somewhere in the group) at value 54. Sometimes it may make sense to give a more precise estimate. The girls listed with height 54 inches probably range in height from 53.5 inches to 54.5 inches, with 54 being just the height rounded to the nearest inch. In this case, the division would be 3/9 of the way from 53.5 to 54.5, so $53.5 + \frac{1}{3} = 53.5 + 0.33 = 53.83$.

What if we have a situation like this:

51	2
52	4
53	6
54	6
55	4
56	2

Here, either 53 or 54 could be said to have half the values above and half below. In a case like this, it is usual to "split the difference" and make the median 53.5. If there are an odd number of data points, the "middle point" will always have one of the listed values; when the number of points is even, there is no middle point as such, but either you will get points on either side of the middle all having the same value (as in the 50-girl sample, where the 25th and 26th heights are the same) or the even split shown in this last example, where the 12th and 13th values (of 24) are different.

Natural measurements like height are examples of **normal distributions**. As you add more measurements, they all center on the mean value, with most of the measurements close to the mean, with fewer and fewer values as you get further away from that. The mean, median, and mode are all close, even in small samples like the preceding one. Other kinds of data are "skewed" in comparison to the normal distributions. For example, here is a histogram of U.S. household incomes for 2005. Each bar represents the percentage of U.S. households with yearly incomes in the range between the numbers shown on either side of the horizontal axis.

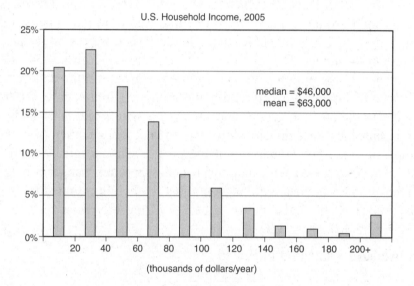

This graph has its peak, its mode, between $20,000 and $40,000 annual income, where about 23% of American households appear. The first two bars add up to 44%, and the fraction between $40,000 and $60,000 is 18%. One-third of that 18% is enough to reach 50%; so the graph can show that the median is about $40,000 plus $20,000/3, or $46,666. (U.S. government statistics give the median as $46,326, which is rounded to $46,000 in the legend on the graph.) The mean is higher still because even though there are fewer and fewer households with the larger incomes, each one adds more to the average than the households below the median do.

Practice

Directions: Use the table below, giving the heights for 20 boys at age 15, to answer the next three questions.

Height (inches)	59	61	62	63	64	65	66	67	68	69	70	73
Number	1	1	1	1	2	2	2	3	2	2	2	1

1. What is the median height of this group of boys?

(1) 65

(2) 65.5

(3) 66

(4) 66.5

(5) 67

1. ① ② ③ ④ ⑤

2. What is the modal value of the boys' heights?

(1) 65

(2) 66

(3) 67

(4) 68

(5) 69

2. ① ② ③ ④ ⑤

3. What is the mean height, to the nearest inch, of the data in this table?

(1) 65

(2) 66

(3) 67

(4) 68

(5) 67

3. ① ② ③ ④ ⑤

Answers

1. **4**   2. **3**   3. **2**

VI. E. Correlation and Trends

It is common to see lines drawn on scatter plots to show a formula for the relationships in the graph. For example, the Old Faithful Eruptions graph at the start of this section has a line through the cluster of points on the lower left of the graph, bending to a line with lower slope through the cluster on the upper right. These lines allow a prediction of the expected eruption length for a given wait time (or the other way around). Since the points are scattered widely around the lines in that graph, the prediction in this case is quite loose. From the line on the graph, you would expect an eruption that lasts for 3 minutes to have a waiting time before it of about 63 minutes—but it would not be surprising for the wait to be as much as 10 minutes more or less than that.

For the two scatter plots used for practice in Section VI. B., we get:

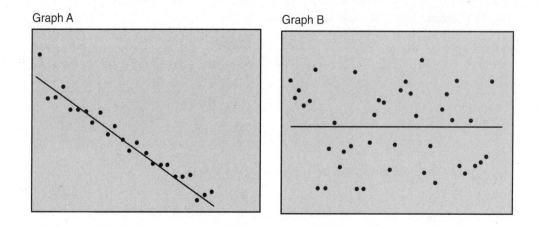

Graph A

Graph B

For Graph A, the points are generally quite close to the line; for Graph B, they are not. The "tightness" of this fit is an indication of how close the relationship is between the x values and the y values on the graph. For Graph A, the y values tend to decrease as the x values increase. That relationship is called a **negative correlation**, meaning that the slope of the best-fitting line is negative and that x and y tend to change in opposite directions (one increases when the other decreases). For Graph C, the relationship is a **positive correlation** with x and y both increasing or decreasing together. The points are not as tightly bound to the line as for Graph A, but there is a clear tendency for the data to follow the straight line up as you look right along the x-axis. By contrast, Graph D has no good fit to a straight line, but unlike Graph B, there does seem to be a relation between the x and y values.

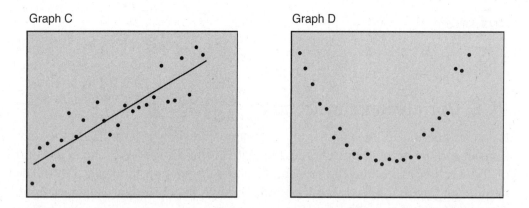

Graph C

Graph D

A quadratic formula ($y = ax^2 + bx + c$) might be a good fit for Graph D. In any case, we can say that there is a negative correlation (y decreases as x increases) on the left of the graph, and a positive correlation on the right.

When the *x*-axis represents time, it is usual to connect the data values in a line graph, to show the change from one time to the next. In that situation, any correlations, across the whole graph or some part of it, indicate trends in the data, that is, changes over time. For example, the car registration graph in Section III. C. shows the trend of increasing registration across the whole period. For a more complex example, here is a graph of the Dow Jones Industrial Average (DJIA) stock index for the end of each month from January 2000 to December 2006.

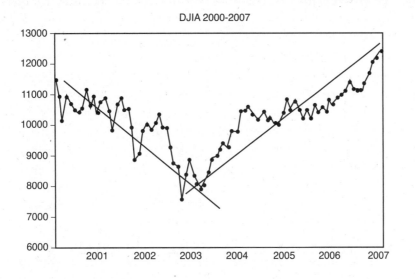

There are a lot of ups and downs from month to month in this data, and the points are not as closely correlated as for Graph A or even Graph C. However, there is a fairly clear downward trend till about the start of 2003 and then an upward trend after that.

Practice

Directions: Use the DJIA graph above to select the best answer for the next two questions.

1. What was the average rate of decline in the DJIA from 2000 to 2003?

    (1) 900 points/year
    (2) 1200 points/year
    (3) 1500 points/year
    (4) 1800 points/year
    (5) 3600 points/year

1. ① ② ③ ④ ⑤

2. What was the average rate of increase in the DJIA from 2003 to 2007?

(1) 1100 points/year   (4) 2400 points/year
(2) 1400 points/year   (5) 4800 points/year
(3) 1700 points/year

2. ① ② ③ ④ ⑤

Use the CPI graph below to select the best answer for the next two questions.

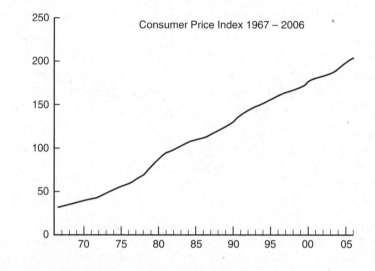

Consumer Price Index 1967 – 2006

3. What was the average percentage rate of increase per year for the CPI over this period?

(1) 2%   (4) 5%
(2) 3%   (5) 6%
(3) 4%

3. ① ② ③ ④ ⑤

4. The CPI is figured with a reference base set to 100 for a particular year or range of years. What is the reference year for this CPI graph?

(1) 1967   (4) 1985
(2) 1975   (5) 2005
(3) 1980

4. ① ② ③ ④ ⑤

Answers

1. **2**   2. **1**   3. **3**   4. **3**

VII. PROBABILITY

VII. A. Basics

Probabilities are measures of how likely certain outcomes or events are, particularly in repeated "trials" of the same circumstances—repeated coin tosses, rolls of dice, or poker hands for example. They also show up in "sampling" from a large population. For example, the 50 ten-year-old girls of Section VI. C. are a sample from the whole population of girls in the United States. Given such a sample, we expect about one-third of the girls to be between 52.5 inches and the national average height of 54.5, and another one-third to be between 54.5 and 56.5 inches tall. In other words, two times out of three, you would predict/expect a randomly chosen ten-year-old girl to be between 52.5 and 56.5 inches tall. In general, the **probability** of an outcome is defined as the number of ways that outcome can be reached divided by the total number of possible outcomes.

EXAMPLE

Coin tosses. If a coin is "fair" then each time you toss it, it should come up heads (H) or tails (T) equally often, on the average. However, that doesn't mean that each time you toss it, you will get one of these and the next time get the other one! In fact, the outcomes get more complex the more times you toss the coin:

Tosses	Possible Outcomes	Total Number
1	H, T	2
2	HH, HT, TH, TT	4
3	HHH, HHT, HTH, THH, HTT, THT, TTH, TTT	8

Each toss has two possible outcomes. The probability of H on the first toss is $\frac{1}{2}$, but the probability of H on the second toss is also $\frac{1}{2}$. Therefore, $\frac{1}{2} \times \frac{1}{2} = \frac{1}{4}$ of the time, you expect to get HH (which is one of the four equally likely outcomes of two coin tosses). Each additional toss doubles the number of outcomes—each of the outcomes for n tosses now has two final possibilities

$$\text{outcome} + \text{H, outcome} + \text{T}$$

n tosses gives $2 \times 2 \times \ldots \times 2 = 2^n$ outcomes, each one exactly as probable as any other. With 4 tosses, there are $2^4 = 16$ outcomes, each equally likely. The outcomes can be grouped in a number of ways for different probability calculations. In the table of outcomes for 3 tosses, there are exactly 3 that have two heads and one tail {HHT HTH THH}, so the probability of 2 heads is $\frac{3}{8}$.

EXAMPLE

Rolling Dice. Standard dice are cubes (six sided) with one to six marks called "pips" on the sides. If a die (singular of "dice") is fair, any one of the six possible outcomes is equally likely, so the probability is 1/6. When rolling two dice, there are $6 \times 6 = 36$ outcomes; with three dice, $6 \times 6 \times 6 = 216$. For most situations in rolling dice, it is the total number of pips showing that matters. The probability of rolling a "lucky 7" with two dice is the number of ways that can happen out of the 36 possible outcomes; whatever happens on the first die, there is a way to get 7 total: $\{1 + 6, 2 + 5, 3 + 4, 4 + 3, 5 + 2, 6 + 1\}$. That is, there are 6 outcomes over 36 possible, for a probability of $\frac{6}{36} = \frac{1}{6}$. To find the probability of a 7 total for rolling three dice, go through the possibilities systematically:

First	First + Second	All Three
1	1 + 1	1 + 1 + 5
	1 + 2	1 + 2 + 4
	1 + 3	1 + 3 + 3
	1 + 4	1 + 4 + 2
	1 + 5	1 + 5 + 1
2	2 + 1	2 + 1 + 4
	2 + 2	2 + 2 + 3
	2 + 3	2 + 3 + 2
	2 + 4	2 + 4 + 1
3	3 + 1	3 + 1 + 3
	3 + 2	3 + 2 + 2
	3 + 3	3 + 3 + 1
4	4 + 1	4 + 1 + 2
	4 + 2	4 + 2 + 1
5	5 + 1	5 + 1 + 1

There are 15 ways to total 7 in the 216 outcomes for rolling three dice; the probability of rolling 7 is 7/216 (≈ 0.03, or 3%).

Note: Probabilities are always in the range between 0 (impossible) to 1 (certain). They may be written as fractions, decimals, or percentages.

EXAMPLE

Drawing numbers from a hat. If there are numbered slips of paper (or colored balls, or whatever) in a hat, and people draw one after another without putting their choice back into the hat, the later choices are not independent of what has already been drawn. That makes the situation a bit different than rolling dice. Suppose there are six balls, each one a different color {red orange yellow green blue violet} in the hat:

Draw	Outcomes	Total, All Draws
First	6	6
Second	5	$6 \times 5 = 30$
Third	4	$6 \times 5 \times 4 = 120$
Fourth	3	$6 \times 5 \times 4 \times 3 = 360$
Fifth	2	$6 \times 5 \times 4 \times 3 \times 2 = 720$

There is no choice at the last draw here, so the total number of outcomes is 720. Any specific sequence of colors, such as the "color wheel" order listed, has a probability of 1/720 (about 0.14%).

EXAMPLE

Mouse in a maze. Any kind of "multiple-choice" situation gives rise to an analysis in terms of probability. If a lab mouse is introduced into a maze at one corner and is hunting for the cheese at the opposite corner, it has a number of possible routes. Suppose it has to go along the vertical or horizontal pathways in this diagram:

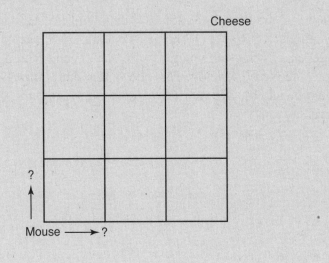

Presumably the mouse won't take a turn that will take it further away from the cheese that it smells waiting at the goal. At each corner, it could move up (U) to get closer vertically, or right (R) to get closer horizontally. At one extreme, it could go straight up and then straight across (UUURRR), and at the other extreme straight across and then up (RRRUUU). Any route that doesn't move away from the cheese will have three moves right and three moves up. We need to find how many ways it is possible to have 3 R moves and 3 U moves in any order. One method for doing this is to use a **decision tree**—make a choice of first move, then "branch" for each choice of the second move, and so on until no more choices can be made.

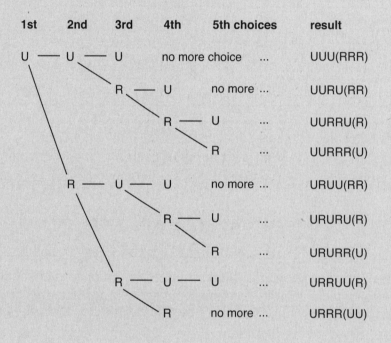

1st	2nd	3rd	4th	5th choices	result
U	U	U	no more choice ...		UUU(RRR)
		R	U	no more ...	UURU(RR)
			R	U ...	UURRU(R)
				R ...	UURRR(U)
	R	U	U	no more ...	URUU(RR)
			R	U ...	URURU(R)
				R ...	URURR(U)
		R	U	U ...	URRUU(R)
			R	no more ...	URRR(UU)

This shows all the branches after an initial choice of U, systematically choosing U before R at each choice. We could do the same starting with R and get exactly the same picture with each U and R in the tree shown "switched" to the other letter. This shows that there must be a total of 18 possible routes to the cheese (the 9 shown above, and the 9 starting with R choices instead).

Practice

1. What is the probability of getting 3 heads in 4 coin tosses with a fair coin?

   (1) 1/2   (4) 3/8
   (2) 1/4   (5) 3/16
   (3) 5/32

   1. ① ② ③ ④ ⑤

2. How many different ways can you get two heads and two tails in four tosses of a fair coin?

   (1) 2   (4) 8
   (2) 4   (5) 12
   (3) 6

   2. ① ② ③ ④ ⑤

3. What is the probability of rolling a total of 9 with two fair dice?

   (1) 1/12   (4) 1/5
   (2) 1/9   (5) 1/4
   (3) 1/6

   3. ① ② ③ ④ ⑤

4. If a laboratory mouse runs a 2 × 2 maze (like the 3 × 3 maze in the example, just with one less intersection in each direction), how many possible routes are there to the cheese?

   (1) 2   (4) 8
   (2) 4   (5) 12
   (3) 6

   4. ① ② ③ ④ ⑤

Answers

1. **2**   2. **3**   3. **2**   4. **3**

VII. B. Sampling, Permutations, and Combinations

B-1

When tossing coins or rolling dice, some number of times, we are doing "repeating trials" of the same basic setup, and each toss or roll is independent. The numbers of heads and tails, or the sum of the "pips" in the dice form a "distribution" of possible values. Each roll of the dice or toss of the coins is a "sample" of that distribution. Similarly, wildlife managers will "sample" a population under study (wolves, eagles, seals, etc.), often tagging the captured individuals and releasing them, possibly to be sampled again later. This kind of sampling is called "sampling with replacement."

It is also possible to do "sampling without replacement." For example, a quality control engineer may pull a sample (one, or many items) from a production run to analyze whether the product is within the allowable tolerances. Even if the analysis is not destructive, the items in the sample will not usually be put back into the production run for sale.

The study of sampling statistics is beyond the scope of the CHSPE. However, there are some simple cases of sampling without replacement that do show up. Card games and lotteries, like coin tossing and dice, are part of the original background for the study of probability and statistics. Each time a card is dealt in a card game, the probabilities for the remaining cards changes; each time a numbered ball is picked in a lottery, the chances of the remaining balls also changes.

For example, if there are 10 balls, and you are picking 3 at random:

1st ball:	there are 10 equally likely choices, each has probability of 1/10
2nd ball:	only 9 left, each with probability of 1/9 (about 11%)
3rd ball:	only 8 left; each with probability of 1/8 (12.5%)

That is, the total number of choices of 3 balls is $10 \times 9 \times 8 = 720$, and the probability of any specific sequence of choices, say ball 7, then ball 2, and finally ball 5 would be:

$$1/10 \times 1/9 \times 1/8 = \frac{1}{10 \times 9 \times 8} = 1/720$$

Note that in a lottery, the actual sequence in which the balls are drawn doesn't matter, just which ones wind up chosen. The sequence $\{2\ 5\ 7\}$ is the "same" result as the $\{7\ 2\ 5\}$ sequence in the example above. As a matter of vocabulary, when the ordering of the result *does* matter, it is called a "permutation," and when it *doesn't* (as in our lottery example), it is called a "combination." (***Note:*** this is technical terminology in mathematics; ordinary English doesn't usually make this distinction. The "combination" on a combination lock in fact does depend on the order of the digits, and it also allows repeats of digits.)

How many different ways can our specific three numbers (2, 5, and 7) be chosen? There are three equally likely first choices, two second choices, and the last one is determined by the first two. So there are $3 \times 2 \times 1 = 6$ different *permutations* out of the total number (720) of possibilities that give the same *combination*. The probability of choosing these 3 out of the 10 numbers is therefore $6/720 = 1/120$.

number of permutations of 3 balls out of 10: $10 \times 9 \times 8$
number of 3-ball combinations out of 10: $10 \times 9 \times 8 / 3 \times 2 \times 1$

If we pick 4 balls instead of three, the numbers change to reflect that:

$$10 \times 9 \times 8 \times 7$$
$$\text{and}$$
$$10 \times 9 \times 8 \times 7 / 4 \times 3 \times 2 \times 1$$

B-2

Factorial Notation

There is special short-hand notation for the total number of permutations of n items, namely $n!$ (pronounced "n factorial"). It just means $n \times n - 1 \times n - 2 \times \ldots \times 3 \times 2 \times 1$. There is no equally short notation for the permutations of a *subset* of n items, but there is a formula that is intended to suggest a short-cut to the calculation:

$$\text{number of permutations of } r \text{ out of } n \text{ items} = \frac{n!}{(n-r)!}$$

Instead of multiplying out all the numbers from n on down, and all of those from $n - r$ on down, and dividing, just notice that every factor in the denominator will cancel against the *same* factor in the numerator. In other words, the value of the formula is obtained by multiplying n by $n - 1$, *etc.* **until** you have multiplied r factors (i.e., until just before you would multiply by $n - r$). Sometimes you will see a special notation for this formula with a capital P for "permutation" and small n and r for the total number of items and the number $r <= n$ to be chosen:

$P(n,r) = nPr = $ number of permutations of r out of n items $= n!/(n - r)!$

To get a formula for the combinations of r out of n items, the discussion above shows we need to take account of all the ways the chosen items might be arranged – that is, the total number $r!$ of permutations of the chosen items. That gives the formula:

$C(n,r) = nCr = $ number of combinations of r out of n items
$= nPr/r! = n!/r!(n - r)!$

EXAMPLE

Mary's sewing box has 6 spools of thread of different colors (red, green, yellow, blue, white, and black). How many different combinations of two colors are possible with this set up?

There are 6 ways to choose the first spool and 5 to choose the second. Given $6 \times 5 = 30$ ordered choices, there are two ways to get each pair of spools, so the total number of different color combinations is $30/2 = 15$. This is $C(5,2)$, which has the formula:

$$\frac{6!}{2! \times 4!} = \frac{6 \times 5 \times 4 \times 3 \times 2 \times 1}{(2 \times 1) \times (4 \times 3 \times 2 \times 1)} = \frac{6 \times 5}{2 \times 1} = \frac{30}{2} = 15$$

EXAMPLE

Calculate $P(8,3)$, the number of permutations (ways to arrange) 3 out of 8 different items.

$$P(8,3) = \frac{8!}{(8-3)!} = \frac{8 \times 7 \times 6 \times 5 \times 4 \times 3 \times 2 \times 1}{5 \times 4 \times 3 \times 2 \times 1} = 8 \times 7 \times 6 = 8 \times 42 = 336$$

EXAMPLE

Calculate $\dfrac{12!}{10!}$

$$\frac{12!}{10!} = \frac{12 \times 11 \times 10 \times \ldots \times 1}{10 \times \ldots \times 1} = 12 \times 11 = 132$$

Practice

1. In a race with 5 equally good runners, how many different outcomes (1st, 2nd, & 3rd places) are possible?

   (1) 120   (4) 40
   (2) 90   (5) 30
   (3) 60

   1. ① ② ③ ④ ⑤

2. A bowl contains 6 balls, marked with the numerals 1 through 6. If two balls are picked out at random, what is the probability that numbers 5 and 6 will both be picked?

    (1) 1/30   (4) 1/6

    (2) 1/15   (5) 1/12

    (3) 1/5   **2.** ① ② ③ ④ ⑤

3. How many combinations are there of 3 items picked from a set of 12?

    (1) $\dfrac{12!}{3! \times 9!}$ (4) $\dfrac{12!}{3!}$

    (2) $\dfrac{9! \times 3!}{12!}$ (5) $\dfrac{9!}{12!}$

    (3) $\dfrac{12!}{9!}$ **3.** ① ② ③ ④ ⑤

4. How many permutations are there of 4 items picked from a set of 10?

    (1) 10,000   (4) 5,000

    (2) 9,600   (5) 4,800

    (3) 5,040   **4.** ① ② ③ ④ ⑤

5. Calculate $\dfrac{11!}{9!}$

    (1) 999   (4) 119

    (2) 990   (5) 110

    (3) 445   **5.** ① ② ③ ④ ⑤

6. Calculate $\dfrac{12!}{9! \times 3!}$

    (1) 220   (4) 440

    (2) 12/27   (5) 4/9

    (3) 1320   **6.** ① ② ③ ④ ⑤

7. Calculate $P(8,3)$ *(the number of permutations of 8 items, 3 at a time).*

    (1) 350   (4) 1680

    (2) 336   (5) 56

    (3) 512   **7.** ① ② ③ ④ ⑤

8. Calculate $C(8,3)$ *(the number of combinations of 8 items, 3 at a time).*

    (1) 336   (4) 168
    (2) 512   (5) 56
    (3) 50

8. ① ② ③ ④ ⑤

9. Calculate $C(15,4)$ *(the number of combinations of 15 items, 4 at a time).*

    (1) 1235   (4) 1365
    (2) 1345   (5) 1645
    (3) 1234

9. ① ② ③ ④ ⑤

10. Calculate $P(25,2)$ *(the number of permutations of 25 items, 2 at a time).*

    (1) 2400   (4) 300
    (2) 1200   (5) 120
    (3) 600

10. ① ② ③ ④ ⑤

Answers

1. **3**   2. **2**   3. **1**   4. **3**   5. **5**
6. **1**   7. **2**   8. **5**   9. **4**   10. **4**

Answer Sheet

MODEL TEST A

ENGLISH LANGUAGE ARTS SECTION

Language Subtest

1 Ⓐ Ⓑ Ⓒ Ⓓ	13 Ⓐ Ⓑ Ⓒ Ⓓ	25 Ⓐ Ⓑ Ⓒ Ⓓ	37 Ⓐ Ⓑ Ⓒ Ⓓ
2 Ⓐ Ⓑ Ⓒ Ⓓ	14 Ⓐ Ⓑ Ⓒ Ⓓ	26 Ⓐ Ⓑ Ⓒ Ⓓ	38 Ⓐ Ⓑ Ⓒ Ⓓ
3 Ⓐ Ⓑ Ⓒ Ⓓ	15 Ⓐ Ⓑ Ⓒ Ⓓ	27 Ⓐ Ⓑ Ⓒ Ⓓ	39 Ⓐ Ⓑ Ⓒ Ⓓ
4 Ⓐ Ⓑ Ⓒ Ⓓ	16 Ⓐ Ⓑ Ⓒ Ⓓ	28 Ⓐ Ⓑ Ⓒ Ⓓ	40 Ⓐ Ⓑ Ⓒ Ⓓ
5 Ⓐ Ⓑ Ⓒ Ⓓ	17 Ⓐ Ⓑ Ⓒ Ⓓ	29 Ⓐ Ⓑ Ⓒ Ⓓ	41 Ⓐ Ⓑ Ⓒ Ⓓ
6 Ⓐ Ⓑ Ⓒ Ⓓ	18 Ⓐ Ⓑ Ⓒ Ⓓ	30 Ⓐ Ⓑ Ⓒ Ⓓ	42 Ⓐ Ⓑ Ⓒ Ⓓ
7 Ⓐ Ⓑ Ⓒ Ⓓ	19 Ⓐ Ⓑ Ⓒ Ⓓ	31 Ⓐ Ⓑ Ⓒ Ⓓ	43 Ⓐ Ⓑ Ⓒ Ⓓ
8 Ⓐ Ⓑ Ⓒ Ⓓ	20 Ⓐ Ⓑ Ⓒ Ⓓ	32 Ⓐ Ⓑ Ⓒ Ⓓ	44 Ⓐ Ⓑ Ⓒ Ⓓ
9 Ⓐ Ⓑ Ⓒ Ⓓ	21 Ⓐ Ⓑ Ⓒ Ⓓ	33 Ⓐ Ⓑ Ⓒ Ⓓ	45 Ⓐ Ⓑ Ⓒ Ⓓ
10 Ⓐ Ⓑ Ⓒ Ⓓ	22 Ⓐ Ⓑ Ⓒ Ⓓ	34 Ⓐ Ⓑ Ⓒ Ⓓ	46 Ⓐ Ⓑ Ⓒ Ⓓ
11 Ⓐ Ⓑ Ⓒ Ⓓ	23 Ⓐ Ⓑ Ⓒ Ⓓ	35 Ⓐ Ⓑ Ⓒ Ⓓ	47 Ⓐ Ⓑ Ⓒ Ⓓ
12 Ⓐ Ⓑ Ⓒ Ⓓ	24 Ⓐ Ⓑ Ⓒ Ⓓ	36 Ⓐ Ⓑ Ⓒ Ⓓ	48 Ⓐ Ⓑ Ⓒ Ⓓ

Reading Subtest

1 Ⓐ Ⓑ Ⓒ Ⓓ	22 Ⓐ Ⓑ Ⓒ Ⓓ	43 Ⓐ Ⓑ Ⓒ Ⓓ	64 Ⓐ Ⓑ Ⓒ Ⓓ
2 Ⓐ Ⓑ Ⓒ Ⓓ	23 Ⓐ Ⓑ Ⓒ Ⓓ	44 Ⓐ Ⓑ Ⓒ Ⓓ	65 Ⓐ Ⓑ Ⓒ Ⓓ
3 Ⓐ Ⓑ Ⓒ Ⓓ	24 Ⓐ Ⓑ Ⓒ Ⓓ	45 Ⓐ Ⓑ Ⓒ Ⓓ	66 Ⓐ Ⓑ Ⓒ Ⓓ
4 Ⓐ Ⓑ Ⓒ Ⓓ	25 Ⓐ Ⓑ Ⓒ Ⓓ	46 Ⓐ Ⓑ Ⓒ Ⓓ	67 Ⓐ Ⓑ Ⓒ Ⓓ
5 Ⓐ Ⓑ Ⓒ Ⓓ	26 Ⓐ Ⓑ Ⓒ Ⓓ	47 Ⓐ Ⓑ Ⓒ Ⓓ	68 Ⓐ Ⓑ Ⓒ Ⓓ
6 Ⓐ Ⓑ Ⓒ Ⓓ	27 Ⓐ Ⓑ Ⓒ Ⓓ	48 Ⓐ Ⓑ Ⓒ Ⓓ	69 Ⓐ Ⓑ Ⓒ Ⓓ
7 Ⓐ Ⓑ Ⓒ Ⓓ	28 Ⓐ Ⓑ Ⓒ Ⓓ	49 Ⓐ Ⓑ Ⓒ Ⓓ	70 Ⓐ Ⓑ Ⓒ Ⓓ
8 Ⓐ Ⓑ Ⓒ Ⓓ	29 Ⓐ Ⓑ Ⓒ Ⓓ	50 Ⓐ Ⓑ Ⓒ Ⓓ	71 Ⓐ Ⓑ Ⓒ Ⓓ
9 Ⓐ Ⓑ Ⓒ Ⓓ	30 Ⓐ Ⓑ Ⓒ Ⓓ	51 Ⓐ Ⓑ Ⓒ Ⓓ	72 Ⓐ Ⓑ Ⓒ Ⓓ
10 Ⓐ Ⓑ Ⓒ Ⓓ	31 Ⓐ Ⓑ Ⓒ Ⓓ	52 Ⓐ Ⓑ Ⓒ Ⓓ	73 Ⓐ Ⓑ Ⓒ Ⓓ
11 Ⓐ Ⓑ Ⓒ Ⓓ	32 Ⓐ Ⓑ Ⓒ Ⓓ	53 Ⓐ Ⓑ Ⓒ Ⓓ	74 Ⓐ Ⓑ Ⓒ Ⓓ
12 Ⓐ Ⓑ Ⓒ Ⓓ	33 Ⓐ Ⓑ Ⓒ Ⓓ	54 Ⓐ Ⓑ Ⓒ Ⓓ	75 Ⓐ Ⓑ Ⓒ Ⓓ
13 Ⓐ Ⓑ Ⓒ Ⓓ	34 Ⓐ Ⓑ Ⓒ Ⓓ	55 Ⓐ Ⓑ Ⓒ Ⓓ	76 Ⓐ Ⓑ Ⓒ Ⓓ
14 Ⓐ Ⓑ Ⓒ Ⓓ	35 Ⓐ Ⓑ Ⓒ Ⓓ	56 Ⓐ Ⓑ Ⓒ Ⓓ	77 Ⓐ Ⓑ Ⓒ Ⓓ
15 Ⓐ Ⓑ Ⓒ Ⓓ	36 Ⓐ Ⓑ Ⓒ Ⓓ	57 Ⓐ Ⓑ Ⓒ Ⓓ	78 Ⓐ Ⓑ Ⓒ Ⓓ
16 Ⓐ Ⓑ Ⓒ Ⓓ	37 Ⓐ Ⓑ Ⓒ Ⓓ	58 Ⓐ Ⓑ Ⓒ Ⓓ	79 Ⓐ Ⓑ Ⓒ Ⓓ
17 Ⓐ Ⓑ Ⓒ Ⓓ	38 Ⓐ Ⓑ Ⓒ Ⓓ	59 Ⓐ Ⓑ Ⓒ Ⓓ	80 Ⓐ Ⓑ Ⓒ Ⓓ
18 Ⓐ Ⓑ Ⓒ Ⓓ	39 Ⓐ Ⓑ Ⓒ Ⓓ	60 Ⓐ Ⓑ Ⓒ Ⓓ	81 Ⓐ Ⓑ Ⓒ Ⓓ
19 Ⓐ Ⓑ Ⓒ Ⓓ	40 Ⓐ Ⓑ Ⓒ Ⓓ	61 Ⓐ Ⓑ Ⓒ Ⓓ	82 Ⓐ Ⓑ Ⓒ Ⓓ
20 Ⓐ Ⓑ Ⓒ Ⓓ	41 Ⓐ Ⓑ Ⓒ Ⓓ	62 Ⓐ Ⓑ Ⓒ Ⓓ	83 Ⓐ Ⓑ Ⓒ Ⓓ
21 Ⓐ Ⓑ Ⓒ Ⓓ	42 Ⓐ Ⓑ Ⓒ Ⓓ	63 Ⓐ Ⓑ Ⓒ Ⓓ	84 Ⓐ Ⓑ Ⓒ Ⓓ

Answer Sheet
MODEL TEST A

Model Test A Answer Sheet

MATHEMATICS SECTION

1 Ⓐ Ⓑ Ⓒ Ⓓ
2 Ⓐ Ⓑ Ⓒ Ⓓ
3 Ⓐ Ⓑ Ⓒ Ⓓ
4 Ⓐ Ⓑ Ⓒ Ⓓ
5 Ⓐ Ⓑ Ⓒ Ⓓ
6 Ⓐ Ⓑ Ⓒ Ⓓ
7 Ⓐ Ⓑ Ⓒ Ⓓ
8 Ⓐ Ⓑ Ⓒ Ⓓ
9 Ⓐ Ⓑ Ⓒ Ⓓ
10 Ⓐ Ⓑ Ⓒ Ⓓ
11 Ⓐ Ⓑ Ⓒ Ⓓ
12 Ⓐ Ⓑ Ⓒ Ⓓ
13 Ⓐ Ⓑ Ⓒ Ⓓ

14 Ⓐ Ⓑ Ⓒ Ⓓ
15 Ⓐ Ⓑ Ⓒ Ⓓ
16 Ⓐ Ⓑ Ⓒ Ⓓ
17 Ⓐ Ⓑ Ⓒ Ⓓ
18 Ⓐ Ⓑ Ⓒ Ⓓ
19 Ⓐ Ⓑ Ⓒ Ⓓ
20 Ⓐ Ⓑ Ⓒ Ⓓ
21 Ⓐ Ⓑ Ⓒ Ⓓ
22 Ⓐ Ⓑ Ⓒ Ⓓ
23 Ⓐ Ⓑ Ⓒ Ⓓ
24 Ⓐ Ⓑ Ⓒ Ⓓ
25 Ⓐ Ⓑ Ⓒ Ⓓ
26 Ⓐ Ⓑ Ⓒ Ⓓ

27 Ⓐ Ⓑ Ⓒ Ⓓ
28 Ⓐ Ⓑ Ⓒ Ⓓ
29 Ⓐ Ⓑ Ⓒ Ⓓ
30 Ⓐ Ⓑ Ⓒ Ⓓ
31 Ⓐ Ⓑ Ⓒ Ⓓ
32 Ⓐ Ⓑ Ⓒ Ⓓ
33 Ⓐ Ⓑ Ⓒ Ⓓ
34 Ⓐ Ⓑ Ⓒ Ⓓ
35 Ⓐ Ⓑ Ⓒ Ⓓ
36 Ⓐ Ⓑ Ⓒ Ⓓ
37 Ⓐ Ⓑ Ⓒ Ⓓ
38 Ⓐ Ⓑ Ⓒ Ⓓ
39 Ⓐ Ⓑ Ⓒ Ⓓ

40 Ⓐ Ⓑ Ⓒ Ⓓ
41 Ⓐ Ⓑ Ⓒ Ⓓ
42 Ⓐ Ⓑ Ⓒ Ⓓ
43 Ⓐ Ⓑ Ⓒ Ⓓ
44 Ⓐ Ⓑ Ⓒ Ⓓ
45 Ⓐ Ⓑ Ⓒ Ⓓ
46 Ⓐ Ⓑ Ⓒ Ⓓ
47 Ⓐ Ⓑ Ⓒ Ⓓ
48 Ⓐ Ⓑ Ⓒ Ⓓ
49 Ⓐ Ⓑ Ⓒ Ⓓ
50 Ⓐ Ⓑ Ⓒ Ⓓ

Model Tests

Model Test A

English Language Arts Section

WRITING TASK

The local board of education has made a rule forbidding students to bring cell phones to school. Do you agree or disagree? Write a letter to your high school newspaper to convince your fellow students to agree with your position on this issue. Be specific about your reasons for taking your position.

LANGUAGE SUBTEST

Directions: Look at the underlined words in each sentence. You may see a mistake in punctuation, capitalization, or word usage. If you spot a mistake in the underlined section of a sentence, select the answer choice that corrects the mistake. If you find no mistake, choose Choice D, *Correct as is*.

1. The chick broke open <u>its'</u> shell

    (A) it is
    (B) it's
    (C) its
    (D) *Correct as is*

2. Everyone has a cell phone except <u>I</u>.

    (A) me
    (B) she
    (C) they
    (D) *Correct as is*

3. Maya passed her driving <u>test she had wanted</u> a driver's license for years.

    (A) test she has wanted
    (B) test, she had wanted
    (C) test; she had wanted
    (D) *Correct as is*

4. The workers asked for a <u>raise, their</u> boss refused to give it to them.

    (A) raise their boss
    (B) raise, but their boss
    (C) raise; but their boss
    (D) *Correct as is*

5. Although Brad is older than Bob, Bob <u>is tallest</u>.

    (A) is most tallest
    (B) is most tall
    (C) is taller
    (D) *Correct as is*

6. When I am old enough to vote, <u>I will register</u> as an Independent.

    (A) I am registered
    (B) I would register
    (C) I will have registered
    (D) *Correct as is*

7. The new uniforms are hanging in the <u>Marching bands dressing</u> room.

    (A) marching bands dressing
    (B) marching band's dressing
    (C) Marching Bands dressing
    (D) *Correct as is*

8. Tommy <u>and me</u> have the highest scores on the test.

    (A) and I
    (B) and mine
    (C) and myself
    (D) *Correct as is*

9. <u>"Why do I have to take this stupid test?"</u> grumbled Cecily when her parents told her about the CHSPE.

    (A) "Why do I have to take this stupid test"?
    (B) "Why do I have to take this stupid test"
    (C) 'Why do I have to take this stupid test'?
    (D) *Correct as is*

10. After Luke danced <u>with Maria: he asked</u> Judy to dance.

    (A) with Maria; he asked
    (B) with Maria, he asked
    (C) with Maria. He asked
    (D) *Correct as is*

11. <u>Their</u> going to lose the game if they don't play better.

    (A) There
    (B) They'll
    (C) They're
    (D) *Correct as is*

12. Most jobs today <u>demands</u> some familiarity with computers.

    (A) demand
    (B) does demand
    (C) is demanding
    (D) *Correct as is*

13. The <u>Golden gate bridge needs</u> to be painted every year.

    (A) Golden Gate Bridge needs
    (B) golden Gate bridge needed
    (C) Golden gate Bridge needs
    (D) *Correct as is*

14. The school bus waited for Martha's brother and <u>she</u>.

    (A) herself
    (B) her
    (C) I
    (D) *Correct as is*

15. The blue bowl holds <u>fewer</u> soup than the green one.

    (A) fewest
    (B) least
    (C) less
    (D) *Correct as is*

16. Do you think that <u>she and I</u> both should get an A in math?

    (A) herself and I
    (B) her and me
    (C) me and she
    (D) *Correct as is*

17. Students learn to drive <u>more carefuller</u> in drivers' education classes.

    (A) carefully
    (B) carefullest
    (C) careful
    (D) *Correct as is*

18. Miss California was the <u>beautifulest</u> of all the Miss America contestants.

    (A) more beautiful
    (B) most beautiful
    (C) most beautifulest
    (D) *Correct as is*

Directions: Look at each sentence. You may see a mistake in sentence structure. If you spot a mistake in the sentence's structure, select the answer choice that rewrites the sentence so that it is clear, concise, and correct. If you find no mistake, choose Choice D, *Correct as is*.

19. The magician took off his hat, turned it upside down, and, with a flourish, pulled out a rabbit.

    (A) The magician took off his hat and he turned it upside down and pulled out a rabbit with a flourish.
    (B) The magician took off his hat turned it upside down and pulled out a rabbit with a flourish.
    (C) Taking off his hat and turning it upside down, the magician with a flourish pulling out a rabbit.
    (D) *Correct as is*

20. Some insects standing still as a stick or leaf are able to hide from insect-eating birds.

    (A) Standing still as a stick or leaf, some insects are able to hide from insect-eating birds.
    (B) Able to hide from insect-eating birds, some insects standing still as a stick or leaf.
    (C) Some insects stand still as a stick or leaf they are able to hide from insect-eating birds.
    (D) *Correct as is*

Model Test A

21. Monica told us about her trip to San Antonio to visit her parents at our club meeting.

    (A) At our club meeting, Monica told us about her trip to San Antonio to visit her parents.

    (B) Monica told us about her trip to San Antonio at our club meeting to visit her parents.

    (C) At our club meeting Monica told about her trip to San Antonio to visit her parents to us.

    (D) *Correct as is*

22. When Johnny completes twelfth grade next year, he has attended Community High School for four years.

    (A) Johnny completes twelfth grade next year, he has attended Community High School for four years.

    (B) When Johnny completes twelfth grade next year, he would have attended Community High School for four years.

    (C) When Johnny completes twelfth grade next year, he will have attended Community High School for four years.

    (D) *Correct as is*

23. Juanita cannot go with us to the play on account of the fact that she has a previous appointment.

    (A) Juanita cant to go with us to the play on account of the fact that she has a previous appointment.

    (B) On account of the fact that she has a previous appointment, Juanita cannot go with us to the play.

    (C) Because she has a previous appointment, Juanita cannot go with us to the play.

    (D) *Correct as is*

24. There were extra pillows on the bed that were both needless and unnecessary.

    (A) There were extra and unnecessary pillows that were on the bed.

    (B) The extra pillows on the bed are both unneeded and unnecessary.

    (C) There were extra pillows on the bed.

    (D) *Correct as is*

25. If the catcher would of made fewer errors, the team would have won the game.

    (A) If the catcher will have made fewer errors, the team will have won the game.

    (B) If the catcher had made fewer errors, the team would have won the game.

    (C) If the catcher had made fewer errors, the team will have won the game.

    (D) *Correct as is*

26. Lying down in the afternoon sun, a feeling of complete relaxation came over her.

    (A) She was lying down in the afternoon sun, a feeling of complete relaxation came over her.

    (B) As she was lying down in the afternoon sun, a feeling of complete relaxation came over her.

    (C) Laying down in the afternoon sun, a feeling of complete relaxation came over her.

    (D) *Correct as is*

27. Sue's duties as a classroom aide include taking attendance, collecting homework, and helping students with their assignments.

    (A) Sue's duties as a classroom aide include taking attendance, collecting homework, and to help students with their assignments.
    (B) Sue's duties include taking attendance, collecting homework, and helping students with their assignments as a classroom aide.
    (C) Sue's duties as a classroom aide include taking attendance, she also collects homework and helps students with their assignments.
    (D) *Correct as is*

28. The murals of Diego Rivera combining figures from Mexican folklore and images from modern working class life.

    (A) The murals of Diego Rivera combine figures from Mexican folklore and images from modern working class life.
    (B) Diego Rivera's murals combining figures from Mexican folklore and images from modern working class life.
    (C) The murals of Diego Rivera that combine figures from Mexican folklore and images from modern working class life.
    (D) *Correct as is*

29. A wind blew off Bob's cap while mowing the lawn.

    (A) Mowing the lawn, a wind blew off Bob's cap.
    (B) While mowing the lawn, a wind blew off Bob's cap.
    (C) While Bob was mowing the lawn, a wind blew off his cap.
    (D) *Correct as is*

30. The necklace of carved beads Sharon wants in the jewelry box.

    (A) Wanted by Sharon, the necklace of carved beads in the jewelry box.
    (B) Sharon wants the necklace of carved beads that is in the jewelry box.
    (C) Sharon wants the necklace of carved beads, it is in the jewelry box.
    (D) *Correct as is*

31. In this book on winter sports, the author describes ice-skating, skiing, snowboarding, and how to fish in an ice-covered lake.

    (A) The author of this book on winter sports describes in it ice-skating, skiing, snowboarding, and how to fish in an ice-covered lake.
    (B) In this book on winter sports, the author describes ice-skating, skiing, snowboarding, and fishing in an ice-covered lake.
    (C) In this book on winter sports, the author has described ice-skating, skiing, snowboarding, and how to fish in an ice-covered lake.
    (D) *Correct as is*

32. Racing after the gangster whom he had spotted, the policeman crashed into a panhandler.

    (A) Racing after the gangster who he has spotted, the policeman crashed into a panhandler.
    (B) The policeman crashed into a panhandler racing after the gangster whom he had spotted.
    (C) The policeman, racing after the gangster, has spotted him and he crashed into a panhandler.
    (D) *Correct as is*

Model Test A

33. Because he was living in his apartment for four years, his landlord agreed to paint the premises.

    (A) Although he was living in his apartment for four years, his landlord agreed to paint the premises.

    (B) His landlord agreed to paint the premises, because he was living in his apartment for four years.

    (C) Because he had been living in his apartment for four years, his landlord agreed to paint the premises.

    (D) *Correct as is*

34. Rodents, to some a source of disease and plague, to others a source of information about human psychology.

    (A) To some, rodents are a source of disease and plague; to others, they are a source of information about human psychology.

    (B) Although rodents are to some a source of disease and plague, to others a source of information about human psychology.

    (C) A source of disease and plague to some: to others rodents are a source of information about human psychology.

    (D) *Correct as is*

35. Back from their cruise, our neighbors told us that they enjoyed making new friends on board ship, relaxing on the deck chairs, and to visit different Caribbean ports.

    (A) Back from their cruise, our neighbors told us that they enjoyed making new friends on board ship, relaxing on the deck chairs, and they visited different Caribbean ports.

    (B) Back from their cruise, our neighbors told us that they enjoyed making new friends on board ship, relaxing on the deck chairs, and visiting different Caribbean ports.

    (C) Back from their cruise, our neighbors tell us that they enjoy making new friends on board ship, relaxing on the deck chairs, and to visit different Caribbean ports.

    (D) *Correct as is*

36. Chasing after the car, the speeding vehicle soon outdistanced my excited dog.

    (A) Chasing after the car, my excited dog was soon outdistanced by the speeding vehicle.

    (B) The speeding vehicle soon outdistanced my excited dog, it was chasing after the car.

    (C) It chased after the car, and the speeding vehicle soon outdistanced my excited dog.

    (D) *Correct as is*

Directions: Read the passage. Then read the questions that come after the passage. Choose the correct answer based on what you know about writing good essays.

National Voting Rights

When Pastor Thomas Johnson of Gainesville, Florida, tried to register to vote, he was turned away. Pastor Johnson is a minister with a calling. His calling is to help ex-convicts make the transition from jail into working life. He knows how rough it can be, because he himself is an ex-convict who once sold drugs in New York City. Pastor Johnson would have been allowed to vote in New York because that state permits ex-convicts who have served their sentences to participate in elections. However, he was not allowed to vote in Florida.

Pastor Johnson's difficulty demonstrates a serious problem in the way our federal elections are conducted. Elections for President, House, and Senate are national, yet state and local authorities determine who is eligible to vote in these elections. Irregardless of whether one believes that ex-convicts should be entitled to vote, it makes little sense for a person's voting status to change simply because he or she has moved to a new home. In elections for national office, national standards should determine voter eligibility.

37. Which of these statements would BEST summarize the main point of this passage?

   (A) Voting rights are different in New York and Florida.
   (B) Pastor Johnson's right to vote was violated.
   (C) Voting rights in national elections should be the same in all states.
   (D) Ex-convicts should have the right to vote.

Pastor Johnson is a minister with a calling. His calling is to help ex-convicts make the transition from jail into working life.

38. What is the BEST way to combine the two sentences shown above?

   (A) Pastor Johnson is a minister, his calling is to help ex-convicts make the transition from jail into working life.
   (B) A minister, Pastor Johnson is a person with a calling, which is to help ex-convicts make the transition from jail into working life.
   (C) Pastor Johnson is a minister with a calling, since his calling is to help ex-convicts make the transition from jail into working life.
   (D) Pastor Johnson is a minister whose calling is to help ex-convicts make the transition from jail into working life.

39. Which sentence would NOT belong in this passage?

   (A) State law should not determine who is eligible to vote in national elections.
   (B) Pastor Johnson received an award from Florida's Governor Jeb Bush for community service.
   (C) Voter eligibility rules can affect the outcome of elections.
   (D) If voting is a right, the right to vote should not vary depending on where a person lives.

He knows <u>how rough it can be</u>, because he himself is an ex-convict who once sold drugs in New York City.

40. Good writing is clear and precise. Choose the answer that replaces the underlined words in the sentence above with clearer, more precise wording.

   (A) how difficult doing this may be
   (B) how hard it can be doing anything like this
   (C) how difficult making this transition can be
   (D) how rough this kind of thing can be

<u>Irregardless of whether</u> one believes that ex-convicts should be entitled to vote, it makes little sense for a person's voting status to change simply because he or she has moved to a new home.

41. Which phrase would BEST replace the underlined phrase in the sentence above?

   (A) Irregardless of whether or not
   (B) Without regarding whether or not
   (C) Regardless of whether
   (D) Without regard for if

42. The passage as a whole can best be described as

   (A) descriptive
   (B) persuasive
   (C) narrative
   (D) lyrical

Anna Katharine Green, Mother of Detective Fiction

Who then should be called detective fiction's mother? Some mystery readers say it should be Agatha Christie. Others say it should be Dorothy Sayers. However, long before Christie and Sayers wrote their classic British whodunits, a young American named Anna Katharine Green wrote a best seller about the murder of a Fifth Avenue millionaire. The name of the book was The Leavenworth Case, *which was an instant success. It sold over 150,000 copies. Also, it marked the first appearance of Inspector Ebenezer Gryce, the first serial detective in the history of the mystery novel.*

Anna Katharine Green originally dreamed of becoming a poet. Her father, a well-known trial lawyer, approved of her ambition to write poetry. What he did not know was that in secret she also was working on writing a detective novel. It took Green six years to finish the novel. She had to hide everything in her closet so her father wouldn't find out her secret.

Green was not the first woman to write detective fiction. In England, twenty years after Edgar Allan Poe wrote Murders in the Rue Morgue, *Mrs. Henry Wood and Mary Elizabeth Braddon wrote suspense novels, creating* East Lynne *(1861) and* Lady Audley's Secret *(1862), respectfully. In America, Metta Fuller Victor, who is often given credit for being the first American woman writer of detective fiction, wrote* The Dead Letter *(1866), featuring a New York City private detective. Green, however, went beyond her predecessors, writing with authority about criminal law and forensic police procedure. As the daughter of a trial lawyer, she was able to inject a note of realism into her tales, which were widely popular.*

Over the years, fashions in detective fiction changed. Green's mysteries fell out of favor with readers, and eventually went out of print. The mother of detective fiction was all but forgotten. Today, however, with two novels back in print after nearly a century, this long neglected author is finally beginning to receive the recognition she deserves.

43. Which sentence would BEST begin this essay?

(A) This essay is about Anna Katharine Green, a famous mystery writer.
(B) Critics call Edgar Allan Poe the father of detective fiction.
(C) Most people today enjoy reading detective fiction.
(D) One special kind of fiction is known as mystery or detective fiction.

The name of the book was The Leavenworth Case, *which was an instant success. It sold over 150,000 copies.*

44. What is the BEST way to combine the two sentences shown above?

(A) An instant success, *The Leavenworth Case* sold over 150,000 copies.
(B) The name of the book was *The Leavenworth Case*, which was an instant success that sold over 150,000 copies.
(C) An instant success, the book was named *The Leavenworth Case*, and it sold over 150,000 copies.
(D) The name of the book was *The Leavenworth Case*, which was an instant success, selling over 150,000 copies.

45. Which of the following sentences would NOT belong in the second paragraph?

(A) Writing verse was considered a respectable occupation for young women.
(B) She met the poet and essayist Ralph Waldo Emerson, who encouraged her poetic aspirations.
(C) Green's older sister and two older brothers and their wives also shared the family home.
(D) In college, she was elected president of the Washington Irving Association, a society of would-be writers.

She had to hide everything *in a closet so her father wouldn't find out her secret.*

46. Consider the underlined word in sentence above. Good writing uses concrete examples. Choose the answer that replaces the underlined word with a concrete example.

(A) the pieces
(B) her writing stuff
(C) the whole thing
(D) the manuscript

In England, twenty years after Edgar Allan Poe wrote Murders in the Rue Morgue, *Mrs. Henry Wood and Mary Elizabeth Braddon wrote suspense novels, writing* East Lynne *(1861) and* Lady Audley's Secret *(1862),* respectfully.

47. Which word or phrase would BEST replace the underlined word in the sentence above?

(A) with respect
(B) respectably
(C) respectively
(D) being respected

48. What source is BEST for finding out the details of how Anna Katharine Green's first mystery novel was received by the public?

(A) an encyclopedia article on Green
(B) a book on how to write detective fiction
(C) a biography of Green
(D) a chapter in a textbook on women's studies

Model Test A

READING SUBTEST

Directions: Read the passage. Then read each question about the passage. Make up your mind which is the best answer to the question. Then mark the answer you have chosen on your answer sheet.

THE MILLER, HIS SON, AND THE DONKEY
A Fable from Greece

One day, a long time ago, an old miller and his son were on their way to market with a donkey which they hoped to sell. They drove him very slowly, for they thought they would have a better chance to sell him if they kept him in good condition. As they walked along the highway, some travelers laughed loudly at them.

"How silly," cried one, "to walk when they might as well ride. The most stupid of the three is not the one you would expect it to be."

The miller did not like to be laughed at, so he told his son to climb up and ride.

They had gone a little farther along the road, when three merchants passed by.

"Oho, what have we here?" they cried. "Respect old age, young man! Get down, and let the old man ride."

Though the miller was not tired, he made the boy get down and climbed up himself to ride, just to please the merchants.

At the next turnstile they overtook some women carrying market baskets loaded with vegetables and other things to sell.

"Look at the old fool," exclaimed one of them. "Perched on the donkey, while that poor boy has to walk."

The miller felt a bit vexed, but to be agreeable he told the boy to climb up behind him.

They had no sooner started out again than a loud shout went up from another company of people on the road.

"What a crime," cried one, "to load up a poor dumb beast like that! They look more able to carry the poor creature, than he to carry them."

"They must be on their way to sell the poor thing's hide," said another.

The miller and his son quickly scrambled down, and a short time later, the market place was thrown into an uproar as the two came along carrying the donkey slung from a pole. A great crowd of people ran out to get a closer look at the strange sight.

The donkey did not dislike being carried, but so many people came up to point at him and laugh and shout, that he began to kick and bray, and then, just as they were crossing a bridge, the ropes that held him gave way, and down he tumbled into the river.

The poor miller now set out sadly for home. By trying to please everybody, he had pleased nobody, and lost his donkey besides.

1. What did the miller originally plan to do with the donkey?

   (A) give it away
   (B) ride it
   (C) carry it
   (D) sell it

2. The miller wanted the donkey to get to the market

   (A) swiftly
   (B) cheaply
   (C) by itself
   (D) in good shape

Model Test A

3. The merchants scolded the miller's son because they thought he was

    (A) dishonest
    (B) disrespectful
    (C) unintelligent
    (D) tired

4. The women assumed that the miller

    (A) was ignoring the needs of his son
    (B) preferred walking to riding
    (C) was too old to ride on a donkey
    (D) weighed more than his son did

5. The donkey began to kick because

    (A) the miller and his son were too heavy
    (B) he was afraid of falling in the river
    (C) the noisy crowd frightened him
    (D) he disliked being slung from a pole

6. People like the miller in this story can be described as

    (A) willing to work
    (B) quick to anger
    (C) kind and generous
    (D) easy to influence

7. The best moral for this story is

    (A) "Actions speak louder than words."
    (B) "Waste not, want not."
    (C) "If you try to please all, you please none."
    (D) "Don't count your chickens before they are hatched."

EARLY MEMORIES
From a Memoir by Ethel Weiner

Six months after my birth, our family of four moved to what was then the outskirts of Brooklyn. My earliest memories concern the large vacant lot adjoining the five-story white brick building in which we lived. I can clearly recall the cows browsing in the background. I can still see the occasional train puff by.

The few years we spent in Brooklyn marked the high water mark of my family's fortunes. The treachery of Pop's business partner cost us our half ownership of the white house and compelled us to return to the immigrant-packed Lower East Side of Manhattan to one of the only two private houses which stood near the top of Pitt Street hill, where it approached Grand Street.

The Hyman family occupied the adjoining two-story and attic red brick house. The two buildings, ours and the Hymans', were exact replicas except that our parlor floor and basement was occupied by Pop's upholstery shop, whereas "Judge" Hyman's local Democratic club was installed on the Hymans' lower floor.

The Hyman children were eight in number. They ranged in age from Gus, aged 20, down to Becky, aged nine, who was my special friend. What an industrious family they were! Every leisure moment was spent in rolling pinwheel paper into cylindrical rolls and slipping paper rings around the middle. The "Judge" paid regular wages, and this enabled the seven Hyman boys and Becky, the youngest and the only girl, to work their way through school within the confines of their home.

8. The writer looks back on her early days in Brooklyn with

    (A) distaste
    (B) nostalgia
    (C) indifference
    (D) glee

9. The writer's family moved from Brooklyn

   (A) because they needed room to expand
   (B) to get away from the railroad tracks
   (C) out of financial necessity
   (D) because they were immigrants

10. For the writer and her family, the move to the Lower East Side was

    (A) an adventure
    (B) a setback
    (C) a reunion
    (D) a mistake

11. The writer blames the move from Brooklyn on

    (A) her father
    (B) Judge Hyman
    (C) a dishonest businessman
    (D) herself

12. The writer's new home was

    (A) larger than the white house
    (B) very similar to the Hymans' house
    (C) lacking a basement
    (D) a tenement apartment

13. The Hymans impressed the writer because they were

    (A) wealthy
    (B) democratic
    (C) hard-working
    (D) neighborly

14. The Hyman children spent their time at home turning pinwheel paper into rolls

    (A) as part of their education
    (B) because their father paid them
    (C) for the sheer enjoyment of the task
    (D) because they were forbidden to play outdoors

OFF-HIGHWAY VEHICLES: THE NEW RECREATION CHALLENGE

Over the last three decades, Californians have witnessed the explosive growth of the new form of outdoor recreation—the use of off-highway recreational vehicles. The most common types of off-highway recreational vehicles are motorcycles, dune buggies, and four-wheel-drive vehicles. These key types of recreational vehicles, along with their derivatives (minibikes, go-karts) and a few exotics (gyrocopters, hovercraft) are now estimated to number more than a million and a half in California.

Field surveys have shown that the popularity of this recreational activity is tremendous. While some participants are interested only in competition and in the machines themselves, the majority of users prefer more casual touring and sightseeing or using their vehicles as an aid in such other activities as hunting, fishing, and camping. For such people, off-highway vehicles are popular because they allow them great mobility in the out-of-doors, as well as a variety of satisfactions ranging from socialization with fellow vehicle users to the development of personal skills in mechanical repair work.

Despite its popularity, however, off-highway vehicle recreation is not without its problems. There has been a good deal of public protest and opposition to uncontrolled use of these vehicles. Property owners are sensitive to trespass, especially when off-highway vehicle use results in property destruction. Many observers are offended by the noise created by these vehicles, noise that is especially intrusive in the natural outdoor setting. Conservationists and land management officials are most concerned with the harm that unrestricted off-highway vehicle use may cause through soil erosion, vegetative damage, and disruption of wildlife patterns. All of these interests call for some limitation of the use of off-highway vehicles.

15. According to this article, which of the following off-highway vehicles is LEAST commonly in use?

    (A) dune buggy
    (B) four-wheel-drive vehicle
    (C) gyrocopter
    (D) motorcycle

16. Most off-highway vehicle users enjoy the vehicles because they allow their drivers

    (A) a chance to compete
    (B) great mobility in the out-of-doors
    (C) inexpensive urban transportation
    (D) opportunities for property destruction

17. Conservationists fear unrestricted off-highway vehicle use may damage the land through

    (A) mechanical problems
    (B) protest demonstrations
    (C) excessive noise
    (D) wearing away the soil

18. Property owners are concerned about off-highway vehicle use because vehicle users

    (A) need to develop skills in mechanical repair work
    (B) disrupt wildlife patterns in wilderness areas
    (C) prevent vegetative damage
    (D) trespass on privately owned land

19. The article suggests that, if current problems caused by off-highway vehicle recreation continue, we may see

    (A) an expansion of off-highway vehicle use
    (B) a lessening of public protest
    (C) the proportion of gyrocopters to dune buggies increase
    (D) restrictions placed on off-highway vehicle use

EIGHT O'CLOCK*
A Poem by A. E. Housman

He stood, and heard the steeple
Sprinkle the quarters on the morning town.
One, two, three, four, to market place and
     people
It tossed them down.

Strapped, noosed, nighing his hour,
He stood and counted them and cursed his luck;
And then the clock collected in the tower
Its strength, and struck.

A. E. Housman (1859–1936)

20. In line 1, "He" most likely refers to

    (A) an observer
    (B) the condemned man
    (C) the executioner
    (D) a guard

21. The quarters referred to in line 2 are

    (A) coins
    (B) housing accommodations
    (C) divisions of an hour
    (D) districts of a city

22. The poem suggests that the central character will die by

    (A) being tossed from a tower
    (B) being beheaded
    (C) injection
    (D) hanging

*Eight A.M. was the customary time in England for executions.

Model Test A

23. The poem's central character curses his luck because he

    (A) dislikes having to wait
    (B) cannot escape his fate
    (C) is late for an appointment
    (D) has lost his wager

24. The poem provides information about all of the following EXCEPT

    (A) the emotions of the condemned man
    (B) the manner of his execution
    (C) the nature of his crime
    (D) the physical setting

RATINGS: COAST GUARD JOB DESCRIPTIONS

YEOMAN—The Coast Guard's effective administration depends on the efficient performance of a highly trained clerical staff. Yeomen fill that need. They prepare records and keep the Coast Guard's vast amount of letters of messages and reports flowing smoothly.

Qualifications: Yeomen need qualifications similar to those of secretaries, stenographers, and typists in private industry. Yeomen should be above average in general learning ability, should possess a degree of manual dexterity, and must be able to work harmoniously with others in an office organization. Courses in English and in business subjects such as keyboarding and filing are very useful.

MARINE SCIENCE TECHNICIAN—Marine Science Technicians observe, collect, analyze, and disseminate meteorological and oceanographic observations. They make visual and instrumental weather and oceanographic observations, and they conduct routine chemical analysis. Their analysis and interpretation of weather and sea conditions furnish advice used in search and rescue operations.

Qualifications: Marine Science Technicians should be above average in general learning ability and should have an aptitude for mathematics. School courses in algebra, trigonometry, chemistry, physics, and keyboarding are very helpful.

PORT SECURITY SPECIALIST—Port Security Specialists supervise and control the safe handling, transportation, and storage of explosives and other dangerous cargoes. They are well versed in the regulations and equipment responsible for the security of vessels, harbors, and waterfront facilities. They are also experts in the field of fire prevention and extinguishment.

Qualifications: Port Security Specialists should be average or above average in general learning ability and should have normal hearing and vision. School courses in practical mathematics, chemistry, and English are helpful.

25. Which of the following school courses would be useful for BOTH a Marine Science Technician and a Port Security Specialist?

    (A) algebra
    (B) chemistry
    (C) English
    (D) keyboarding

26. Which of the following is NOT part of the job of a Marine Science Technician?

    (A) analyzing sea conditions
    (B) collecting meteorological observations
    (C) handling explosives
    (D) interpreting the weather

27. Which of the following civilian jobs is LEAST related to the work of a Port Security Specialist?

    (A) clerk
    (B) firefighter
    (C) security guard
    (D) warehouse worker

IN THE RAPIDS
From *The Call of the Wild* by Jack London

Later on, in the fall of the year, Buck saved John Thornton's life in quite another fashion. The three partners were lining a long and narrow poling-boat down a bad
(5) *stretch of rapids on the Forty-Mile Creek. Hans and Pete moved along the bank, snubbing with a thin Manila rope from tree to tree, while Thornton remained in the boat, helping its descent by means of a pole, and*
(10) *shouting directions to the shore. Buck, on the bank, worried and anxious, kept abreast of the boat, his eyes never off his master.*

At a particularly bad spot, where a ledge of barely submerged rocks jutted out into
(15) *the river, Hans cast off the rope, and, while Thornton poled the boat out into the stream, ran down the bank with the rope-end in his hand to snub the boat when it had cleared the ledge. This it did, and was*
(20) *flying down-stream in a current as swift as a mill-race, when Hans checked it with the rope and checked too suddenly. The boat flirted over and snubbed in to the bank bottom up, while Thornton, flung sheer out of*
(25) *it, was carried down-stream toward the worst part of the rapids, a stretch of wild water in which no swimmer could live.*

Buck had sprung in on the instant; and at the end of three hundred yards, amid a mad
(30) *swirl of water, he overhauled Thornton. When he felt him grasp his tail, Buck headed for the bank, swimming with all his splendid strength. But the progress shoreward was slow; the progress down-stream*
(35) *amazingly rapid. From below came the fatal roaring where the wild current went wilder and was rent in shreds and spray by the rocks which thrust through like the teeth of an enormous comb. The suck of the water*
(40) *as it took the beginning of the last steep pitch was frightful, and Thornton knew that the shore was impossible. He scraped furiously over a rock, bruised across a second, and struck a third with crushing force. He*

(45) *clutched its slippery top with both hands, releasing Buck, and above the roar of the churning water shouted: "Go, Buck! Go!"*

28. What were the three partners trying to do?

   (A) get directions to find their way home
   (B) compete in a boat race
   (C) move their boat downstream safely
   (D) tie up their boat at the dock

29. Buck watched his master from the bank because Buck

   (A) had been forbidden to ride in the boat
   (B) was concerned for his master's safety
   (C) did not know how to swim
   (D) was too nervous to pole the boat

30. Why did the boat overturn?

   (A) A sudden wave crashed into it.
   (B) It hit some submerged rocks.
   (C) Thornton flipped it with his pole.
   (D) Hans stopped its motion too suddenly.

31. A clue that Buck is actually a dog occurs when

   (A) he is worried and anxious
   (B) he leaps into the river
   (C) his master grabs on to him
   (D) his master releases him

32. In line 41, the word "pitch" most nearly means

   (A) high tone
   (B) sticky substance
   (C) level of intensity
   (D) downward slope

33. Buck's master lets go of Buck in order to

   (A) swim for the shore
   (B) grab a rock with both hands
   (C) be carried further down-stream
   (D) save the overturned boat

34. In the final sentence of the passage, Thornton's tone can best be described as

    (A) lyrical
    (B) informative
    (C) urgent
    (D) angry

35. Which of the following does NOT characterize the San Diego coastline?

    (A) rocky headlands
    (B) sandy beaches
    (C) steep cliffs
    (D) dense rainforests

36. The major value of San Diego County's lagoons today is their use as

    (A) commercial harbors
    (B) sewage disposal areas
    (C) sites for naval bases
    (D) wildlife habitat

37. How does Mission Bay differ from San Diego Bay?

    (A) Mission Bay has been set aside as a wildlife refuge.
    (B) Mission Bay has less commercial importance than San Diego Bay does.
    (C) Mission Bay has suffered from the dumping of industrial and municipal sewage.
    (D) Mission Bay has been developed as a major naval base.

38. According to the last paragraph, local government took a positive stance on water pollution by

    (A) encouraging its growth
    (B) increasing its frequency
    (C) banning actions that caused it
    (D) prohibiting water-associated recreation

39. Water pollution regulations concerning San Diego Bay have led to

    (A) an increase in naval vessels
    (B) an increase in sewage dumping
    (C) an increase in its recreational use
    (D) a decrease of pleasure craft

THE SAN DIEGO COASTLINE

The Pacific Ocean forms the western border of San Diego County. This 76 mile coastline is characterized by long stretches of open sandy beaches interrupted by rocky headlands. In many areas the beaches and headlands are backed by precipitous cliffs several hundred feet high.

There is also a series of lagoons and bays extending along the entire coastline. Included in this series are a number of small marshy estuaries fed by intermittent streams, intertidal lagoons of moderate size, and two large bays. The estuaries and lagoons are valuable mainly as wildlife habitat, while Mission and San Diego Bays are of major significance for recreation and commerce.

Mission Bay is the result of a reclamation project by the city of San Diego. About 5000 acres of marshland were dredged and filled to produce a modern recreation complex. Mission Bay now provides extensive water surfaces for boating and fishing, and the adjacent shoreline is highly developed for recreational purposes.

San Diego Bay is the district's largest natural harbor, the site of a major naval base, a busy center of commerce, and an important recreational complex. Local government has taken a positive stance on water pollution and has prohibited the dumping of municipal and industrial sewage into the bay. Direct dumping of sewage from naval vessels is being phased out, and pleasure craft will soon be required to have sewage holding tanks. These measures have resulted in a marked improvement in the water quality of the bay, and, as a result, all types of water-associated recreation are increasing.

THE COYOTE
From *Roughing It* by Mark Twain

The coyote is a long, slim, sick and sorry-looking skeleton, with a gray wolf-skin stretched over it, a tolerably bushy tail that forever sags down with a despairing
(5) *expression of forsakenness and misery, a furtive and evil eye, and a long, sharp face, with slightly lifted lip and exposed teeth. He has a general slinking expression all over. The coyote is a living, breathing allegory of*
(10) *Want. He is always hungry.*
He is always poor, out of luck and friendless. The meanest creatures despise him, and even the fleas would desert him for a velocipede. He is so spiritless and cowardly
(15) *that even while his exposed teeth are pretending a threat, the rest of his face is apologizing for it. And he is so homely!—so scrawny, and ribby, and coarse-haired, and pitiful. When he sees you he lifts his lip and*
(20) *lets a flash of his teeth out, and then turns a little out of the course he was pursuing, depresses his head a bit, and strikes a long, soft-footed trot through the sage-brush, glancing over his shoulder at you, from*
(25) *time to time, till he is about out of easy pistol range, and then he stops and takes a deliberate survey of you; he will trot fifty yards and stop again—another fifty and stop again; and finally the gray of his glid-*
(30) *ing body blends with the gray of the sage-brush, and he disappears. All this is when you make no demonstration against him; but if you do, he develops a livelier interest in his journey, and instantly electrifies his*
(35) *heels and puts such a deal of real estate between himself and your weapon, that by the time you have raised the hammer you see that you need a minie rifle, and by the time you have got him in line you need a*
(40) *rifled cannon, and by the time you have "drawn a bead" on him you see well enough that nothing but an unusually long-winded streak of lightning could reach him where he is now.*

40. The passage above can best be characterized as a

    (A) scientific report
    (B) sentimental anecdote
    (C) humorous sketch
    (D) lyrical description

41. The word "meanest" (line 12) most nearly means

    (A) most ordinary
    (B) most stingy
    (C) most effective
    (D) most contemptible

42. Someone who acts like the coyote can best be described as

    (A) spineless
    (B) menacing
    (C) pitiless
    (D) irritable

43. The coyote bares his teeth to

    (A) devour his prey
    (B) make himself look dangerous
    (C) apologize for his manner
    (D) beg for a handout

44. What is the purpose of this passage?

    (A) to inform
    (B) to persuade
    (C) to express opinion
    (D) to entertain

45. What characteristic of the coyote does the final sentence of the passage emphasize?

    (A) determination
    (B) speed
    (C) ugliness
    (D) hunger

MARJORY DOUGLAS AND
THE RIVER OF GRASS

Pioneering conservationist Marjory Stoneman Douglas called it the River of Grass. Stretching south from Lake Okeechobee, fed by the rain-drenched Kissimmee River Basin, the Everglades is a water marsh, a slow moving river of swamps and sawgrass flowing southward to the Gulf of Mexico. It is a unique ecosystem, whose enduring value has come from its being home to countless species of plants and animals: cypress trees and mangroves, wood storks and egrets, snapping turtles and crocodiles. For the past 60 years, however, this river has been shrinking. Never a torrent, it has dwindled as engineering projects have diverted the waters feeding it to meet agricultural and housing needs.

In her 1947 book The Everglades: River of Grass, *Douglas tried to give people everywhere a sense of why the Everglades mattered. "The Everglades is a test," she wrote. "If we pass it, we get to keep the planet." Poetically she set the scene: "The miracle of the light pours over the green and brown expanse of saw grass and of water, shining and slow-moving below, the grass and water that is the meaning and the central fact of the Everglades of Florida." What others saw as a worthless swamp, she saw as a miracle of nature. "There are no other Everglades in the world," she wrote. "They are, they have always been, one of the unique regions of the earth; remote, never wholly known. Nothing anywhere else is like them. . . ."*

Douglas dedicated her life to preserving this unique region. She defended the Everglades against the invasions of the developers, the sugar planters, and her special foes, the Army Corps of Engineers. (In the 1950s, in an effort to prevent the normal seasonal flooding of former marshlands that were now used for real estate and agricultural development, the U.S. Army Corps of Engineers constructed a complex system of pump stations, levees, canals and dams. In process, the army engineers managed to destroy thousands of acres of wetlands, upsetting the natural cycles on which the Everglades depended.) A true environmentalist, Marjory Stoneman Douglas well deserves her title "mother of the Everglades."

46. What did Douglas want to do about the Everglades?

    (A) protect it
    (B) develop it
    (C) divert it
    (D) divide it up

47. Someone like Douglas can be described as

    (A) committed
    (B) proud
    (C) distrustful
    (D) gentle

48. According to paragraph 1, the River of Grass has been shrinking because

    (A) the Everglades has had less rainfall than normal
    (B) it is part of a unique ecosystem
    (C) countless species of plants and animals depend on it for water
    (D) its water supply has been redirected to serve other purposes

49. Douglas wrote her book, *The Everglades: River of Grass,* chiefly because she

    (A) wanted to win fame as an author
    (B) wished to leave behind a record of her life
    (C) hoped to influence her readers
    (D) wanted to entertain an audience

50. The passage tells the reader

    (A) why Douglas valued the Everglades
    (B) how the Everglades grew
    (C) how the developers fought Douglas
    (D) who discovered the Everglades

51. In the last paragraph, the sentences within the curved lines (the parentheses) explain

 (A) how the Army Corps of Engineers responded to Douglas
 (B) why the developers and agricultural interests opposed seasonal flooding
 (C) what Douglas's goals were for the Army Corps of Engineers
 (D) why Douglas looked on the Army Corps of Engineers as her enemies

RICHARD KIRKLAND:
THE ANGEL OF MARYE'S HEIGHTS
A Story of the American Civil War

The morning after the Battle of Fredericksburg, the ground before the stone wall at the base of Marye's Heights was covered with wounded, dead, and dying Northerners. Hours passed by as soldiers from both sides listened to the cries for water and pleas for help. Finally, Richard Kirkland, a young Confederate sergeant, could bear it no more. He approached his commanding officer, Brigadier General Joseph Kershaw, and said, "General, I can't stand this."

"What's the matter, Sergeant?" asked the general.

"All day I have heard those poor people crying for water, and I can stand it no longer," Kirkland replied. "I come to ask permission to go and give them water."

"Kirkland, don't you know that you would get a bullet through your head the moment you stepped over the wall?" responded the general.

"Yes," said the sergeant, "I know that I may, but if you will let me, I am willing to try it."

The general was moved by Kirkland's request and allowed him to go. However, he refused to allow him to carry a white flag of truce that would have ensured his safety. Despite the danger, Kirkland ventured over the wall, bringing with him as many canteens of water as he could carry. Under Northern fire, he reached the nearest sufferer and gave him water. As soon as they understood his intent, the enemy ceased fire, and for an hour and a half Kirkland tended the wounded unharmed.

52. The general gave Sergeant Kirkland permission to go because the general

 (A) was too busy to go himself
 (B) realized that the battle was over
 (C) could not let him carry a white flag of truce
 (D) was stirred by Kirkland's nobility

53. People like the sergeant in this story can be described as

 (A) dangerous
 (B) impatient
 (C) compassionate
 (D) unpatriotic

54. The Northerners stopped firing because they

 (A) had been defeated in the battle
 (B) needed to save their ammunition
 (C) obeyed the white flag of truce
 (D) respected the sergeant's errand of mercy

Directions: Select the word or group of words that has the same, or nearly the same meaning as the word that is in **boldface.**

55. **Tyrant** most nearly means

    (A) outstanding artist
    (B) cruel or unjust ruler
    (C) foreign citizen
    (D) cowardly fighter

56. **Rebuke** most nearly means

    (A) neglect
    (B) embarrass
    (C) pamper
    (D) scold

57. **Stifle** most nearly means

    (A) let out
    (B) suppress
    (C) laugh
    (D) gargle

58. **Hoard** most nearly means

    (A) store up
    (B) spend carelessly
    (C) give away
    (D) melt down

59. **Eminent** most nearly means

    (A) poetic
    (B) mellow
    (C) mature
    (D) outstanding

60. **Identical** most nearly means

    (A) delicate
    (B) easily visible
    (C) exactly alike
    (D) numerous

61. **Radiant** most nearly means

    (A) shining
    (B) reddened
    (C) wide open
    (D) blinking

62. **Considerably** most nearly means

    (A) mentally
    (B) constantly
    (C) thoughtfully
    (D) significantly

63. **Glisten** most nearly means

    (A) sparkle
    (B) shatter
    (C) be transparent
    (D) be damp

64. **Pretense** most nearly means

    (A) good effort
    (B) false show
    (C) best guess
    (D) promise

Model Test A

Directions: Read the sentences below, paying special attention to the words in **boldface.** Then look at the answer choices. Select the answer choice in which the **boldfaced** word is used in the same way that it is in the original sentence.

The social worker took **charge** *of the abandoned infant.*

65. In which sentence does the word "charge" mean the same thing that it does in the sentence above?

   (A)   Teddy Roosevelt led his troops in a charge up San Juan Hill.
   (B)   The head nurse was in charge of the psychiatric ward.
   (C)   The hotel provides wireless Internet service at no extra charge.
   (D)   Lucy asked the librarian how many books she could charge at one time.

Trying desperately to lighten the ship, the crew struggled to **cast** *their cargo into the angry sea.*

66. In which sentence does the word "cast" mean the same thing that it does in the sentence above?

   (A)   After the play, the members of the cast changed out of their costumes.
   (B)   When Sherry broke her ankle, she had her foot in a cast for two months.
   (C)   She cast a quick glance over her shoulder at the odd-looking man.
   (D)   David ripped up the junk mail and cast the pieces into the wastebasket.

Hate sometimes can **stem** *from envy.*

67. In which sentence does the word "stem" mean the same thing that it does in the sentence above?

   (A)   The economist proved that the increase in the national debt did in fact stem from the costs of the recent war.
   (B)   When Michael dropped his wine glass, its stem shattered.
   (C)   With the aid of the troops, Prince Rupert managed to stem the rebellion.
   (D)   If you hold the rose by the smooth portion of its stem, you can avoid touching its thorns.

It is Helen's **practice** *to go jogging every morning before breakfast.*

68. In which sentence does the word "practice" mean the same thing that it does in the sentence above?

   (A)   The marching band has to practice every day after school.
   (B)   Felipe liked to make a practice of reading bedtime stories to his two sons every night.
   (C)   Gwen has been highly successful in building up her dental practice.
   (D)   Before you are allowed to practice law, you must pass the bar exam.

Johnny's baseball coach praised him for his **application** *to his pitching drills.*

69. In which sentence does the word "application" mean the same thing that it does in the sentence above?

   (A)   Henry thought he had discovered an unusual application for shoe polish.
   (B)   Please use black ink when you fill out your application for a driver's license.
   (C)   Application to your studies will help you pass the test.
   (D)   After a second application of varnish, the gym floor looked good as new.

Model Test A

*Monica plans to **mount** a campaign to raise funds for her son's nursery school.*

70. In which sentence does the word "mount" mean the same thing that it does in the sentence above?

    (A) Every time Billy tried to mount his pony, he fell off.
    (B) Sue tried to economize, but her expenses continued to mount.
    (C) The hikers all cheered when they reached the top of the mount.
    (D) The general planned to mount a surprise attack on the unsuspecting enemy forces.

*Convinced that Mayor Madeleine is really Jean Valjean, Detective Javert stubbornly sets out to **stalk** the escaped galley slave.*

71. In which sentence does the word "stalk" mean the same thing that it does in the sentence above?

    (A) Some species of spiders do not spin webs; instead, they stalk their prey on the ground.
    (B) Threshing or thrashing separates the grain from the stalk on which it grows.
    (C) Whenever Susie was upset, she would stalk off in a temper.
    (D) In our car, the turn-signal stalk is located on the left-hand side of the steering wheel.

*The French and German governments have reached a tentative agreement about the proposed economic **compact** between the two countries.*

72. In which sentence does the word "compact" mean the same thing that it does in the sentence above?

    (A) When I rent an automobile for a business trip, I prefer a compact car to a midsize one.
    (B) Katya had a hard time digging in the garden because the soil was so compact.
    (C) The pilgrims aboard the *Mayflower* signed a compact binding them to obey the rules of the new colony.
    (D) The wrestler's compact, muscular body gleamed with sweat as he struggled to pin his opponent to the mat.

*On cold, wintry mornings, I often have a hard time trying to **start** my engine.*

73. In which sentence does the word "start" mean the same thing that it does in the sentence above?

    (A) In the Scouts, Toby learned how to start a fire and how to extinguish one as well.
    (B) The movie will start at seven o'clock and will be over by nine.
    (C) When the conductor tapped Julia on the shoulder, she woke up with a start.
    (D) A bell gave the signal for the start of the race.

*The museum curators decided it would be artistically effective to **suspend** the mobile from the highest point in the building.*

74. In which sentence does the word "suspend" mean the same thing that it does in the sentence above?

    (A) People blame Ben for his divorce from Kathy, but I think that we should suspend judgment until we've heard his side of the story.
    (B) How will we be able to get from Alameda to San Francisco if they suspend ferry service?
    (C) When the judge threatened to suspend Tanya's driving license, she told him to go right ahead.
    (D) We plan to suspend the chandelier from a hook attached to the ceiling.

> **Directions:** In each of the sentences below, the word in **boldface** may be unfamiliar to you. Use the other words in the sentence to help you decide what the word in **boldface** means.

*The sea was so rough that the safest thing to do was to grab the railing of the ship and hang on; walking was too **precarious** a pastime.*

75. As used in the sentence above, "precarious" most nearly means

    (A) ordinary
    (B) leisurely
    (C) tempting
    (D) risky

*An **insipid** dish lacks flavor; it needs a touch of spice to make it pleasing to the taste.*

76. As used in the sentence above, "insipid" most nearly means

    (A) salty
    (B) bland
    (C) aromatic
    (D) uncooked

*Absorbed in her book, Nancy was **oblivious** to the noisy quarrels of her younger brothers.*

77. As used in the sentence above, "oblivious" most nearly means

    (A) unaware
    (B) unafraid
    (C) uncertain
    (D) undeserving

*The glitter and **opulence** of the ballroom took Cinderella's breath away.*

78. As used in the sentence above, "opulence" most nearly means

    (A) great size
    (B) popularity
    (C) deep silence
    (D) luxuriousness

*Charlie Brown's friend Pigpen was **intractable**: he absolutely refused to take a bath.*

79. As used in the sentence above, "intractable" most nearly means

    (A) unattractive
    (B) impolite
    (C) tidy
    (D) stubborn

Model Test A

The airline customer service agent tried to **mollify** *the angry passenger by offering her a seat in first class.*

80. As used in the sentence above, "mollify" most nearly means

   (A) change somewhat
   (B) turn back
   (C) discharge
   (D) soothe

The police fired tear gas into the crowd to **disperse** *the protesters.*

81. As used in the sentence above, "disperse" most nearly means

   (A) scatter
   (B) distress
   (C) provoke
   (D) soak

After the earthquake, they searched the **debris**, *hunting for survivors in the wreckage.*

82. As used in the sentence above, "debris" most nearly means

   (A) rubble
   (B) basement
   (C) neighborhood
   (D) caverns

After several **abortive** *attempts to fix the old computer, Sharon decided it was time to buy a new laptop.*

83. As used in the sentence above, "abortive" most nearly means

   (A) premature
   (B) unsuccessful
   (C) rudimentary
   (D) naive

Because she felt no urge to marry, she was **indifferent** *to his constant proposals.*

84. As used in the sentence above, "indifferent" most nearly means

   (A) unusual
   (B) uninterested
   (C) immoral
   (D) impulsive

MATHEMATICS SECTION

Directions: Each of the following statements, questions, or problems is followed by four suggested answers or completions. Choose the *one* that best completes each of the statements or answers the question. Mark the oval on the answer sheet whose letter corresponds to the answer you have selected.

1. The first 5 terms of a geometric series are:

$$2 \quad -1 \quad \frac{1}{2} \quad -\frac{1}{4} \quad \frac{1}{8} \quad \ldots$$

What is the eighth term of this series?

(A) $\dfrac{1}{32}$

(B) $-\dfrac{1}{32}$

(C) $\dfrac{1}{64}$

(D) $-\dfrac{1}{64}$

2. For the series in the previous question, what is the sum of the first six terms?

(A) It must be between $1\dfrac{1}{8}$ and $1\dfrac{1}{4}$

(B) It must be between $1\dfrac{1}{4}$ and $1\dfrac{3}{8}$

(C) It must be between $1\dfrac{3}{8}$ and $1\dfrac{1}{2}$

(D) It must be greater than $1\dfrac{1}{2}$

3. The International Space Station (ISS) orbits the Earth at an average altitude of 354 kilometers (220 miles). The circumference of the Earth is close to 40,000 kilometers. Which of the numbers below is the best estimate of the circumference of the ISS orbit?

(A) 4.1×10^4 km
(B) 4.2×10^4 km
(C) 4.4×10^4 km
(D) 4.2×10^5 km

4. Felipe is rolling a pair of dice (the usual six-sided kind, with one to six pips on the sides). If the dice are fair, what is the probability of rolling a 6 (total of the pips on the two dice adding to 6)?

(A) $\dfrac{5}{36}$

(B) $\dfrac{5}{18}$

(C) $\dfrac{1}{6}$

(D) 1

5. Simplify the expression $\dfrac{x^2 + x^4}{1 - (x+1)(x-1)}$

(A) $\dfrac{x^6}{x^2 + 1}$

(B) $1 + x^2$

(C) $\dfrac{x^2 + x^4}{2 - x^2}$

(D) $1 + x^2$

6. The Carpenters bought an air conditioner on sale for $390, receiving a discount of 25% on the list price. What is the ratio of the sale price to the list price?

(A) 2:3
(B) 3:5
(C) 3:4
(D) 1:3

7. If it takes 3.3 quarts to water 1 square foot of a vegetable garden, how many gallons does it take to water a garden 10 feet by 12 feet?

(A) 96
(B) 99
(C) 39.6
(D) 396

Refer to the graph below to answer the next three questions.

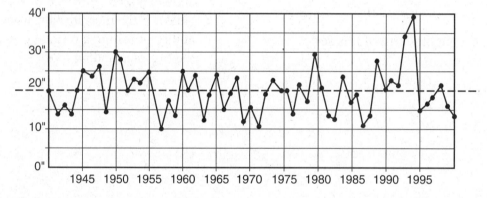

Annual Precipitation, San Joaquin Drainage, 1941–2000

8. The lowest recorded precipitation (rainfall) in the San Joaquin Valley during this period was about

(A) 10 inches
(B) 15 inches
(C) 20 inches
(D) 25 inches

9. The average annual precipitation in the San Joaquin Valley during this period was about

(A) 15 inches
(B) 20 inches
(C) 25 inches
(D) 30 inches

10. Roughly how many years shown in this graph had precipitation less than 15 inches?

(A) 10
(B) 15
(C) 20
(D) 25

11. If a man who is x years old now is three times the age of his son, how old will his son be five years from now?

(A) $(x + 15)$ years
(B) $(3x + 5)$ years
(C) $(x + 5/3)$ years
(D) $(x/3 + 5)$ years

Model Test A

12. Which of the following solid figures has the greatest volume?

    (A) A rectangular solid 11 inches by 13 inches by 1 foot
    (B) A sphere 1 foot in diameter
    (C) A cone 1 foot in diameter and 1 foot high
    (D) A cube 1 foot on a side

Refer to the graph below to answer the next two questions.

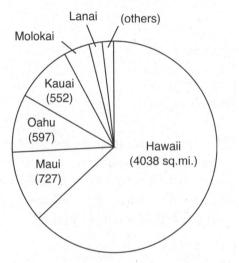

Land Area of the Hawaiian Islands

13. From the data shown in this pie chart, what is the best estimate below for the total land area of the Hawaiian Islands?

    (A) 5000 square miles
    (B) 5900 square miles
    (C) 6400 square miles
    (D) 8000 square miles

14. Using the data in the Hawaiian Islands pie chart, what is the best estimate below for the land area of Molokai Island?

    (A) 100 square miles
    (B) 250 square miles
    (C) 500 square miles
    (D) It is not possible to estimate the area of Molokai

15. What is the slope of the line $4x + 3y = 2$?

    (A) $\dfrac{3}{4}$

    (B) $-\dfrac{3}{4}$

    (C) $\dfrac{4}{3}$

    (D) $-\dfrac{4}{3}$

16. What is the closest estimate below of the area of the ballroom shown in this diagram?

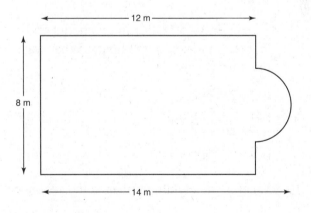

    (A) 96 m²
    (B) 99 m²
    (C) 102 m²
    (D) 116 m²

17. Ms. Wright's history class took a 10-question quiz. The distribution of the test scores was:

Test Score (%)	Number of Students
35	2
40	1
45	3
50	3
55	6
60	5
65	4
70	4
75	3
80	2
85	2
90	1

What was the median score on this quiz?

(A) 55%
(B) 60%
(C) 65%
(D) 70%

18. A man drove 50 miles in two hours and then 150 miles in three hours. What was his average speed?

(A) 25 mph
(B) 37.5 mph
(C) 40 mph
(D) 50 mph

19. What is the eighth number in the sequence below?

2   5   8   11   14 ...

(A) 17
(B) 20
(C) 23
(D) 29

20. In the diagram to the right, Rosebud Avenue meets San Simeon at an angle of 30°, and 23rd Street crosses San Simeon at right angles. Rosebud runs for 60 yards between 23rd and San Simeon. Approximately how long is the stretch on San Simeon between the intersections?

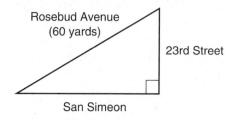

Rosebud Avenue
(60 yards)

23rd Street

San Simeon

(A) 30 yards
(B) 50 yards
(C) 52 yards
(D) 60 yards

21. If the price of potatoes drops 30¢ per pound, you will be able to buy six more pounds for $8 than you were able to when you paid the higher price. What was the original, higher price per pound?

(A) 50¢
(B) 60¢
(C) 80¢
(D) $1

22. California has an area of 423,970 square kilometers, and a population recorded in the Federal Census of 2010 as 37,253,956. Which of the following gives the California population density (people per square kilometer) correct to 3 significant digits?

(A) 8.79×10^2
(B) 1.14×10^{-2}
(C) 8.79×10^1
(D) 1.14×10^{-1}

Refer to the graph below to answer the next three questions.

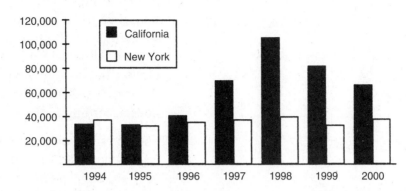

Persons Naturalized as U.S. Citizens in New York and California, 1994–2000

23. In which year did New York naturalize more U.S. citizens than California did?

    (A) 1994
    (B) 1996
    (C) 1998
    (D) 2000

24. Which statement below best describes the number of citizens naturalized in California during this period?

    (A) The number of citizens naturalized each year increased throughout the period.
    (B) The number of citizens naturalized each year decreased steadily after 1994.
    (C) The number of citizens naturalized increased and then decreased during the period.
    (D) The number of citizens naturalized decreased and then increased during the period.

25. About how many citizens were naturalized in California from 1994 through 2000?

    (A) 100,000
    (B) 200,000
    (C) 300,000
    (D) 400,000

26. Every three minutes on the average someone sets off a false alarm. Approximately how many false alarms are set off during an eight-hour shift?

    (A) 160
    (B) 120
    (C) 24
    (D) 16

27. Phil buys some items at the local ReadyMart for a total purchase of $9.53. If he pays with a $10 bill, what is the *smallest* number of coins he could get as correct change?

    (A) 5
    (B) 6
    (C) 7
    (D) 8

28. What is the slope of line *L* in the graph below?

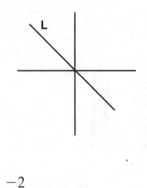

(A) −2
(B) −1
(C) 1
(D) 2

29. The five best sprinters on the boys' track team (Shawn, Morgan, Johnny, Brad, and Tony) are running a trial heat to select two of them to go to a statewide tournament. Assuming the runners are equally matched, what is the probability that Morgan and Brad will be chosen?

(A) 1/25
(B) 1/20
(C) 1/10
(D) 1/5

30. A man buys a condo for $63,000. He pays $2,500 for plumbing and $4,000 for rewiring. If he wants to make a profit of 20%, at what price must he sell the condo?

(A) $70,000
(B) $75,600
(C) $83,400
(D) $83,600

31. A car is to make a 240-mile trip. The driver estimates he will be traveling at an average rate of 25 miles per hour in the city, but at an average of 50 miles per hour on the freeway. If only 15 miles will be driven in city traffic, how long will it take this driver to make the 240-mile trip if everything goes according to his estimate?

(A) 5 hours and 6 minutes
(B) 4 hours and 48 minutes
(C) 4 hours and 30 minutes
(D) 4 hours and 21 minutes

32. Mrs. Brown is 20 years older than her daughter. Five years ago, she was three times as old. How old is the daughter now?

(A) 15
(B) 16
(C) 18
(D) 20

33. Amy's living room is 25 feet by 30 feet, with the ceiling 10 feet high. If she is painting the walls and ceiling the same color, what is the area she must buy paint to cover?

(A) 750 square feet
(B) 1500 square feet
(C) 1750 square feet
(D) 1850 square feet

34. A triangle has one angle of 55° and one of 40°. What is the third angle?

(A) 75°
(B) 85°
(C) 90°
(D) 95°

Refer to the following graph to answer the next six questions.

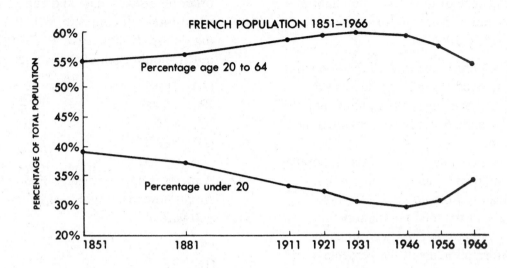

FRENCH POPULATION 1851–1966

35. Which of the following statements about the makeup of the French population in the period from 1851 to 1966 is true?

   (A) The percentage of the French population under 20 decreased, while the percentage between the ages of 20 and 64 increased.
   (B) The percentage of the French population between the ages of 20 and 64 remained the same, while the percentage under 20 changed.
   (C) The percentage of the French population under 20 decreased and then increased, while the percentage of the population between the ages of 20 and 64 first increased and then decreased.
   (D) The percentage of the French population under 20 increased and then decreased; the percentage of the population between the ages of 20 and 64 did the same.

36. In what year was the percentage of the French population under 20 years of age at its *highest* point?

   (A) 1966
   (B) 1946
   (C) 1881
   (D) 1851

37. In 1851, approximately what percentage of the total population was made up of persons between the ages of 20 and 64?

   (A) 38%
   (B) 40%
   (C) 55%
   (D) 60%

38. In 1851, approximately what percentage of the total population was made up of persons aged 65 and over?

   (A) 7%
   (B) 12%
   (C) 38%
   (D) 55%

39. Which of the following statements about the percentage of the French population aged 65 and over is true for the period from 1851 to 1966?

    (A) The percentage of the French population aged 65 and over decreased.
    (B) The percentage of the French population aged 65 and over remained the same.
    (C) The percentage of the French population aged 65 and over increased steadily from about 7% to about 12% of the total population.
    (D) It is impossible to determine any information about the percentage of the French population aged 65 and over from the graph given.

40. Which of the following statements about the percentage of the French population under the age of 20 is obviously *false*?

    (A) In the year 1851, persons under 20 made up approximately 38% of the total French population.
    (B) In the year 1931, the percentage of the French population under 20 was lower than it was in 1946.
    (C) In the year 1931, the percentage of the French population under 20 was higher than it was in 1966.
    (D) In the years after 1946, the portion of the French population under 20 grew as a result of the post-World War II baby boom.

41. Three women eat lunch together, each ordering a salad plate and cup of coffee. Their total bill comes to $20.40, not counting the tip. If they leave a 15% tip, how much should each of the women pay?

    (A) $6.80
    (B) $7.48
    (C) $7.82
    (D) $22.46

42. A meter is approximately 39.36 inches. About how many meters are there in 100 yards?

    (A) 50
    (B) 91
    (C) 110
    (D) 300

Refer to the diagram below for the next question.

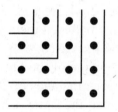

43. Johnny is arranging coins in the pattern shown and has done four repetitions of the pattern. How many additional coins are needed to complete the fifth repetition?

    (A) 5
    (B) 9
    (C) 12
    (D) 25

44. What is the slope of the line in the diagram below?

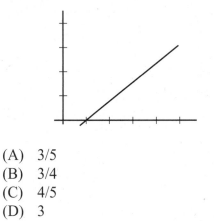

(A) 3/5
(B) 3/4
(C) 4/5
(D) 3

45. A Marin County resident goes shopping and purchases $56 worth of goods, only $8 of which is taxable. How much will his total bill be, including the 6% sales tax?

(A) $48.00
(B) $56.48
(C) $60.48
(D) $64.00

Refer to the graph below to answer the next five questions.

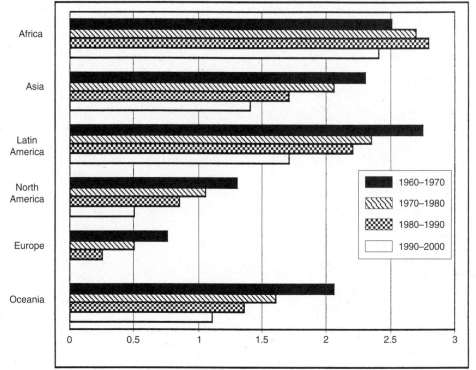

World Population–Annual Growth Rate by Continent: 1960–2000

46. Which region shown on this graph had the smallest annual growth rate throughout the period from 1960 to 2000?

(A) Africa
(B) Asia
(C) North America
(D) Europe

47. Which region had the highest growth rate from 1970 to 1980?

(A) Africa
(B) Asia
(C) Latin America
(D) Oceania

48. Which region reversed the trend of its annual growth rate in the 1990s, as compared to previous decades?

    (A) Africa
    (B) Latin America
    (C) North America
    (D) Europe

49. Which of the conclusions below is NOT supported by this graph?

    (A) Growth rates have decreased on all continents since the sixties.
    (B) Population is increasing in all major regions of the world.
    (C) No region's population is growing more than 3% per year.
    (D) Europe's growth rate has been less than half that of most other regions in the world throughout the time period shown.

50. Approximately how many times greater was the population growth rate in Africa than in Europe during the seventies?

    (A) 2
    (B) 3
    (C) 4
    (D) 5

ANSWER KEY
English Language Arts Section
LANGUAGE SUBTEST

[There is no correct answer for the Writing Task.]

1. C	9. D	17. A	25. B	33. C	41. C
2. A	10. B	18. B	26. B	34. A	42. B
3. C	11. C	19. D	27. D	35. B	43. B
4. B	12. A	20. A	28. A	36. A	44. A
5. C	13. A	21. A	29. C	37. C	45. C
6. D	14. B	22. C	30. B	38. D	46. D
7. B	15. C	23. C	31. B	39. B	47. C
8. A	16. D	24. C	32. D	40. C	48. C

READING SUBTEST

1. D	10. B	19. D	28. C	37. B	46. A
2. D	11. C	20. B	29. B	38. C	47. A
3. B	12. B	21. C	30. D	39. C	48. D
4. A	13. C	22. D	31. C	40. C	49. C
5. C	14. B	23. D	32. D	41. D	50. A
6. D	15. C	24. C	33. B	42. A	51. D
7. C	16. B	25. B	34. C	43. B	52. D
8. B	17. D	26. C	35. D	44. D	53. C
9. C	18. D	27. A	36. D	45. B	54. D

55. B	60. C	65. B	70. D	75. D	80. D
56. D	61. A	66. D	71. A	76. B	81. A
57. B	62. D	67. A	72. C	77. A	82. A
58. A	63. A	68. B	73. A	78. D	83. B
59. D	64. B	69. D	74. D	79. D	84. B

Mathematics Section

1. D	11. D	21. C	31. A	41. C
2. B	12. D	22. C	32. A	42. B
3. B	13. C	23. A	33. D	43. B
4. A	14. B	24. C	34. B	44. B
5. D	15. D	25. D	35. C	45. B
6. C	16. C	26. A	36. D	46. D
7. B	17. B	27. A	37. C	47. A
8. A	18. C	28. B	38. A	48. A
9. B	19. C	29. C	39. C	49. B
10. B	20. C	30. C	40. B	50. D

Model Test A

ANSWER EXPLANATIONS

English Language Arts Section

LANGUAGE SUBTEST

1. **(C)** its
Don't confuse the contraction *it's* (short for *it is*) with the possessive pronoun *its. The chick broke open its shell* is correct.

2. **(A)** me
Incorrect pronoun form. In this sentence, the pronoun is the object of the preposition *except*. Therefore, the correct answer is Choice A, *me*.

3. **(C)** test; she had wanted
Run-on sentence. Do not run two sentences together without any punctuation. Inserting the semicolon between the two independent clauses corrects the error.

4. **(B)** raise, but their boss
Comma splice. Do not link two sentences with only a comma. The insertion of the conjunction *but* after the comma corrects the comma splice.

5. **(C)** is taller
In making a comparison, use the correct form of the adjective. How many persons does this sentence compare? Only two: Brad and Bob. *Tallest*, the superlative form of the adjective *tall*, is used in comparing three or more persons; *taller*, the comparative form, is used in comparing two.

6. **(D)** Correct as is
The future tense is used correctly here.

7. **(B)** marching band's dressing
Choice B corrects both the error in punctuation and the error in capitalization.

8. **(A)** and I
Incorrect pronoun form. In this sentence, the pronoun is the subject of the sentence and should be in the subjective case. You wouldn't say "Me have the highest score on the test," would you? No. You'd say, "I have the highest score on the test." Similarly, you want to say "Tommy and I have the highest scores on the test."

9. **(D)** Correct as is
The rule is to use double quotation marks to set off direct quotations. Choice C uses single quotation marks; you can eliminate Choice C. The rule is to use a question mark after direct questions. Choice B has no question mark; you can eliminate Choice B. The rule is that, when the question mark applies only to the quoted material, the question mark goes inside the quotation marks. Choice A places the question mark outside the quotation marks; you can eliminate Choice A. Only the original sentence follows all the rules correctly; the sentence is correct as it stands.

10. **(B)** with Maria, he asked
Error in punctuation. Use a comma, not a colon, after an introductory adverb clause.

11. **(C)** They're
Don't confuse the contraction *they're* (short for *they are*) with the possessive pronoun *their* (as in *their team)* or the adverb *there* (as in *Here! Not there!*). Choice C is correct. If they don't play better, *they are* going to lose.

12. **(A)** demand
Subject-verb agreement. The subject of the sentence, *jobs*, is plural; the verb should be plural as well. Most jobs today *demand* familiarity with computers.

13. **(A)** Golden Gate Bridge needs
Error in capitalization. As it is used here, the word *bridge* is part of a proper name. Therefore, it must be capitalized.

14. **(B)** her
Error in pronoun case. The pronoun is the object of the preposition *for.* It must be in the objective case. The school bus waited for *her*.

15. **(C)** less
Error in usage. In formal writing, *fewer* refers to things you can count (how many), while *less* refers to amount or extent (how much). The blue bowl holds *fewer* jelly

beans than the green bowl does. (One jelly bean, two jelly beans, three jelly beans . . .) It also holds *less* soup.

16. **(D)** Correct as is
The pronoun here is part of the subject of the subordinate clause and should be in the subjective case. The wording *she and I* is correct.

17. **(A)** carefully
The adverb *carefully* modifies the verb *to drive*. It answers the question, "How?" How do the students learn to drive? They learn to drive *carefully*.

18. **(B)** most beautiful
Error in adjective comparison. You are comparing one beauty queen with 49 others. Therefore, you should use the superlative form of the adjective *beautiful*. Polysyllabic adjectives like *beautiful* form the superlative by adding the word *most* (or *least*). Miss California was the *most beautiful* of all.

19. **(D)** Correct as is
Choice A is wordy and awkward. Choice B omits necessary punctuation. Choice C is a sentence fragment; it lacks a main verb. Only Choice D is left. The original sentence uses parallel structure correctly. It is correctly punctuated. The correct answer is Choice D.

20. **(A)** Standing still as a stick or leaf, some insects are able to hide from insect-eating birds.
Misplaced modifier. By recasting the sentence in this way, you make it clear that the insects are able to hide from insect-eating birds *because* they stand so still.

21. **(A)** At our club meeting, Monica told us about her trip to San Antonio to visit her parents.
Misplaced modifier. Was Monica visiting her parents at the club meeting? No. She was telling her friends at the club meeting about her visit to her parents in San Antonio. Choice A recasts the sentence and corrects the confusion.

22. **(C)** When Johnny completes twelfth grade next year, he will have attended Community High School for four years.

Error in sequence of tenses. The future perfect tense (*will have attended*) is used to indicate a time that comes after the present moment and before a time in the future.

23. **(C)** Because she has a previous appointment, Juanita cannot go with us to the play.
Wordiness. Do not use many words when a few will make your point. The phrase "on account of the fact that" is wordy. Replace it with "because."

24. **(C)** There were extra pillows on the bed.
Wordiness (again!). Do not use many words when a few will make your point.

25. **(B)** If the catcher had made fewer errors, the team would have won the game.
Errors in usage and verb form. Do not use "of" in place of an unstressed "have." In addition, do not use "would have" in place of "had."

26. **(B)** As she was lying down in the afternoon sun, a feeling of complete relaxation came over her.
Dangling participle. Was a feeling lying down in the afternoon sun? No. *She* was lying down. Choice B corrects the dangling participle without introducing fresh errors.

27. **(D)** Correct as is
The original sentence correctly uses parallel structure in listing Sue's duties.

28. **(A)** The murals of Diego Rivera combine figures from Mexican folklore and images from modern working class life.
Sentence fragment. The original sentence needs a main verb. By changing the participle *combining* to the verb *combine,* you correct the error.

29. **(C)** While Bob was mowing the lawn, a wind blew off his cap.
Dangling participle. Ask yourself who was mowing the lawn. It certainly wasn't the wind!

30. **(B)** Sharon wants the necklace of carved beads that is in the jewelry box.
What is wrong with the original sentence? It is a sentence fragment. You correct it by supplying the missing verb. You can do so in several ways. Here is one correction: "The necklace of carved beads that Sharon

wants is in the jewelry box." Correcting the sentence in this way emphasizes *where* the object Sharon wants is located. Here is another: "Sharon wants the necklace of carved beads that is in the jewelry box." This is Choice B, the correct answer choice. This sentence has a slightly different emphasis. It emphasizes exactly *which* object Sharon wants.

The other sentences contain errors. Like the original sentence, Choice A is a sentence fragment. Choice C is a comma splice. Only Choice B is grammatically correct.

31. **(B)** In this book on winter sports, the author describes ice-skating, skiing, snowboarding, and fishing in an ice-covered lake. Lack of parallelism. *Ice-skating, skiing,* and *snowboarding* are gerunds, verb forms that end in *–ing* and function like nouns. *Ice-skating, skiing,* and *snowboarding* are the first three items in a series of four items; all four items in the series should be gerunds.

32. **(D)** Correct as is
Choice A contains an error in the case of the relative pronoun and an error in the tense of the verb. Choice B alters the sense of the original sentence and is unclear as to who is racing after whom. Choice C is wordy, awkward, and unclear. The original sentence is error-free. Therefore, Choice D, *Correct as is,* is the right answer.

33. **(C)** Because he had been living in his apartment for four years, his landlord agreed to paint the premises.
Error in sequence of tenses. The *had* before *been living* correctly indicates a time before the landlord finally *agreed.*

34. **(A)** To some, rodents are a source of disease and plague; to others, they are a source of information about human psychology.
Sentence fragment. Choice A corrects the fragment by adding the verb "are" and supplying a semicolon to link the two independent clauses that have been created.

35. **(B)** Back from their cruise, our neighbors told us that they enjoyed making new friends on board ship, relaxing on the deck chairs, and visiting different Caribbean ports.

Lack of parallelism. *Making* and *relaxing* are gerunds, verb forms that end in *–ing* and function like nouns. *Making* and *relaxing* are the first two items in a series of three items; all three items in the series should be gerunds.

36. **(A)** Chasing after the car, my excited dog was soon outdistanced by the speeding vehicle.
Dangling participle. Ask yourself who was chasing after the car. The car certainly wasn't chasing after itself!

37. **(C)** Voting rights in national elections should be the same in all states.
Throughout the passage, the author's thrust is that national standards, not state or local standards, should decide who gets to vote. Her point is that, no matter what state you live in, your right to vote should stay the same. Choice D is incorrect. The second paragraph states that it does not matter "whether one believes that ex-convicts should be able to vote." What matters is that the rules determining who gets to vote in national elections should be the same, no matter where you live.

38. **(D)** Pastor Johnson is a minister whose calling is to help ex-convicts make the transition from jail into working life.
Use the process of elimination to answer this question. Choice A incorrectly links two independent clauses with a comma (the dreaded comma splice). Therefore, you can eliminate Choice A. Choice B is wordy and awkward. Therefore, you can eliminate Choice B. Choice C uses an illogical conjunction to link the two independent clauses. Therefore, you can eliminate Choice C. Choice D neatly links the two clauses and in the process cuts out unnecessary verbiage. The correct answer is Choice D.

39. **(B)** Pastor Johnson received an award from Florida's Governor Jeb Bush for community service.
The major thrust of this passage concerns the need to have national standards to determine who is to vote in national elections. Choices A, C, and D all touch on the ques-

tion of voting rights. Choice B does not; it merely provides information about Pastor Johnson's career in Florida. It does not belong in the passage.

40. **(C)** how difficult making this transition can be
What can be hard? *Making the transition* from prison life to life outside prison can be hard. Choice C replaces the indefinite pronoun *it* with a specific phrase.

41. **(C)** Regardless of whether
Error in usage. *Irregardless* is nonstandard for *regardless*. Regardless of how you may feel about this question, please avoid using *irregardless*.

42. **(B)** persuasive
Throughout the passage, the author is trying to convince the reader that her point is valid. If, after reading her argument, you now agree that voting rights in national elections should be the same in all states, she has succeeded in making her point. The passage is clearly *persuasive*.

43. **(B)** Critics call Edgar Allen Poe the father of detective fiction.
You might expect that the opening sentence of this essay would mention Anna Katharine Green. Instead, it leads up to discussing this relatively unknown woman writer by dropping the name of Edgar Allen Poe, a far more famous writer. This opening sentence is not a typical topic sentence. Instead, it is a "hook" to catch the reader's interest. Think of it as a literary variation on "bait and switch": the bait thrown out by the author is the suggestion that she is going to discuss Poe; the switch comes when she discusses Green instead.

44. **(A)** An instant success, *The Leavenworth Case* sold over 150,000 copies.
Choices B, C, and D all suffer from awkwardness and redundancy. Only Choice A is clear and concise.

45. **(C)** Green's older sister and two older brothers and their wives also shared the family home.
The second paragraph deals with Green's literary aspirations: Choices A, B, and D,

which all pertain to writing, would be appropriate in this context. Choice C, which deals with Green's siblings, would not.

46. **(D)** the manuscript
What did Green hide in her closet? She hid a specific, concrete object, something she could pick up in her two hands and shove behind a hatbox. In a word, she hid her *manuscript*.

47. **(C)** respectively
Do not confuse *respectively* with *respectfully*. *Respectively* means in precisely the order given: Mrs. Henry Wood wrote *East Lynne*, while Mary Elizabeth Braddon wrote *Lady Audley's Secret*. *Respectfully*, however, means courteously and considerately.

48. **(C)** A biography of Green
A full-length biography of a woman writer should provide more details about her life than either an encyclopedia article or a chapter in a textbook on women's studies. It certainly should provide more information than a "how-to" book on mystery writing would!

READING SUBTEST

1. **(D)** Sell it
The word "originally" is your clue that you will find the answer to this question near the beginning of this story. The miller and his son were "on their way to market with a donkey which they hoped to sell." What did the miller originally plan to do with the donkey? He planned to sell it.

2. **(D)** in good shape
The passage goes on to describe how they traveled. Guiding the mule's movements, they drove him to market "very slowly." Why did they choose to travel so slowly? The sentence goes on to give their reasoning: "they thought they would have a better chance to sell him if they kept him in good condition." In other words, they wanted the donkey to get to the market in good shape.

3. **(B)** disrespectful
Where can you find the answer to this question? The key word here is "merchants."

Scan the passage for the word "merchants." Your eye will be drawn to the words "three merchants passed by." The miller's son is riding the donkey. The merchants shout at him, telling him to "Respect old age." They are scolding him for being disrespectful to his father by riding while the old miller is forced to walk.

4. **(A)** was ignoring the needs of his son
Where can you find the answer to this question? The key word here is "women." Scan the passage for the word "women." Your eye will be drawn to the words "they overtook some women." The miller is riding the donkey. One of the women exclaims or cries out when she sees him "Perched on the donkey, while that poor boy has to walk." She feels sorry for the miller's son, and blames the miller for ignoring the needs of his son.

5. **(C)** the noisy crowd frightened him
Where can you find the answer to this question? The key word here is "kick." Scan the passage for the word "kick." Your eye will be drawn to the words "kick and bray." Read the whole sentence up to this point: "The donkey did not dislike being carried, but so many people came up to point at him and laugh and shout, that he began to kick and bray." Now use the process of elimination to find the correct answer.
Did the donkey kick because the miller and his son were too heavy? No. He was not carrying them; they were carrying him. You can eliminate Choice A. Did the donkey kick because he was afraid of falling in the water? No. Nothing in the passage suggests that the donkey feared falling in. You can eliminate Choice B. Did the donkey kick because the noisy crowd frightened him? That sounds possible: you know that when the laughing, pointing, shouting people surrounded him, the donkey "began to kick and bray." The correct answer may be Choice C.
Look at the final answer choice. Did the donkey kick because he disliked being slung from a pole? No. The sentence explicitly states that the donkey "did not dislike

being carried." Therefore, being carried slung from a pole did not cause him to kick. You can eliminate Choice D.
Only Choice C is left. It is the correct answer.

6. **(D)** easy to influence
The miller listens to the comments of every person passing by and tries to make everyone happy. When he is criticized for walking, he rides. When he is criticized for making his son walk while he rides, he lets his son ride with him. When he is criticized for overloading the donkey with two riders, he and his son carry the beast instead. Wishing to do whatever everyone wants of him, the miller is easy to influence. The correct answer is Choice D.

7. **(C)** "If you try to please all, you please none."
The miller tried to please everyone. He ended by pleasing no one, for the onlookers thought him a fool, and he and his son lost their chance to sell the donkey.

8. **(B)** nostalgia
The writer of this memoir is fondly looking back on her days in the big, white house in Brooklyn. She has happy memories of cows grazing and of trains puffing by. She feels nostalgia, a sentimental longing for the happiness of a former place or of a time gone by.

9. **(C)** out of financial necessity
Look closely at the second paragraph. Why did the writer's family move back to the Lower East Side? They were compelled or forced to do so. What forced them to do so? Something cost them their half ownership of the Brooklyn house, and so they had to move for money reasons. In other words, they had to move out of financial necessity.

10. **(B)** a setback
If the time in Brooklyn marked the high point or high-water mark of the family fortunes, then the move to the Lower East Side marked a reversal in the family fortunes. It was a setback, an unexpected reverse or defeat that they were compelled to endure.

11. **(C)** a dishonest businessman
    The writer does not blame her father (Pop) for the change in the family fortunes. Instead, in the second paragraph she states explicitly that it "was the treachery of Pop's business partner" that caused the family to lose their Brooklyn home. According to the writer, her father's business partner had betrayed Pop's trust, swindling him out of his money and costing him the half-ownership of the house in Brooklyn. Thus, she blames the move from Brooklyn on a dishonest businessman.

12. **(B)** very similar to the Hymans' house
    Again, go back to the text. Where does the writer first mention the Hymans' house? She first mentions it in paragraph 3: it was "the adjoining two-story and attic red brick house." Not only were the two houses located next to one another, but also they resembled one another. In fact, except for some minor differences, the two buildings "were exact replicas" or duplicates. Clearly, the writer's new home was very similar to the Hymans' house.

13. **(C)** hard-working
    What impresses the writer most about the Hymans? In paragraph 4 she discusses the Hyman family and exclaims, "What an industrious family they were!" The exclamation point at the end of the sentence expresses strong emotion: the writer is extremely impressed by how industrious (hard-working) they were.

14. **(B)** because their father paid them
    The writer states that the "Judge" paid regular wages to his children for creating the pinwheel paper rolls.

15. **(C)** Gyrocopter
    When you are answering questions about a reading passage, it is a good plan to read the passage quickly, or to skim over it, paying special attention to the first and last paragraphs and to the opening and closing sentences of each paragraph. In this passage, the first paragraph introduces the topic (the growth in the number of off-highway recreational vehicles) and then goes on to give the main types of these vehicles and to estimate their numbers. The second paragraph says that these vehicles are tremendously popular and then goes on to give some of the reasons for their popularity. The last paragraph says that these vehicles cause problems and goes on to list some of the problems. The very last sentence says that various interests "call for some limitation of the use of off-highway vehicles." If you have a good overview of what the passage says and where it says it, you will be able to find the answers to detailed questions more easily.
    Question 15 asks which of four possible choices is the least commonly used recreational vehicle. Turn back to the first paragraph, which introduces the different types of vehicles. Its second sentence says, "The most common types of off-highway recreational vehicles are motorcycles, dune buggies, and four-wheel-drive vehicles." You are looking for the least commonly used recreational vehicle. Therefore, you should be able to rule out the most commonly used vehicles, Choices A, B, and D. The gyrocopter, Choice C, was not listed as one of the most commonly used vehicles. This suggests that, of the four vehicles given, it may be the one least commonly in use. In fact, later in the paragraph, gyrocopters are listed with hovercraft among the "few exotics." They are unusual recreational vehicles, far less common than dune buggies, four-wheel-drive vehicles, and motorcycles.

16. **(B)** great mobility in the out-of-doors
    The second paragraph of the reading passage gives people's reasons for liking off-highway vehicles. Read through these reasons and compare them with the possible answers to determine the reason most users enjoy their vehicles. Choice A, a chance to compete, is something that numbers of off-highway-vehicle users enjoy. However, the paragraph's second sentence states that "while some participants are interested only

in competition . . . , the majority of users prefer more casual touring and sightseeing." This means that some are interested in a chance to compete, but most are not. Therefore, you can rule out Choice A. Choice C, inexpensive urban transportation, is not supported by the passage, which stresses the usefulness of off-highway vehicles in hunting, fishing, camping, and other non-urban activities. Therefore, you can rule out Choice C. While off-highway vehicle use can result in property destruction, most off-highway vehicle users are not out there looking for opportunities for property destruction. Therefore, you can rule out Choice D. Only Choice B is left. For the majority of users (those people who prefer more casual touring and outdoor activities to the joys of competition), "off-highway vehicles are popular because they allow them great mobility in the out-of-doors." Choice B is the correct answer.

17. **(D)** wearing away the soil
The last paragraph of the passage mentions the problems in using off-highway vehicles. Read through it again to find out which problem most concerns conservationists. The next-to-last sentence of the passage states plainly that they are "most concerned with the harm that unrestricted off-highway vehicle use may cause through soil erosion." Clearly, Choice D (wearing away the soil, that is, soil erosion) is the correct answer.
In answering this sort of question, you may find it helpful to make a guess about the correct answer and then to skim back over the passage just to test out whether your guess was accurate. From just a quick glance at the four answer choices, you could probably guess that a conservationist would most likely fear the wearing away of the soil or soil erosion as a possible problem. Thus, you could immediately scan the passage, looking for phrases like "soil erosion" and "wearing away the soil," and, on locating the phrase, read through that part of the passage quickly to confirm your guess.

18. **(D)** trespass on privately owned land
The same strategy mentioned above for question 17 works well here also: guess which of the four answer choices is most likely to concern property owners, and then check back in the third paragraph to see if your guess was right. A property owner is likely to be concerned about someone's trespassing on his or her privately owned land, so Choice D is a good guess. The third sentence of the paragraph discussing the problems of off-highway vehicle use says "property owners are sensitive to trespass." That means they can get pretty touchy when someone intrudes on their land. The wording isn't exactly the same here as it is in the question, but the meaning is very close: you can assume your guess is correct. (Besides, Choices B and C are mentioned as concerns of conservationists and land management officials, not of property owners, so you can rule them out. What's more, Choice A makes no sense in the context, so you can rule it out as well.)

19. **(D)** restrictions placed on off-highway vehicle use
This question asks you to reason a little bit beyond what is actually said in the passage. The passage's concluding paragraph deals with the problems of off-highway vehicle use. The second sentence of this paragraph says that "there has been a good deal of public protest in opposition to uncontrolled use of these vehicles." Then, after describing some of the protests, the paragraph concludes with the statement that "all of these interests call for some limitation of the use of off-highway vehicles." What you need to do at this point is to think things through. If the problems caused by off-highway vehicle use continue, what is likely to occur? The protests in opposition are likely to continue, and even to increase. As a result of this growing opposition, there will likely be some limitation of off-highway vehicle use. Thus, Choice D is a likely result if the problems continue.

Check the other answers to see whether any of them is a likely result of continued problems. Choice A, an expansion of off-highway vehicle use, actually might be a cause of continued or intensified problems, not a result of them. You can eliminate Choice A. Continuing problems should lead to an increase of protest, not a lessening of complaints. You can eliminate Choice B. Continuing problems caused by off-highway vehicles in general wouldn't be likely to lead to an increase in numbers of one particular kind of recreational vehicle. You can eliminate Choice C. Only Choice D is left; it is the correct answer.

20. **(B) the condemned man**
The "he" in line 1 is also the "he" in line 6 who curses his luck. He is the man condemned to death.

21. **(C) divisions of an hour**
Think of quarter hours. Every quarter hour, the steeple tells the people of the town the time: one stroke for 15 minutes past the hour, two strokes for half-past, three strokes for three-quarters-past, four strokes for the hour's close.

22. **(D) hanging**
How is the man described? He is both "strapped" (tied up) and "noosed." In other words, his head is in a noose. What is a noose? It is a loop made with a slipknot, often used as a hangman's halter. This suggests that the subject of the poem is to die by hanging.

23. **(D) cannot escape his fate**
The condemned man is waiting to be executed. He curses his luck because he has been captured and condemned to death. There is no way out for him. He cannot escape his fate.

24. **(C) the nature of his crime**
Although we know a great deal about the condemned man, we do not know what crime he committed that led him to his fate. Murder? Treason? The poem gives us no clue. We do have information about his emotions: he "cursed his luck." He resents

his fate. Therefore, Choice A is incorrect. We also have information about the manner of his execution: he is "noosed" and is going to be hanged. Therefore, Choice B is incorrect. We definitely have information about the setting: the marketplace, with a clock tower overlooking the gallows. Therefore, Choice D is incorrect. Only Choice C is left. It is the correct choice.

25. **(B) chemistry**
Notice that the three job descriptions all follow the same form: they begin with a general statement of the nature of the job, go on to give the qualifications for filling the job, and finally conclude with a sentence that lists the courses that it would be useful for someone to have as qualifications for the job. Therefore, when you encounter this question asking which course would be useful for both marine science technicians and port security specialists, you know just where to look for the answer: go to the last sentence of each job description and compare the two course lists given there. For marine science technician, the courses suggested are algebra, trigonometry, chemistry, physics, and keyboarding. For port security specialist, the courses suggested are practical mathematics, chemistry, and English. The only course common to both lists is chemistry. Choice B must be the correct answer.

26. **(C) handling explosives**
Check each of the four answer choices by looking through the first part of the job description for a Marine Science Technician. Remember, you are looking for something that is not a part of the science tech's job. Therefore, if an answer choice is a task that a science tech would do, you can eliminate that choice.
Choice A—analyzing sea conditions. This task is listed in the Marine Science Technician's job description. The last sentence of the description begins, "their analysis and interpretation of weather and sea conditions furnish advice." You can cross out Choice A. Choice B—collecting meteorological obser-

Model Test A

vations. This task appears in the second sentence of the job description: "They make visual and instrumental weather and oceanographic observations." You can cross out Choice B.

Choice C—handling explosives. This is not part of the job description for a marine science technician. (In fact, it is listed in the Port Security Specialist's job description.) As soon as you come to this answer choice, you know that you have found the task that is not part of the technician's job. This is the correct answer to the question.

27. **(A)** clerk
This question requires you to compare the job description for a Port Security Specialist with what you know of other (civilian) jobs. If aspects of the civilian job resemble aspects of the Port Security Specialist's work, you can rule out that answer choice. First look at the Port Security Specialist's job description. What does a Port Security Specialist do? A Port Security Specialist is an expert in "fire prevention and extinguishment": the job is like a firefighter's; therefore, you can eliminate Choice B. A Port Security Specialist is knowledgeable ("well-versed") in the regulations and equipment for safeguarding "vessels, harbors, and waterfront facilities": the job is like a security guard's; therefore, you can eliminate Choice C. A Port Security Specialist deals with the storage and transportation of dangerous cargoes: the job is like a warehouse worker's; therefore, you can eliminate Choice D. Only Choice A, clerk, is left. A Port Security Specialist is not someone who specializes in filing and similar office work. The least related civilian job clearly is that of a clerk.

28. **(C)** move their boat downstream safely
The opening paragraph sets the stage for what is to come. The second sentence states that the "three partners were lining a long and narrow poling-boat down a bad stretch of rapids." In other words, using rope lines and a pole, the three men are trying to move the poling-boat safely down the creek.

29. **(B)** was concerned for his master's safety
The opening paragraph's final sentence describes the way in which Buck watches his master. Thornton is in the boat, using his pole to help the boat move safely through a bad stretch of rapids. Buck is described as "worried and anxious." He never takes his eyes off his master. What does this suggest about Buck's reason for watching his master? Clearly, Buck was concerned for his master's safety.

30. **(D)** Hans stopped its motion too suddenly.
Reread the section of the second paragraph that describes how the boat overturned: "The boat flirted over and snubbed in to the bank bottom up." To find out why the boat overturned, go to the previous sentence. The boat "was flying down-stream in a current as swift as a mill-race, when Hans checked it with the rope and checked too suddenly." To check something is to bring it to a halt, to stop its motion. By stopping the boat's motion so suddenly, Hans manages to flip the boat, unintentionally overturning it.

31. **(C)** his master grabs on to him
Use the process of elimination to answer this question. Does Buck's anxiety about his master give you a clue that he is a dog? Not necessarily; servants and apprentices also have masters. Do not assume that Choice A is the correct answer, but move on to the next answer choice. Does Buck's leap into the river give you a clue that he is a dog? No. Cross out Choice B. Does the way his master grabs on to Buck give you a clue that Buck is a dog? Yes. Describing Buck's attempt to rescue his master, the second sentence of paragraph 3 states: "When he felt him grasp his tail, Buck headed for the bank." Buck's master has grabbed hold of Buck's tail and is hanging on to it for dear life. The sentence is your clue that Buck is a loyal dog and not a human being. The correct answer is Choice C.

32. **(D)** downward slope
Have you ever gone white-water rafting? If you have, you can probably visualize the scene described here. The fast and furious

stream is racing downhill, heading for the rocks below. (Think of a waterfall.) London describes what is taking place: "The suck of the water as it took the beginning of the last steep pitch was frightful." Pitch here has nothing to do with high tones (as in a musical pitch) or sticky substances (as in tar and pitch). It has nothing to do with levels of intensity. The steep pitch is the steep downward slope toward which Thornton and Buck are hurtling.

33. **(B)** grab a rock with both hands
Hanging on to Buck's tail, Thornton realizes that it is impossible for the dog to fight the force of the rapids and swim to the shore hauling his master's weight. Tossed by the current from one rock onto the next, Thornton desperately clutches the rock's "slippery top with both hands, releasing Buck." He thus lets go of Buck in order to grab a rock with both hands.

34. **(C)** urgent
As he shouts, "Go, Buck! Go!" Thornton's tone is clearly urgent: he is urging Buck on, ordering the dog to save himself.

35. **(D)** dense rainforests
This passage consists of four paragraphs; you need to have a general idea what each of the paragraphs says about the coastline of San Diego County. Each paragraph discusses a particular aspect of the coastline.
Paragraph 1: Landforms of the coastline (beaches, headlines, cliffs)
Paragraph 2: Coastal waters (bays, lagoons, estuaries)
Paragraph 3: Mission Bay
Paragraph 4: San Diego Bay
Question 35 asks which of its four possible answers is not found on the coast of San Diego County: rocky headlands, sandy beaches, steep cliffs, or dense rainforests. From a quick overview of the passage, you know you can find the answer to this question in paragraph 1. Use the process of elimination here. Are there rocky headlands along the coastline? Yes, the stretches of open beaches are "interrupted by rocky

headlands." Cross out Choice A. Are there sandy beaches? Certainly there are. Cross out Choice B. Are there steep cliffs? Paragraph 1's final sentence mentions "precipitous cliffs several hundred feet high." That sounds steep. Cross out Choice C. Only Choice D is left. There are no tropical rainforests along San Diego County's coast.

36. **(D)** wildlife habitat
Which paragraph in the passage discusses lagoons? Paragraph 2. Read this paragraph over again looking for anything that explains why the lagoons are valuable. The last sentence of the paragraph begins, "the estuaries and lagoons are valuable mainly as wildlife habitat." Clearly, the correct answer is wildlife habitat, Choice D.

37. **(B)** Mission Bay has less commercial importance than San Diego Bay does. Since its shoreline is highly developed for recreational purposes, Mission Bay clearly has not been set aside as a wildlife refuge. Therefore, Choice A is incorrect. Though San Diego Bay has had to be protected from the dumping of industrial and municipal sewage, nothing in the passage suggests that Mission Bay has suffered from such pollution. Choice C is incorrect. Not Mission Bay, but San Diego Bay, is the site of a major naval base. Choice D is incorrect. While Mission Bay is highly developed for recreation, it is not, as San Diego is, a busy center of commerce. Thus, it has less commercial importance than San Diego Bay does. Choice B is correct.

38. **(C)** banning actions that caused it
Since water pollution is bad, the way you do something positive about it is to get rid of it. San Diego has "prohibited the dumping of municipal and industrial sewage into the bay." Thus, the government has banned actions that caused water pollution.

39. **(C)** an increase in its recreational use.
This final question on the passage concerns San Diego Bay. To answer it, turn to paragraph 4. The middle sentences of this paragraph discuss what water pollution

regulations have been enacted; these mostly concern limiting the dumping of sewage by the city, by industry, and by naval and private boats. The paragraph's concluding sentence discusses what effects these regulations have had: there has been "a marked improvement in the water quality," and "all types of water-associated recreation are increasing." Compare this statement with the answer choices given. The correct answer is Choice C: the recreational use of San Diego Bay has grown as its pollution has lessened.

40. **(C)** humorous sketch
Think of Wile E. Coyote in the Road Runner cartoons when you read this passage. With his folksy, down-home language and his wild exaggerations ("even the fleas would desert him for a velocipede"), Twain has written a humorous sketch—a shaggy coyote story, if not a shaggy dog story.

41. **(D)** most contemptible
Scan the passage for the word "meanest." You will find it in the second sentence of the second paragraph. "The meanest creatures despise him, and even the fleas would desert him for a velocipede." Not even the lowly fleas will stick with him. This sorry-looking creature is scorned by everyone. Even the meanest, most contemptible creatures despise him.

42. **(A)** spineless
The third sentence of the second paragraph describes the coyote as "spiritless and cowardly." In other words, he is a spineless creature.

43. **(B)** make himself look dangerous
Scan the passage for the word "teeth." The third sentence of the second paragraph states that "while his exposed teeth are pretending a threat, the rest of his face is apologizing for it." Thus, he bares or exposes his teeth to pretend he is a threat. In other words, he bares his teeth to try to make himself look dangerous.

44. **(D)** to entertain
In this passage, Twain is cheerfully spinning a yarn, humorously exaggerating in order to entertain his readers. His purpose is entertainment, pure and simple. He is not simply expressing opinions; he is creating an image of the coyote that will amuse his readers.

45. **(B)** speed
Fear definitely gives wings to the heels of this coyote. If you make a demonstration against him, that is, start pulling out a weapon, he takes off like lightning and goes faster and faster until he is well out of reach of any weapon you may have. Clearly, the characteristic of the coyote emphasized in the final sentence of this passage is speed.

46. **(A)** protect it
The opening sentence of the final paragraph sums up Douglas's relationship to the Everglades. She dedicated her life to preserving the Everglades, writing books and giving speeches in defense of this unique region. Clearly, she wanted to protect it.

47. **(A)** committed
A committed person is someone who is dedicated and loyal, devoted to a cause. Given her lifelong dedication to the cause of the Everglades, Douglas certainly deserves to be described as committed.

48. **(D)** its water supply has been redirected to serve other purposes
Scan the opening paragraph for the word "shrinking." You'll find it in the next-to-last sentence. The River of Grass has been shrinking. Why? The final sentence of the paragraph gives the reason: "it has dwindled as engineering projects have diverted the waters feeding it to meet agricultural and housing needs." The engineers have diverted or redirected the waters to serve other purposes. The correct answer is Choice D.

49. **(C)** hoped to influence her readers
Scan the passage for the title of Douglas's book. You'll find it in the opening sentence of the second paragraph. There, it explains that through her book Douglas "tried to give people everywhere a sense of why the Everglades mattered." She was attempting to convert her readers to her point of view.

In other words, she hoped to influence her readers, turning them into friends of the Everglades.

50. **(A)** why Douglas valued the Everglades
Use the process of elimination to answer this question. Does the passage tell you why Douglas valued the Everglades? Yes. She valued it because it was unique, a miracle of nature. This is probably the correct answer, but you should check the other answers to be sure. Does the passage tell you how the Everglades grew? No. You can cross out Choice B. Does the passage tell you how the developers fought Douglas? No. It tells you that Douglas fought the developers but gives you no idea about how the developers may have fought back. You can cross out Choice C. Does the passage tell you who discovered the Everglades? No. You can cross out Choice D. Only Choice A is left. As you suspected, it is the correct answer.

51. **(D)** why Douglas looked on the Army Corps of Engineers as her enemies
Why have these two sentences been enclosed between parentheses? Remarks in parentheses (that's the plural of parenthesis) generally serve to set off definitions, related additional information, and examples. To understand the purpose of the sentences here, you need to look closely at the sentence that comes just before the opening parenthesis. According to this sentence, Douglas "defended the Everglades against the invasions of the developers, the sugar planters, and her special foes, the Army Corps of Engineers." The parenthetical sentences go on to tell what the Army Corps of Engineers did to the Everglades that angered Douglas. The writer has included these sentences to help you understand why Douglas looked on the Army Corps of Engineers as her enemies or special foes.

52. **(D)** was stirred by Kirkland's nobility
Look at the sentence in which the general gives Kirkland permission to go on his errand of mercy. "The general was moved by Kirkland's request and allowed him to go." In other words, he was stirred or moved emotionally by Kirkland's nobility in being willing to risk his own life to ease the suffering of others.

53. **(C)** compassionate
In risking his own life to ease the suffering of others, Kirkland showed that he was merciful or compassionate.

54. **(D)** respected the sergeant's errand of mercy
The Northerners, that is, the Union soldiers, fired at the Confederate sergeant when he came out from behind the stone wall. Then, "as soon as they understood his intent," the Northerners ceased fire. Once they realized that the Confederates were not launching another attack and understood that Kirkland intended only to help the wounded, they stopped shooting at him. Clearly, they respected the sergeant's errand of mercy.

55. **(B)** cruel or unjust ruler
A tyrant is a cruel or unjust ruler, someone who oppresses the people. Think of "a wicked tyrant."

56. **(D)** scold
To rebuke is to scold or reprimand. Think of "being rebuked for cheating."

57. **(B)** suppress
To stifle something is to suppress or restrain it. Think of "stifling a cough."

58. **(A)** store up
To hoard is to store up or accumulate something, hiding it away. Think of "hoarding food."

59. **(D)** outstanding
Eminent means distinguished or outstanding. Think of "eminent scholars."

60. **(C)** exactly alike
Identical means exactly alike, impossible to tell apart. Think of "identical twins."

61. **(A)** shining
Radiant means shining or dazzling. Think of "radiant smiles."

62. **(D)** significantly
Considerably means noticeably or significantly. Think of becoming "considerably fatter."

63. **(A)** sparkle
To glisten is to sparkle or shine. Think of "eyes glistening with tears."

64. **(B)** false show
A pretense is a false show, a kind of deception or make-believe. Think of "false pretenses."

65. **(B)** The head nurse was in charge of the psychiatric ward.
As used in both sentences, charge has to do with care or supervision: both the social worker and the head nurse are supervising the care of people. Charge is a noun.

66. **(D)** David ripped up the junk mail and cast the pieces into the wastebasket.
As used in both sentences, to cast is to toss or throw away. It is a verb.

67. **(A)** The economist proved that the increase in the national debt did in fact stem from the costs of the recent war.
As used in both sentences, to stem from something is to arise from it or come into being. It is a verb.

68. **(B)** Felipe liked to make a practice of reading bedtime stories to his two sons every night.
As used in both sentences, a practice is a habit or custom. It is a noun.

69. **(D)** Application to your studies will help you pass the test.
As used in both sentences, application means persistent effort, hard work combined with constant attention. It is a noun.

70. **(D)** The general planned to mount a surprise attack on the unsuspecting enemy forces.
As used in both sentences, to mount something is to prepare to launch or organize it. Mount here is a verb.

71. **(A)** Some species of spiders do not spin webs; instead, they stalk their prey on the ground.
As used in both sentences, to stalk something is to hunt it down. Stalk here is a verb.

72. **(C)** The pilgrims aboard the *Mayflower* signed a compact binding them to obey the rules of the new colony.

As used in both sentences, a compact is a formal agreement. It is a noun.

73. **(A)** In the Scouts, Toby learned how to start a fire and how to extinguish one as well.
As used in both sentences, to start something is to get it going, to set it in operation. It is a verb.

74. **(D)** We plan to suspend the chandelier from a hook attached to the ceiling.
As used in both sentences, to suspend something is to hang it by attaching it to something above. It is a verb.

75. **(D)** risky
Precarious means risky or dangerous. Think of "precarious footing."

76. **(B)** bland
Insipid means tasteless or bland. Think of "insipid hospital food."

77. **(A)** unaware
Oblivious means unconscious or unaware. Think of being "oblivious to danger."

78. **(D)** luxuriousness
Opulence means luxuriousness or extreme wealth. Think of "luxurious opulence."

79. **(D)** stubborn
Intractable means obstinate or stubborn. Think of someone "as intractable as a mule."

80. **(D)** soothe
To mollify is to pacify or soothe. Think of "mollifying someone's anger."

81. **(A)** scatter
To disperse is to drive off or scatter. Think of "dispersing a mob."

82. **(A)** rubble
Debris means ruins or rubble. Think of "picking through debris."

83. **(B)** unsuccessful
Abortive means fruitless or unsuccessful. Think of "an abortive plot."

84. **(B)** uninterested
Indifferent means uninterested or unconcerned. Think of being "indifferent to human suffering."

Mathematics Section

1. **(D)** $-\dfrac{1}{64}$

    In a geometric series, each term is derived from the previous one by multiplying it by a fixed ratio. In this case, each term is half the magnitude of the previous one, and it also switches from positive to negative and back again. You could probably just write out the next few terms by recognizing this pattern. Or you could figure out that the fixed ratio in this case is $-\dfrac{1}{2}$. The next few terms of the series after the ones given in the question are:

    sixth term $\quad -\dfrac{1}{16}$

    seventh term $\quad \dfrac{1}{32}$

    eighth term $\quad -\dfrac{1}{64}$

2. **(B)** It must be between $1\dfrac{1}{4}$ and $1\dfrac{3}{8}$
    As you add up the terms,
    the sum keeps "bouncing" around—from 2, to 1, to $1\dfrac{1}{2}$, to $1\dfrac{1}{4}$, etc., because of the alternating positive and negative contributions. When you get to the fourth term, $-\dfrac{1}{4}$, and the sum that far ($1\dfrac{1}{4}$), you should see that the next term will push it up again (by $\dfrac{1}{8}$), and the sixth term will drop back again. So without even adding in the last two terms, you should be able to pick out choice B. (And if you did add up all 6, you just got some more practice with fractions, so that is OK, too.)

3. **(B)** 4.2×10^4 km
    All the answers are given in scientific notation. The circumference of the ISS orbit must be more than that of the Earth, which is 4.0×10^4 in scientific notation (4 followed by four zeros $= 4 \times 10^4$). Choice D is easily ruled out; it is more than ten times as large as the circumference of the Earth, while the ISS orbits only a short distance above the surface of the Earth.

    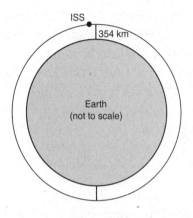

    You should remember that the circumference of a circle is π (about 3.14) times the diameter of the circle, and the diameter of the ISS orbit is approximately 700 km larger than the diameter of the earth (350 km wider on each side). Therefore,

    $$C_{ISS} \approx \pi \times (D_{Earth} + 700) =$$
    $$\pi \times D_{Earth} + \pi \times 700 = C_{Earth} + \pi \times 700$$

    $\pi \times 700$ is a bit more than 2100 (you don't need to use more than the first digit of π to choose the right answer here, since all answers are only given to thousands of km, the first decimal place after the 4 in $4.n \times 10^4$).

4. **(A)** $\dfrac{5}{36}$

    With two 6-sided dice, there are $6 \times 6 = 36$ possible outcomes, all equally likely if the dice are fair. Except for the "extreme" results ("snake-eyes" with single pips on each die, or a 12 from both dice landing with 6 pips showing), any other sum (3 to 11) can happen in more than one way.

The 5 outcomes with a sum of 6, giving a probability of $\dfrac{5}{36}$, are

Die 1	Die 2	Sum
1	5	6
2	4	6
3	3	6
4	2	6
5	1	6

5. **(D)** $1 + x^2$

Do any possible simplifications in the numerator and denominator separately, then see what else can be done.

Numerator: Both terms have x^2 as a factor: $x^2 + x^4 = x^2(1 + x^2)$

Denominator: Multiply $(x + 1)(x - 1) = x^2 - 1$
Subtract $1 - (x^2 - 1) = 1 - x^2 + 1 = x^2$

Finally: $\dfrac{x^2(1 + x^2)}{x^2} = 1 + x^2$

Note: The factorization $x^2 - 1 = (x + 1)(x - 1)$ or the more general $x^2 - n^2 = (x + n)(x - n)$ is worthwhile memorizing; it can help in a fair number of cases.

6. **(C)** $3 : 4$

The ratio of two numbers is a comparison of the two reduced to lowest terms. In this case, the sale price is 1/4 (25%) off the list price, so it is easy to see that it compares to the full price as 3/4 to 1. Multiplying by 4, 3/4 : 1 becomes 3 : 4.

7. **(B)** 99 gallons

First you must find the area of the garden in square feet. Multiplying the length by the width, you get 120 square feet. Then multiply by the number of quarts required per square foot (3.3 quarts for each).

$$
\begin{array}{r}
120 \\
\underline{3.3} \\
36\ 0 \\
\underline{360} \\
396.0
\end{array}
$$

To convert 396 quarts to gallons, you must remember that a gallon is 4 quarts. 396/4 = 99.

8. **(A)** 10 inches

Look for the lowest point on the graph; it isn't necessary to be absolutely certain which point is lowest, if there are several at about the same height. When there are a lot of points, it may help to cover most of the graph with a piece of paper (for example, your answer sheet) and move it down parallel to the *x*-axis until only one point or a very few points are visible. There are three points below all the others, with one in the late 1950s (about 1957) being almost exactly on the 10-inch line.

9. **(B)** 20 inches

The average rainfall is in the center of the range of yearly rainfall numbers. For every year with more rainfall, there must be one or more other years that "balance" it on the other side. So, to find the average on a graph, look for a level that has about as many points above it as below it. A piece of paper helps in this question, as it did for the previous one. Setting it at the 15-inch level, you will see a large majority of the points lying above 15. At 20 inches, it looks like about half of the points are covered (but try the other answers before being too quick to jump at this one). At the 25-inch-level, there are no more than 9 or 10 points above the sheet of paper, and at 30 inches only two. The graph does center on 20 inches.

10. **(B)** 15

Count the number of points that are below the 15-inch line on the graph. If you're not sure whether a point is exactly on the line or below it, count it anyway, and check whether that makes a difference in the answer you would choose. In this case, there are thirteen points that are definitely below the line, one that probably is below it (1949) and a couple that are hard to tell exactly (1966 and 1994). The answer *must* be more than 10 (Choice A), and it cannot be as high as 20 (Choice C). The only reasonable choice is 15.

11. **(D)** $(x/3 + 5)$ years

You need to write an expression for the *son's* age in five years, given the information presented in the questions. Since it is the son's age that is asked for, start by writing an expression for the son's age now. We are told that the man's age (x) is three times the son's age now. Using y for the son's age, that statement becomes: $x = 3y$, or dividing by 3 to get y:

$$y = \text{the son's age now} = x/3$$

In five years, the son will be $y + 5 = x/3 + 5$.

12. **(D)** A cube 1 foot on a side
You do not need to remember formulas for the volume of a sphere or a cone to answer this question. What you need is to imagine the figures, or make a sketch of them on paper. Both the cone and the sphere will fit inside the cube (each is 1 foot at the longest in height, width, and depth, the same as the cube); but the sphere and the cone reach their longest value at only one point in each dimension. (You could carve either the cone or the sphere out of a 1-foot cube of wood; doing that would remove volume from the cube to get to the other figure.)
A picture doesn't help for comparing the rectangular solid with the cube, as that is larger in one dimension than the cube, but smaller in another. Here, you do have to remember that the volume of a rectangular solid is width × depth × height. The solid in A has a volume of $11 \times 13 \times 12\,\text{in.}^3$, and the cube has volume $12 \times 12 \times 12\,\text{in.}^3$. The last dimension is the same in both, so it "cancels out" in deciding which solid has the larger volume; you just need to calculate that $11 \times 13 = 143$ and $12 \times 12 = 144$. The cube is larger than solid A as well as the other figures.

13. **(C)** 6400 square miles
There are several ways to make the estimate. One quick way is to notice that Hawaii and Maui together make up very close to $\frac{3}{4}$ of the "pie." These two islands together are a bit less than 4,800 square miles, so $\frac{1}{4}$ of the area is $4800 \div 3 = 1600$, and 4 times that is 6400.
A more straightforward way to estimate the total land area is to add the sizes given in the graph and then make your best guess of the size of the unlabeled slices of the pie chart. Lanai, Molokai, and "others" together make up a piece about the same size as Kauai or Oahu, so they are about 550 square miles or so. You can round off the other sizes to make the addition quicker; for example, if you round to the nearest 50, you get:

```
  4050
+ 700      4750 up to here...
+ 600      5350
+ 550      5900
+ 550?
  6450
```

6450 rounds off to Choice C. Note that if you add the islands one at a time, you can already see by the time Kauai's 550 is added that Choice B is too small, and that Choice D is much too large (the unlabeled pieces are obviously less than the 2100 square miles needed to go from 5900 to 8000).

14. **(B)** 250 square miles
You can compare the slice for Molokai to one of the other slices that gives a value for area. The easiest one to use for this purpose is Kauai, right next to Molokai; Kauai should look roughly twice as large. (You can also lay the edge of your answer sheet across the outer edge of the slices, and compare them that way.) In any case, for the answers given, it is clear that Molokai is not 100 sq. miles (less than 1/5 the size of Kauai), and not 500 sq. miles (almost the same size as Kauai). Choice B (250 sq. miles) is reasonable as an estimate, so it must be the correct choice.

15. **(D)** $-\dfrac{4}{3}$
You can use algebra to find the "slope-intercept" equation of the line, $y = mx + b$, with slope m:

Subtract $4x$ from both sides of the equation:
$3y = 2 - 4x$

Divide both sides by 3:

$$y = \frac{2}{3} - \frac{4x}{3} = (-\frac{4}{3})x + \frac{2}{3}$$

This shows that the slope is $-\dfrac{4}{3}$.

16. **(C)** 102 m²
The rectangular portion of the room is 8 meters by 12 meters, and the semicircular stage area adds some additional area. You can rule out Choices A ($96 = 8 \times 12$) and D ($116 = 8 \times 14$) right away; to choose B or C, estimate the size of the semicircle. Because the total length of the room is 14 meters, the radius of the circle must be 2 meters. A full circle with radius 2 meters has the area $\pi r^2 = 2 \times 2 \times \pi = 4\pi$. Half of that is $2\pi \approx 2 \times 3.14 = 6.28$. Therefore, the room is about $8 \times 12 + 6$ square meters, giving Choice C as the best estimate.

17. **(B)** 60%
The median score is the score that has half the students getting that percentage or less, and half the students scoring that percentage or better. You need to know how many students there are in the class. With this many rows in the table, it is probably easiest to keep a "running total" of the sum going line by line. Just keep track to the side as you add in each new row:

35%	2	
40%	+1	3
45%	+3	6
50%	+3	9
55%	+6	15
60%	+5	20
65%	+4	24
70%	+4	28
75%	+3	31
80%	+2	33
85%	+2	35
90%	+1	36

You need to locate where in the list the 18th highest or lowest score is found. Notice that as you add up the number of students, when you get to 55% and add in the 6 students with that score, there are 15 students with that score or lower. As soon as you include the students with a score of 60%, you have covered more than half the class, so the median score is 60%.

18. **(C)** 40 mph
The man's average speed is the total distance divided by the total time it took (speed is the rate, which is distance over time). In this case, the man drove 50 miles at one rate, and then 150 miles at another rate. But his total distance was 200 miles, and the total time was $2 + 3 = 5$ hours, so that his average rate of travel was 200 miles/5 hours = 200/5 mph = 40 mph.

19. **(C)** 23
Find the change from each number to the next one. In this case, the difference is always 3 (such a sequence is called an arithmetic sequence). To find the eighth number in the sequence, it is simplest to just continue for a few terms and then count the positions:

1st	2nd	3rd	4th	5th	
6th	7th	8th	9th . . .		
2	5	8	11	14	17
20	23	26 . . .			

20. **(C)** 52 yards
Since the angle between Rosebud and San Simeon is 30°, and that between 23rd and San Simeon is 90°, the other angle must be 60°. The 23rd Street side of the triangle is half of a side of an equilateral triangle, so it is 30 yards long. If x stands for the San Simeon side, then the Pythagorean formula gives $x^2 + 30^2 = 60^2$, or $x^2 = 3600 - 900 = 2700$. You can eliminate Choices A and D without any arithmetic; the San Simeon side of the triangle has to be shorter than Rosebud (the hypotenuse) and longer than the 23rd Street side, because it is opposite a larger angle. The choice is between B and C, and you can check by squaring them that

52 yards (52 × 52 = 2704) is closer than 50 yards (50 × 50 = 2500).

You could also find the answer by remembering that a 30–60 right triangle has its sides in the ratio of $1 : \sqrt{3} : 2$, and that $\sqrt{3}$ is approximately 1.73; therefore, the San Simeon side is about $1.73 \times 30 = 51.9$ yards.

21. **(C)** 80¢

Algebraic solution:

Let c be the original price per pound (the number you are asked to figure out), and let n be the original number of pounds that you could buy for $8. You can write this initial condition as

$$c \times n = \$8 = 80¢$$

(n pounds at c per pound costs n times c)

The price drops 30¢ a pound (and so, it becomes $c - 30$, if we take c in cents), and the same $8 or 800 cents buys $(n + 6)$ pounds. That is the same as

$$(c - 30) \times (n + 6) = 800¢ = c \times n$$

Simplify the left side: $(c - 30) \times n = cn - 30n$, and $(c - 30) \times 6 = 6c - 180$. Putting these together you get

$$cn - 30n + 6c - 180 = cn$$
or (canceling the cn) $6c - 30n = 180$

But what can you do now? Don't forget the original equation: $c \times n = 800¢$. You can use this to replace either c or n in the last equation. Since we want to find c, use $n = 800/c$ to write

$$6c - 30 \times 800/c = 180$$

Multiply by c to get

$$6c^2 - 24000 = 180c \quad \text{or}$$
$$6c^2 - 180c = 24000$$

Divide by 6:

$$c^2 - 30c = 4000 \quad \text{or} \quad c^2 - 30c - 4000 = 0$$

At this point, you can use the quadratic formula, or try to factor this to solve for c.

$$c^2 - 30c - 4000 = (c - 80)(c + 50) = 0.$$

From this, c must be either 80¢ or −50¢ (which is not realistically possible); so $c = 80¢$.

Checking the given answers:

Doing all the above is a significant amount of work. Is there an easier way? Yes, in fact. Work "backwards" from the choices, to find one that meets the terms of the problem.

A. If the original price is 50¢ per pound, then for $8 you can buy 16 pounds (800¢/50¢). If the price drops 30¢ per pound, the cost is 20¢ per pound, and $8 buys 800¢/20¢ = 40 pounds. That is 40 − 16 = 24 pounds more than before, not 6 as the question states.

B. If the original price is 60¢ per pound, $8 buys $800/60 = 80/6 = 13\frac{2}{3}$ pounds, and a drop of 30¢ buys 800/30—twice as much (i.e., $13\frac{2}{3}$ pounds more), not six pounds more.

C. If the original price is 80¢ per pound, $8 buys $800/80 = 10$ pounds, and a drop of 30¢ buys $800/(80 - 30) = 800/50 = 80/5 = 16$ pounds, six pounds more than before, just what the question requires.

D. If the original price is $1 per pound, $8 buys 8 pounds, and a price of $1 − 30¢ = 70¢ buys $800/70 = 80/7 = 11\frac{3}{7}$ pounds, not six pounds more than the original price. This is a case in which you are better off testing each answer than in solving the problem, unless you happen to be a whiz at algebra.

22. **(C)** 8.79×10^1

You do not need to perform the full division (37,253,956 people ÷ 423,970 square kilometers), even if you have a calculator. Just set it up in scientific notation with a few digits: $\dfrac{3.7 \times 10^7}{4.2 \times 10^5}$. You can immediately rule out Choice B or Choice D, as they look more like the digits that result from 4.2 ÷ 3.7. To choose between A and C, divide the power of 10 in the numerator against that in the denominator: $10^7 \div 10^5 = 10^2$. The result will be about $3.7 \times 10^2 \div 4.2 = 370 \div 4.2$. That will be less than 100 but more than 10; 8.79×10^2 is obviously too big, while Choice C has the right "order of magnitude."

23. **(A)** 1994

Compare the white bars for New York with the black bars for California. You must look for the year, or years, when the white bar is higher than the black bar. Only 1994, Choice A, can be correct.

24. **(C)** The number of citizens naturalized increased and then decreased

For this question, you can ignore the white New York bars. All the choices deal with the increase or decrease of naturalizations in California. The black bars increase in height to 1998 and then get lower. You can immediately rule out Choices A and B, which say that increase or decrease was continuous. The numbers on the scale to the left of the graph show that the higher bars stand for more naturalized citizens (over 100,000 in 1998; fewer in other years). So only Choice C states what is actually visible in the chart.

25. **(D)** 400,000

You need to add the approximate values for the naturalizations in each year to get the total. Choice A can be ruled out right away, as naturalizations in 1998 alone were more than 100,000 and adding other years can only increase that. You can add the numbers in any order you like, but it may be simplest to start with the largest bars and go down from there: in 1999 there were about 80,000; in 1997 about 70,000; in 2000 maybe a bit less than 70,000. Adding just these years gives $100,000 + 80,000 + 70,000 + 70,000 = 320,000$. This is already more than any answer except D, and if you go on to add in 40,000 for 1996 and about 30,000 for 1994 and 1995 you come out to a bit more than 400,000. Choice D must be the correct answer.

26. **(A)** 160

An alarm once every three minutes is a rate of $60/3 = 20$ alarms per hour. In eight hours, this gives $8 \times 20 = 160$ alarms.

27. **(A)** 5

The change is $\$10.00 - \$9.53 = \$0.47$. He will get the smallest number of coins possible if the clerk uses the largest denomina-

tion coin available at each step of making the change:

47¢ largest coin less than this is a quarter
$47¢ - 25¢ = 22¢$
22¢ largest usable coin is a dime
$22¢ - 10¢ = 12¢$
12¢ largest usable coin is a dime
$12¢ - 10¢ = 2¢$
2¢ largest usable coin is a penny
$2¢ - 1¢ = 1¢$
1¢ largest usable coin is a penny
$1¢ - 1¢ = $ none.

28. **(B)** −1

The slope of a line is the ratio of change in the vertical (y) direction to change in the horizontal (x) direction. In this case, y is decreasing while x increases; therefore, the slope will be a negative number (there is a negative change in y as x changes positively). To decide between Choices A and B, you need to estimate how fast y is changing with respect to a change in x. A slope of -2 would mean that as x goes some distance to the right, y would go down *twice* as much, but a look at the line shows that it is always about as far away from the origin in y as it is in x. The y coordinates change at about the same rate as the x coordinates do; hence the magnitude of the slope is about 1, and since we know that it is negative (sloping down), the correct answer is Choice B, -1.

29. **(C)** $\dfrac{1}{10}$

The order in which the boys place does not matter in this case (the two front-runners are chosen), and since we are assuming that all the runners have equal chances, the probability of each possible outcome (combination of two runners) is 1 divided by the number of different outcomes. If you recognize this as "the number of combinations of 2 out of 5 items," C(5,2), and the formula for that as 5!/2! $\times$ 3!, you can rewrite this as $\dfrac{5 \times 4}{2 \times 1} = \dfrac{20}{10} = 10$.

The probability of each outcome is therefore $\dfrac{1}{10}$.

You don't have to remember the formulas or definitions to get this result. If you have time to think about it, you can figure it out from the basics of probability calculations: Morgan has 1 chance out of 5 to come in first, and then Brad has 1 chance out of the 4 remaining runners for 2nd. So the outcome {Morgan 1st, Brad 2nd} has a probability of $\frac{1}{5} \times \frac{1}{4} = \frac{1}{20}$. Similarly, the other order {Brad 1st, Morgan 2nd} also has a probability of $\frac{1}{20}$, and these two cases add up to $\frac{1}{20} + \frac{1}{20} = \frac{1}{10}$ as the probability they both make the cut.

30. **(C)** $83,400

To make a profit of 20%, the man must add 20% to the total amount he spent on the condo; that is, he must add 20% of ($63,000 + $2,500 + $4,000) = $69,500. 20% is the same as 0.2, so you can multiply $69,500 by 0.2.

$$\begin{array}{r} \$69,500 \\ \times\ 0.2 \\ \hline \$13,900.0 \end{array}$$

(You can also do this in your head by noticing that 20% = 2 × 10%, and 10% × 69,500 = 6,950.) The price at which the man must sell the condo to get the 20% profit is

$$\begin{array}{r} \$69,500 \\ +\ \$13,900 \\ \hline \$83,400 \end{array}$$

31. **(A)** 5 hours and 6 minutes

The man drives 15 miles in the city at 25 miles per hour, and the rest of the trip (240 − 15 = 225 miles) on the freeway at 50 miles per hour. Since distance = rate × time, you can get the time he spent at each of these rates as time = distance / time. The freeway time is 225/50 hours. Instead of dividing this out directly, reduce the frac-

tion by dividing numerator and denominator by 5 to get 45/10 = 4.5 hours. The city time is 15/25, which reduces to 3/5. You don't actually have to calculate the minutes to get the answer in this case. 3/5 hours is more than half an hour (that would be 2.5/5!), so that the two sections of the man's trip take $4\frac{1}{2}$ plus something over one half hour, and the answer must be over 5 hours. Only Choice A satisfies this requirement. ALWAYS delay doing calculations until you are sure you need the exact answer; many times you will be able to decide the correct answer to a question without doing any hard work.

32. **(A)** 15

Write each statement in terms of the number you want to determine, the daughter's current age (x). The first statement is that Mrs. Brown is $x + 20$ years old. The next statement is about five years ago, and so you can write expressions for their ages at that time:

	Mrs. Brown	Daughter
ages now	$x + 20$	x
5 years ago	$x + 20 - 5$	$x - 5$

and the statement is that Mrs. Brown's age was three times that of her daughter:

$$\begin{aligned} x + 15 &= 3(x - 5) \\ x + 15 &= 3x - 15 \\ x + 30 &= 3x \\ 30 &= 2x \end{aligned}$$

and therefore $x = 15$.

33. **(D)** 1850 square feet

Amy has the ceiling and four walls to paint. The ceiling is 25 feet by 30 feet, with area 25 × 30 = 750 square feet. The two longer walls are 30 feet long by 10 feet high, adding 2 × 30 × 10 = 600 square feet. Finally, the two shorter walls are 25 feet by 10 feet. The total area is

$$25' \times 30' + 2 \times 30' \times 10' + 2 \times 25' \times 10' =$$
$$750 + 600 + 500 \text{ square feet}$$
$$= 1850 \text{ square feet}$$

34. **(B)** 85°
The sum of the angles of the triangle must be 180° (this is one of the geometrical facts you need to memorize). The two angles you know, from the statement of the question, are 55° and 40°. The remaining angle is 180 − (55 + 40) = 180 − 95 = 85°.

35. **(C)** The percentage of the French population under 20 decreased and then increased, while the percentage between the ages of 20 and 64 first increased and then decreased. Looking at the graph, you see the top line (labeled "percentage age 20 to 64") going up from about 55% to about 60% and then dropping back down; the lower line (labeled "percentage under 20") first drops and then from 1946 to 1966 it rises. Comparing these lines to the choices given we find:
A. Choice A is not correct for the part of the graph from 1946 to 1966 (the percentage under 20 increases and the 20 to 64 part decreases, exactly the opposite of the statement in A).
B. Choice B is incorrect since the 20 to 64 percentage also changed during this period.
C. Choice C is correct; that is just how we described the graph above.
D. Choice D is incorrect; the graph gives percentages for people under 20, and for people from 20 to 64. Subtracting those percentages from 100% gives the percentage of people 65 and over in the French population during the years covered by the graph.

36. **(D)** 1851
The "percentage under 20" line begins high, drops lower, and then rises again. To decide where it is highest, compare the 1851 value with the 1966 value by laying a pencil or a piece of paper on the graph, level with the bottom axis. Since the percentage drops after 1851, the only possibility for a higher percentage is at the 1966 end, after the percentage has had some time to rise again. But you will see that the 1851 value is still higher (about 38% or 39%) than the 1966 value (about 35%).

37. **(C)** 55%
The line labeled "percentage age 20 to 64" starts out (in 1851) at the level of the 55% tick mark on the *y*-axis of the graph. Therefore, about 55% of the French population in 1851 was between the ages of 20 and 64.

38. **(A)** 7%
There is no line on the graph for people age 65 and over, but you can figure out the percentage in this group since the whole population (100%) must be made up of the people under 20, the people between 20 and 64, and the people 65 and over. The percentage between 20 and 64 was 55% in 1851 (see the previous question). Likewise, the percentage under 20 was about 38%. (You don't have to be exact about these numbers, as long as you are fairly close; the choices are far enough apart that being off by one or two percentage points in estimating the values shouldn't matter.) After adding 55% and 38%, you get 93% for the combined percentage of the population that is 64 or under; therefore, the population 65 and over is 100% − 93% = 7%.

39. **(C)** The percentage of the French population aged 65 and over increased steadily from about 7% to about 12% of the total population
To answer this question, with statements about the history of the French population age 65 or over, you may need to repeat for other dates the kind of reasoning used for the last question. The choices are for a decreasing (Choice A), unchanging (Choice B), or increasing percentage of the 65 and over segment of the population. Choice D (that we can't determine this from the graph) is wrong from the start, since Question 74 shows how we can go about finding out what happened to this age group during the period covered by the graph. The first thing to do is to compare the end of the graph to its start; if that doesn't give us enough information, we can look at points in the middle as well.

In 1966, about 54% of the population is in the 20–64 age group, and about 34% in the under-20 age group. Together, these are 54 + 34 = 88%, leaving 12% for the part of the French population aged 65 and over. This is distinctly larger than the 7% in 1851, so it is clear that Choices A (that the over-64 population decreased) and B (that it remained the same) are wrong, and Choice C (increase from 7% to 12%) is likely correct. (To be absolutely certain, you could check intermediate dates to see that they have percentages between 7% and 12%; this is unnecessary here, since you have already eliminated the other choices.)

40. **(B)** In the year 1931, the percentage of the French population under 20 was lower than it was in 1946.

Look at each of the answers, and mark any that could be false. It is likely (with a question phrased this way) that there will be only one obviously false statement.

A. In 1851, the percentage under 20 was about 38%; this is clearly TRUE from the graph.

B. In 1931, the percentage under 20 was lower than it was in 1946. TRUE. The values are not too far apart, but the graph goes down from 1931 to 1946, so the percentage under 20 in 1931 must have been higher.

C. In 1931, the percentage under 20 was higher than in 1966. FALSE. This is just the reverse of B.

D. After 1946, the portion under 20 grew as a result of the post-World War II baby boom. You can't tell from the graph whether the reason given (the baby boom) is correct, but it is TRUE that the under-20 fraction grew after 1946; the low point of the under-20 line is 1946 at about 30%, and in 1956 and 1966, the values on this line are greater.

41. **(C)** $7.82

The total bill is $20.40 and they leave a 15% tip:

$$\begin{array}{r} \$20.40 \\ \times \;\;.15 \\ \hline 102\;00 \\ 204\;0 \\ \hline \$3.06 \end{array}$$

Each woman's share is $\frac{1}{3}$ of $20.40 (= $6.90) plus her $\frac{1}{3}$ share of the tip ($\frac{1}{3}$ of 3.06 = 1.02); $6.80 + $1.02 = $7.82, Choice C.

42. **(B)** 91

A yard is 36 inches (a bit less than a meter, which is 39.36 inches). 100 yards is therefore 3,600 inches, and it must be less than 100 meters. This rules out Choices C and D. Choice A is also impossible, since 100 yards would equal 50 meters only if a meter were equal to 2 yards. In fact, the conversion given (1 meter = 39.36 inches) means that 1 meter is a bit less than 1.1 yards (a meter would be exactly 1.1 yards if it were 36 + 3.6 = 39.6 inches). 100 meters is about 110 yards; 100 yards has to be *less* than 100 meters.

43. **(B)** 9

In the four earlier stages, the number of coins added each time was 1, 3, 5 and 7; the number increased by two each time. Therefore, nine coins are needed at the fifth stage. You can also see this by looking at the overall pattern of the figure, which is a square of coins at each stage, with N by N coins at the Nth stage, so the fifth repetition will have a total of 25 coins, 9 more than the 16 coins shown in the diagram.

44. **(B)** 3/4

Slope is "rise over run"—vertical change divided by horizontal change. In this case, the line goes through the points (1,0) on the *x*-axis and (5,3) at the highest point shown on the graph. So it changes 3 units in the vertical direction (from 0 to 3), while changing 4 units horizontally (from 1 to 5). The slope is therefore 3 divided by 4, Choice B.

45. **(B)** $56.48
Only $8 out of the total purchases of $56 is taxable; the tax on this $8 is $8 \times .06 =$ $0.48. Add this to the purchase amount to get his total bill, $56 + $0.48 = $56.48.

46. **(D)** Europe
The bars on the graph go from 0 on the left to 3.0% on the right. As you scan down the regions on the graph, you should notice that the bars for Europe are shorter (always less than 1.0%) than any others. With the exception of the 0.5% growth rate for North America in 1990–2000, all the bars for Europe are smaller than all others on the graph.

47. **(A)** Africa
The growth rates for 1970–1980 are given by the second bar for each region. Consider each of the choices in turn:
A. Africa 1970–1980 growth rate is about $2\frac{3}{4}$%.
B. Asia 1970–1980 growth rate is a bit more than 2%.
C. Latin America 1970–1980 growth rate is about $2\frac{1}{3}$%.
D. Oceania 1970–1980 growth rate is about $1\frac{1}{2}$%.
The largest growth rate among these was Africa's $2\frac{3}{4}$%.

48. **(A)** Africa
For all regions other than Africa, the pattern in the graph is a steady decline in the annual growth rate, with the black bar for the sixties longer than the next lower one (for the seventies), and that one longer than the next, and so on. In Africa, the trend is for an increasing growth rate from the sixties through the eighties, and then a reversal in the nineties, with the growth rate declining for the first time in the period shown.

49. **(B)** Population is increasing in all major regions of the world

There are two problems with Choice B. First, the growth rate in Europe in the nineties is near zero (there is no visible "white bar" for Europe), and the rate at the end of the nineties suggests that Europe is *not* growing now. The other problem is that you have to guess what is happening now, past the end of the graph. It is probably a reasonable guess that the regions with more than 1% growth rate in 1990–2000 are likely to be growing still, even if at a smaller rate—but that requires conclusions beyond the actual data on the graph. To confirm that Choice B is correct, you should at least briefly consider the other choices:
A. Growth rates have decreased on all continents since the sixties. True; even Africa, which was increasing that rate in the seventies and eighties, fell below the growth rate of the sixties in 1990–2000.
C. No region's population is growing more than 3% a year. Fairly clear from the graph—all growth rates in the nineties are below 2.5% and would need to increase very dramatically to pass 3% now.
D. Europe's growth rate has been less than half that of most other regions in the world throughout the time period shown. Compare Europe to the next smaller growth rate area, North America. Even there the statement is true except for the 1960–1970 period (with Europe at about 0.75% and North America at about 1.3%), and all the other regions are much larger than North America in all comparable periods.

50. **(D)** 5
During the seventies, the growth rate in Africa was more than $2\frac{1}{2}$% (maybe as much as 2.7%), and the growth rate of Europe was about $\frac{1}{2}$%. Since $\frac{2.5}{0.5} = \frac{25}{5} = 5$, the best choice is Choice D.

Answer Sheet
MODEL TEST B

ENGLISH LANGUAGE ARTS SECTION

Language Subtest

1 Ⓐ Ⓑ Ⓒ Ⓓ	13 Ⓐ Ⓑ Ⓒ Ⓓ	25 Ⓐ Ⓑ Ⓒ Ⓓ	37 Ⓐ Ⓑ Ⓒ Ⓓ
2 Ⓐ Ⓑ Ⓒ Ⓓ	14 Ⓐ Ⓑ Ⓒ Ⓓ	26 Ⓐ Ⓑ Ⓒ Ⓓ	38 Ⓐ Ⓑ Ⓒ Ⓓ
3 Ⓐ Ⓑ Ⓒ Ⓓ	15 Ⓐ Ⓑ Ⓒ Ⓓ	27 Ⓐ Ⓑ Ⓒ Ⓓ	39 Ⓐ Ⓑ Ⓒ Ⓓ
4 Ⓐ Ⓑ Ⓒ Ⓓ	16 Ⓐ Ⓑ Ⓒ Ⓓ	28 Ⓐ Ⓑ Ⓒ Ⓓ	40 Ⓐ Ⓑ Ⓒ Ⓓ
5 Ⓐ Ⓑ Ⓒ Ⓓ	17 Ⓐ Ⓑ Ⓒ Ⓓ	29 Ⓐ Ⓑ Ⓒ Ⓓ	41 Ⓐ Ⓑ Ⓒ Ⓓ
6 Ⓐ Ⓑ Ⓒ Ⓓ	18 Ⓐ Ⓑ Ⓒ Ⓓ	30 Ⓐ Ⓑ Ⓒ Ⓓ	42 Ⓐ Ⓑ Ⓒ Ⓓ
7 Ⓐ Ⓑ Ⓒ Ⓓ	19 Ⓐ Ⓑ Ⓒ Ⓓ	31 Ⓐ Ⓑ Ⓒ Ⓓ	43 Ⓐ Ⓑ Ⓒ Ⓓ
8 Ⓐ Ⓑ Ⓒ Ⓓ	20 Ⓐ Ⓑ Ⓒ Ⓓ	32 Ⓐ Ⓑ Ⓒ Ⓓ	44 Ⓐ Ⓑ Ⓒ Ⓓ
9 Ⓐ Ⓑ Ⓒ Ⓓ	21 Ⓐ Ⓑ Ⓒ Ⓓ	33 Ⓐ Ⓑ Ⓒ Ⓓ	45 Ⓐ Ⓑ Ⓒ Ⓓ
10 Ⓐ Ⓑ Ⓒ Ⓓ	22 Ⓐ Ⓑ Ⓒ Ⓓ	34 Ⓐ Ⓑ Ⓒ Ⓓ	46 Ⓐ Ⓑ Ⓒ Ⓓ
11 Ⓐ Ⓑ Ⓒ Ⓓ	23 Ⓐ Ⓑ Ⓒ Ⓓ	35 Ⓐ Ⓑ Ⓒ Ⓓ	47 Ⓐ Ⓑ Ⓒ Ⓓ
12 Ⓐ Ⓑ Ⓒ Ⓓ	24 Ⓐ Ⓑ Ⓒ Ⓓ	36 Ⓐ Ⓑ Ⓒ Ⓓ	48 Ⓐ Ⓑ Ⓒ Ⓓ

Reading Subtest

1 Ⓐ Ⓑ Ⓒ Ⓓ	22 Ⓐ Ⓑ Ⓒ Ⓓ	43 Ⓐ Ⓑ Ⓒ Ⓓ	64 Ⓐ Ⓑ Ⓒ Ⓓ
2 Ⓐ Ⓑ Ⓒ Ⓓ	23 Ⓐ Ⓑ Ⓒ Ⓓ	44 Ⓐ Ⓑ Ⓒ Ⓓ	65 Ⓐ Ⓑ Ⓒ Ⓓ
3 Ⓐ Ⓑ Ⓒ Ⓓ	24 Ⓐ Ⓑ Ⓒ Ⓓ	45 Ⓐ Ⓑ Ⓒ Ⓓ	66 Ⓐ Ⓑ Ⓒ Ⓓ
4 Ⓐ Ⓑ Ⓒ Ⓓ	25 Ⓐ Ⓑ Ⓒ Ⓓ	46 Ⓐ Ⓑ Ⓒ Ⓓ	67 Ⓐ Ⓑ Ⓒ Ⓓ
5 Ⓐ Ⓑ Ⓒ Ⓓ	26 Ⓐ Ⓑ Ⓒ Ⓓ	47 Ⓐ Ⓑ Ⓒ Ⓓ	68 Ⓐ Ⓑ Ⓒ Ⓓ
6 Ⓐ Ⓑ Ⓒ Ⓓ	27 Ⓐ Ⓑ Ⓒ Ⓓ	48 Ⓐ Ⓑ Ⓒ Ⓓ	69 Ⓐ Ⓑ Ⓒ Ⓓ
7 Ⓐ Ⓑ Ⓒ Ⓓ	28 Ⓐ Ⓑ Ⓒ Ⓓ	49 Ⓐ Ⓑ Ⓒ Ⓓ	70 Ⓐ Ⓑ Ⓒ Ⓓ
8 Ⓐ Ⓑ Ⓒ Ⓓ	29 Ⓐ Ⓑ Ⓒ Ⓓ	50 Ⓐ Ⓑ Ⓒ Ⓓ	71 Ⓐ Ⓑ Ⓒ Ⓓ
9 Ⓐ Ⓑ Ⓒ Ⓓ	30 Ⓐ Ⓑ Ⓒ Ⓓ	51 Ⓐ Ⓑ Ⓒ Ⓓ	72 Ⓐ Ⓑ Ⓒ Ⓓ
10 Ⓐ Ⓑ Ⓒ Ⓓ	31 Ⓐ Ⓑ Ⓒ Ⓓ	52 Ⓐ Ⓑ Ⓒ Ⓓ	73 Ⓐ Ⓑ Ⓒ Ⓓ
11 Ⓐ Ⓑ Ⓒ Ⓓ	32 Ⓐ Ⓑ Ⓒ Ⓓ	53 Ⓐ Ⓑ Ⓒ Ⓓ	74 Ⓐ Ⓑ Ⓒ Ⓓ
12 Ⓐ Ⓑ Ⓒ Ⓓ	33 Ⓐ Ⓑ Ⓒ Ⓓ	54 Ⓐ Ⓑ Ⓒ Ⓓ	75 Ⓐ Ⓑ Ⓒ Ⓓ
13 Ⓐ Ⓑ Ⓒ Ⓓ	34 Ⓐ Ⓑ Ⓒ Ⓓ	55 Ⓐ Ⓑ Ⓒ Ⓓ	76 Ⓐ Ⓑ Ⓒ Ⓓ
14 Ⓐ Ⓑ Ⓒ Ⓓ	35 Ⓐ Ⓑ Ⓒ Ⓓ	56 Ⓐ Ⓑ Ⓒ Ⓓ	77 Ⓐ Ⓑ Ⓒ Ⓓ
15 Ⓐ Ⓑ Ⓒ Ⓓ	36 Ⓐ Ⓑ Ⓒ Ⓓ	57 Ⓐ Ⓑ Ⓒ Ⓓ	78 Ⓐ Ⓑ Ⓒ Ⓓ
16 Ⓐ Ⓑ Ⓒ Ⓓ	37 Ⓐ Ⓑ Ⓒ Ⓓ	58 Ⓐ Ⓑ Ⓒ Ⓓ	79 Ⓐ Ⓑ Ⓒ Ⓓ
17 Ⓐ Ⓑ Ⓒ Ⓓ	38 Ⓐ Ⓑ Ⓒ Ⓓ	59 Ⓐ Ⓑ Ⓒ Ⓓ	80 Ⓐ Ⓑ Ⓒ Ⓓ
18 Ⓐ Ⓑ Ⓒ Ⓓ	39 Ⓐ Ⓑ Ⓒ Ⓓ	60 Ⓐ Ⓑ Ⓒ Ⓓ	81 Ⓐ Ⓑ Ⓒ Ⓓ
19 Ⓐ Ⓑ Ⓒ Ⓓ	40 Ⓐ Ⓑ Ⓒ Ⓓ	61 Ⓐ Ⓑ Ⓒ Ⓓ	82 Ⓐ Ⓑ Ⓒ Ⓓ
20 Ⓐ Ⓑ Ⓒ Ⓓ	41 Ⓐ Ⓑ Ⓒ Ⓓ	62 Ⓐ Ⓑ Ⓒ Ⓓ	83 Ⓐ Ⓑ Ⓒ Ⓓ
21 Ⓐ Ⓑ Ⓒ Ⓓ	42 Ⓐ Ⓑ Ⓒ Ⓓ	63 Ⓐ Ⓑ Ⓒ Ⓓ	84 Ⓐ Ⓑ Ⓒ Ⓓ

Answer Sheet

MODEL TEST B

MATHEMATICS SECTION

1 Ⓐ Ⓑ Ⓒ Ⓓ   14 Ⓐ Ⓑ Ⓒ Ⓓ   27 Ⓐ Ⓑ Ⓒ Ⓓ   40 Ⓐ Ⓑ Ⓒ Ⓓ
2 Ⓐ Ⓑ Ⓒ Ⓓ   15 Ⓐ Ⓑ Ⓒ Ⓓ   28 Ⓐ Ⓑ Ⓒ Ⓓ   41 Ⓐ Ⓑ Ⓒ Ⓓ
3 Ⓐ Ⓑ Ⓒ Ⓓ   16 Ⓐ Ⓑ Ⓒ Ⓓ   29 Ⓐ Ⓑ Ⓒ Ⓓ   42 Ⓐ Ⓑ Ⓒ Ⓓ
4 Ⓐ Ⓑ Ⓒ Ⓓ   17 Ⓐ Ⓑ Ⓒ Ⓓ   30 Ⓐ Ⓑ Ⓒ Ⓓ   43 Ⓐ Ⓑ Ⓒ Ⓓ
5 Ⓐ Ⓑ Ⓒ Ⓓ   18 Ⓐ Ⓑ Ⓒ Ⓓ   31 Ⓐ Ⓑ Ⓒ Ⓓ   44 Ⓐ Ⓑ Ⓒ Ⓓ
6 Ⓐ Ⓑ Ⓒ Ⓓ   19 Ⓐ Ⓑ Ⓒ Ⓓ   32 Ⓐ Ⓑ Ⓒ Ⓓ   45 Ⓐ Ⓑ Ⓒ Ⓓ
7 Ⓐ Ⓑ Ⓒ Ⓓ   20 Ⓐ Ⓑ Ⓒ Ⓓ   33 Ⓐ Ⓑ Ⓒ Ⓓ   46 Ⓐ Ⓑ Ⓒ Ⓓ
8 Ⓐ Ⓑ Ⓒ Ⓓ   21 Ⓐ Ⓑ Ⓒ Ⓓ   34 Ⓐ Ⓑ Ⓒ Ⓓ   47 Ⓐ Ⓑ Ⓒ Ⓓ
9 Ⓐ Ⓑ Ⓒ Ⓓ   22 Ⓐ Ⓑ Ⓒ Ⓓ   35 Ⓐ Ⓑ Ⓒ Ⓓ   48 Ⓐ Ⓑ Ⓒ Ⓓ
10 Ⓐ Ⓑ Ⓒ Ⓓ   23 Ⓐ Ⓑ Ⓒ Ⓓ   36 Ⓐ Ⓑ Ⓒ Ⓓ   49 Ⓐ Ⓑ Ⓒ Ⓓ
11 Ⓐ Ⓑ Ⓒ Ⓓ   24 Ⓐ Ⓑ Ⓒ Ⓓ   37 Ⓐ Ⓑ Ⓒ Ⓓ   50 Ⓐ Ⓑ Ⓒ Ⓓ
12 Ⓐ Ⓑ Ⓒ Ⓓ   25 Ⓐ Ⓑ Ⓒ Ⓓ   38 Ⓐ Ⓑ Ⓒ Ⓓ
13 Ⓐ Ⓑ Ⓒ Ⓓ   26 Ⓐ Ⓑ Ⓒ Ⓓ   39 Ⓐ Ⓑ Ⓒ Ⓓ

Model Test B

English Language Arts Section

WRITING TASK

Some people who believe that competition is a destructive force in society are in favor of eliminating grades as a method of measuring students' performance. Do you agree or disagree? Write a letter to your local board of education to convince the members of the board to agree with your position on this issue. Be specific about your reasons for taking your position.

_____

_____

_____

_____

_____

_____

_____

_____

_____

LANGUAGE SUBTEST

Directions: Look at the underlined words in each sentence. You may see a mistake in punctuation, capitalization, or word usage. If you spot a mistake in the underlined section of a sentence, select the answer choice that corrects the mistake. If you find no mistake, choose Choice D, *Correct as is*.

1. I think that <u>their</u> going to Reno.

   (A) they
   (B) they're
   (C) there
   (D) *Correct as is*

2. Four cars <u>don't</u> fit in a three-car garage.

   (A) dont
   (B) do'nt
   (C) doesn't
   (D) *Correct as is*

3. Everybody loves Raymond except his brother <u>and I</u>.

   (A) and me
   (B) and myself
   (C) or I
   (D) *Correct as is*

4. In the circus parade, the clowns <u>precede</u> the elephant.

   (A) proceed
   (B) proceeds
   (C) precedes
   (D) *Correct as is*

5. The twins are polite and friendly to <u>strangers however, they</u> are nasty and rude to their big sister.

   (A) strangers, however, they
   (B) strangers: however they
   (C) strangers; however, they
   (D) *Correct as is*

6. Tell me when <u>its</u> time to go.

   (A) it
   (B) it's
   (C) its'
   (D) *Correct as is*

7. Who says that <u>me and Monica</u> can't win the race?

   (A) Monica and me
   (B) Monica and I
   (C) myself and Monica
   (D) *Correct as is*

8. If Cinderella <u>accepts</u> the prince's proposal, they will have a big wedding.

   (A) excepts
   (B) accepted
   (C) excepted
   (D) *Correct as is*

9. At King Henry's death, his kingdom <u>was divided between</u> his three nephews.

   (A) was dividing among
   (B) were divided between
   (C) was divided among
   (D) *Correct as is*

10. The school had a bad reputation <u>for their large numbers</u> of students involved with gangs.

    (A) for there large numbers
    (B) for its large number
    (C) for it's large number
    (D) *Correct as is*

11. Have you heard about <u>Harvard colleges</u> new admissions policy?

    (A) Harvard colleges'
    (B) Harvard College's
    (C) Harvard college's
    (D) *Correct as is*

12. Morgan wants the following toys for his <u>birthday racing cars,</u> stuffed animals, and a football.

   (A) birthday: racing cars,
   (B) birthday, racing cars,
   (C) birthday; racing cars,
   (D) *Correct as is*

13. I <u>can't hardly wait</u> to complete this assignment.

   (A) cant hardly wait
   (B) can hardly wait
   (C) cannot hardly wait
   (D) *Correct as is*

14. <u>The Getty Museums new exhibit</u> has received a great deal of attention.

   (A) The Getty museums new exhibit
   (B) The Getty Museum's new exhibit
   (C) The Getty museum's new Exhibit
   (D) *Correct as is*

15. "When do you think the mail <u>will arrive," she asked?</u>

   (A) will have arrived," she asked?
   (B) will arrive"? she asked.
   (C) will arrive?" she asked.
   (D) *Correct as is*

16. <u>You were supposed to</u> do the dishes.

   (A) You was supposed to
   (B) You were suppose to
   (C) You was suppose to
   (D) *Correct as is*

17. Do the police know <u>who done it?</u>

   (A) who did it?
   (B) who done did it?
   (C) who done it.
   (D) *Correct as is*

18. <u>You're guess is</u> as good as mine.

   (A) Youre guess is
   (B) Your guess is
   (C) Your' guess is
   (D) *Correct as is*

Directions: Look at each sentence. You may see a mistake in sentence structure. If you spot a mistake in the sentence's structure, select the answer choice that rewrites the sentence so that it is clear, concise, and correct. If you find no mistake, choose Choice D, *Correct as is.*

19. After managing the team for several years, its operation was understood by him.

   (A) After he has managed the team for several years, he understood how it should be operated.
   (B) After managing the team, for several years, he understood how they were operated.
   (C) After managing the team for several years, he understood its operation.
   (D) *Correct as is*

20. The reason why I arrived late was due to the fact that the bus was delayed by heavy traffic.

   (A) The reason that I arrived late was because the bus was delayed by heavy traffic.
   (B) The reason that I arrived late was due to the fact that heavy traffic delayed the bus.
   (C) The reason why I arrived late was that the bus was delayed by heavy traffic.
   (D) *Correct as is*

Model Test B

21. While walking along the road, a car traveling at well over the speed limit nearly hit me.

    (A) I was nearly hit while I was walking along the road by a car that was traveling at well over the speed limit.
    (B) While I was walking along the road, a car traveling at well over the speed limit nearly hit me.
    (C) A car was traveling at well over the speed limit, and it nearly hit me while I was walking along the road.
    (D) *Correct as is*

22. When I called him, he doesn't answer the phone.

    (A) When I call him, he didn't answer the phone.
    (B) When I am calling him, he didn't answer the phone.
    (C) When I call him, he doesn't answer the phone.
    (D) *Correct as is*

23. Sherry opened the box of candy, peeked inside, and, with great delight, pulled out a chocolate truffle.

    (A) Opening the box of candy, peeking inside, Sherry pulling out a chocolate truffle with great delight.
    (B) Sherry opened the box of candy peeked inside and pulled out a chocolate truffle with great delight.
    (C) Sherry opened the box of candy and she peeked inside and pulled out a chocolate truffle with great delight.
    (D) *Correct as is*

24. Since Susie was feeling ill, she did extremely well on the big test.

    (A) Provided Susie was feeling ill, she does extremely well on the big test.
    (B) Even though Susie was feeling ill, she did extremely well on the big test.
    (C) Because Susie was feeling ill, she did extremely well on the big test.
    (D) *Correct as is*

25. A braggart is a person who is conceited, self-centered, and likes to boast.

    (A) A braggart is a person who is conceited, self-centered, and boasted.
    (B) A braggart is a person who is conceited, likes to be self-centered, and to boast.
    (C) A braggart is a person who is conceited, self-centered, and boastful.
    (D) *Correct as is*

26. Cook the omelet in a Teflon pan. The pan should be copper-bottomed.
    (A) Cook the omelet in a Teflon pan and copper-bottomed.
    (B) Cook the omelet in a copper-bottomed Teflon pan.
    (C) Cook the omelet in a pan that is Teflon and it is copper-bottomed.
    (D) *Correct as is*

27. If the Confederate Army will have won the day at Gettysburg, the history of America would have been profoundly altered.

   (A) If the Confederate Army will win the day at Gettysburg, the history of America would have been profoundly altered.

   (B) The Confederate Army having won the day at Gettysburg, the history of America will be profoundly altered.

   (C) Had the Confederate Army won the day at Gettysburg, the history of America would have been profoundly altered.

   (D) *Correct as is*

28. Before starting an exercise program, a consultation with your physician is advisable.

   (A) Before starting an exercise program, it is advisable to have a consultation with your physician.

   (B) Before starting an exercise program, a physician's consultation is advisable.

   (C) Before starting an exercise program, you should consult your physician.

   (D) *Correct as is*

29. The doctor is accused of issuing unnecessary prescriptions, abusing drugs, and he overcharges.

   (A) The doctor is accused of issuing unnecessary prescriptions, drug abuse, and he also overcharges.

   (B) The doctor is accused of issuing unnecessary prescriptions, abusing drugs, and overcharging.

   (C) The doctor is accused of issuing prescriptions unnecessarily, abusing drugs, and he overcharges.

   (D) *Correct as is*

30. Reaching for the book, the ladder on which he stood slipped out from under him.

   (A) Reaching for the book, he stood on the ladder and so it slipped out from under him.

   (B) When he reached for the book, the ladder on which he stood slipped out from under him.

   (C) He reached for the book, the ladder on which he stood slipped out from under him.

   (D) *Correct as is*

31. The water vole can be distinguished from the common rat by the smallness of its ears and looking at the bluntness of its face.

   (A) The water vole may be distinguished from the common rat by the smallness of its ears and looking at the bluntness of its face.

   (B) The water vole can be distinguished from the common rat by the smallness of its ears and the bluntness of its face.

   (C) One can distinguish the water vole from the common rat by the smallness of its ears and looking at how blunt its face is.

   (D) *Correct as is*

32. Shakespeare wrote many plays, they are now being presented on public television.

   (A) Shakespeare wrote many plays, and so they have now been presented on public television.

   (B) Now being presented on public television, Shakespeare wrote many plays.

   (C) Shakespeare wrote many plays that are now being presented on public television.

   (D) *Correct as is*

33. Although most Californians believe that they are due to have a serious earthquake in the near future, they are not frightened by that possibility.

    (A) Because most Californians believe that they are due to have a serious earthquake in the near future, they are not frightened by that possibility.
    (B) Although most Californians believe a serious earthquake is due to be had by them in the near future, that possibility does not frighten them.
    (C) Since in the near future most Californians believe that they are due to have a serious earthquake, they are not frightened by that possibility.
    (D) *Correct as is*

34. Thinking that I had done poorly on the examination, all hopes of winning the scholarship were abandoned.

    (A) Although I thought I had done poorly on the examination, all hopes of winning the scholarship were abandoned.
    (B) Thinking that I had done poorly on the examination, I abandoned all hopes of winning the scholarship.
    (C) Thinking in my mind that I have done poorly on the examination, all hopes of winning the scholarship were abandoned by me.
    (D) *Correct as is*

35. At his advanced age, he found driving to the supermarket less strenuous than to walk.

    (A) At his advanced age, he found driving to the supermarket less strenuous than walking.
    (B) At his advanced age, he finds driving to the supermarket less strenuous than to walk.
    (C) He found that driving to the supermarket was less strenuous than it was to walk at his advanced age.
    (D) *Correct as is*

36. As the setting sun slowly sank behind the snow-covered peaks of the towering mountains.

    (A) The setting sun slowly sank behind the snow-covered peaks of the towering mountains.
    (B) As the setting sun sunk slowly behind the snow-covered peaks of the towering mountains.
    (C) Behind the snow-covered peaks of the towering mountains as the setting sun slowly sank.
    (D) *Correct as is*

Directions: Read the passage in the box. Then read the questions that come after the passage. Choose the correct answer based on what you know about writing good essays.

Contra Dancing

Contra dancing is a sociable and exhilarating form of dance. It gives a sense of community to dancers that is really unique. In contra dancing, dancers interact with each other socially as they dance. A couple will dance one round of the dance with another couple and then move on to dance with the next couple in the line. Sometimes partners turn holding on to each other in a swing; sometimes they turn away from each other to swing with somebody new. Whether or not the dancers are actually holding each other, they are connected with one another. They are always looking at each other. They look out for each other, too, because it is important for the experienced dancers to help new dancers so the new dancers don't get lost during the dance. That is how the new dancers learn that they are part of a community, when experienced dancers guide them through a dance.

Contra dancing is especially exhilarating because there is live music. A lot of people enjoy dancing to recorded music, especially if there is a deejay. For contra dancing, live music is best. Instead of playing the same tune over and over, contra musicians play medleys of tunes. They switch from one tune to another to crank up the energy, or they improvise. When the tune changes or the musicians go off on an improvisation, the dancers can improvise, too. They get so involved with the music that they do all sorts of extra stuff. They have to respond to the musicians' energy. On the contrary, the musicians respond to the dancers' increased energy, becoming even more inventive as they improvise.

37. What would be the BEST title for this essay?

    (A) Contra Dancing in America Today
    (B) How I Learned to Contra Dance
    (C) Making Friends by Contra Dancing
    (D) Contra, an Exciting, Communal Dance Form

Contra dancing is a sociable and exhilarating form of dance. It gives a sense of community to dancers that is really unique.

38. Which of the following is the BEST way to combine the sentences above?

    (A) Contra dancing is a sociable and exhilarating form of dance that gives a sense of community to dancers that is really unique.
    (B) Being that it is a sociable and exhilarating form of dance, contra dancing gives a really unique sense of community to dancers.
    (C) Contra dancing, a sociable and exhilarating form of dance, gives dancers a unique sense of community.
    (D) A sociable and exhilarating form of dance that gives dancers a really unique sense of community, that is what contra dancing is.

For contra dancing, live music is best.

39. In context, what is the BEST way to revise the sentence above?

    (A) Change "For" to "Regarding."
    (B) Insert "Clearly" at the beginning of the sentence.
    (C) Insert "however" after "dancing."
    (D) Insert "the" after "is."

They get so involved with the music that they do all sorts of extra stuff.

40. Consider the underlined words in the sentence above. Good writing uses concrete examples. Choose the answer that replaces the underlined words with a concrete example.

    (A) do way more than what they normally do
    (B) have to express how involved they get
    (C) try a lot of different extra movements
    (D) throw in twirls or swing with extra energy

On the contrary, the musicians respond to the dancers' increased energy, becoming even more inventive as they improvise.

41. Which word or phrase would BEST replace the underlined phrase in the sentence above?

    (A) For instance,
    (B) In turn,
    (C) Otherwise,
    (D) In brief,

Model Test B

42. Which of the following sentences would NOT belong in the second paragraph?

    (A) You do not need to have a partner to attend a contra dance.
    (B) All the tunes are lively jigs and reels.
    (C) The spontaneity and energy of the musicians and dancers are amazing.
    (D) The musicians play on all sorts of instruments: fiddles, guitars, pianos, accordions, even saxophones.

Shopaholics

The word "addict" conjures up images of desperate individuals committing crimes in order to afford their next fix and of down and out alcoholics on Skid Row. The prob-
(5) *lem of addiction is not, consequently, limited to drugs and alcohol. Many of us jokingly describe ourselves as "shopaholics," but for the true shopping addict, this is no laughing matter. Studies demon-*
(10) *strate that over five percent of Americans are compulsive shoppers, and the impact of shopping addiction can be quite serious. New York psychologist April Benson has seen patients lose their jobs for spending*
(15) *too much time on eBay. Many compulsive shoppers build up substantial credit card debt that they cannot support, and so they wind up having to file for bankruptcy. It is also common for compulsive shopping to*
(20) *wreck marriages.*
Beating a shopping addiction is difficult, at least in part because one cannot simply stop shopping. There are factors that mean that the recovering shopping addict will face
(25) *temptation regularly and unavoidably. Adding to this challenge is the lack of support and treatment options available to shopping addicts because hardly anyone takes their affliction seriously.*

The problem of addiction is not, <u>consequently</u>, limited to drugs and alcohol.

43. Which word or phrase would BEST replace the underlined word in the sentence above?

    (A) however
    (B) furthermore
    (C) similarly
    (D) *Leave as is*

44. Which of these statements would BEST summarize the main point of this passage?

    (A) Addiction is harmful.
    (B) Shopping is a relatively harmless addiction.
    (C) No one really notices shopping addicts.
    (D) Shopping addiction is a serious problem.

45. Which sentence would NOT belong in this passage?

    (A) Consumer spending promotes the economic health of the nation.
    (B) Shopping addiction is not as different from drug or alcohol addiction as we assume.
    (C) Mental health professionals should treat compulsive shopping as a serious problem.
    (D) Shopping addicts may appear well put together, but their lives are out of control.

46. In line 21, the word "Beating" most nearly means

    (A) punishing
    (B) overcoming
    (C) stirring
    (D) striking

There are factors that mean that the recovering shopping addict will face temptation regularly and unavoidably.

47. Good writers use specific terms rather than generalities. How can the underlined words be rewritten to make them more specific and less vague?

    (A) Something about American culture seems to determine that
    (B) Things invariably turn out so that
    (C) The need to put food on the table and clothes on one's back means that
    (D) Shopping is an everyday occurrence, and so

48. Which of the following ideas is supported by details or evidence in this essay?

    (A) New support groups for shopaholics are springing up every day.
    (B) Shopaholics risk financial ruin as a result of their addiction.
    (C) Compulsive shopping is an even riskier addiction than drug or alcohol addiction.
    (D) April Benson lost her job because she spent too much time shopping on eBay.

READING SUBTEST

> **Directions:** Read the passage. Then read each question about the passage. Make up your mind which is the best answer to the question. Then mark the answer you have chosen on your answer sheet.

THE LION'S SHARE
A Fable from Greece

A long time ago, the Lion, the Fox, the Jackal, and the Wolf agreed to go hunting together, sharing with each other whatever they found.

One day the Wolf ran down a stag. He immediately called his comrades to divide the spoil.

Without being asked, the Lion placed himself at the head of the feast to do the carving, and, with a great show of fairness, began to count the guests.

"One," he said, counting on his claws, "that is myself, the Lion. Two, that's the Wolf, three, is the Jackal, and the Fox makes four."

He then very carefully divided the stag into four equal parts.

"I am King Lion," he said, when he had finished, "so of course I get the first part. This next part falls to me because I am the strongest; and this is mine because I am the bravest."

He now began to glare at the others very savagely. "If any of you have any claim to the part that is left," he growled, stretching his claws meaningfully, "now is the time to speak up."

1. What did the Lion, the Wolf, the Fox, and the Jackal agree to do?

   (A) They agreed to hunt one another.
   (B) They agreed to obey one another.
   (C) They agreed to show one another whatever they found.
   (D) They agreed to divide what they caught with each other.

2. The Wolf called the Lion, the Fox, and the Jackal because

   (A) he wanted to go hunting with them
   (B) he respected their agreement
   (C) the dead stag had begun to spoil
   (D) he needed their help to catch the stag

3. A clue to predicting the outcome of this story occurs when

   (A) the Wolf calls the Lion, the Fox, and the Jackal
   (B) the Lion starts carving without being asked
   (C) the Wolf runs down a stag
   (D) the Lion divides the stag into four parts

4. Someone like the Lion in this story can be described as

   (A) brave
   (B) fair
   (C) selfish
   (D) careful

5. When he told his three comrades that now was the time to speak up, the Lion was

   (A) encouraging them
   (B) threatening them
   (C) fooling himself
   (D) obliging them

6. The story tells the reader

   (A) why the Wolf, the Fox, and the Jackal had trusted the Lion
   (B) which beast was the best hunter
   (C) how the beasts agreed to make the Lion their king
   (D) what the Lion took as his share

7. The best moral for this story is

   (A) "He who hesitates is lost."
   (B) "Waste not, want not."
   (C) "If you try to please all, you please none."
   (D) "Might makes right."

Model Test B

GRAY WATER: USE EVERY DROP

"Gray water" is slightly used water—the water you have collected at the bottom of the tub after you have showered or the rinse water from the washing machine. It is still useful, and we cannot afford to let it go down the drain.

The best use for soapy water is in stretching your irrigation water allotment. The University of California Agricultural Cooperative Extension advises that gray water, regardless of whether it has detergent or soap in it, can be used on your plants without too much worry. There are some things to remember, however.

1. *Don't put the soapy rinse water directly on the plant. Pour it on the earth at the base of the plant, but not on the leaves. You should not pour it on the lawn or on leafy ground covers.*
2. *If the rinse water contains borax soap, do not use it for irrigation.*
3. *If chlorine bleach is in the rinse water, you can use it for irrigation, but you should be sure to pour it on different spots each day. Too much chlorine is not good; letting the rinse water stand for a day will help.*

Plumbing and health codes also have a few requirements:

1. *Don't rearrange your plumbing to lead the gray water outside. Use buckets or trash pails to carry it outdoors. A garden hose siphon will work handily to get the used water outside where you need it.*
2. *There must not be any way for gray water to contaminate the water system. To avoid this, don't pump used water into the sprinkler system, and don't hook up a pump to any part of the household plumbing.*
3. *You must not allow the gray water to flow onto your neighbor's property. Keep it on your own plants and there is no problem.*

8. Which of the following is an example of gray water?

   (A) carbonated water
   (B) rain water
   (C) soapy water
   (D) tap water

9. As used in the second paragraph, "stretching" most nearly means

   (A) drawing tight
   (B) increasing in quantity
   (C) making longer
   (D) slowing down

10. What is NOT a good use for gray water?

    (A) drinking
    (B) irrigating fields
    (C) rinsing sidewalks
    (D) watering house plants

11. Rinse water should not be used for irrigation if it

    (A) contains borax soap
    (B) contains chlorine bleach
    (C) does not contain borax soap
    (D) does not contain chlorine bleach

12. To reduce the ill effects of chlorine-containing rinse water, you should

    (A) concentrate it in one area
    (B) mix it with borax soap
    (C) not put too much in any one spot
    (D) pour it directly on the plants

13. The health department does not want gray water to

    (A) be used for irrigation
    (B) be carried outdoors in buckets
    (C) contain detergent or soap
    (D) pollute the water system

Model Test B

14. To get used water outside your house, you should

    (A) let it flow onto your neighbor's property
    (B) pump it into your sprinkler system
    (C) reposition the plumbing to lead the used water outdoors
    (D) use a garden hose siphon or buckets

MY DRAGON

A Feature Story by Sharon Green

I have a dragon in my house. It is small but powerful. When it first showed up at my house, I was a little bit nervous. Dragons were huge mythological beasts that breathed fire, I thought, not invisible creatures hanging on your every word.

I had never talked to a dragon before, and I wasn't sure it would understand me. I wasn't sure where to start.

Now I can spend hour after hour talking to my dragon. It's even learned to recognize my voice. I take my time when I talk to my dragon, and it understands every word. I love the way my dragon pays attention to what I'm saying: it makes me think that I have special things to say.

My dragon is a voice-recognition software program that lives in my computer. It is called Dragon Naturally Speaking. The program takes my spoken words and turns them into text that materializes on my computer screen. Sometimes the dragon types words that sound like what I have said but are a little bit off. I had to learn how to help my dragon fix whatever he'd got wrong. Here's what I learned. It doesn't help to YELL. It doesn't help to s-p-e-a-k s-l-o-w-l-y. It really doesn't help to, say, just, one, word, at, a, time. The only thing that works is to speak clearly and naturally and to be patient with the dragon, who is doing the best he can.

My dragon was not born; he did not hatch from an egg. My small, clever dragon was manufactured, made by a software company called Nuance. I know this is true, but I don't care. When I dictate into the microphone, I speak clearly and naturally and talk to my dragon. And when I talk to my dragon, I feel my words come alive.

15. The writer's initial reaction to the Dragon Naturally Speaking software program was one of

    (A) terror
    (B) uneasiness
    (C) indifference
    (D) hostility

16. What does the writer do with her dragon?

    (A) She speaks to it.
    (B) She punishes it.
    (C) She pets it.
    (D) She threatens it.

17. As used in the third paragraph, "even"

    (A) expresses how little progress has been made
    (B) means having no irregularities
    (C) gives a sense of fairness
    (D) indicates something unexpected

18. The writer describes

    (A) how the software program was manufactured
    (B) why she acquired the software program
    (C) what she learned about fixing errors in the text
    (D) how the dragon came to show up at her house

Model Test B

19. The writer writes "yell" in capital letters to

    (A) demonstrate how to correct an error
    (B) give a visual equivalent of speaking in a loud voice
    (C) provide an example of a typical software error
    (D) express how happy she is to have acquired this software program

20. Working with the software program

    (A) teaches the writer what to say
    (B) makes the writer feel good about her writing
    (C) is something the writer always wanted to do
    (D) takes too much of the writer's time

21. Which of the following sentences best expresses the writer's overall attitude toward her dragon?

    (A) It is a useful tool.
    (B) It is a captive slave.
    (C) It is a powerful beast.
    (D) It is a friendly helper.

MINIGARDENS FOR VEGETABLES

Containers

To start a minigarden of vegetables, you will need a container large enough to hold each plant when it is fully grown. You can use plastic or clay pots, an old pail, a plastic bucket, a bushel basket, a wire basket, or a wooden box. Almost any container is satisfactory, from tiny pots for your kitchen windowsill to large wooden boxes for your patio.

The size and number of the containers can vary with the space you have and the number of plants you want to grow. Six-inch pots are satisfactory for chives. Radishes, onions, and a variety of tomato (Tiny Tim) will do well in ten-inch pots. For the average patio, five-gallon plastic cans are suitable. They are easy to handle and provide enough space for the larger vegetable plants.

Light

Vegetable plants grow better in full sunlight than in the shade. Some vegetables need more sun than others. Leafy vegetables (lettuce, cabbage, mustard greens) can stand more shade than root vegetables (beets, radishes, turnips). Root vegetables can stand more shade than vegetable fruit plants (cucumbers, peppers, tomatoes), which do very poorly in the shade. Plant your vegetable fruit plants where they will get the most sun, and your leafy vegetables and root vegetables in the shadier areas.

Starting Plants Indoors

You can give some plants a jump on the growing season by starting them indoors on windowsills that have plenty of sunlight. Then, after the weather gets warmer, you can transplant them into larger containers and move them outdoors.

Hardening

Plants should be gradually "hardened," or toughened, for two weeks before being moved outdoors. This is done by withholding water and lowering the temperature. Hardening slows down the plants' rate of growth to prepare them to withstand such conditions as chilling, drying winds, or high temperatures.

Lettuce, cabbage, and many other plants can be toughened to withstand frosts; others, such as tomatoes and peppers, cannot be hardened.

22. Which of the following statements are TRUE?

    I.   Lettuce does better in the shade than tomatoes do.
    II. Plants started indoors need some toughening time before you move them outdoors.
    III. Radishes grow well in six-inch pots.

    (A) Statements I and II only
    (B) Statements I and III only
    (C) Statements II and III only
    (D) All of the statements

23. You toughen a seedling by

    (A) putting it in a cooler environment
    (B) putting it in a six-inch pot
    (C) watering it thoroughly
    (D) increasing its rate of growth

24. To "give some plants a jump on the growing season" is to

    (A) shake off the effects of transplanting them
    (B) get them off to an early start
    (C) skip a necessary stage in their growth
    (D) keep them in the shade

25. Which of the following statements are FALSE?

    I. Some plants do well if you start them indoors.
    II. Green peppers can be hardened by withholding water.
    III. Root plants need more sun than vegetable fruit plants do.

    (A) Statements I and II only
    (B) Statements I and III only
    (C) Statements II and III only
    (D) All of the statements

26. Who is the most likely intended audience for this article?

    (A) an experienced farmer
    (B) a botany student
    (C) a novice gardener
    (D) an authority on gardening

SEATTLE

Nestled between the craggy Olympic Mountains to the west and the volcanic peaks of the Cascade Range to the east, the city of Seattle sits on a narrow strip of land between Puget Sound and 18-mile-long Lake Washington. Just north of downtown Seattle these bodies of water are linked by a system of locks and a ship canal leading into Lake Union, which bisects the city.

Although early maritime voyagers caught sight of the Washington coast before the close of the 18th century, Seattle itself was settled comparatively late. With an entire continent to cross, the first families did not reach what was to be Seattle until 1851, when they settled at Alki Point. The windswept town was soon moved around the point next to the protected waters of Elliott Bay.

The city prospered, but by 1865 it was noticeable something was missing: the busy lumberjacks, trappers, and traders had no brides. Asa Mercer, founder of the Territorial University, went east and recruited 11 brave and eligible young ladies to return with him; a second group of 57 women made their way to the growing city a year later.

Built almost entirely of wood, the young city was destroyed in 1889 when a painter's glue pot boiled over and started the Great Fire. Seattle was soon rebuilt, this time using more stone, iron, and concrete than wood. By 1893 the first transcontinental railroad had reached Seattle, and maritime trade had been established with the Orient.

Swift growth followed the 1897 Klondike gold rush, for which Seattle served as a jumping off point. Seattle's population increased sixfold from 1890 to 1910; tide flats were filled and steep slopes were leveled to create more livable areas. In 1909 the city was host to its first world's fair, the Alaska-Yukon-Pacific Exhibition; the University of Washington now occupies the site.

27. The main purpose of the opening paragraph is to

    (A) praise Seattle's scenic attractions
    (B) portray Seattle as it was seen by the earliest explorers
    (C) explain the basis of Seattle's economy
    (D) introduce Seattle's geographic location

28. The first families reached Seattle

    (A) as part of a maritime expedition
    (B) after having taken an overland route
    (C) after having been recruited by Asa Mercer
    (D) through a system of locks and canals

29. Why was the town of Seattle moved near Elliott Bay?

    (A) because it needed rebuilding after the Great Fire of 1889
    (B) because the new site offered more shelter from wind
    (C) because Elliott Bay was closer to Alki Point
    (D) because women were expected to arrive shortly

30. A "jumping-off point" (last paragraph) most likely is

    (A) a place from which one departs on a journey
    (B) an introduction to a particular subject
    (C) a steep slope that needs to be leveled
    (D) a craggy mountain peak

31. Population growth in the 1890s led to a need for

    (A) more industry
    (B) more trade with the Orient
    (C) better housing sites
    (D) stronger universities

In the following selection from her novel Jo's Boys, *Louisa May Alcott concludes the story of the March family and their friends that she began in her famous novel* Little Women.

HAPPY ENDINGS
A Selection from *Jo's Boys*
by Louisa May Alcott

 It is a strong temptation to the weary historian to close the present tale with an earthquake which should engulf Plumfield and its environs so deeply in the bowels of
(5) *the earth that no youthful Schliemann could ever find a vestige of it. But as that somewhat melodramatic conclusion might shock my gentle readers, I will refrain, and forestall the usual question, 'How did they*
(10) *end?' by briefly stating that all the marriages turned out well. The boys prospered in their various callings; so did the girls, for Bess and Josie won honors in their artistic careers, and in the course of time*
(15) *found worthy mates. Nan remained a busy, cheerful, independent spinster, and dedicated her life to her suffering sisters and their children, in which true woman's work she found abiding happiness. Dan never*
(20) *married, but lived, bravely and usefully, among his chosen people till he was shot defending them, and at last lay quietly asleep in the green wilderness he loved so well, with a lock of golden hair upon his*
(25) *breast, and a smile on his face which seemed to say that the constant knight had fought his last fight and was at peace. Stuffy became an alderman, and died suddenly of apoplexy after a public dinner. Dolly was a*
(30) *society man of mark till he lost his money, when he found congenial employment in a fashionable tailoring establishment. Demi became a partner, and lived to see his name above the door, and Rob was a professor at*
(35) *Laurence College; but Teddy eclipsed them all by becoming an eloquent and famous*

clergyman, to the great delight of his aston-
ished mother. And now, having endeavored
to suit everyone by many weddings, few
(40) deaths, and as much prosperity as the eter-
nal fitness of things will permit, let the
music stop, the lights die out, and the cur-
tain fall forever on the March family.

32. This selection is best described as

    (A) biography
    (B) essay
    (C) fiction
    (D) history

33. The author provides details about what
    happened to her characters in order to

    (A) increase interest in a subsequent book
    (B) prevent her readers from bothering
        her with questions
    (C) demonstrate the depth of her knowl-
        edge of the subject
    (D) share a true experience

34. In line 12, the word "callings" most nearly
    means

    (A) shouts
    (B) impulses
    (C) professions
    (D) decisions

35. People like Nan in this passage can be
    described as

    (A) proud
    (B) selfless
    (C) suffering
    (D) unwomanly

36. Dan dies

    (A) in his sleep
    (B) lost in the wilderness
    (C) from a bullet wound
    (D) from a stroke

37. The nickname "Stuffy" most likely refers
    to the character's

    (A) breathing problems
    (B) taste in clothing
    (C) eating habits
    (D) career choice

38. The statement "Teddy eclipsed them all"
    most nearly means

    (A) Teddy outshone them all.
    (B) Teddy concealed them all.
    (C) Teddy escaped them all.
    (D) Teddy followed them all.

39. In the final sentence, the narrator rules out
    the possibility of any

    (A) weddings
    (B) funerals
    (C) prosperity
    (D) sequels

The following article was written about the 2002
Oakland mayoral race between then mayor
Jerry Brown and his challenger, Wilson Riles Jr.

**ELECTION BATTLE: THE HOME
STRETCH**

In an apparently one-sided race to become
Oakland's next mayor, former City Councilman
Wilson Riles Jr. is scrambling to loosen incum-
bent Jerry Brown's grip on City Hall.

California's former Governor Brown defeated
a field of 10 mayoral opponents in 1998,
actively campaigning and winning 59% of the
city's vote. This year, however, Brown has run a
low-key, "stealth" campaign without lawn signs
or even a storefront campaign office. Instead, he
has participated in debates and sent out a scat-
tering of mailings that stress his record.

Riles, for his part, has relied on radio ads,
mailers, and newsletters pushed under car
windshield wipers to get his message across. He

has also hit the city streets, shaking hands with passersby, taking his message directly to the voting public.

These differences in campaign style merely hint at the extent of the candidates' differences.

Riles, most recently head of a Quaker peace and justice organization, contends that Brown has ignored the plight of Oakland's working-class families, who no longer can afford to buy homes in the city. According to the former City Councilman, the city should require all new developments to include a certain number of lower-priced homes so that low-income families are not priced out of the market.

Brown for his part maintains that more housing, including affordable housing, has been erected during his term in office than in previous years. He opposes subjecting developers to new, potentially burdensome, requirements, stating that several current housing developments are having problems getting financing as things stand.

Riles also has criticized Brown's record on education, maintaining that establishing charter schools and small magnet schools may help a handful of students, but does nothing for the majority of the 54,000 pupils enrolled in Oakland's public school system, who need after-school programs and tutoring support.

Brown, however, denies Riles's claim. Instead, he argues that charter schools and small schools not only give families a good alternative to local public schools but also put pressure on the public schools to improve in order to compete.

Riles asserts that Brown's Oakland achievements are more shadow than substance. "It's past time for theatrics, past time for showboating and lightweight celebrity," he declared.

Brown, however, maintains that Oakland is headed in the right direction. On Election Day, he believes, the majority of voters will show that they agree.

40. A synonym for the word "incumbent" is

(A) city councilman
(B) future mayor
(C) current office holder
(D) former state governor

41. Riles's reforms are aimed at providing help to all of the following EXCEPT

(A) low-income families
(B) developers
(C) members of the working class
(D) public school students

42. Which of the following statements are TRUE?

I. Riles has been campaigning more actively than Brown.
II. Brown was elected governor of California in 1998.
III. Brown failed to set up a storefront campaign office.

(A) Statements I and II only
(B) Statements I and III only
(C) Statements II and III only
(D) All of the statements

43. Which of the following statements are FALSE?

I. Brown made no use of mailers in his campaign.
II. Riles stresses the dangers of putting burdens on developers.
III. Oakland's 54,000 students all are enrolled in charter schools.

(A) Statements I and II only
(B) Statements I and III only
(C) Statements II and III only
(D) All of the statements

44. By asserting that Brown's Oakland achievements are "more shadow than substance," Riles suggests they are

    (A) shady
    (B) substantial
    (C) ill-omened
    (D) deceptive

THE INDIANS OF CALIFORNIA

California's Indians have lived under the governments of the three countries—Spain, Mexico, and the United States. Each of these governments recognized the rights of the Indians and attempted to deal fairly and justly with them, at least in theory, but their good intentions were never adequately administered.

Many Indians were held in peonage during the Spanish and Mexican regimes. The Spanish mission life into which the South California Indians were drawn cut their numbers by over 70 percent. For several decades after the United States acquired California, Indians were threatened with extinction by massacre and starvation. Nonetheless, Spain conceded the validity of the Indians' rights to use the land. Mexico recognized the Indians as Mexican citizens. When California became part of the United States, Indians were to become citizens and their liberty and property were to be accorded full protection under the laws of their new government.

Despite these good intentions, by 1860 the Indians of California were destitute, landless, and without any ratified treaties with the federal government. They remained in that unenviable position for the next 60 years until, in the early decades of the 20th century, the insistence of a church group prompted the federal government to purchase home sites, or rancherias, for the "landless Indians of California."

The rancherias purchased were small, generally inadequate to support the residents, and scattered throughout the northern and central part of the state. Nevertheless, they were places to which the Indians could move, reasonably secure in the knowledge that no one could drive them away as they had so often been driven away from other homes.

45. The passage blames the injustices suffered by California's Indians on

    (A) Mexico's recognition of Indians as citizens
    (B) the insistence of church groups
    (C) the poor motivation of the Indians
    (D) flawed administrative practices

46. According to the above passage, Spanish mission life was so hard on Southern California Indians that

    (A) large numbers of them died
    (B) their numbers increased by over 70 percent
    (C) they chose to become ranchers
    (D) they moved to the northern and central parts of the state

47. In the 1860s the Indians of California faced hardship because

    (A) they were held in peonage during the Spanish regime
    (B) they were illegal aliens
    (C) they had no ratified treaties with the federal government
    (D) their homesites were scattered throughout the northern and central parts of the state

48. The ownership of the Indians' rancherias belongs to

    (A) a church group
    (B) the federal government
    (C) the three governments of Spain, Mexico, and the United States
    (D) the residents of the homesites

49. One strong advantage of the rancherias was their

    (A) nearness to ancestral Indian hunting grounds in Southern California
    (B) stability as homesites from which the Indians could not be driven away
    (C) capability to support a large Indian population
    (D) ample size

CHOCOLATE

The Mayans and Aztecs considered chocolate the food of the gods, but today's lovers of sweets would not find the earliest chocolate heavenly. Chocolate is made from the roasted and ground seeds of the cacao tree. Until the sixteenth century, ground chocolate was mixed with water and spices, including chili peppers, to make a bitter, frothy beverage which Spanish explorers termed fitter for hogs than men. Not until Cortez brought chocolate back to Spain in 1526 was sugar added to the mix, but once it was, European royalty prized hot chocolate drinks. Over the next two centuries, hot chocolate became fashionable; chocolate houses (like coffeehouses) sprang up throughout Europe.

50. The comment that "today's lovers of sweets would not find the earliest chocolate heavenly" is meant to be

    (A) humorous
    (B) critical
    (C) offensive
    (D) sentimental

51. The initial attitude of the Spaniards toward the Aztec chocolate beverage can best be characterized as

    (A) appreciative
    (B) resentful
    (C) objective
    (D) scornful

52. The Spaniards' attitude toward chocolate changed

    (A) once the beans had been roasted
    (B) once the beverage had been heated
    (C) after the drink had been sweetened
    (D) after chili peppers were added to the mixture

53. The passage does all of the following EXCEPT

    (A) describe a process
    (B) mention a date
    (C) ask a question
    (D) name a historical figure

54. This passage most likely was taken from a

    (A) work of fiction
    (B) biography
    (C) feature story
    (D) technical report

Directions: Select the word or group of words that has the same, or nearly the same meaning as the word that is in **boldface**.

55. **Complex** most nearly means

    (A) difficult
    (B) ridiculous
    (C) appropriate
    (D) obvious

56. **Vicinity** most nearly means

    (A) downtown
    (B) urban area
    (C) region nearby
    (D) metropolis

57. **Span** most nearly means

    (A) expand
    (B) avoid
    (C) go around
    (D) extend across

58. **Corrupt** most nearly means

    (A) radical
    (B) lazy
    (C) cowardly
    (D) wicked

59. **Hazard** most nearly means

    (A) creature
    (B) peril
    (C) riches
    (D) water

60. **Authorize** most nearly means

    (A) order
    (B) give power
    (C) write off
    (D) forbid

61. **Modify** most nearly means

    (A) renovate
    (B) intensify
    (C) change somewhat
    (D) repent for

62. **Confide** most nearly means

    (A) put trust
    (B) be mistaken
    (C) be disappointed
    (D) take pains

63. **Ponder** most nearly means

    (A) answer
    (B) regret
    (C) ignore completely
    (D) consider carefully

64. **Isolate** most nearly means

    (A) console
    (B) inject
    (C) watch closely
    (D) separate from others

Directions: Read the sentences below, paying special attention to the words in **boldface**. Then look at the answer choices below it. Select the answer choice in which the **boldfaced** word is used in the same way that it is in the original sentence.

Did you know that, when you shake hands with someone you have just met, you are following an old **convention**?

65. In which sentence does the word "convention" mean the same thing that it does in the sentence above?

    (A) Jerry decided to wear his Darth Vader costume to BayCon, the local science fiction convention.
    (B) Feminist leader Gloria Steinem challenged any man who dared to observe the convention of holding a door open for her.
    (C) The Geneva Convention is an international agreement about the ways in which prisoners of war should be treated.
    (D) Calling the convention to order, the Presiding Bishop welcomed the delegates.

*It takes **character** to stand up for what is right.*

66. In which sentence does the word "character" mean the same thing that it does in the sentence above?

    (A) How many young people today have sufficient character to resist peer pressure?
    (B) As word of her arrest spread, Martha began to feel as if she could never wipe out the stain on her character.
    (C) Sir Ian McKellen plays the title character in the Royal Shakespeare Company's production of *King Lear*.
    (D) In nursery school Morgan practiced writing out the alphabet, character after character.

*Joan's will specifies that, after her funeral expenses have been paid, she wants the **balance** of her estate to go to Doctors Without Borders, her favorite charity.*

67. In which sentence does the word "balance" mean the same thing that it does in the sentence above?

    (A) Performing her Tai Chi exercises, Norma tried to achieve a sense of both emotional and physical balance.
    (B) As a gymnast in training, Paula excelled at doing handstands on the balance beam.
    (C) When Joe won the lottery, he immediately paid off the balance of his mortgage.
    (D) No matter how hard I have tried, I have never been able to balance my checkbook.

*In college, Lorena has been exploring two very different **disciplines**, psychology and astronomy.*

68. In which sentence does the word "disciplines" mean the same thing that it does in the sentence above?

    (A) Although Donald disciplines his son, he never uses force.
    (B) Through obedience training, the dog owner disciplines his pet, teaching the animal control.
    (C) Painter, inventor, poet, engineer, Leonardo da Vinci was a master of many disciplines.
    (D) The best student does not look to the teacher for schooling; instead, she disciplines herself.

*It is time to **register** to take the proficiency test.*

69. In which sentence does the word "register" mean the same thing that it does in the sentence above?

    (A) If you want a job as a cashier, you had better learn to operate a cash register.
    (B) When Ella first was allowed to hold her baby sister, we all saw her face register her delight.
    (C) Although the principal warned Henry he was in danger of being expelled, the warning clearly failed to register.
    (D) As soon as I turn 18 years old, I intend to register to vote.

*Teachers often try to **mold** the minds of their students.*

70. In which sentence does the word "mold" mean the same thing that it does in the sentence above?

    (A) Influential commentators are able to mold public opinion.
    (B) A mold growing in Alexander Fleming's laboratory produced a substance that killed a number of disease-causing bacteria.
    (C) The sculptor carefully poured the hot metal into a plaster mold.
    (D) John left the casserole in the refrigerator for so long that it began to mold.

*Barbara reread the article three times to make sure she understood the author's **drift**.*

72. In which sentence does the word "drift" mean the same thing that it does in the sentence above?

    (A) Huck and Tom let the raft drift slowly down stream.
    (B) Lying flat on her back, Jo moved her arms and legs to make an angel in the snow drift.
    (C) Bored by the dull lecture, Sharon realized that her attention was beginning to drift.
    (D) Despite her wandering attention, she still managed to catch the lecturer's general drift.

*The writer told the heroic young woman's story, but, wanting to **spare** her embarrassment, would not reveal her name.*

71. In which sentence does the word "spare" mean the same thing that it does in the sentence above?

    (A) The condemned traitor begged the king to spare his life.
    (B) I stripped the sheets from the guest room bed to spare my hostess the bother.
    (C) Do you have any spare books to donate to the library's book drive?
    (D) When my car had a flat tire, I was very grateful that I had a spare in the trunk.

*The concentration of pollutants in the water has reached an unsafe **level**.*

73. In which sentence does the word "level" mean the same thing that it does in the sentence above?

    (A) Too high a level of sound can damage people's eardrums.
    (B) A billiard table must be absolutely level.
    (C) Jim handled himself well in a crisis; he always kept a level head.
    (D) The developers intend to level the run-down tenements and build new townhouses in their place.

*Mitch never allowed anyone else to **shoulder** his burdens.*

74. In which sentence does the word "shoulder" mean the same thing that it does in the sentence above?

    (A) Amy allowed the unhappy child to cry on her shoulder.
    (B) The highway patrol officer signaled Matt to pull off onto the shoulder of the highway.
    (C) In the army hospital, Miss Nightingale's volunteers worked shoulder to shoulder with the natives in tending the wounded.
    (D) It was time for the hiker to shoulder his backpack and head down the trail.

Directions: In each of the sentences below, the word in **boldface** may be unfamiliar to you. Use the other words in the sentence to help you decide what the word in **boldface** means.

*Uncertain which suitor she ought to marry, the princess **vacillated**, saying now one, now the other.*

75. As used in the sentence above, "vacillated" most nearly means

    (A) wavered
    (B) anticipated
    (C) returned home
    (D) grew ill

*Some people thought Salvador Dali was a brilliant painter; others **dismissed** him as a conceited fake.*

76. As used in the sentence above, "dismissed" most nearly means

    (A) praised
    (B) scattered
    (C) exasperated
    (D) rejected

*Contrary to her usual **gregarious** behavior, Susan began avoiding parties and family gatherings and started to spend her evenings alone in her room.*

77. As used in the sentence above, "gregarious" most nearly means

    (A) outgoing
    (B) polite
    (C) sleepy
    (D) unfriendly

*The most critical issue for wildlife in this dry land is their need for **unimpeded** access to water.*

78. As used in the sentence above, "unimpeded" most nearly means

    (A) uncertain
    (B) unacceptable
    (C) unhindered
    (D) untreated

*During the last forty years of Tennyson's long life, his creative powers never **flagged**; he did some of his best work after he reached the age of 70.*

79. As used in the sentence above, "flagged" most nearly means

    (A) improved
    (B) waved
    (C) flowered
    (D) dwindled

*Lovejoy is an antiques dealer who gives his customers advice on how to tell **spurious** antiques from objects that are genuinely old.*

80. As used in the sentence above, "spurious" most nearly means
    (A) former
    (B) ancient
    (C) fake
    (D) crude

*For many years an **obscure** researcher, Barbara McClintock gained international fame when she won the Nobel Prize.*

81. As used in the sentence above, "obscure" most nearly means

    (A) incomprehensible
    (B) penniless
    (C) unknown
    (D) hard-working

*Trying to prove the witness a liar, the district attorney repeatedly questioned her **veracity**.*

82. As used in the sentence above, "veracity" most nearly means

    (A) skill
    (B) intelligence
    (C) truthfulness
    (D) intensity

*Because the damage to his car had been **negligible**, Michael decided that he wouldn't bother to report the dented fender to his insurance company.*

83. As used in the sentence above, "negligible" most nearly means

    (A) intentional
    (B) insignificant
    (C) expensive
    (D) permanent

*Though she tried to be happy living in the city with Clara, Heidi **pined** for her beloved mountains and for her gruff but loving grandfather.*

84. As used in the sentence above, "pined" most nearly means

    (A) headed
    (B) longed
    (C) bloomed
    (D) settled

MATHEMATICS SECTION

Directions: Each of the following statements, questions, or problems is followed by four suggested answers or completions. Choose the *one* that best completes each of the statements or answers the question. Mark the oval on the answer sheet whose letter corresponds to the answer you have selected.

1. Which number below is the correct simplification of
    $(\frac{1}{4} + 1\frac{2}{3}) \div (1 - \frac{1}{6})$?

    (A) $\frac{10}{23}$

    (B) $\frac{19}{10}$

    (C) 2.3
    (D) 3.2

2. Which expression below is equal to $((2 - 2x) - (1 - x))(1 + x) + 2x(x + 1)$?

    (A) $(x + 1)^2$
    (B) $(x + 1)(x - 1)$
    (C) $2x^2 + 2x - 1$
    (D) $1 - 2x - x^2$

3. The Avalanche Gulch trail on Mt. Shasta rises from 2060 meters above sea level at the Bunny Flat trailhead to 4320 meters at the summit of the mountain, 4.5 miles to the northeast.

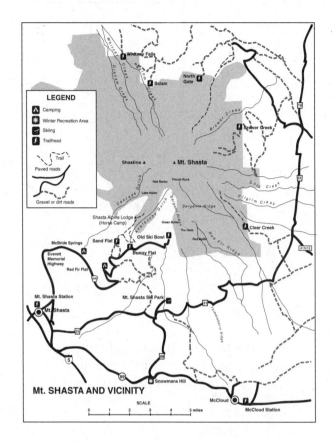

What is the closest estimate below for the average slope of the mountain from the trailhead to the summit?
(**Note:** 1 mile ≈ 1.6 kilometers.)

    (A) 0.3%
    (B) 0.5%
    (C) 30%
    (D) 50%

Refer to the graph below to answer the next two questions.

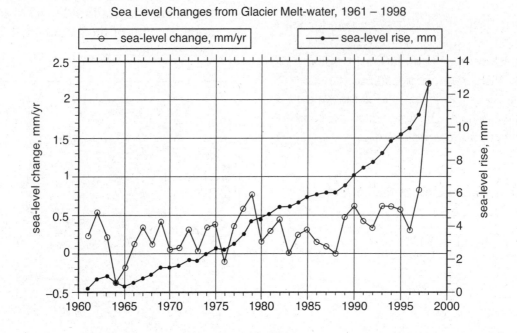

Sea Level Changes from Glacier Melt-water, 1961 – 1998

4. What is the best estimate below for the average rate of increase from glacial melting in the period from 1961 to 1998?

   (A) 0.25 mm/yr
   (B) 0.30 mm/yr
   (C) 0.50 mm/yr
   (D) 2 mm

5. Which statement below is supported by this graph?

   (A) Sea level did not change over the period 1961–1998.
   (B) Sea level rose every year from 1961 to 1998.
   (C) Sea level fell more than 5 years in the period 1961–1998.
   (D) Sea level tended to rise throughout 1961–1998.

6. For the triangle in this diagram, what is the best estimate of the length of side *AC*?

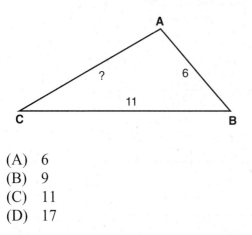

(A) 6
(B) 9
(C) 11
(D) 17

7. The boys in Mr. Rice's biology class prepared a table of their heights, recording the results by the number of boys at each height:

Height (inches)	Number
63	1
65	2
69	1
70	2
71	3
73	1

What is the median height of the boys?

(A) 69 inches
(B) 70 inches
(C) 71 inches
(D) 73 inches

8. For the table of heights in Question 7, what is the mode?

(A) 69 inches
(B) 70 inches
(C) 71 inches
(D) 73 inches

9. What is the mean height of the boys in Mr. Rice's class?

(A) 41.1 inches
(B) 68.5 inches
(C) 68.8 inches
(D) 69.0 inches

10. Which of the following four graphs represents the linear equation $y = -x/2 - 1$?

(A)

(B)

(C)

(D)

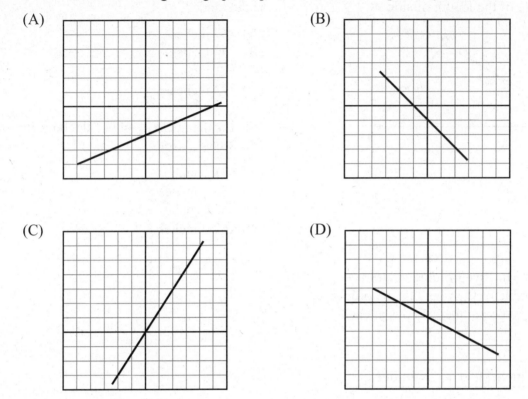

Refer to the graph below to answer the next two questions.

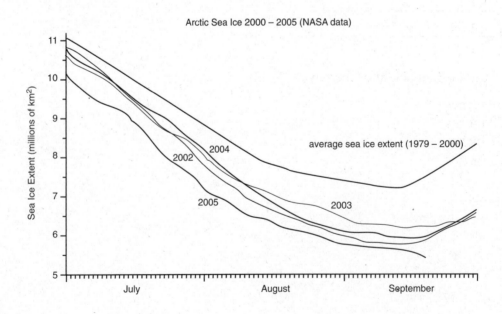

Arctic Sea Ice 2000 – 2005 (NASA data)

11. Compared to the references graph for sea ice in the Arctic Ocean from 1979 to 2000, there was about 9% less sea ice at the start of July 2005 than there was at the start of July in the reference period (about 1 million square kilometers less compared to the total of about 11 million at the left edge of the graph). Which answer below is the best estimate of the percentage change at the start of September 2005 as compared to the reference period?

    (A) 10%
    (B) 25%
    (C) 33%
    (D) 45%

12. The graph above shows the sea ice extent for 2005 from the start of July through about September 20. Which of the following is a reasonable projection of what happened later in the fall of 2005?

    (A) The extent of sea ice continued to fall throughout the rest of the year.
    (B) The extent of sea ice remained the same throughout the rest of the year.
    (C) The extent of sea ice began to increase again by the end of September.
    (D) The extent of sea ice did not increase until winter began in December.

13. A triangle has one angle of 55° and one of 40°. How many degrees is the third angle?

    (A) 75°
    (B) 85°
    (C) 90°
    (D) 95°

14. What is the next number, *N*, in this sequence?

    8   6   10   4   12   2   *N*?

    (A) 0
    (B) 10
    (C) 14
    (D) 16

15. A woman is 62 years old. Her daughter is 29 years old. In how many years will the mother be exactly twice as old as her daughter?

    (A) 3
    (B) 4
    (C) 5
    (D) 6

16. How many miles apart are the cities of Philipstown and De Witt, shown on the map below as 3/4 inch apart? The scale of miles on the map is 1 inch = 100 miles.

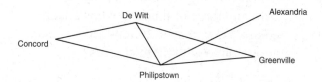

    (A) 3/4 mile
    (B) 30 miles
    (C) 75 miles
    (D) 750 miles

17. Smart's latex paint can cover 400 square feet of wall surface per gallon. Al needs to paint a wall that measures 59 feet by 15 feet, with two circular holes in the wall, each one 4 feet in diameter. He needs to do two coats of paint. Approximately how many gallons of paint will he need to do this job?

    (A) 2.2 gallons
    (B) 4.1 gallons
    (C) 4.3 gallons
    (D) 4.4 gallons

18. What is 8.312×10^{-4} in standard decimal notation (without exponents of 10)?

    (A) 0.00008312
    (B) 0.0008312
    (C) 0.008312
    (D) 0.08312

19. A "tricolor" flag is one with three equal width horizontal stripes of different colors. An on-line flag company allows orders with any three of their twelve available colors. How many different tricolor flags are possible with these choices?

    (A) 1,230
    (B) 1,320
    (C) 1,000
    (D) 220

20. A librarian has 72 books to catalog. He can catalog six books an hour, and his assistant can catalog two books an hour. They can spend up to three hours a day on cataloging. Which of the following cannot be answered from this information?

    (A) What is the shortest time, in days, that it would take them working together to complete the cataloging of this set of books?
    (B) What is the shortest time, in days, that it would take the assistant to do the cataloging by herself?
    (C) How many days per month should be scheduled for cataloging?
    (D) What is the maximum average rate, in books per day, at which the librarian and his assistant can catalog books?

21. In the figure below, the line *BC* is perpendicular to both *AB* and *CD*. What is the shortest possible distance from *A* to *D*?

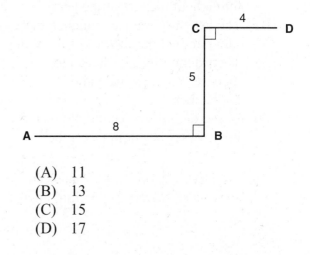

    (A) 11
    (B) 13
    (C) 15
    (D) 17

22. Three men had an average age of 36. The oldest was 39, while the youngest was 32. How old was the third man?

    (A) 33
    (B) 34
    (C) 36
    (D) 37

Refer to the chart below to answer the next three questions.

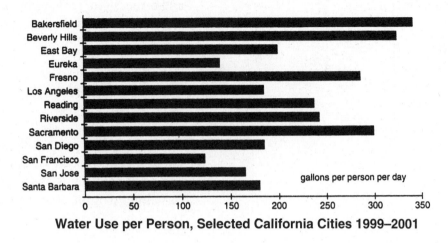

Water Use per Person, Selected California Cities 1999–2001

23. Water use per person in Santa Barbara was about what fraction of the use in Bakersfield?

    (A) 1/2
    (B) 1/3
    (C) 1/4
    (D) 1/5

24. Which of the following cities had lower water use per person than Los Angeles?

    (A) Eureka
    (B) Fresno
    (C) Reading
    (D) Riverside

25. How many of the cities listed had water usage of 200 or more gallons per person per day?

    (A) 5
    (B) 7
    (C) 9
    (D) 11

26. What is $(8.3 \times 10^{-4}) \times (4.7 \times 10^{15})$ in standard scientific notation?

    (A) 39.01×10^{12}
    (B) 3.901×10^{12}
    (C) 39.01×10^{11}
    (D) 3.901×10^{11}

27. Two cars are heading south on Highway 5, one at 65 miles per hour, the other at 50 miles per hour. The car traveling at 50 miles per hour is 48 miles ahead of the faster car. In how many hours will the faster car catch up with the slower car?

    (A) $4\frac{4}{5}$ hours
    (B) $3\frac{1}{2}$ hours
    (C) $3\frac{1}{5}$ hours
    (D) $2\frac{4}{5}$ hours

Model Test B

28. What is the product of the slope of line *B* and the slope of line *A*?

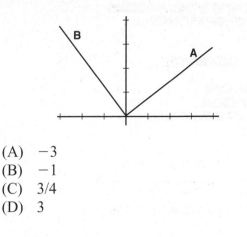

(A) −3
(B) −1
(C) 3/4
(D) 3

29. Thom has a cylindrical barrel 4 feet across and 5 feet high. About how many cubic feet of water will the barrel hold?

(A) 30 cubic feet
(B) 40 cubic feet
(C) 50 cubic feet
(D) 60 cubic feet

30. A carpenter has to cut a stick one meter long into two pieces. He wants to have one piece four times as long as the other. How long will the shorter piece be?

(A) $16\frac{2}{3}$ cm
(B) 20 cm
(C) 20 in.
(D) $33\frac{1}{3}$ cm

Refer to the following graph to answer the next two questions.

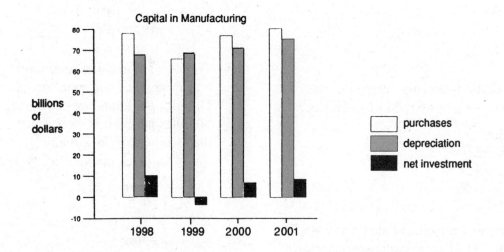

31. The net investment in manufacturing capital is the amount spent on new capital investments (purchases) minus the depreciation on existing capital. Which year had negative net investment?

(A) 1998
(B) 1999
(C) 2000
(D) 2001

32. In which year did manufacturers spend about $10 billion more on purchases than they lost in depreciation?

(A) 1998
(B) 1999
(C) 2000
(D) 2001

33. A highway was built in Kern County at a cost of $132,000. The costs were borne by the county, the state, and the federal governments. The state paid twice as much as the county, and the federal government paid four times as much as the state. How much did the county pay?

    (A) $11,000
    (B) $12,000
    (C) $13,200
    (D) $18,500

34. What is the eighth number in the sequence of numbers below?

    1   3   6   10   15   21 . . .

    (A) 25
    (B) 28
    (C) 32
    (D) 36

Refer to the following graph to answer the next four questions.

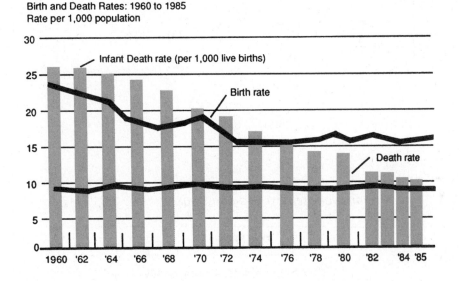

Birth and Death Rates: 1960 to 1985
Rate per 1,000 population

35. Which of the following statements about birth and death rates in the United States is NOT true?

    (A) The infant death rate decreased steadily from 1960 to 1985.
    (B) Births exceeded deaths by at least 5 per thousand for the period shown.
    (C) The birth rate decreased steadily from 1960 to 1985.
    (D) The death rate in 1985 was less than it had been in 1960.

36. In 1968, the population of the United States was about 200 million people. Approximately how many Americans died in 1968?

    (A) 1 million
    (B) 2 million
    (C) 5 million
    (D) 10 million

37. The infant death rate in 1985 was about what percent of the rate in 1960?

    (A) 20%
    (B) 30%
    (C) 40%
    (D) 50%

Model Test B

38. From 1960 to 1975, the birth rate decreased every year EXCEPT

    (A) 1966
    (B) 1968
    (C) 1970
    (D) 1972

39. What is the area of the triangle formed by the three points with coordinates (2,5), (−2,−3), and (4,−3)?

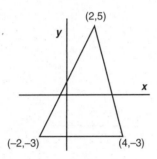

    (A) 12
    (B) 24
    (C) 36
    (D) 48

40. An aluminum mine gets a yield of $1\frac{1}{4}$ pounds of metal for each ton of ore. How many tons must be processed to produce 200 pounds of the metal?

    (A) 125 tons
    (B) 160 tons
    (C) 250 tons
    (D) 320 tons

41. The debate team at Johnny's high school went from 25 in his first year to 30 in his second year. What was the percentage increase the second year?

    (A) 2%
    (B) 5%
    (C) 10%
    (D) 20%

Refer to the following table to answer the next two questions.

RAINFALL				
Precipitation data, 4 P.M. Monday for selected California Stations				
City	Last 24 hours	Season to Date	Normal to Data	Seasonal Norm
Oakland	0	5.43	6.98	18.69
San Jose	0	2.33	4.84	13.65
Fresno	0	1.68	3.32	10.24
Los Angeles	0	0.24	4.49	14.05
(Season: July 1 to June 30)				

42. Which city NORMALLY has had the least amount of rainfall by this date in the season?

    (A) Oakland
    (B) San Jose
    (C) Fresno
    (D) Los Angeles

43. What percentage of its normal rainfall for the year has Oakland had so far this season?

    (A) 5%
    (B) 29%
    (C) 48%
    (D) 78%

Model Test B

44. A quart is 32 ounces and a liter is approximately 30.3 ounces. About what percent of a liter is one quart?

(A) 90%
(B) 95%
(C) 105%
(D) 110%

Refer to the following table to answer the next three questions.

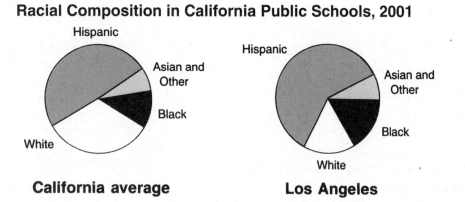

Racial Composition in California Public Schools, 2001

California average   **Los Angeles**

45. Which group had the largest fraction of the students in Los Angeles schools in 2001?

(A) White
(B) Black
(C) Asian and Other
(D) Hispanic

46. Which group averaged the smallest fraction of students in all California schools in 2001?

(A) White
(B) Black
(C) Asian and Other
(D) Hispanic

47. How did the proportion of Hispanic students in the average California school in 2001 compare with that in Los Angeles?

(A) It was about 1/2 as big.
(B) It was about 80% as big.
(C) It was about the same size.
(D) It was about twice as big.

48. It takes a crew of four painters 15 hours to prepare an apartment for painting. How many hours would it take a crew of six?

(A) $7\frac{1}{2}$ hours
(B) 8 hours
(C) 10 hours
(D) 12 hours

Model Test B

49. Jordan walks home from the bus stop at Alameda and Pasadena, along any one of the possible shortest routes in the diagram below.

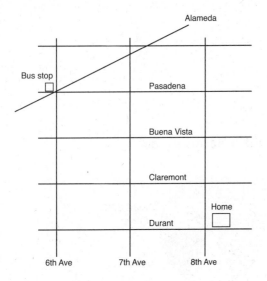

If Jordan chooses his route at random, what is the probability that he will walk south on 6th Ave. and east on Durant on any particular day?

(A) 8%
(B) 10%
(C) 12%
(D) 25%

50. Given the following table of values:

y	0	2	1.5	0
x	−2	0	1	2

which of the answers below is a possible graph of the table?

(A)

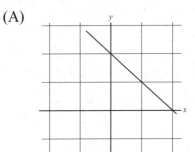

(B)

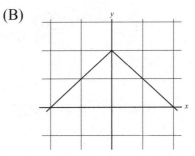

(C)

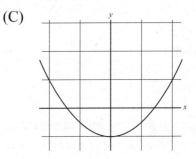

(D)

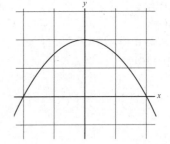

ANSWER KEY

English Language Arts Section

LANGUAGE SUBTEST

[There is no correct answer for the Writing Task.]

1. B	9. C	17. A	25. C	33. D	41. B
2. D	10. B	18. B	26. B	34. B	42. A
3. A	11. B	19. C	27. C	35. A	43. A
4. D	12. A	20. C	28. C	36. A	44. D
5. C	13. B	21. B	29. B	37. D	45. A
6. B	14. B	22. C	30. B	38. C	46. B
7. B	15. C	23. D	31. B	39. C	47. C
8. D	16. D	24. B	32. C	40. D	48. B

READING SUBTEST

1. D	10. A	19. B	28. B	37. C	46. A
2. B	11. A	20. B	29. B	38. A	47. C
3. B	12. C	21. D	30. A	39. D	48. B
4. C	13. D	22. A	31. C	40. C	49. B
5. B	14. D	23. A	32. C	41. B	50. A
6. D	15. B	24. B	33. B	42. B	51. D
7. D	16. A	25. C	34. C	43. D	52. C
8. C	17. D	26. C	35. B	44. D	53. C
9. B	18. C	27. D	36. C	45. D	54. C

55. A	60. B	65. B	70. A	75. A	80. C
56. C	61. C	66. A	71. B	76. D	81. C
57. D	62. A	67. C	72. D	77. A	82. C
58. D	63. D	68. C	73. A	78. C	83. B
59. B	64. D	69. D	74. D	79. D	84. B

Mathematics Section

1. C	11. B	21. B	31. B	41. D
2. A	12. C	22. D	32. A	42. C
3. C	13. B	23. A	33. B	43. B
4. B	14. C	24. A	34. D	44. C
5. D	15. B	25. B	35. C	45. D
6. B	16. C	26. B	36. B	46. C
7. B	17. C	27. C	37. C	47. B
8. C	18. B	28. B	38. C	48. C
9. C	19. B	29. D	39. B	49. B
10. D	20. C	30. B	40. B	50. D

Model Test B

ANSWER EXPLANATIONS

English Language Arts Section

LANGUAGE SUBTEST

1. **(B)** they're
   Don't confuse the contraction *they're* (short for *they are*) with the possessive pronoun *their* (as in *their team*) or the adverb *there* (as in *Here! Not there!*). Choice B is correct. *They're going* to Reno.
2. **(D)** Correct as is
   The subject of the sentence, *Four cars*, is plural; the verb, *don't fit*, is plural as well.
3. **(A)** and me
   Incorrect pronoun form. In this sentence, the pronoun is the object of the preposition *except*. Therefore, the correct answer is Choice A, *and me*.
4. **(D)** Correct as is
   The subject of the sentence, *clowns*, is plural; the verb, *precede*, is plural as well. The clowns *precede* (go before) the elephant.
5. **(C)** strangers; however, they
   Run-on sentence. The insertion of the semicolon between the two independent clauses corrects the run-on sentence.
6. **(B)** it's
   Don't confuse the contraction it's (short for *it is*) with the possessive pronoun *its*. The phrase *it's time to go* is correct.
7. **(B)** Monica and I
   Error in pronoun case. The pronoun here is part of the subject of the subordinate clause and should be in the subjective case. The wording *Monica and I* is correct.
8. **(D)** Correct as is
   Do not confuse the verb *except* (to make an exception of or exclude) with the verb *accept* (to approve or agree to; to receive). In accepting the prince's proposal, Cinderella agrees to marry him.
9. **(C)** was divided among
   Use *between* when referring to only two objects; use *among* when referring to groups of three or more.
10. **(B)** for its large number.
    Error in pronoun-antecedent agreement. *School* is a collective noun, here being used in a singular sense. The singular pronoun *its* is therefore correct.
11. **(B)** Harvard College's
    Error in capitalization and punctuation. As it is used here, the word *college* is part of the proper name Harvard College. Therefore, it must be capitalized. Also, the apostrophe is needed to signal that the noun is in the possessive case.
12. **(A)** birthday: racing cars,
    The colon here is used correctly to direct attention to the series or list of toys that follow.
13. **(B)** can hardly wait
    Double negative. *Hardly* and *scarcely* are words that have negative force. If you use them with an unnecessary negative (for example, *not*, *nothing*, or *without*), most grammarians consider the result nonstandard. Eliminate the unnecessary negative.
14. **(B)** The Getty Museum's new exhibit
    Error in punctuation. Use the apostrophe followed by the letter *–s* to indicate the possessive case of a singular noun.
15. **(C)** will arrive?" she asked.
    The rule is that, when the question mark applies only to the quoted material, the question mark goes inside the quotation marks. Choice B places the question mark outside the quotation marks; you can eliminate Choice B. Choice A and the original sentence also both misplace the question mark, putting it after the expression *she asked*; you can eliminate Choices A and D. Only Choice C is left. It is the correct answer.
16. **(D)** Correct as is
    The term "suppose to" is nonstandard. Always add the *–d*.
17. **(A)** who did it?
    The sentence "Do the police know who did it?" is correct. Here's why. *Done* is standard as the past participle of the verb *do*. However, it is nonstandard as a substitute for *did*. Did you understand that? I hope you have done so.

18. **(B)** Your guess is
Do not confuse the contraction *you're* (short for *you are,* as in "You are guessing") with the possessive pronoun *your* (as in "Your guess is as good as mine").

19. **(C)** After managing the team for several years, he understood its operation.
Use the process of elimination to answer this question. The original sentence contains a dangling modifier; therefore, it is not correct. You can eliminate Choice D. Choice A introduces an error involving the sequence of tenses. You can eliminate Choice A. Choice B recasts the sentence, changing its meaning, and throws in an unnecessary comma. You can eliminate Choice B. Only Choice C is left. It is the correct answer.

20. **(C)** The reason that I arrived late was that the bus was delayed by heavy traffic.
Wordiness. The expression *the reason . . . was because* is both informal and redundant (unnecessarily wordy). Avoid *the reason . . . is because* constructions and their variants. Either substitute *that* for *because* (as in Choice C) or totally reword the sentence.

21. **(B)** While I was walking along the road, a car traveling at well over the speed limit nearly hit me.
Dangling modifier. Who was walking along the road? Not the car! Choice C correctly indicates that *I* was walking.

22. **(C)** When I call him, he doesn't answer the phone.
Error in sequence of tenses. The present tense here indicates a habitual action: When I, as I customarily do, call him, he, as is his usual practice, doesn't answer the phone.

23. **(D)** Correct as is
The original sentence uses the commas correctly to separate items in a series and to set off the parenthetical phrase "with great delight." Choice D is the correct answer.

24. **(B)** Even though Susie was feeling ill, she did extremely well on the big test.
Incorrect conjunction. The author is setting up a contrast between what was expected ("Susie was feeling ill, so she did badly on the test.") and what actually happened ("Susie was feeling ill, but she aced the test anyway!"). The conjunction *Even though* signals this contrast.

25. **(C)** A braggart is a person who is conceited, self-centered, and boastful.
Lack of parallelism. *Conceited* and *self-centered* are both adjectives, words that modify nouns. *Conceited* and *self-centered* are the first two items in a series of three items; all three items in the series should be adjectives. Replace *likes to boast* with the adjective *boastful*.

26. **(B)** Cook the omelet in a copper-bottomed Teflon pan.
Choice B effectively combines two short, choppy sentences into a smoother, more concise whole.

27. **(C)** Had the Confederate Army won the day at Gettysburg, the history of America would have been profoundly altered.
Error in shift of mood. Use the subjunctive mood to express a situation that is contrary to fact. The Confederate Army did not win the day at Gettysburg. The history of America has not been altered. The verbs of both clauses should be in the subjunctive mood. Choice C corrects the error.

28. **(C)** Before starting an exercise program, you should consult your physician.
Dangling modifier. Ask yourself who is going to start the exercise program. Choice C provides the sentence with a subject (*you*).

29. **(B)** The doctor is accused of issuing unnecessary prescriptions, abusing drugs, and overcharging.
Lack of parallelism. *Issuing unnecessary prescriptions* and *abusing drugs* are gerunds, verb forms that end in *–ing* and function like nouns. *Issuing unnecessary prescriptions* and *abusing drugs* are the first two items in a series of three items; all three items in the series should be gerunds as well.

30. **(B)** When he reached for the book, the ladder on which he stood slipped out from under him.

Ask yourself just who reached for the book. The ladder? No way! To correct this dangling participle, change the participial phrase into a subordinate clause.

31. **(B)** The water vole can be distinguished from the common rat by the smallness of its ears and the bluntness of its face.
Lack of parallelism. The noun phrase "the smallness of its ears" is the first item in a series of two. The other item in this series should be a plain noun phrase as well. To correct the error, you simply delete the words "looking at."

32. **(C)** Shakespeare wrote many plays that are now being presented on public television.
Comma splice. Use the process of elimination to answer this question. The original sentence incorrectly links two independent clauses with a comma (the dreaded comma splice). Therefore, you can eliminate Choice D. Choice A corrects the comma splice but changes the sentence's meaning. You can eliminate Choice A. Choice B corrects the comma splice but introduces a fresh error, a misplaced modifier. You can eliminate Choice B. Choice C corrects the comma splice and introduces no fresh errors. It is the correct answer.

33. **(D)** Correct as is
The original sentence is correct. The use of the conjunction *Although* signals a contrast between what you would expect and what is actually the case. Because most Californians believe in the possibility of an imminent earthquake, you would expect them to be frightened. They are not.

34. **(B)** Thinking that I had done poorly on the examination, I abandoned all hopes of winning the scholarship.
Dangling participle. Who was thinking? Certainly not the hopes! Ask yourself who abandoned all hopes of winning the scholarship. Clearly, "I" did. Choice B recasts the sentence, making the pronoun *I* the subject of the sentence and placing the opening participial phrase ("Thinking that I had done poorly on the examination") near the pronoun it modifies.

35. **(A)** At his advanced age, he found driving to the supermarket less strenuous than walking.
Lack of parallelism. Choice A correctly balances the gerund *driving* with the gerund *walking*.

36. **(A)** The setting sun slowly sank behind the snow-covered peaks of the towering mountains.
Sentence fragment. Removing the conjunction *As* corrects the sentence fragment.

37. **(D)** Contra, an Exciting, Communal Dance Form
A good title is neither too broad nor too narrow. The title *Contra Dancing in America Today* suggests that the essay discusses contra dancing as a national phenomenon, dealing with it from a historical perspective. The title is too broad in scope to be appropriate for this essay. You can eliminate Choice A. The title *How I Learned to Contra Dance* is too narrow in scope to be appropriate for this essay. You can eliminate Choice B. The title *Making Friends by Contra Dance* is appropriate as a title for the first paragraph, but inappropriate as a title for the second paragraph. Therefore, you can eliminate Choice C. The title *Contra, an Exciting, Communal Dance Form* covers all the bases: it refers both to the communal nature of contra dancing (the subject of paragraph 1) and the excitement and energy of contra dancing (the subject of paragraph 2). Choice D is the correct answer.

38. **(C)** Contra dancing, a sociable and exhilarating form of dance, gives dancers a unique sense of community.
Choice C correctly combines the two sentences into a single grammatical whole. In addition, it eliminates the adverb *really*, so that it no longer modifies the adjective *unique*. (Many writers consider *unique* an absolute adjective: something is either unique or it is *not* unique; there are no degrees of comparison.)

39. **(C)** Insert "however" after "dancing."
Look at the context in which the sentence under question is found. "For contra danc-

ing, live music is best" immediately follows a sentence about dancing to recorded music. To indicate the shift from talking about recorded music to talking about live music, you need a transition word that signals a contrast. The final sentence would read as follows: "For contra dancing, however, live music is best."

40. **(D)** throw in twirls or swing with extra energy
What specifically do the dancers do when they respond to the musicians' improvisations? They twirl, they spin, they swing faster: these are concrete examples of specific actions that the dancers perform.

41. **(B)** In turn,
The writer is describing a series of actions: one action leads to the next, which *in turn* leads to yet another action. The phrase *in turn* means in the proper order or sequence. It is used correctly here.

42. **(A)** You do not need to have a partner to attend a contra dance.
The subject of the second paragraph is the relationship between live music and contra dancing. A sentence about whether you need to bring a partner with you to attend the dance is inappropriate in this context.

43. **(A)** however
Look at the context in which the sentence under question is found. It immediately follows the opening sentence, which states that most people identify addiction with alcohol and drug addiction. The second sentence rejects what "most people" think: "The problem of addiction is not . . . limited to drugs and alcohol." It is setting up a contrast. The transitional word you want in this context is *however,* which signals such a contrast.

44. **(D)** Shopping addiction is a serious problem.
Use the process of elimination to answer this question. "Addiction is harmful" is far too broad a statement to summarize the passage's main point; the passage is discussing shopping addiction, not addiction in general. You can eliminate Choice A. The point

of the passage is that shopping addiction *is* harmful. You can eliminate Choice B. The statement that "no one really notices shopping addicts" is irrelevant to the passage's main point. You can eliminate Choice C. Only Choice D is left. It is the correct answer: the passage's main point is that shopping addiction is a serious problem.

45. **(A)** Consumer spending promotes the economic health of the nation.
The passage as a whole points out the dangers of compulsive consumer spending. A sentence in favor of consumer spending definitely would be out of place in the context.

46. **(B)** overcoming
To beat a shopping addiction is to conquer or overcome it.

47. **(C)** The need to put food on the table and clothes on one's back means that
What specific factors make it unavoidable that recovering shopping addicts will regularly face temptation? They need to buy food. They need to buy clothes. Therefore, they have to shop.

48. **(B)** Shopaholics risk financial ruin as a result of their addiction.
The opening paragraph clearly states that "Many compulsive shoppers build up substantial credit card debt that they cannot support, and so they wind up having to file for bankruptcy." Because of their shopping addiction, they borrow so much money that they end up bankrupt, ruined financially. This supports the statement that "Shopaholics risk financial ruin as a result of their addiction."

READING SUBTEST

1. **(D)** They agreed to divide what they caught with each other.
The four beasts agreed to go hunting, "sharing with each other whatever they found." Thus, *they agreed to divide what they caught with one another.*

2. **(B)** he respected their agreement
The Wolf ran down a stag. In other words, he had caught and killed a deer. Rather than

eating the deer by himself, he called his three comrades to join him. He was living up to their agreement; clearly, *he respected their agreement.*

3. **(B)** the Lion starts carving without being asked.
Even though the Wolf had killed the deer, the Lion takes the Wolf's place at the head of the table and starts to carve the deer. The Lion does not wait to be asked. The Lion does what he wants, assuming the others will give way to him. Just as the Lion ignores the others' wishes when he *starts carving without being asked*, he likewise ignores their wishes when he takes the Lion's share of the food. Thus, the Lion's starting to carve without being asked is a clue that enables us to predict how the story will turn out.

4. **(C)** selfish.
In taking the entire deer as his share, the Lion is clearly being *selfish*.

5. **(B)** threatening them
Consider the Lion's actions when he tells his comrades that now is the time to speak up. First, he glares at them very savagely. He growls, and he stretches his claws meaningfully. He is not simply inviting them to speak; instead, he is conveying the threat that, if they speak, they will have to face those powerful claws in a battle over the deer's carcass. Clearly he is *threatening them.*

6. **(D)** what the Lion took as his share
By the end of the story, it is clear to the reader that the Lion's share is the entire carcass of the deer.

7. **(D)** "Might makes right."
What gives the Lion the right to devour the entire deer, leaving nothing for his three comrades? The Lion's strength or might allows him to do what he wants, ignoring the rights and wrongs of the situation. Thus, *might makes right.*

8. **(C)** soapy water
With this and later passages, we will assume that you have read the passage to get a general idea of its meaning and to

have a sense of where in the passage to look for specific details to answer the individual questions. You can usually get a good idea of the contents of a paragraph by reading just its first sentence (generally the topic sentence of the paragraph), so your first skimming of the passage doesn't have to be complete or take a lot of time.
The very first sentence of the passage explains what "gray water" is: water left over after showers or baths or in washing machines. Such water is soapy and a bit dirty. Question 8 asks you for an example of gray water. The possible choices are:
A. Carbonated water. Not gray water. It is not something left over after washing. It is what you drink as sparkling water or seltzer.
B. Rain water. Not gray water. Rainwater, in fact, is usually quite clean.
C. Soapy water. This is the type of water left after showering or washing. Clearly, Choice C is an example of gray water.
D. Tap water. Not gray water. This is the water that comes out of the tap *before* you wash.

9. **(B)** increasing in quantity
The paragraph advises you to add soapy water to the amount of water you are allowed or allotted for irrigation. By doing so you stretch your irrigation water allotment, increasing it in quantity. The correct answer is B.

10. **(A)** drinking
Use the process of elimination to begin answering this question. The second paragraph of the passage says that gray water "can be used on your plants." Therefore, Choice B, *irrigating fields*, is a good use for gray water, as is Choice D, *watering houseplants*. You can eliminate Choices B and D. Choices A and C (*drinking* and *rinsing sidewalks*) are not mentioned in the passage, so you have to think a bit to see which one would be an appropriate use for gray water and which one would not. There is no obvious reason why you couldn't use slightly soapy water to rinse your sidewalks. There are several reasons why you probably

shouldn't drink the stuff. (At the very least, it would taste bad; at worst, the cleaning agents in the water might do you some real harm.) Clearly, the best answer is Choice A: *drinking* would not be a good use for gray water.

11. **(A)** contains borax soap

To answer this question, you should scan the passage looking for three key words: "irrigation," "chlorine," and "borax soap." You may remember seeing them in the second paragraph; you may even remember what the passage has to say about them. Even if you don't remember what the passage says, you can catch it on a second detailed reading as you check out each answer choice.

The second paragraph recommends that gray water be used for irrigation, but gives three points to remember. Point 2 is: "If the rinse water contains borax soap, do not use it for irrigation." Point 3 is: "If chlorine bleach is used in the rinse water, you can use it for irrigation" as long as you are careful to pour it on different spots each day. Thus, chlorine is all right to use (if you take some precautions); borax is not. The correct answer is Choice A.

12. **(C)** not put too much in any one spot

The passage states that "you should be sure to pour it on different spots each day." By doing so, you do not put too much in any one spot. The correct answer is C.

13. **(D)** pollute the water system

You can find what the health department wishes or requires in the second list of three points given in the passage. This list is introduced in the passage by the sentence "Plumbing and health codes also have a few requirements." Point 2 states that "There must not be any way for gray water to contaminate the water system." This suggests that Choice D is correct. To double-check, look at the other answers and see how they agree or disagree with the contents of the passage.

A. be used for irrigation. This is exactly what the passage suggests should be done with gray water, and nothing in the list of

plumbing and health code requirements says you should not do this.

B. be carried outdoors in buckets. This is the method Point 1 suggests you use to satisfy the plumbing and health requirements: "Use buckets or trash pails to carry it outdoors."

C. contain detergent or soap. Gray water by definition is used water that contains soap or detergent. It makes no sense for the health department to wish gray water not to contain these substances.

The only possible answer is Choice D. It is the correct answer.

14. **(D)** Use a garden hose siphon or buckets

The passage specifically states "You must not allow the gray water to flow onto your neighbor's property." Thus, Choice A is incorrect. Similarly, the passage warns the reader not to "pump used water into the sprinkler system." Choice B is incorrect. The passage also cautions the reader, "Don't rearrange your plumbing to lead the gray water outside." Choice C is incorrect. However, the passage does suggest the helpfulness of garden hose siphons to get gray water outside the house and recommends the use of buckets or trash pails. The correct answer is D.

15. **(B)** uneasiness

The writer states that when the dragon first showed up at her house, she "was a little bit nervous." Thus, her initial or first reaction to the Dragon Naturally Speaking software program was one of uneasiness.

16. **(A)** She speaks to it.

The writer spends "hour after hour talking to my dragon." Clearly, she speaks to it.

17. **(D)** indicates something unexpected

To have the dragon learn to recognize the writer's voice comes as a surprise to the writer. Here "even" is being used as an adverb modifying the verb "learned." It would be remarkable for a mythological beast to learn to recognize a human being's voice; it certainly is remarkable for a software program to recognize someone's voice.

Model Test B

18. **(C)** what she learned about fixing errors in the text

In the fourth paragraph, the writer states that she "had to learn how to help my dragon fix whatever he'd got wrong." She describes all of the methods that did not work, and then goes on to explain what does work. Thus, she is describing "what she learned about fixing errors in the text." The correct answer is C.

19. **(B)** give a visual equivalent of speaking in a loud voice.

By putting the word "yell" in capital letters, the writer makes the word look very big and emphatic. This is a visual equivalent of yelling or speaking in a loud voice.

20. **(B)** makes the writer feel good about her writing

At the end of the third paragraph, the writer states that the way the dragon pays attention to what she's saying makes her think that she has special things to say. In the concluding paragraph, she states that when she talks to her dragon, she feels her words come alive. Both these statements suggest that working with the software program makes the writer feel good about her writing. You can use the process of elimination to come up with the correct answer. The writer speaks to the software program, teaching it what to write down. The software program does not teach the writer what to say. You can eliminate Choice A. When the software program initially showed up at the writer's house, the writer was nervous about using it. Therefore, working with the software program was not something the writer always wanted to do. You can eliminate Choice C. Although the writer can spend hour after hour talking to her dragon, nothing in the paragraph suggests that working with the software program takes too much of the writer's time. You can eliminate Choice D. Only Choice B is left. It is the correct answer.

21. **(D)** It is a friendly helper.

To this writer, the voice recognition software program is more than a useful tool.

The writer does not care that it was manufactured. She thinks of it in personal terms as someone who pays attention to her and encourages her to think that she has special things to say. Thus, to her the dragon is a friendly helper, not a captive slave or powerful beast.

22. **(A)** Statements I and II only

Use the process of elimination to answer this question. In the paragraph on "Light," it is stated that leafy vegetables, such as lettuce, can stand more shade than root vegetables, and that root vegetables in turn can stand more shade than vegetable fruit plants, such as tomatoes. Thus, it logically follows that lettuce does better in shade than tomatoes do. Statement I is true. Therefore, you can eliminate Choice C. Likewise, the opening sentence of the section on "Hardening" asserts that "plants should be gradually 'hardened,' or toughened, for two weeks before being moved outdoors." If indoor plants should be hardened or toughened for two weeks, clearly they need this toughening time. Statement II is true. Therefore, you can eliminate Choice B. The second paragraph, however, states that although chives do well in six-inch pots, radishes flourish in ten-inch pots. Statement III is false. Therefore, you can eliminate Choice D. Only Choice A is left. It is the correct answer.

23. **(A)** putting it in a cooler environment

In the next-to-last paragraph you are advised to harden your seedlings "by withholding water and lowering the temperature." One way to lower the temperature of a plant is to put the plant in a cooler environment.

24. **(B)** get them off to an early start.

Think of what happens when you get a jump on your competition—you get a head start. Similarly, when you give plants a jump on the growing season, you get them to start growing earlier than normal: you get them off to an early start.

25. **(C)** Statements II and III only

To answer this question, you discover which statements are false by eliminating those statements that you can prove to be true. The paragraph entitled "Starting Plants Indoors" states that you can "give some plants a jump on the growing season by starting them indoors." Thus, it is true that some plants do well if you start them indoors. Statement I clearly is NOT false; it is true. You immediately can eliminate Choices A, B, and D; the only possible answer is Choice C.

26. **(C)** A novice gardener
Neither an experienced farmer nor an authority on gardening would need such basic information on growing vegetables. Choices A and D are incorrect. Students of botany would have more interest in plants as scientific specimens than in plants as garden crops. Choice B is incorrect. Remember, the title of the passage is "Minigardens for Vegetables." It is intended for an audience of novice or beginner gardeners.

27. **(D)** introduce Seattle's geographic location
Use the process of elimination to answer this question. Though the opening paragraph mentions several of Seattle's scenic attractions (Lake Washington, the Olympic Mountains, the Cascade Range), it merely names them; it does not praise them. You can cross off Choice A. Though the earliest explorers would have seen the mountains, they could not have seen the system of locks and canals built by later settlers. You can cross off Choice B. The opening paragraph explains nothing about Seattle's economy. You can cross off Choice C. With its emphasis on directions and physical dimensions ("to the west," "to the east," "18-mile-long"), the paragraph clearly tries to give the reader a sense of the city's physical setting and introduce Seattle's geographic location. The correct answer is Choice D.

28. **(B)** after having taken an overland route
Although the Washington coast was first glimpsed from the sea, Seattle's first settlers did not belong to a maritime expedition. Eliminate Choice A. Asa Mercer recruited brides for the unmarried lumbermen and traders 14 years after the first families set-

tled Alki Point. Eliminate Choice C. The system of locks and canals was built many years after Seattle's founding in 1851. Eliminate Choice D. Choice B is correct. The first families had "an entire continent to cross." They thus reached what was to be Seattle after having taken an overland route.

29. **(B)** because the new site offered more shelter from wind
The last sentence of paragraph 2 indicates why the first families moved their original settlement. The town's original location was "windswept." The settlers relocated the town "next to…protected waters." Clearly, they wanted more shelter from the wind.

30. **(A)** a place from which one departs on a journey
The news of the discovery of gold in the Klondike led thousands of people to head for Alaska to get rich quick. For these hopeful prospectors, Seattle was a jumping-off point, a place in which they could equip themselves for the gold fields and from which they could depart on their northern journey.

31. **(C)** better housing sites
The "tide flats were filled and steep slopes were leveled to create more livable areas." Given the sudden growth in population, Seattle needed more dry, level places on which people could build homes. In other words, the city needed better housing sites.

32. **(C)** fiction
Although the narrator refers to herself as a "weary historian," the tale she narrates is not a history but a fictional story. Unlike a writer of nonfiction (history or biography, for example), the narrator does not have to stick to the facts; instead, she can present her gentle reader with a melodramatic conclusion involving earthquakes or with a less dramatic but equally fictional conclusion in which all the characters live happily ever after.

33. **(B)** prevent her readers from bothering her with questions
The writer is attempting to "forestall the usual question" about the fate of her characters. By describing her characters' ends, she

satisfies her readers' curiosity and prevents them from bothering her with questions.

34. **(C)** professions
To prosper in one's calling is to do well in one's profession or vocation.

35. **(B)** selfless
Nan dedicates her life to the service of others. How would you describe such a person? Altruistic, unselfish—in a word, selfless.

36. **(C)** from a bullet wound
Carefully read the sentence that describes Dan's death. What causes his death? He is "shot defending" his people; in other words, he dies from a bullet wound. However, even though he dies a violent death, he looks peaceful in death, as if he is sleeping.

37. **(C)** eating habits
What do we know about Stuffy? He dies of an apoplexy or stroke "after a public dinner." This suggests that Stuffy habitually stuffs himself with food, overeating until his body finally collapses after one banquet too many.

38. **(A)** Teddy outshone them all
To eclipse others is to surpass or outshine them. By becoming a famous and eloquent clergyman, young Teddy outshines the other boys, who have less prominent careers.

39. **(D)** sequels
The narrator closes with the wish that "the curtain fall forever on the March family." The image here comes from the theater. The curtain will not rise again to reveal the new adventures of these characters. The story of the March family is over; there will be no follow-ups or sequels.

40. **(C)** current officeholder
An incumbent is somebody currently in office, the officeholder or elected official.

41. **(B)** developers
By requiring developers to build a set number of units of affordable housing, Riles hopes to help low-income home buyers and working-class families. By stressing the need for after-school programs and tutorial support, he hopes to help public school students. None of his suggested reforms explicitly benefits developers.

42. **(B)** Statements I and III only
Use the process of elimination to answer this question. Putting together the information contained in the first three paragraphs, you can easily infer that Riles has been a more active campaigner than Brown: Riles has been scrambling; Brown has been low-key. Thus, Statement I is true, and you can eliminate Choice C. The second paragraph states that Brown defeated 10 mayoral opponents in 1998: he was running for mayor, not governor, in 1998. Therefore, Statement II is false, and you can immediately eliminate Choices A and D. The correct answer must be Choice B.

43. **(D)** All of the statements
Again, use the process of elimination to choose the correct answer. Statement I is false: Brown did send out a scattering of mailings. Therefore, you can eliminate Choice C. Statement II is false: it was not Riles, but Brown who was concerned with burdening developers with excessive requirements. Therefore, you can eliminate Choice B. Statement III is also false: only some of Oakland's 54,000 students attend charter schools. Therefore, you can eliminate Choice A. Only Choice D is left; it is the correct answer.

44. **(D)** deceptive
Something that is "more shadow than substance" has less substance to it than has been claimed for it. Thus, Riles asserts that Brown's achievements are deceptive: they are exaggerated, illusory achievements, not solid ones.

45. **(D)** flawed administrative practices
The opening paragraph states that, although the various governments attempted to treat the Indians justly, the governments' "good intentions were never adequately administered." In other words, the injustices suffered by California's Indians were due to flawed or faulty administrative practices.

46. **(A)** large numbers of them died
The passage's second paragraph states that many Indians were held in peonage (this means that they were agricultural workers

who were unable to leave the land they worked on) and that "mission life . . . cut their numbers by over 70 percent." This means that, for every hundred Indians who came under the control of the Spanish missionaries, at the end of the Spanish regime fewer than 30 were left. Clearly, Spanish mission life was so hard on the Indians that "large numbers of them died."

47. **(C)** they had no ratified treaties with the federal government

Scan the passage for the key date "1860" or a phrase indicating the mid-19th century. Does the opening sentence of the next-to-last paragraph jump out at you? Describing the situation of the Indians at that time, it states that "by 1860 the Indians of California were destitute, landless, and without any ratified treaties with the federal government." Checking the answers, you can immediately rule out Choice A: by 1860 the Spanish and Mexican regimes were past. You can also eliminate Choice B: once California became part of the United States, its Indians were not foreign nationals or illegal aliens, but natives who "were to become citizens." Similarly, you can cross out Choice D: by 1860, the Indians were landless; they had been driven away from their original territories. It was not until the early 1900s that the federal government purchased homesites for them in the northern and central parts of the state. Only choice C is left. It is the correct answer. Lacking ratified treaties with the federal government, the Indians were at a major disadvantage.

48. **(B)** the federal government

The homesites or rancherias were purchased in the early decades of the 20th century at the insistence of a church group. The next-to-last paragraph describes the origins of this program. The second sentence of the paragraph clearly states that the federal government purchased the homesites. The government owned the lands. Thus, Choice B is correct.

49. **(B)** their stability as homesites from which the Indians could not be driven away

Use the process of elimination to answer this question. Were the rancherias near ancestral Indian hunting grounds in Southern California? No. They were in the northern and central part of the state, not the south. Cross out Choice A. Were the rancherias capable of supporting a large Indian population? No. They were "generally inadequate to support the residents." Cross out Choice C. Were they ample or extensive in size? No. They were small. Cross out Choice D. Only Choice B is left. As the passage's last sentence states, "they were places to which the Indians could move, reasonably secure in the knowledge that no one could drive them away." Thus, they offered security or stability as homesites. The correct answer is Choice B.

50. **(A)** humorous

What we have here is a play on words. The Mayans and Aztecs considered chocolate the food of the gods. We commonly associate gods with heaven. Thus, the food of the gods might playfully be called heavenly. In stating that "today's lovers of sweets would not find the earliest chocolate heavenly," the writer is attempting to be humorous.

51. **(D)** scornful

In describing the Aztec beverage as "fitter for hogs than men," the explorers were being scornful or mocking.

52. **(C)** after the drink had been sweetened.

The passage states that once sugar was "added to the mix," people valued the hot chocolate drinks. Thus, the attitude toward chocolate changed "after the drink had been sweetened."

53. **(C)** ask a question

Use a process of elimination to answer this question. Does the passage describe a process? Yes. It describes how ground chocolate, "was mixed with water and spices including chili peppers" to make a beverage. You can cross out Choice A. Does the passage mention a date? Yes. It mentions the year 1526. You can cross out Choice B. Does the passage name a historical figure? Yes. It mentions the explorer

Cortez. You can cross out Choice D. Does the passage ask a question? No, it does not. By process of elimination, the correct answer is C.

54. **(C)** feature story
Again, use the process of elimination to answer this question. The passage is dealing straightforwardly with facts; it is not taken from a work of fiction. You can cross out Choice A. The passage is focused on chocolate, a food; it is not focused on a person. It is not taken from a biography. You can cross out Choice B. The passage is not dry and technical; it is not taken from a technical report. You can cross out Choice D. Although the passage deals straightforwardly with facts, it is light in tone and even humorous. This suggests that it is most likely taken from a feature story, an article written with a personal slant.

55. **(A)** difficult
Complex means difficult or complicated. Think of "a complex problem."

56. **(C)** region nearby
Vicinity means a region nearby or surrounding area. Think of having "no stores in the vicinity."

57. **(D)** extend across
To span means to extend or reach across. Think of "spanning a gap."

58. **(D)** wicked
Corrupt means wicked or dishonest. Think of "a corrupt judge."

59. **(B)** peril
Hazard means peril or danger. Think of "fire hazard."

60. **(B)** give power
To authorize means to give power or authority. Think of "an authorized biography."

61. **(C)** change somewhat
To modify means to change somewhat or alter. Think of "modifying a contract."

62. **(A)** put trust
To confide in someone is to put trust in that person. Think of "confiding secrets" to a friend.

63. **(D)** consider carefully
To ponder is to consider something carefully, to weigh its importance. Think of "pondering important decisions."

64. **(D)** separate from others
To isolate something is to separate it or set it apart. Think of being "isolated in quarantine."

65. **(B)** Feminist leader Gloria Steinem challenged any man who dared to observe the convention of holding a door open for her. Convention as used in both sentences means an accepted custom or practice, a usual way of doing things. It is a noun.

66. **(A)** How many young people today have sufficient character to resist peer pressure? Character as used in both sentences means courage or moral fiber. It is a noun.

67. **(C)** When Joe won the lottery, he immediately paid off the balance of his mortgage. Balance as used in both sentences means the remainder or what is left over. It is a noun.

68. **(C)** Painter, inventor, poet, engineer, Leonardo da Vinci was a master of many disciplines.
Disciplines as used in both sentences means branches of learning or academic fields. It is a noun. Think of "scholarly disciplines."

69. **(D)** As soon as I turn 18 years old, I intend to register to vote.
Register as used in both sentences means to enroll or sign up. It is a verb.

70. **(A)** Influential commentators are able to mold public opinion.
Mold as used in both sentences means to influence or shape. It is a verb.

71. **(B)** I stripped the sheets from the guest room bed to spare my hostess the bother. Spare as used in both sentences means to save from strain or discomfort. It is a verb.

72. **(D)** Despite her wandering attention, she still managed to catch the lecturer's general drift.
Drift as used in both sentences means the general meaning or sense. It is a noun.

73. **(A)** Too high a level of sound can damage people's eardrums.
Level as used in both sentences is a measure or degree of intensity. It is a noun.

74. **(D)** It was time for the hiker to shoulder his backpack and head down the hill.
Shoulder as used in both sentences means to support or carry on the shoulders. It is a verb.

75. **(A)** wavered
Someone who vacillates goes back and forth, wavering between alternative choices. Think of "vacillating about a decision."

76. **(D)** rejected
Dismissed as used here means rejected someone as not being worth considering. Think of "dismissing a suitor."

77. **(A)** outgoing
Gregarious means outgoing or sociable. Think of "gregarious partygoers."

78. **(C)** unhindered
Something unimpeded is unhindered; it is not slowed down or prevented. Think of "unimpeded progress."

79. **(D)** dwindled
To flag is to dwindle or wane. Think of "flagging energy."

80. **(C)** fake
Spurious means fake or bogus. Think of "spurious claims."

81. **(C)** unknown
Obscure as used here means unknown or undistinguished; it is the opposite of famous. Think of "an obscure street musician."

82. **(C)** truthfulness
Veracity means truthfulness or honesty. Think of "trusting someone's veracity."

83. **(B)** insignificant
Negligible means insignificant or trifling. Think of "negligible expenses."

84. **(B)** longed
To pine for something is to long or yearn for it. Think of "pining for one's family."

Mathematics Section

1. **(C)** 2.3
Convert both terms to simple fractions, rather than mixed numbers, and then divide. For the first term, the fractions need to be expressed with a common denominator, in this case 12, the least common denominator of $\frac{1}{4}$ and $\frac{5}{3}$:

$$\frac{1}{4} + \frac{(3+2)}{3} = \frac{1}{4} + \frac{5}{3} = \frac{3 \times 1 + 4 \times 5}{12} = \frac{23}{12}$$

The second term as a simple fraction is $\frac{5}{6}$. To divide $\frac{23}{12}$ by $\frac{5}{6}$, multiply $\frac{23}{12}$ by the reciprocal of $\frac{5}{6}$, namely $\frac{6}{5}$:

$$\frac{23}{12} \times \frac{6}{5} = \frac{23}{2} \times \frac{1}{5} = \frac{23}{10} = 2\frac{3}{10} = 2.3$$

2. **(A)** $(x+1)^2$
Work outwards from the innermost nested parentheses, simplifying as you go. That is, first simplify $(2 - 2x) - (1 - x)$ before multiplying it by $1 + x$:

$$
\begin{array}{r}
-(1 - x) = -1 + x \\
+2 - 2x \\
\hline
1 - x
\end{array}
$$

Now, multiply this result by $(1 + x)$

$(1 - x) \times (1 + x) = 1 \times (1 + x) - x \times (1 + x) = 1 + x - (x + x^2) = 1 + x - x - x^2 = 1 - x^2$

Finally, add the second term, which itself simplifies to $2x^2 + 2x$: $1 - x^2 + 2x^2 + 2x = 1 + x^2 + 2x$, or in a more standard order: $x^2 + 2x + 1$.
This clearly doesn't match Choice C or D; you can pick the right one (A) if you remember one or both of the factorizations $x^2 - 1 = (x + 1)(x - 1)$ and $x^2 + 2x + 1 = (x + 1)(x + 1)$, but even if don't have these memorized, you should be able to see that $(x + 1)(x - 1)$ has to have −1 as its constant (no factors of x) term. You shouldn't need to take the time to multiply out either of the two potential answers.

3. **(C)** 30%
The slope from the trailhead to the summit of the mountain is the vertical distance

(4320 meters – 2060 meters) divided by the horizontal distance (4.5 miles), that is, the "rise" over the "run." These two numbers need to be in the same units for the division to make sense. The vertical distance is 2260 meters or 2.26 kilometers. You need to either convert this distance to miles, or convert the horizontal distance from miles to kilometers. Converting to kilometers is probably easier (it is easier to multiply 4.5 times 1.6 than to divide 2.26 by 1.6).

$$4.5 \text{ miles} \times 1.6 \ \frac{\text{km}}{\text{mile}} = 7.2 \text{ km}$$

The slope is 2.26/7.2. You don't need to do a long division to select the correct answer. Just notice that 2.26 is significantly less than half (50%) of 7.2 (which would be 3.6) and just a bit less than one-third (33%) (which would be 2.4). Choices A and B confuse the slope computed as a decimal value (0.3) and the percentage equivalent (30%); Choices B and D are incorrect because they used 4.5 miles, instead of 7.2 km, as the "run" for the rise/run calculation.

4. **(B)** 0.30 mm/yr

The change each year is given in the graph with open circle markers, mostly contained between 0 and 0.75 on the sea-level change scale (the left-side scale here). Choice D is clearly ruled out; the units are wrong for a rate of increase in any case. (The scale on the right gives the total change in mm over the period, for the graph with solid circle representing the data points.) You could make an estimate of the average change by moving your answer sheet up the graph and seeing how the open-circled points are distributed above and below the level of the three remaining answers. However, it is simpler to make your estimate using the solid-circled "sea-level rise" graph. This starts just above 0 for 1961, and reaches approximately 13 mm in 1998. That is a change of 13 mm in 38 years, a bit less than 13/39 = 1/3 mm/yr (Choice B). For 0.5 mm/yr over 38 years, the total rise would be 38/2 = 19; for 0.25 mm/yr over that time period, the total rise would be 19/2 = 9.5

mm/yr. Choice B is the only reasonable estimate.

5. **(D)** Sea level tended to rise throughout 1961–1998.

Consider each statement in turn, and see how it matches, or does not match, the graphs:
A. *Sea level did not change . . . .* In fact, there was change each year from the year before, and over the full period, most change was in the direction of increased sea level. A is incorrect.
B. *Sea level rose every year . . . .* In fact, some years (notably 1964 and 1965) had sea level changes less than 0 mm/yr (the scale on the left axis starts at –0.5, not at 0!) B is incorrect.
C. *Sea level fell more than 5 years . . . .* In fact, the only years for which it is clear that the level fell were 1964, 1965, and 1976; the change was near zero, possibly a bit below, for 1983 and 1988. No other years were less than zero; all but 5 years out of 38 had a rise in sea level. C is incorrect.
D. *Sea level tended to rise . . . .* With sea level rising in all but 5 years, the graph has an almost continual rise. If you try to match the data with the edge of your answer sheet used as a rule, you can get a very good match on the first 25 years (1961–1985) by connecting those two end points (for a rise of 6 mm in 25 years), with the remaining points tending to fit an even steeper slope.

6. **(B)** 9

Eliminate the answers that can't be correct. Choice D (17) is impossible because that is the sum of the lengths of the other two sides of a triangle, and one of the basic facts about triangles is that each side is less than the sum of the other two. Choices A and C (6 and 11) would make the triangle an "isosceles" triangle, with two sides the same length. The equal sides would make the triangle more "symmetrical" than the one in the diagram, with angles opposite the equal sides also equal. The angles in the diagram are clearly unequal. Only Choice B is possible. You can confirm that by using your answer sheet to compare *AC* with *AB*.

7. **(B)** 70 inches.
The total number of boys in the class is 10 (add the numbers in the "#" column of the table). The median is the height at which half of the boys are taller and half shorter; that would be the height mid-way between the 5th and 6th tallest in the table. Counting up from 63 inches, there are 4 boys up to a height of 69 inches, and the 5th and 6th are both at 70 inches.

8. **(C)** 71 inches.
The "mode" in a distribution of data values like the table of heights is the value which has the largest number of samples in the table (or sometimes, a range of values with the largest number of samples among other ranges of the same size). Sometimes, there are bimodal distributions with more than one mode. However, in this case, there is a single data value with the largest number of boys' heights (3 boys at 71 inches).

9. **(C)** 68.6 inches.
To calculate the mean, you can add the heights of all 10 boys and divide by 10. Don't forget that there are 10 values! $63 + 65 + 65 + 69 + 70 + 70 + 71 + 71 + 71 + 73 = 686$, mean $= 688/10 = 68.8$
Note: it is probably easier to figure this out by adding the differences of the heights above the shortest height of 63 inches, and then adding the mean difference to 63 to get the final result. You can do this by making a running total of the differences next to the table:

Height (inches)	Number	Difference	Total	Note
63	1	0	0	
65	2	4	4	$2 \times (65 - 63)$
69	1	6	10	
70	2	14	24	$2 \times (70 - 63)$
71	3	24	48	$3 \times (71 - 63)$
73	1	10	58	

Thus, the mean difference is 5.8 inches, so the mean height is $63 + 5.8 = 68.8$ inches.

10. **(D)**

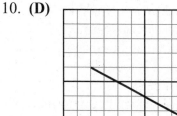

The equation of the line is in the "slope-intercept" form, $y = -x/2 - 1$. When x is 0, the line intercepts (crosses) the y-axis, in this case, at $y = -1$. Choice B also intercepts the axis at -1, but it has a different slope. The slope of the line is given by the coefficient of x in this form (where the coefficient of y is 1), namely $-1/2$. As x increases two units to the right, y decreases by 1 (changes by -1). Choice B also has a negative slope, but in that case the decrease in y is the same amount as the increase in x.

11. **(B)** 25%
Use your answer sheet to align vertically across the graph for the start of September (the large "tick" 2/3 of the way along the data axis) and mark that position on the 2005 graph and the "average sea ice extent" reference graph. Then mark where those heights are on the vertical axis (again, use the answer sheet, this time keeping parallel to the horizontal axis at the height of your marks on the two graphs). You should find that the Sept. 1 extent of sea ice for the reference period was a bit less than 7.5 million square km, and for 2005 somewhat more than 5.5 million square km. The difference is close to (somewhat less than) 2 million square km. Therefore the change is a decrease of approximately 2/7.5. You can rule out the wrong answers fairly quickly without doing a long division here:
A *wrong*; 10% decrease would be 7.5/10 = 0.75, much less than 2
B *close*; 25% decrease would be 7.5/4 (or more simply, 15/8), a bit less than 2

C *wrong*; 33% decrease would be 7.5/3 = 2.5, but we know the decrease is < 2
D *wrong* – must be higher than C, which we've already seen is too high.
The answer must be B.

12. **(C)** The extent of sea ice began to increase again by the end of September
All the pre-2005 graphs reach a low point and begin rising during the September portion of the graph. The graph for 2005 is a bit lower than the earlier ones, but it shares the same general shape for the portion shown, and the same general climate pattern can be expected to continue through the end of the year. Each of the other descriptions (A, B, and D) would need some special cause, and the graph has no indication of any unusual circumstances that would change the pattern.

13. **(B)** 85°
The sum of the angles of the triangle must be 180°; the two known angles have 55 + 40 = 95 degrees. The third angle must have 180 − 95 = 85 degrees.

14. **(C)** 14
Find the change from each number to the next in the sequence:

from 8 to 6	subtract 2	−2
from 6 to 10	add 4	+4
from 10 to 4	subtract 6	−6
from 4 to 12	add 8	+8
from 12 to 2	subtract 10	−10

To follow this pattern, the next number should add 12, to give 2 + 12 = 14.

15. **(B)** 4
In an unknown number of years ("x"), the mother's age will be twice the daughter's. The mother is now 62 and the daughter 29. Add x years to each and make an equation:

$62 + x = 2(29 + x)$ $62 + x = 58 + 2x$
Subtracting x from both sides, and then 58, gives $x = 4$.

16. **(C)** 75 miles
The towns are 3/4 inch apart on the map, and 1 inch stands for 100 miles; therefore, the towns are really 3/4 × 100 miles = 75 miles apart.

17. **(C)** 4.3 gallons
Al must get enough paint to cover the area of the wall twice over. The area is that of a rectangle 59 feet by 15 feet *minus* the area of the two circular holes. The holes are 4 feet in diameter, so each has a radius of 2 feet. The area of each circular hole is πr^2 or, in this case, $\pi \times 2 \times 2 = 4\pi$ square feet. Each circle has an area of about 4 × 3.14 . . . square feet, or roughly $12\frac{1}{2}$ square feet. The two circles together take about 25 square feet from the total area of the rectangle. That is 59 × 15 = 885 square feet (notice that it is easier to calculate this as 60 × 15 = 900 *minus* 15 than to use brute force to do the multiplication). Subtracting the circle area of 25 square feet, the wall has 860 square feet to be painted. Two coats require 1,720 square feet of coverage, and each gallon covers 400 square feet. So the final answer is the result of dividing 1,720 square feet by 400:

$$\begin{array}{r} 4.3 \\ 400)\overline{1720.00} \\ \underline{1600} \\ 120\ 0 \end{array}$$

18. **(B)** 0.0008312
Moving the decimal point in 8.312×10^{-4} one place to the left, increases the exponent of 10 by 1; that is, $8.312 \times 10^{-4} = 0.8312 \times 10^{-3} = 0.08312 \times 10^{-2} = 0.008312 \times 10^{-1}$. One last move left gives the final answer: 0.0008312.

19. **(B)** 1,320
The number of ways to pick out 3 of 12 things is called the number of "permutations" of 12 things taken 3 at a time. There is a formula for this, $P(12,3) = 12!/(12 − 3)!$ The "!" means "multiply by all the integers from the one in front of the ! down to 1." However, you do not need this formula to figure out the result. You have to choose three different colors. There are 12 choices for the first one; after that there are 11 left for the second color. Finally, there are 10 colors left for the third one. That gives:

12 × 11 × 10 = 132 × 10 = 1,320.

20. **(C)** How many days per month should be scheduled for cataloging?
The information given in the question only mentions the 72 books currently needing cataloging. There is no information on how many books will come in on a regular basis, or if there is some other backlog, or any kind of information that could be used to make a schedule of the number of days per month to be devoted to cataloging. In case this seems a bit uncertain, you should check over the other choices to confirm that they can be figured out from the data:
A. What is the shortest time, in days, that it would take them, working together, to complete the cataloging of this set of books? All the information is available: they can catalog 6 + 2 books per hour (if both of them do the work), for 3 hours a day. That gives the number of books per day, and dividing the 72 books by that rate gives the number of days.
B. What is the shortest time, in days, that it would take the assistant to do the cataloging by herself? Same reasoning as for Choice A, just omit the librarian.
C. What is the maximum average rate, in books per day, at which the librarian and his assistant can catalog books? Since you know the rate per hour at which the two catalog books, you can find their average rate per hour, and multiplying by three, you can get the average rate per day at which they can do the cataloging.

21. **(B)** 13
The shortest distance from *A* to *D* is along the straight line between them. This is the hypotenuse of a right triangle. (Extend *AB* to the right and draw a line parallel to *BC* to complete a rectangle.) Since the horizontal leg *AE* is 12, and the vertical leg *ED* is 5, this is a 5-12-13 right triangle, and the distance *AD* = 13. You can use the Pythagorean Theorem if you don't remember about 5-12-13 right triangles.

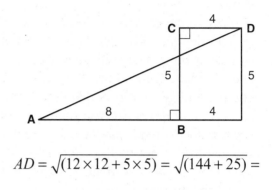

$$AD = \sqrt{(12 \times 12 + 5 \times 5)} = \sqrt{(144 + 25)} =$$

$$\sqrt{169} = 13$$

22. **(D)** 37
The average age is the sum of the men's ages divided by 3. This can be stated in an equation with the unknown age *a* of the third man:

$$\frac{(32 + 39 + a)}{3} = 36$$

Simplify this in stages to find *a*:
(32 + 39) + a = (3 × 36) = 108;
a = 108 − 71 = 37.

23. **(A)** 1/2
Compare the usage for Bakersfield (the top bar of the chart) with Santa Barbara (the bottom bar). The top bar extends nearly to the value of 350 gallons per person per day on the horizontal scale. The bar for Santa Barbara lies between 150 and 200. Half of 350 would be 175, which is a reasonable guess for Santa Barbara. All the other choices would be too small (for example, 1/3 of 350 ≈ 127).

24. **(A)** Eureka
Move a pencil or piece of paper to touch the Los Angeles bar on the right, and look to see which of the cities named as choices has a bar that doesn't reach as far as your marker. This is fairly easy since all the cities named are near L.A. in the chart. You will see that only Eureka has a bar that ends to the left (signifying lower water use than in L.A.).

25. **(B)** 7

A piece of paper helps with this question, as with the previous one. Place the paper so that its bottom edge is along the scale and its right edge is at the 200 mark. Then count the number of bars that go past the right edge of the paper. You should count six bars that extend past the paper, and also see that the bar for the East Bay reaches the paper (if you shift it slightly to the left, you'll see the end of the East Bay bar), making a total of seven cities with water usage of 200 or more.

26. **(B)** 3.901×10^{12}

You can assume that the digits are correct in all of the choices; the question is placement of the decimal point and the power of 10. When multiplying, you add the exponents of 10.

$$8 \times 10^{-4} \times 4 \times 10^{15} = 8 \times 4 \times 10^{(15-4)} =$$
$$32 \times 10^{11}$$

Therefore, Choice C (39.01×10^{11}) is the correct numerical value for the answer, but standard scientific notation uses a single digit before the decimal point. Moving the decimal point one to the left from 39.01 to 3.901 implies multiplying by a factor of 10 ($39.01 \times 10^{11} = 3.901 \times 10 \times 10^{11} = 3.901 \times 10^{12}$). The correct answer is Choice B.

27. **(C)** $3\frac{1}{5}$ hours

The slower car is 48 miles ahead of the faster car. The faster car is going 65 mph and the slower one 50 mph; that is, the faster car is gaining on the slower one at $(65 - 50) = 15$ mph. If x stands for the number of hours needed to overtake the slower car, the *distance* to be covered is 48 miles and the *rate* is 15. Since *distance* = *rate* × *time*, $48 = 15x$, and $x = 48/15 = 16/5 = 3\frac{1}{5}$ hours.

28. **(B)** −1

Find the two slopes and then calculate their product. The slope of a line is its *rise* (vertical change) divided by the *run* (horizontal change). To figure this for the two lines shown, try to find convenient points on the lines by using a piece of paper or a pencil to match points on the line with the tick marks on the x and y axes. Line A rises from the origin a vertical distance of 3 units in a horizontal change of 4 units; the slope of $A = 3/4$. Line B drops 4 units in moving right 3 units; its slope is negative, $−4/3$. The product of the two slopes is $3/4 \times −4/3 = −12/12 = −1$.

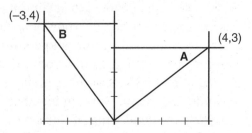

29. **(D)** 60 cubic feet

You need to *estimate* the volume of the cylinder; the exact value involves π, and all choices are suspiciously round numbers, so you need only use an approximate value for π, say 3.1 or 3.14. The volume of the cylinder is its circular area times its height, $V = \pi r^2 h$. The radius of the cylinder is 2 feet (the question states that the barrel is "4 feet across," so its diameter is 4 feet), and it is 5 feet high. $V = \pi(2 \times 2)5 = 20\pi \approx 20 \times 3.14 \approx 63$. This is closer to Choice D than to any of the other choices.

30. **(B)** 20 cm

If the shorter piece has length x, the longer has length $4x$, and the total length is $x + 4x = 5x = 1$ meter $= 100$ cm. Therefore, $x = 100$ cm / 5 $= 20$ cm.

31. **(B)** 1999

Note that all the bars stretch between 0 and another value so that the length of the bar is a measure of the purchases, depreciation, or net investment. The only year in which the black net investment bar goes below 0 is 1999. You can check this by seeing that 1999 is the only year in which the depreciation bar (the gray middle bar of each group) is taller than the bar for purchases.

32. **(A)** 1998

When purchases are $10 billion more than depreciation, the net investment is (positive) $10 billion. In the graph, the difference between the left bar (purchases, in white) and the middle bar (depreciation, in gray) is the black net investment bar on the right. Look for a black bar that just reaches the $10 billion tick mark on the vertical scale of the graph. The only possibility is 1998.

33. **(B)** $12,000

Write the facts given in the question as equations. If you let c, s, and f stand for the county, state, and federal shares in the total cost, you get

$c + s + f = \$132,000$

$s = 2c$

$f = 4s = 8c$

Rewriting the total cost entirely in terms of c (the unknown you need for the answer) gives

$c + 2c + 8c = 11c = \$132,000$

$c = \$132,000 / 11 = \$12,000$

34. **(D)** 36

To figure out the pattern in the numbers given, look at the difference at each step:

$$3 - 1 = 2$$
$$6 - 3 = 3$$
$$10 - 6 = 4$$
$$15 - 10 = 5$$
$$21 - 15 = 6$$

The difference increases by one at each step. The next number in the sequence will be the seventh, and it will be $21 + 7 = 28$. The question asks for the *eighth* number, which will be $28 + 8 = 36$.

35. **(C)** The birth rate decreased steadily from 1960 to 1985.

Check each of the statements, looking for one that you can confirm to be false by looking at the graph:

A. The infant death rate decreased steadily. TRUE. The infant death rate is shown by the gray bars on the graph, and each one is lower than the one before it (to its left).

B. Births exceeded deaths by at least five per thousand for the period shown. TRUE. The line labeled "Birth rate" is always above the 15 per 1,000 line on the graph, while the line labeled "Death rate" is always below or just at the 10 per 1,000 line. The gap between them is always at least five (per 1,000).

C. The birth rate decreased steadily from 1960 to 1985. FALSE. The birth rate line drops from 1960 to 1967, then rises to 1970. The decrease does not continue all the way to 1985.

D. The death rate in 1985 was less than it had been in 1960. Probably TRUE, but hard to tell from the thick lines on the graph—in 1960, the line is close to 10 per 1,000 and in 1985 maybe just a little bit lower than that.

In any case, C is obviously false and must be the correct choice for this question.

36. **(B)** 2 million

The death rate in 1968 was very close to 10 deaths per thousand, or about 1% ($10/1000 = 1/100$). Since the population was about 200 million, the number of deaths that year had to be about 1% of 200 million, or

$$\frac{1}{100} \times 200 \text{ million} = 2 \text{ million}$$

37. **(C)** 40%

In 1960 the infant death rate (given by the gray bar) was about 26 per thousand, and in 1985 it had decreased to about 10 to 11 per thousand. You can make a close guess about the percentage by rounding these numbers to 25 and 10; then the 1985 value is about $10/25 = 2/5$ of the 1960 value, and $2/5 = 40\%$. If you use 26 for the 1960 value and carry out the long division, you can stop as soon as you see that the answer is closer to 40% than to any other of the choices. Be careful to use the gray bars (the infant death rate) and not the lower line, which is the overall death rate.

38. **(C)** 1970

Look on the graph of birth rates for a year between 1960 and 1975 where the curve rises to show a higher birth rate. The bump in the graph occurs at 1970.

39. **(B)** 24
The area of a triangle is $\frac{1}{2}$ (base × height). In this figure, the base is a distance of 6 along the line $y = -3$ from $x = -2$ to $x = 4$, and the height is 8 [5 units from the vertex at (2,5) down to the x-axis and 3 more to reach the base]. Therefore, the area is $\frac{1}{2}(6 \times 8) = 48/2 = 24$.

40. **(B)** 160 tons
One ton produces 5/4 pounds of aluminum. Use a proportion equation to find out how many tons, T, are needed for 200 pounds:

$$T : 200 = 1 : 5/4$$

T must be the same multiple of 1 ton that 200 pounds is of 5/4 pounds; that is, $T = 200 \div (5/4)$. Dividing by 5/4 is the same as multiplying by 4/5. $T = 200 \times (4/5) = (200 \times 4)/5 = 800/5 = 160$.

41. **(D)** 20%
The percentage increase is the change (five students more in the second year) divided by the original number of students (25). This is $5/25 = 1/5 = 2/10 = 20/100$ or 20%.

42. **(C)** Fresno
The column labeled "Normal to Date" gives the amount of rainfall that the cities normally have by this date of the season. The largest value is for Oakland (nearly 7 inches) and the lowest value is the 3.32 inches for Fresno.

43. **(B)** 29%
Oakland has had 5.43 inches of rain in the season so far. The amount of rain it normally gets for the year is the 18.89 inches in the last column of the table—the "season" is the whole year from one July 1st to the next June 30th. Be careful to use this seasonal norm in answering the question ("What percentage of its normal rainfall for the year has Oakland had so far this season?"). That percentage is 5.43/18.89, but before doing a laborious long division, make a rough estimate of the percentage and compare it to the choices given. The easy numbers near 5.43 and 18.89 would

be 5/20 (1/4 = 25%) or 6/18 (1/3 = 33%). 6/18 will actually be a bit large, since the numerator 6 is larger than 5.43 *and* the denominator 18 is smaller than 18.89. Either estimate is good enough to eliminate all the choices except B.

44. **(C)** 105%
A quart is 32 ounces and a liter is ~30.3; therefore, a quart is a fraction 32/30.3 of a liter. You can see immediately that the percentage has to be greater than 100%. You can either do the long division, to find that 32/30.3 = 1.056, or you can test Choices C and D for which one is closer to giving 32 ounces. 110% of 30.3 means 30.3 + 3.03, so Choice D is more than an ounce too big. But 105% adds exactly half as much (1.51 ounces) to the 30.3; that comes out about 31.8 ounces, close to 32 (and *much* closer than Choice D).

45. **(D)** Hispanic
The question concerns only the Los Angeles schools, so you can ignore the pie chart on the left. Look for the largest slice of the pie in the chart on the right. The medium gray shaded Hispanic portion is obviously more than half, so all the other segments must be smaller.

46. **(C)** Asian and Other
This question is a mirror image of the last one; here you need to look at the pie chart on the left (for California average) for the smallest slice of the pie. Hispanic is obviously the largest slice, followed by White and then Black; this leaves Asian and Other as the smallest slice.

47. **(B)** It was about 80% as big.
This question requires you to compare the two pie charts, specifically to compare the size of the gray Hispanic slices in the two pies. In the California average, the Hispanic piece is just under half, maybe about 48% or 49%; in Los Angeles the Hispanic slice is significantly more than half, maybe about 60%. So you can rule out Choices C and D right away. It remains to see whether the gray slice on the left is

half or 80% the size of the one on the right. Try drawing a line cutting the Los Angeles slice in two equal parts; it should be clear that half the Los Angeles piece is noticeably smaller than the California average. If you made numerical estimates of the sizes (such as those above), you can also see that 48% is 12% less than 60%, and 12/60 is 1/5 or 20%, so that the California average is, in fact, somewhere close to 80% of the Los Angeles value. The numbers don't have to be very precise in order to get a ratio that confirms Choice B as the closest one to being correct.

48. **(C)** 10 hours

It takes four painters 15 hours to do the job. Thus, the job requires 4×15 "painter-hours." Any other combination of workers and times must add up to the same 60 painter-hours to get the job done. For a crew of six painters, this means 60 painter-hours ÷ 6 painters = 10 hours.

49. **(B)** 10%

Jordan must walk 3 blocks south and 2 blocks east to reach the corner nearest his home. At the bus stop, he can go either south or east, and at each intersection after that he can also choose his direction until he gets to 8th Ave. going east or to Durant going south. List all the ways he can do 3 south (S) and 2 east (E) legs on his walk. It is best in making such a list to be systematic; for example always list an "S" choice first, then switch that with an "E" if possible. Work the changes from the "last" S first, then the others in turn:

S	S	S	E	E	*make all S choices first*
S	S	E	S	E	*move the 1st E choice forward*
S	S	E	E	S	*move the second E choice up one*
S	E	S	S	E	
S	E	S	E	S	
S	E	E	S	S	
E	S	S	S	E	*make E the first choice...*
E	S	S	E	S	
E	S	E	S	S	
E	E	S	S	S	

When you have both E choices up front, you're done; there is a total of 10 choices, so the probability of any one of them chosen at random is 1/10, or 10%.

50. **(D)**

The correct graph must contain all the points of the table. It is easiest to check the "intercept" points—where the graph crosses the x- or y-axis (therefore, points where either $y = 0$ or $x = 0$). The straight line in Choice A has two of these points, (2,0) and (0,2), but not the point (–2,0). Choice C has none of these points. To choose between Choice B and Choice D, look for the points on these graphs where $x = 1$. Graph B has the point (1,1), so it doesn't match the expected table value (1,1.5). You have to estimate the value of Choice D at $x = 1$, but it should be clear that it is close to 1.5, so Choice D is the correct choice.

Index